The Dental Acquisitions Manual

2021 EDITION

The Complete Guide to Your Acquisition

Addison Killeen, DDS

Mark Costes, DDS

2021 Paperback Edition

© 2021 Addison Killeen, DDS, Mark Costes, DDS

Published in the United States by Kindle Direct Publishing, an imprint of Amazon.

Library of Congress Cataloging-in-Publication Data
Killeen, Addison; Costes, Mark.

The Dental Acquisition Manual / by Addison Killeen, DDS and Mark Costes, DDS.

ISBN-13:9798736780549
1. Dentistry Practice Management 2. Business - Mergers & Acquisitions

Chapters

How to Use the Dental Acquisition Manual

Welcome to The Dental Acquisition Manual! This book is a compilation of our 'in the trenches' experiences combined with many of the top resources we have developed to help dentists as they prepare to make one of the biggest purchases of their life. We wrote this book to encapsulate some of the information that we have learned over the course of owning and managing 25 dental clinics (as of the time of this writing).

It is important to note that we have not always had it all 'figured out'. We have made too many mistakes to count. Some have even cost us months of frustration and thousands of dollars. However, through these experiences and in a decade of coaching more than a thousand dentists, we believe that we have learned the best and most economical way to acquire a dental practice.

This book is just a part of our plan to help dentists. As Co-Founders of the Dental Success Network, our mission is to help improve the lives of dentists and dental professionals. That is what we have the privilege of doing everyday. Inside the Dental Success Network, we strive to make dentists' lives better with three primary areas: by saving them money, by teaching them new skills, and by connecting them with colleagues in a positive, collaborative environment.

As you go through this book, you will find several instances where we have provided access to a customizable, downloadable document. In these instances, simply scan the QR code, sign up for a Free Trial, and then the QR code will take you to the link to download the resources that are paired with this book.

> To get a FREE 45 day trial and receive digital versions of these documents - visit: https://members.dentalsuccessnetwork.com/acquisition-manual-free-45-day-trial-membership/ or Scan the QR Code -->

> Once you begin your free trial, all the documents are then available at this QR code to the left, or at this site- www.dentalsuccessnetwork.com/acquisition-vault/

Best of luck in your practice acquisition journey, and please remember, if you ever have questions about this manual or want to see something in future versions, please don't hesitate to reach out to Addison via www.AddisonKilleen.com or Mark at www.TrueDentalSuccess.com. We are always here to help.

To your Success,

Addison Killeen DDS

Mark Costes, DDS

Chapter 1

Setting the Vision

When considering the next stage of their dental career, we have found that dentists are attracted to practice ownership for countless reasons. Some are looking for a fresh start in a new city or location; some wish to leave an associateship that no longer fulfills them; and some wish to acquire something that they can call their own and begin building an asset that will eventually bring them income, financial stability and equity.

Perhaps you considered doing a startup and decided that it wasn't the path for you. Startups can be challenging, and they're not always the right fit for everyone. Sometimes there are no openings in the market to do a good startup from either a space perspective or a demographics perspective. This could be that the ratio of dentists:patients is too competitive, or that there are not any good real estate opportunities for a new dental office.

There are, however, great opportunities when dentists, who are late in their career, prepare to transition their practices over to a new generation. When handled correctly, these opportunities allow the acquiring doctor to take over an established practice, mold it according to their own vision and preferences, and pay the selling doctor a fair price for it. This scenario is the ultimate win-win.

However, let's not fool ourselves into thinking an acquisition is easier than a startup. Complicated mitigating factors can make it very difficult to properly execute a transition. There are checklists that need to be completed at every stage. There could be existing staff that might not possess your same values or clinical standards. You could pay an average price for equipment that will break the day after you purchase the practice. While acquisitions can be more financially stable in the early stages of ownerships in comparison to startups, they come with their own unique challenges.

Whether an acquisition is the right avenue for your specific situation and personality, we have found it valuable to create a pros and cons list. Here is ours:

Pros:
- Existing team
- Existing patient base
- Existing revenue stream

- Easier to start- no construction
- Practice the dentistry YOU want to practice - maybe not initially, but this can occur quickly
- Financial benefits of ownership
- You are the boss and have complete control
- Ability to help staff grow and realize potential
- Security in choosing own future

Cons:
- Medium-large debt load
- Moderate revenue to start
- Potentially low new patient flow
- Existing team might not possess the same values
- Existing team may not be clinically proficient
- Diagnosing inconsistencies between new and previous owner
- Previous owner and new owner styles/history/persona don't match and patients may leave due to change
- Potentially fixing inadequate or failed dentistry

As you consider all the details of an acquisition, you should remember that although the debt on an acquisition might be higher, the revenues from the first day are **usually** good enough to cover the cost. The graph above shows the startup revenues at the bottom, but the acquisition revenues at the higher line.

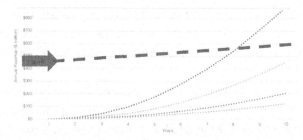

This instant revenue stream is usually what leads people to choose an acquisition over a startup. While this can give you more peace of mind, remember to weigh the factors listed above to see which avenue is going to better match your end goals.

It is very possible that you're not sure what your 'end goals' might be. That is totally normal, and something we do not often consider until someone sits us down and makes us write it down. We do that almost yearly in the Dental Success Institute's Elite Practice Mastermind, and so we've listed the exercise below to complete at your own page. Take about 15 minutes and complete the exercise below.

Ideal Practice Exercise

The second habit from Dr. Stephen Covey's groundbreaking book, *The 7 Habits of Highly Effective People*, is "Begin with the end in mind." Dr. Covey advised that in order to have the greatest likelihood of achieving your desired result, it is important to be able to envision what your ideal outcome looks like, and to put a plan together to achieve your ultimate goal.

Building a successful practice, whether it is a start-up or an acquisition, is no different. Having a clean vision from the beginning of what you want the practice to eventually look like "when it's done" can be one of the most powerful and clarifying exercises that a dentist can perform prior to ownership.

In order to aid with the visualization process, and to help gain a clear visual picture of your ideal dental practice, we have developed the exercise below. Now is the time to allow yourself to dream <u>without practicality and limitations</u>.

At this point, you might be leaning towards keeping this goal 'realistic'. We want to pre-emptively warn against that. Marcus Aurelius, the Roman Emperor whose private journal became the book called *Meditations*, wrote,

> *"Do not think that what is hard for you to master is humanly impossible; and if it is humanly possible, **consider it to be within your reach."***

Remember, every owner of a dental practice, no matter how large architecturally or visually appealing, or successful, started off right where you are right now. If they were able to build their ideal practice, so can you!

Step 1

Start by answering the following questions in as much detail as possible:

Where do you want to live:

What type of patients do you serve (Fee for Service / PPO / Medicaid etc.):

How many practices are in your perfect business:

What's the size of the facility of the business in square feet:

How many operatories:

How is it decorated:

What 'feel' does the office exude when you walk in:

What brands or stores does your dental practice mimic or remind your guests of:

What colors and materials will be the main look of the practice:

How is it unique from the competition:

How many dental (dentist) associates (if any):

How many people are on your team:

What is the annual production and collections:

What is your personal production per month:

What is the overhead and profitability percentage:

How many clinical hours do you work per week:

How many CEO hours do you work per week:

How many weeks do you take off per year:

What is your personal take home income:

Does your practice bring you peace of mind, fulfilment, freedom and joy:

How old are you when you sell the practice and retire:

How will you spend your days during retirement:

The purpose of owning my practice is to:

My business will allow me to:

I will build this practice so that I can:

This practice will give me the ability to:

What skills will I need to improve on:

What habits do I need to remove from my life:

Lastly, What type of owner/dentist/leader do I need to become to achieve the goals set forth above?

Take the answers to these questions and write out your ideal practice vision statement in paragraph form.

Example: On June 14, 2034, at the age of 60 years old, I will transition out of my dental business by selling my group of practices to four dentists who were previously associates and later became minority partners. When the business sells, it will have a total of three affiliated dental practices producing $7M with no debt. The EBITDA will be 20% and the practce group received a 6X valuation. The sales price will be $8.4M. As an 80% owner of the entire group, I will receive a pre-tax check of $6.72M.

Included in your Ideal Practice Vision Statement
- Your Age when "It's Done" and you're ready to transition
- The transaction value of the business and your take home pre/after tax
- Exactly what the practice looks like: physical size, décor, location, team, to the type of services rendered, purchaser...
- Your overall health, your relationships, your mental health (4 Futures Score)
- Plan for what to do with your days
- What's your next chapter?

Create benchmarks with exact dates and specifics that lead to the eventual end goal.

	Financial	Physical Location	Other
Age 30			
Age 40			
Age 50			
Age 60			

Review your Ideal Practice Vision Statement, Benchmarks and Timelines each month from now until your ultimate deadline.

Notes:

_____
_____
_____
_____
_____
_____
_____
_____
_____
_____
_____
_____
_____
_____
_____
_____
_____
_____
_____
_____
_____
_____
_____
_____
_____
_____

Chapter 2

Finding Acquisitions

The next stage of the acquisitions process is to begin identifying possible practices within your desired area that meet your specifications. Once preliminary screenings have been done, you can begin submitting offers. Depending on the location, there may be multiple offices that fit your budget and preferred practice style.

Prior to looking for the right opportunity, it is best to figure out where you want to live, and whether that area has favorable demographics. Even though you will already be purchasing an existing patient base, it is always wise to make sure the general area is not saturated with too many dentists. In areas of over-saturation, you might buy a practice that remains stagnant for many years as you work to grow against external forces that limit potential growth opportunities.

One issue we have seen sometimes is that an acquisition opportunity becomes available, and due to ancillary factors, our minds trick us into thinking that this is 'the one'. Sometimes we jump 10 places ahead and skip the due diligence process in favor of our 'gut feeling'. This can be a disastrous mistake, which could cost you many hundreds of thousands of dollars, and decades of struggle. We encourage, no matter where you are in the process, to go through the steps listed here to ensure that you buy a practice that will lead to long-term growth.

While the next few steps are listed out in this order (1. Demographics, 2. Traffic Numbers, 3. Finding Acquisition offices), this is not always the order that the process occurs. You may find an opportunity in an area where you were not looking, but the opportunity looks solid.

However you approach it, these three steps can be interchangeable, or completed concurrently.

Demographics of Target Areas

Once you have narrowed down your areas of interest to a few different zip codes and neighborhoods, you will need to run demographic reports on each of them. Taking time to do this step will verify and confirm the strength or weakness of your target areas. There can be very significant differences between areas that are relatively close to one another and selecting the one that is right for you could potentially be the difference between a wildly successful practice and one that perpetually struggles.

In the first chapter, you have already begun to identify the type of practice you will eventually want in the future. However, revisiting this shorter list will be helpful when comparing it to the demographics you are looking for.

Below is a list of points to consider:
1. Will you be in network with insurances? Or will you maintain 'out of network' status?
2. What sort of procedures will you perform?
   a. Fillings/simple extractions
   b. Wisdom tooth extractions with sedation
   c. Invisalign
   d. Dentures
   e. Traditional braces
   f. Pediatrics- will this be a special focus
   g. Implants
   h. All on X dentures/prosthetics

You might be able to find acquisitions that match this profile, and you might not. Have no fear!! You can always buy a practice that does one type of dentistry, and gradually change it over to a more comprehensive model. The previous doctor could have been doing all the surgery, and if that is not your passion, you can switch it over to focus on sleep apnea and orthodontics- the possibilities are vast. (Remember, sometimes you will pay a premium for certain practices that add in speciality procedures. If you do not perform some of these procedures, you might be paying for a model that you cannot replicate.)

Your next step is to identify your ideal patient. If you're trending towards wisdom teeth extractions and traditional braces, then you will know that your target demographic is probably younger and proximity to a high school might be a good idea. If your preferred clinical suite includes dentures or all-on-X prosthetics, your ideal demographic might skew towards an older population.

While searching zip codes and cities for your acquisition targets, it's important to ensure that your ideal patient demographic is at the forefront of your mind when evaluating each area. Remember that sometimes a zip code will have great demographics from a national scale, but fail to match the demographic appropriate for the type of dentistry that you want to practice. This inconsistency may lead to more struggle and less long term success.

Once you have your ideal patient demographics, the next step is to start evaluating potential zip codes and areas in the city where you want to live for more detailed demographics and dental competition. Remember that a dentist will generally pull a high density of patients from about a 1 to 3 mile radius range. That small circle around your future practice is where it is the most important to have favorable demographics. When running reports, we will also include the 5 mile range, but that radius is less relevant. These radii also matter more in densely populated areas, where people might not be apt to drive as far. However, in rural spots we tend to see patients drive many more miles to go to the dentist. If you are going to a rural spot like Wahoo,

Nebraska (real place), you will see patients drive 30 miles from adjacent counties to visit a dentist in their closest large town.

We used to run a couple different sets of software to help us decide traffic and demographics. Fortunately now, they have all been rolled into one software, ArcGIS. Below are the instructions to help you run demographics. To access this software, sign up for a Free Trial, and that should allow you to get all the reports for a short time at no cost.

Here are the steps to running these reports:

- Visit Learn ArcGIS to create an account for a free 60 day trial
- Sign up for an account, an email will be sent with your Username info and prompt to create a password
- Once signed into the Learn ArcGIS website, click on the app icon that appears next to your name in the upper right hand corner

- Select the Business Analyst app

After you have accessed the 'Business Analyst' app, click 'Create New Project', give your project a name, then click the 'Create' button.

After a brief load, you are able to open your new project and will be taken to a map. To create your first site, type in an address in the search bar at the top-right to place a pin at that location.

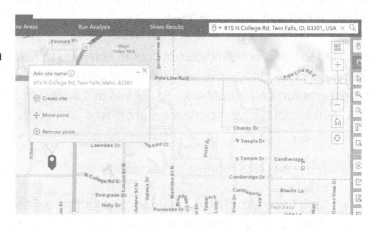

From the menu above your new pin, click 'Create site' and define the boundaries you want to use for your analysis, e.g. mileage rings, drive time, or walk time. After clicking apply, you will see your site as well as the boundaries you just created.

Now that you have created your first site you are able to view reports, infographics, and comparisons for data within that area. You can select these options by clicking on 'Reports' on the toolbar at the top of the page. From the reports screen, click 'Run Reports' in the toolbar to view infographic or classic reports, or click 'Comparison Reports' to compare data from your selected site with data from the same ZIP code, county, state, country or even another created site.

Let's start by running a classic report: from the 'Reports' tab click 'Run Reports' and then 'Run Classic Reports'. Make sure that the site you just created is selected at the top - if not you can click 'Add Sites' to select it.

Now you can choose any one or multiple reports to run from the list below by clicking the checkbox next to each one you want to run. Hover your cursor over the ⓘ to view a summary of the report's contents and click the magnifying glass icon to see a sample version of that report.

You will see all of the reports you have selected in the box on the right. From there, you can choose whether you want to download each report as a PDF, an Excel file, or both.

Once you have made all your selections, click 'Run All' in the bottom-right and ArcGIS will download your selected reports as a .zip file. Find the zipped file in your downloads folder, unzip it, and you will be able to view all of your reports.

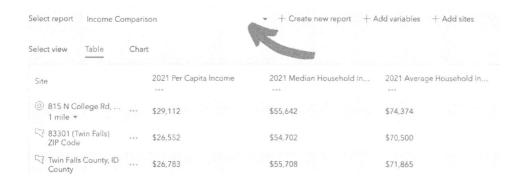

As an alternative to running classic reports, you may also choose to 'Run Infographics' which will display the same data in various interactive infographic formats. Lastly, you can choose 'Comparison Reports' to view comparisons of data such as population growth, average household income and more between your selected site and the same ZIP code, county, state, country, or another created site. Use the dropdown menu in the top-left to change which data you are comparing.

Traffic Numbers

While the demographic statistics can greatly impact the success of your practice, the next largest factor is *visibility* of your practice. Of course you can be in the middle of New York City with a Million people in a 3 mile radius, but if no one can see your practice, it will be challenging to achieve success.

So the next most important factor is visibility and traffic numbers in the zip code and along major routes along an area. We all know that major corporate dental chains prefer to have high visibility spots. They will pay anywhere between $35-45 / Sq. Ft. for lease space each year, and then pay all real estate insurances, property taxes and utilities on top of that!

Remember: As you start to see the traffic numbers in an area, pay attention to which dental offices might have street-frontage visibility. Take note of any that might be for sale or possible acquisition targets. We will address this later, but remember that a practice might be for sale, but the doctor might be keeping it so quiet and confidential that you will not know it is on the market.

Judging the traffic flow, it is important to judge how this metric affects our advertising budget, as well as our facility budget. Our philosophy is that facility and site costs should be under 9%, and advertising should be under 4.5%. However, we always take a holistic approach to the costs, and if we can spend a little more in facility costs to get a spot with better-visibility, we need to then adjust for those costs from the advertising category to balance out and come to the same end-point for profitability of the practice.

Expense Breakdown	Practice Expense	Expense %	Industry Standard
Front/Back Office	$85,767	13.69%	16.0%
Hygiene Salaries	$76,187	12.16%	9.0%
Payroll Taxes & Fees	$13,217	2.11%	2.5%
Fringe Benefits	$0	0.00%	2.5%
Total Payroll	$175,171	27.96%	30.0%
Lab/Specialty	$30,400	4.85%	9.0%
Dental Supplies	$42,041	6.71%	5.0%
Assoc. Dr Salaries	$0	0.00%	N/A
Owner Compensation	$111,382	17.78%	N/A
Total Doctor Salaries	$111,382	17.78%	30.0%
Advertising	$19,856	3.17%	4.5%
Other Minor	$4,108	0.66%	2.0%
Other Expenses	$33,552	5.36%	5.5%
Insurance	$6,335	1.01%	1.5%
Legal & Accounting	$32,026	5.11%	1.5%
Office Expenses	$13,888	2.22%	1.2%
Facility & Equipment	$66,791	10.66%	9.0%
Telephone/Internet	$2,862	0.46%	0.8%

The best software for traffic analysis is also ArcGIS. ArcGIS will give you the traffic counts in specific spots along your roadways at different points in time over the past few years. Once you find a city or part of a city that you want a closer look at, the maps will give you a good idea of the traffic and visibility to expect from any office you may purchase.

To run traffic reports for certain areas, go back to ArcGIS:
- Create/name your project (ie. Traffic Count)
- Your most recent project will be open and displayed on the upper left corner, but you can find all created projects by clicking the three lined drop down menu farthest to the left

- Open your new project (Traffic Count)
  - In the drop down menu that appears, click the ellipses next to Point Locations, and click 'Add New Locations Layer'
  - Create/name your new location

- Narrow down the location of your search by typing the desired address in the search bar in the upper right corner

- Name and Create Site

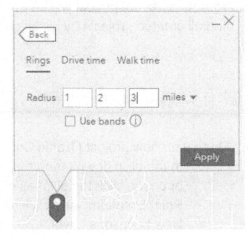

- Select your radius, narrow down as much as possible for cleaner results

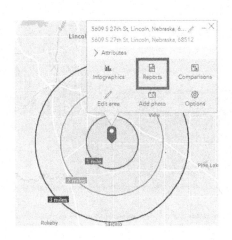

- Click Reports
- Select the drop down menu
- Run reports for:
  - Traffic Count Map
  - Traffic Count Map Close Up
  - Traffic Count Profile

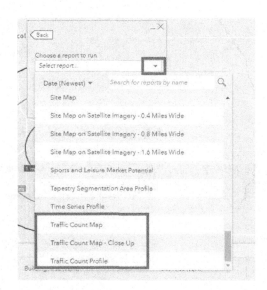

- The reports will save and appear as PDF's on the left hand side menu under the 'Previously Run Reports' tab

Examples:

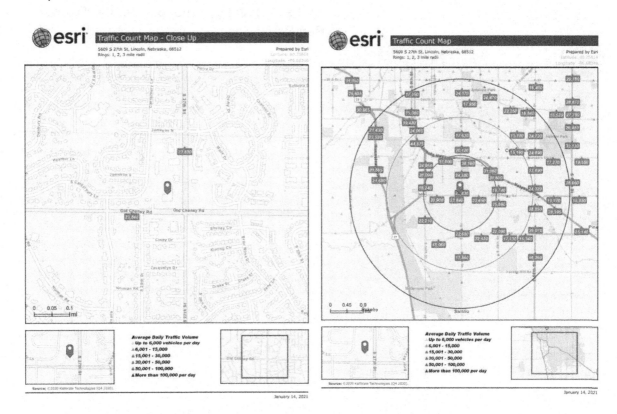

Distance:	Street:	Closest Cross-street:	Year of Count:	Count:
0.11	Old Cheney Rd	S 25th St (0.03 miles E)	2018	23,840
0.13	S 27th St	Jameson N (0.04 miles N)	2018	23,830
0.52	Old Cheney Rd	S 31st St (0.07 miles W)	2018	22,650
0.60	S 27th St	Tierra Dr (0.06 miles S)	2016	24,580
0.64	Old Cheney Rd	S 18th St (0.03 miles E)	2016	20,900
0.93	Nebraska Highway	Pioneers Blvd (0.07 miles NE)	2018	39,190
0.93	State Hwy 2	Rock Island Trl (0.07 miles W)	2017	35,830
0.93	S 27th St	Ridge Line Rd (0.02 miles N)	2018	22,680
0.96	State Hwy 2	Southwood Dr (0.15000001 miles W)	2017	31,460
0.96	S 14th St	Warlick Blvd (0.04 miles N)	2018	1,000
0.99	South 14th Street	Warlick Blvd (0.01 miles NE)	2018	16,240
1.04	Nebraska Highway	Dunn Ave (0.03 miles NE)	2018	37,900
1.07	S 40th St	Duxhall Dr (0.1 miles S)	2018	25,860
1.07	S 33rd St	Pioneers Blvd (0.03 miles N)	2017	7,750
1.08	S 40th St	Wildbriar Ln (0.05 miles S)	2018	19,740
1.08	State Hwy 2	S 33rd Ct (0.31 miles NW)	2017	31,060
1.11	Nebraska Highway	Gertie Ave (0.09 miles NE)	2018	31,600
1.12	S 14th St	Dairy Dr (0.08 miles N)	2015	28,090
1.12	S 14th St	Thunderbird Blvd (0.05 miles S)	2018	22,210
1.21	Pine Lake Rd	S 34th St (0.04 miles E)	2018	22,520
1.21	S 20th St	Burnham St (0.09 miles N)	2002	1,500
1.23	Pioneers Blvd	S 36th St (0.01 miles W)	2016	10,230
1.23	State Hwy 2	S 17th St (0.01 miles E)	2015	33,340
1.25	S 27th St	Stockwell St (0.05 miles N)	2016	20,120
1.27	South 14th Street	S 14th St (0.12 miles N)	2018	24,950
1.29	Old Cheney Rd	Abbott Rd (0.04 miles W)	2018	25,340
1.29	S 33rd St	Prescott Ave (0.03 miles N)	2016	9,130
1.35	Pine Lake Rd	Hazel Scott Dr (0.07 miles E)	2018	18,060
1.36	State Hwy 2	S 48th St (0.25 miles SE)	2018	29,100
1.36	S 40th St	Leesburg St (0.01 miles N)	2018	22,090

If you trial out the 'Business Side' of the software(only allowable if you are using a business email address):

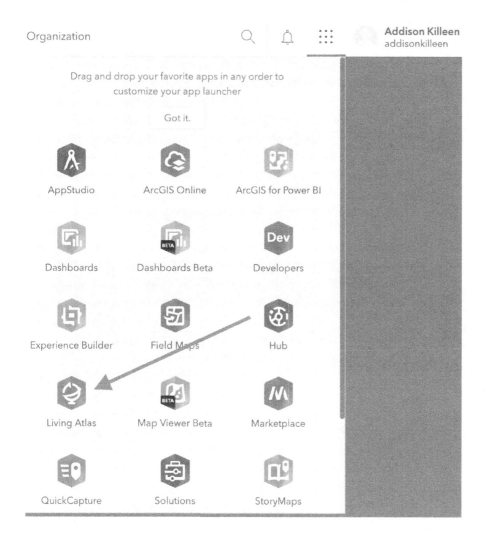

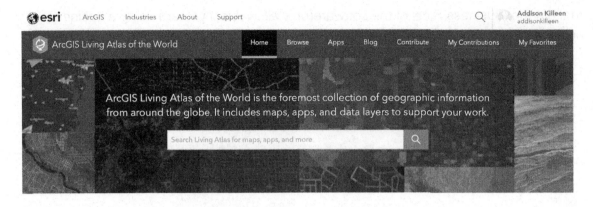

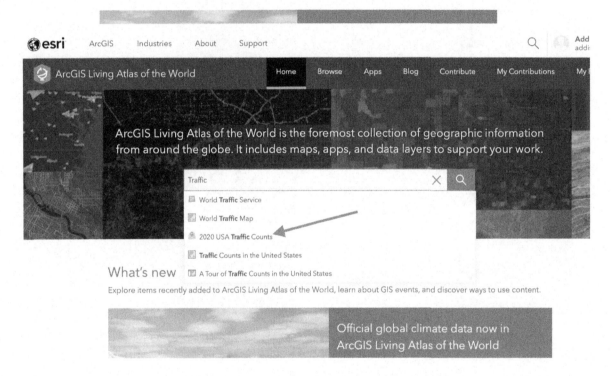

Pick "2020 Traffic Counts" as one option, other option is "Traffic Counts in the United States"

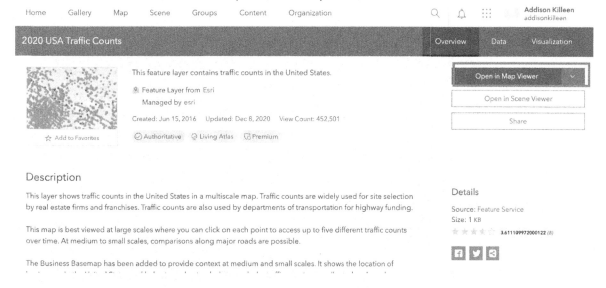

Type in the address you want to search for:

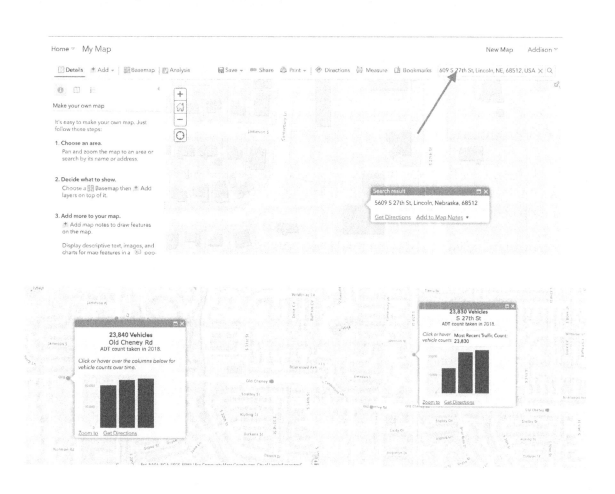

The Heat map below is the option for 'Traffic Counts in the United States'

With all of the traffic reports, print and use them in your evaluation analysis to know exact traffic counts and to make sure you're going to get the visibility you want in any acquisition.

Dental Competition

Now that you have the data for your patient demographics and the traffic patterns in your city, you will want to evaluate the number of dentists and type of dentistry being performed around your target zip codes.

It would be overly simplistic to assume that all dentists are doing the same procedures and in the same manner. Most dentists do varying procedures, have different marketing strategies, and have different target demographics.

To illustrate this point, we will use the restaurant business as an example. Applebees is called a 'Mid-market American-Style Restaurant' by the National Restaurant Association. When they do site research, they really only care about competition with similar 'Mid-market American Style Restaurants'. If there is a Dairy Queen next door to a potential site, they really don't need to worry. Dairy Queen focuses on walk-up and drive through traffic. Dairy Queen's price point is $3-8 a plate, whereas Applebees is $9-23 a plate. So, although they both sell food, they really have no competition between each other.

The same might be true for your new location. A dentist down the street that has been there for 30 years and is trapped in an older medical building might not be the competition that would affect your new startup or acquisition.

To evaluate the competitive landscape, you will need to:

- Evaluate your competition for your **_targeted_** demographic
- Use Google Maps/My
  Maps

    - Create a new map
    - Add in locations for
      other dentists
    - Get a visual
      representation of
      competition
    - Count and Add into
      your spreadsheet

Once you've located all the
dentists within an area around your potential acquisition, categorize these patients into groups.
Remember that any of these offices could potentially be a target for you to acquire, so take note
of the potential age of each doctor who owns the office. While age is not the only factor, it is
usually the most common factor that leads to the sale of an office. Also remember that some
doctors are not the actual owner of the business, and that age is not always the reason for a
sale. For these reasons, do not rule out dentists who are younger or do not look like the typical
seller.

Create three different subsets of dental practices. 1. Dentists like you. 2. Dentists who do not
compete with you. And 3. DSO - Corporate. Remember to evaluate along these competitive
points:

- PPO's vs. FFS
- What are their marketing styles?
- What are their hours?
- Do they have a decent website?
- Do they offer similar services as you will

Remember: your only competition are those dentists in your 'group'.

It is also important to consider future demographics into the quality analysis of a site. While the
current demographics might be very good, the future demographics might be even better and
may be a sound reason to be more aggressive in a certain situation.   On the flip side, the
current demographics of an office might be good currently, but if there are major changes
coming, the office might not be in a good situation in the future. We are reminded of one
situation where an acquisition happened, only to find that a large low-income housing
development occurred across the street immediately after the sale. This office then stagnated
for years with less-than-ideal patients.

To look at future numbers, check with your local planning commission or municipality about plans for future roadways, zoning, or new subdivisions. Here's a few key points to ask about:

- o Will future construction be zoned commercial or residential?
- o Even with commercial construction, will it be for 'Big Box' construction like a Wal-mart or smaller commercial strip malls?
- o Will there be any major roadway construction that will block visibility or access to my site?
- o Will there be any major roadway construction in the next few years that will restrict, even temporarily, access to my site?
- o Are there any tax credits available to build in certain areas?

Looking for Acquisitions

As stated earlier, acquisitions in the dental market can be difficult to find. Due to the complex social factors based around the doctor-patient relationship, many dentists wish to keep the sale of their practice confidential. They fear, and rightfully so, that if word got out publicly that they were selling, that the value of their practice would go down and patients would exit the practice before a new doctor/owner took over. Additionally, they are concerned that staff would potentially leave if word of a practice sale was made public. Because of this, the seller will often tell only a few people, and keep certain specifics very opaque about their location, not mention the size of the patient base, or hide other distinguishing factors. However, typically there are a few places that are good to look for potential acquisitions:

1. Publications like ADA News, Local Dental Journals
2. Dental Supply Representatives - Henry Schein, Patterson, Benco
3. Word of Mouth from Colleagues and Specialists
4. Dental Transition Companies (National or Local representatives)
5. Local Banks

As you start looking for a potential acquisition, you can look in all of the above places. Hopefully you will find a target, or actually a few targets, that have potential. However, if you are not finding anything promising, then you can always employ the last tactic, which is a direct letter to potential dentists in an area.

If you've taken the steps earlier in this chapter, then you have already surveyed the demographics of an area through competitive analysis. This means you should already have a list of addresses of dentists in an area. However, sometimes there may be more practices for sale than you may be able to find or know about. To look for all available options, we also recommend that you send out a personal letter to all potential targets within a zip code.

You might be inclined to only look for the 'prime' practices that have good visibility, but we encourage you to NOT leave any stone unturned. There could be low-performing practices that are for sale that might be good acquisition-merger opportunities. Finding these are harder, but if you can buy and merge two practices together at a good price-point, then you will significantly decrease the time frame of an acquisition and increase the trajectory of your growth.

Here's a draft letter that you can copy and send out to potential acquisition targets:

Example Letter for Targeting Unknown Acquisitions

Example Doctor, DDS
Address
City, STATE 00000

(Fun/personal picture of yourself/family here --->)

Dear Doctor,

My name is _____ and I am a local doctor who has lived in _____ for the past XX Years with my family. (More fluff here.)

I am writing this letter in search of a practice purchase, or transition opportunity with you.

I currently practice in the XXXXXX area and I am looking for an opportunity. I am looking for a XXXX type of practice that will provide me with a place to _____.

The sole focus of my endeavors is to bring high quality care with a 'fantastic' guest experience. I want patients to leave our practice not thinking of me as a dentist, but as a friend and helper along their path to better smiles and healthier teeth. Because of this, I have taken the appropriate education to develop more skills with implants, endodontics, wisdom tooth surgery, sedation, and cosmetic reconstruction.

If you, or a dentist you know, has been thinking about cutting back, selling, retiring, or has a desire to transition into a different role in their practice, you can text or a call: XXX-XXX-XXXX.

Sincerely,

XXXXXXXXXXXXX, DDS

After you've gained a list of at least a few potential acquisitions, you can then start the process of evaluating the practices using the next set of resources. It is important to remember at this stage that you will most likely evaluate many practices before coming to a practice that will be a good match financially for you. In our experience, for each practice purchase, we have gone through an average evaluation of 4-6 practices before finding a practice that was the right fit for the situation. Just as you don't (usually) marry the first person you ever dated, you usually will not buy the first practice you evaluate.

To truly gain a thorough understanding of an acquisition, you will want to go through the next spreadsheet with as much detail as possible. This will give you a good evaluation of the practice, and its financials. We will also address some of the finer points to consider after this evaluation is completed.

Acquisition Analysis

After receiving 'leads' on a few practices, you will need to ask for all relevant information on the practices to start doing proper analysis of each of them. The following documents are required to do a full analysis of the practice:

1. Last 3 years Profit and Loss Statements
2. Last 3 years Tax Returns
3. Codes and Production over the last 3 years
4. Everything in the 'Acquisition Analysis Spreadsheet' for general information

Download this document from the QR Code here→

Acquitision Analysis and Valuation Calculator

	2020			2019		2018
Income	$ 686,433		$	688,818	$	652,290
Lab/Dental Sup	$ 76,656	11%	$	96,167	$	89,130
Wages	$ 200,631	29%	$	207,184	$	204,488
Officers Comp	$ 164,744	24%	$	165,316	$	156,550
Taxes	$ 30,674	4%	$	31,820	$	31,264
Employee Bene	$ 3,300	0%	$	3,450	$	3,200
Office Exp		0%				
Insurance		0%				
Telephone	$ 2,800	0%	$	2,811	$	2,763
Janitorial		0%				
Utilities	$ 5,922	1%	$	5,952	$	6,018
Professional Fees		0%				
Repairs		0%				
Supplies		0%				
City/County Ta	$ 5,114	1%	$	4,570	$	4,280
Interest		0%				
Rent		0%				
Nitrous	$ 950	0%	$	978	$	1,200
Car/Truck		0%				
Advertising		0%				
Uniforms		0%				

The 'Acquisition Analysis' Spreadsheet has many good questions and prompts that you may not have considered when looking at a potential purchase. The first page of the Acquisition analysis is the financial considerations. On this page, you will include any and all information that is generally available about the office. This can be taken from Profit and Loss Statements or from documents such as their previous tax returns.

While we have this information at this stage of the process, it is important to not get too caught up in looking at the final financial valuation at this point. We will address how to get down to the closest valuation method in a later chapter. Right now, it is important to keep an eye on the big picture and just see if there are any major points that are either positive or negative.

After adding some of the financial information, move to the next spreadsheet page and work on answering as much of the information about the practice as possible. See the picture of this sheet on the next page.

This sheet has 88 questions that will get you to the clearest picture of the practice in a relatively short period of time. If any of the questions on this sheet are not a match with your vision, now is the time to make a decision as to whether you want to spend any more time on the evaluation of this practice, or to move on to another one.

Information Needed for Full Appraisal:

Asking Price			Address of Practice	
Previous Years Production		# of Doctors		
T-1				
T-2			Name of Seller	
T-3			Age of Seller	
T-4			Willing to Work post-sale?	
T-5			If so, how long?	
T-6			Date Started/Acquired?	

Overhead %		(As calcualted by you)	
Transition Type	Merger	Sale	Work-out for ___ Yrs

Pts seen in Previous 18 months

Insurances in Network with:

When evaluating multiple practices, it is important to remember aspects of the practice that either a) can be changed in an acquisition, or b) cannot be changed in an acquisition. When we have done acquisitions in the past, we have purchased practices that on the surface seemed like complete mis-matches with our vision. We knew however that we could instantly change many things to more closely align with our vision. During your search, remember the list of things that can be changed: (Not completely exhaustive)

- Softwares used
- Technology used
- Current Staff- can all be changed if needed
- Employee benefits
- Esthetics of the practice
- Brand of the practice
- Labs they are using
- Supplies they use
- Collections policies
- Insurances that you are either in-network or out-of-network with
- Current Marketing
- New patient flow

As you consider the aspects of the practice that can be changed, the list can grow quite quickly. As soon as a new owner comes into the practice, things can begin to look and feel drastically different. For instance the practice could be Fee-for-Service and you could immediately bring on many insurances as in-network status to help grow new patient bases if needed. The entire staff could be people whom you do not see wanting to grow with you. You could change them out quickly for others who would match your style. Keep in mind that you have a lot of freedom as a new owner to make changes.

More importantly is to be able to recognize the things that cannot be changed:

- Location (At least not extremely quickly unless you have another location nearby to merge)
- Rent (Unless the landlord is willing to renegotiate)
- Fixed Equipment and floorplan

As you evaluate the practice, this list is possibly the most important to evaluate. If the location is good and visible, you can be reasonably comfortable to keep progressing through the evaluation. If the practice is hidden, or the floorplan is terrible and the rent is high, it might be best to move onto another acquisition analysis and keep the process moving.

The last step is to do a 'production by procedure' report. This will give you an idea of the untapped opportunities available within the practice being evaluated. In the associated document link from the beginning of the book, you can download the spreadsheet. The spreadsheet gives you the ADA Code analysis page shown on the next page. If the seller is using OpenDental, you can export the production by procedures into an excel spreadsheet. You can then take columns A-F and copy them into this spreadsheet. The spreadsheet then reads all of the codes directly and decides whether it is Diagnostic, Preventative, Restorative, or any of the other major categories.

Date: 01/13/2021

Category	Code	Description	Quantity	Average Fee	Total Fees		Category		
Exams & Xrays	D0120	periodic oral eval	1114	49.91	55,600.00		Diagnostic		
Exams & Xrays	D0140	limited oral evalu	788	41.41	32,631.44		Diagnostic		Income in Category
Exams & Xrays	D0145	oral evaluation fc	6	45.33	272		Diagnostic	Diagnostic	316,064.70
Exams & Xrays	D0150	comprehensive o	745	85.71	63,856.00		Diagnostic	Preventative	187,334.69
Exams & Xrays	D0180	comprehensive p	1	95	95		Diagnostic	Restorative	277,938.93
Exams & Xrays	D0210	intraoral - compl	476	129.76	61,765.00		Diagnostic	Crown and Bridge	573,263.00
Exams & Xrays	D0220	intraoral - periap	846	29.36	24,836.66		Diagnostic	Endodontics	107,406.00
Exams & Xrays	D0230	intraoral - periap	555	25	13,875.00		Diagnostic	Surgery	574,899.56
Exams & Xrays	D0272	bitewings - two r	37	45	1,665.00		Diagnostic	Implants	126,406.00
Exams & Xrays	D0274	bitewings - four r	579	65.08	37,679.00		Diagnostic	Ortho	16,274.00
Exams & Xrays	D0330	panoramic radiog	257	90.39	23,230.60	<-- this is all copied directly	Diagnostic	Perio	56,534.00
Exams & Xrays	D0350	2D oral/facial phc	2	33.5	67	from the Procedures and	Diagnostic	Dentures	62,815.56
Exams & Xrays	D0383	cone beam CT im	1	0	0	codes from OpenDental	Diagnostic	Cosmetics	11,346.00
Exams & Xrays	D9310	consultation - dia	343	2.08	713.1	So columns A-F are all	Other	Sedation	117,848.94
Exams & Xrays	MBR-AD'	Membership Plar	1	444	444	copied into the columns	Other	Other	31,930.10
Exams & Xrays	MEMAV	Membership Disc	11	49	539	directly from Open Dental	Other		
Exams & Xrays	MEMBR	Membership Disc	102	49	4,998.00		Other		
Exams & Xrays	MEMKD	Membership Disc	6	49	294		Other		
Exams & Xrays	MPYR	Membership Plar	19	288	5,472.00		Other		

Once all the data is all entered into each sheet, it will complete all the calculations and then give you a pie chart, shown below, of all the production by dollar amount that the previous doctor has completed.

Doc 1

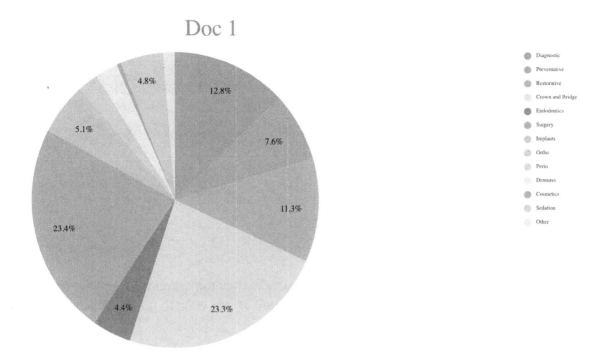

One of the most valuable aspects of this chart is being able to see how their clinical offerings compare with yours and how you might best be able to capture more production by offering a more diverse skill set. Do they do a lot of implant surgery? Do they offer orthodontic services? Do they keep endodontics services in-house or refer them out? If their services are part of your repertoire you can reasonably expect to be able to keep these services in house and grow the revenue of the practice. If they offer services that you do not offer, you have to make a decision. Either you get advanced training in that area or risk overpaying for a practice that generates production from procedures that you cannot perform.

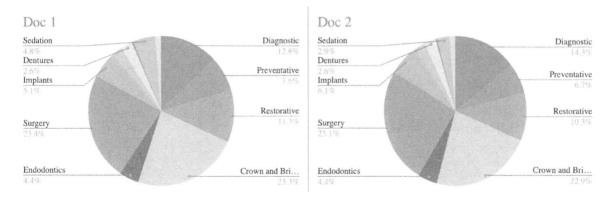

If you have multiple doctors, you can also use the spreadsheet to compare what the different doctors of the practice are completing. Sometimes this looks good in pie chart format, but we have also given you the ability to measure by bar-graph as well because each doctor will produce at varying levels.

	Doc 1	Doc 2	Doc 3	Doc 4	Doc 5
Diagnostic	$316,065	$169,246	$92,748	$316,065	$316,065
Preventative	$187,335	$78,878	$33,829	$187,335	$187,335
Restorative	$277,939	$121,839	$57,645	$277,939	$277,939
Crown and Bridge	$573,263	$270,070	$131,658	$573,263	$573,263
Endodontics	$107,406	$51,691	$25,724	$107,406	$107,406
Surgery	$574,900	$295,914	$168,091	$574,900	$574,900
Implants	$126,406	$71,915	$43,013	$126,406	$126,406
Ortho	$16,274	$7,425	$3,474	$16,274	$16,274
Perio	$56,534	$27,951	$14,764	$56,534	$56,534
Dentures	$62,816	$30,278	$15,634	$62,816	$62,816
Cosmetics	$11,346	$4,705	$2,156	$11,346	$11,346
Sedation	$117,849	$34,332	$12,414	$117,849	$117,849
Other	$31,930	$15,185	$7,383	$31,930	$31,930

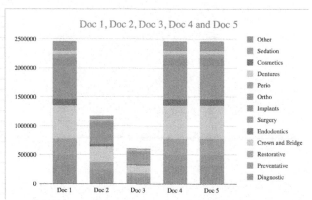

After going through the process on this spreadsheet, as well as the demographics and traffic numbers, you will have enough information to know whether you want to pursue this opportunity or pass on it.

Practice Tour

One of the final stages of the analysis is the live practice visit. Typically, a seller will arrange for this after hours if the sale is confidential. They may ask you to park off-street and be very discreet about the visit. Requests of this nature are normal and should not be cause for alarm.

As you take the tour, keep in mind what aspects are changeable, and which are not. Paint colors, countertops, flooring, and supplies can all be changed very quickly. Even the leather color on chairs can be changed with relative ease with reupholstery. The equipment can be changed if absolutely needed, but there's a good reason to take note of all existing equipment.

Below is the list of details that you should know about each large piece of equipment in the practice. This is used for valuation purposes, negotiation tactics, and as a comprehensive record in the event that you purchase the practice.

- Location
- Date of Evaluation
- Rep or Tech name that installed/sold the equipment
- Type of Equipment
- Model
- Serial #
- Age
- Color/Style
- Recommended replacement?
- Condition
- Notes

Following the tour, you should have a good idea as to whether the practice is a match for you. This can be an exciting moment, but it is always important to remember to remain emotionally unattached, as there are many deals that look good initially, that do not end up working out for one reason or another.

The next chapter will help prepare you for the financial implications of purchasing a new business, before the negotiating process actually begins.

Potential Pitfalls

The numbers of a practice might look really good. The esthetics of the practice are modern and stylish. The team seems upbeat and ready for a new owner. However, there could be things under the surface that would make this acquisition a nightmare rather than a dream.

We have seen many situations over the years where an acquisition turns out to be extremely bad for one reason or another. For these reasons , we want to make sure you learn from the experience of others, rather than learning yourself.

Here's a few simplified examples:

- Doctor selling the practice to 'move back to family'. Production was average to low, and the mix of patients seemed to be PPO and Medicaid. Unfortunately, they hid the fact that they gave extreme discounts on almost everything, and their percentage of medicaid was much higher than in any paperwork they presented early in the process. Acquisition went through and the purchaser found out that it was 80% Medicaid. This office struggled for years and was ultimately closed-merged into another office.
    - How to avoid it? Get the most detailed reports available from the practice management system. Make sure it is not possible for the seller to re-categorize these patients on a separate form, you need actual reports.

- Doctor sold this high-revenue practice for over $1M. New buyer comes in with a similar skillset (probably even better), but different age and ethnicity of the doctor. The selling doctor was an older female from a Eastern European background, spoke Russian, and had a loyal following of Russian-speaking patients. New doctor was a younger male and was not of the same ethnicity, nor did they speak russian. The patient base was quickly weary of the change and it was extremely difficult to achieve the same level of production.
    - How to avoid it? Make sure that you evaluate the 'social' aspect of the patient base and selling doctor. Will the patients feel comfortable switching to you? Is there a language that many of the patients speak that is different from your own?

- Selling Doctor patched all the equipment and real estate issues to look good right up until the sale. In the weeks and months after the sale, equipment broke down weekly. This ended up costing an extra $50,000 to fix all these issues over that time until new equipment could be ordered.
    - How to avoid it? Make sure you have an equipment rep or repair person go with you to an acquisition closer to the closing date to evaluate all the equipment and whether there are any pressing needs. While many things are difficult to find, they should help you evaluate these needs and hopefully ward off any future problems.

- Selling doctor had a great production, but the production was primarily based on crown, bridges and implants. The office sold at a high premium, but the truth was that almost every tooth that needed any work was already crowned. When the new doctor transitioned in, there was very little work that needed to be done. The purchasing doctor was now paying a high loan on a premium practice, but not getting any revenues off the patients that they acquired/obtained.
    - How to avoid it? Make sure to go through the spreadsheet above and do the procedure analysis. You will be able to see if their percentages match the targeted ranges, and whether they have been getting a large percentage of their production from crown and bridge. If so, be weary of paying a high dollar amount for a practice with not many procedures left to do.

Chapter 3

Financials

The next stage in the acquisition process is to get all your financial paperwork together. This can happen when you find an office, but usually even before settling on a final decision. Be ready to take some serious time to get all this together, and start discussions with a finance institution before putting in a final offer on a practice.

It is necessary to have this paperwork organized to ensure that a financial institution or bank will lend you the money it will take to make the acquisition. Although you may not have a final decision on a practice, it's prudent to start this side of the process in order to be able to move quickly once you have decided on a practice and purchase price.

The documents listed are important for this stage of the process and can be accessed by scanning the QR code here -->.

To begin, you'll need these documents:
1. Personal Financial Statement
2. Loan Calculator
3. Pro Forma Spreadsheet (after you've settled on a practice to purchase)
4. Budget + Gameplan (after you've settled on a practice to purchase)
5. Master Formulary
6. Supply Budget

While these are important as you approach banks, it is even worthwhile to update with some frequency after your acquisition is complete. We often keep updated personal finance statements and loan calculators for ourselves each month.

Personal Financial Statement

A PFS is a snapshot in time of your financial picture. It includes:
- ❏ + Cash in banks
- ❏ + Accounts Receivables that are to be paid to you
- ❏ + Securities/stocks/bonds owned by you
- ❏ + Any real estate you own
- ❏ + Any vehicles or other assets you own
- ❏ + Any insurances you own that have cash surrender value
- ❏ - Any debts you owe in student loans

- ❏ - Any real estate debt
- ❏ - Any vehicle or asset debt
- ❏ - Any accounts payable (bills that you have due)

Usually a bank will also want to know your occupation, place of employment, length of employment, income, and your typical monthly living expenses. This will give them a pretty good idea of your risk profile, and credit worthiness.

Here's an example of a PFS:

SUBMITTED TO: _____

TYPE OF CREDIT - CHECK THE APPROPRIATE BOX [ ] Individual - Financial Information only about yourself [X] Joint with: _____

Relationship _____

PERSONAL FINANCIAL STATEMENT OF: Dr. and Mrs. Smith   Soc Sec # _____

Name _____	D. O. B. _____	Statement Date _____
Address _____	City, State, ZIP _____	Soc Sec # _____
Home Phone _____	No. of Dependants _____	Bus. Or Occupation Dentist	Bus. Phone _____

A) CASH IN BANKS AND NOTES DUE TO BANKS (DO NOT INCLUDE REAL ESTATE)

Name of Bank	Type of Account	Type of Ownership	On Deposit	Notes Due to Banks	Collateral (if any) & type of ownership
Bank of America	Checking	Sole	$20,000		
		Cash			
		TOTALS	$20,000	$0	

B) SECURITIES OWNED (Including U.S. Gov. Bonds and all other Stocks and Bonds)

Face Value No. Shares	Description Indicate if not registered in own name	Type of Ownership	Cost	Market Value U.S. Gov. Securities	Market Value Marketable Securities	Market Value Securities Not readily marketable	Amount Pledged to secured loans
100%	Example Dental	LLC	$660			$1,000,000	
		TOTALS	$0	$0	$1,000,000	

C) NOTES AND ACCOUNTS RECEIVABLE (Money payable or Owed to you individually)   Place a check mark in the last box if others have ownership interest ☑

Maker/ Debtor	When Due	Original Amount	Balance Due Good Accts.	Balance Due Doubtful Acct.	Balance Due Notes Relatives & Friends	Security (if any)	Other Owners
	TOTAL	$0	$0	$0			

D) REAL ESTATE OWNED   Place a check mark by the last box if others have ownership interest ☑

Name on Title	Description & Location	Date Acquired	Original Cost	Present Value of Real Estate	Amount of Ins. Carried	MORTGAGE OR CONTRACT PAYABLE Bal. Due	Payment	Maturity	To Whom Payable
		TOTAL	$0		TOTAL	$0			

Here's the second page of the Personal Financial Statement:

COMPANY	Face of Policy	Cash Surrender Value	Policy Loan from Insurance Co.	Other Loans Policy as Collateral	BENEFICIARY
TOTALS	$0		$0		

	ASSETS		Amount			LIABILITIES		Amount
1	Cash on Hand & in Banks	Section A	$20,000		21	Notes Due to Banks	Section A	$0
2	Cash Value of Life Insurance	Section H	$0		22	Notes Due to Relatives & Friends	Section G	
3	U.S. Government Securities	Section B	$0		23	Notes Due to Others	Section G	
4	Other Marketable Securities	Section B	$0		24	Accounts & Bills Payable	Section G	
5	Notes & Accounts Receivable - Good	Section C	$0		25	Unpaid Income Taxes Fed___State___		
6	Other Assets Convertible to Cash		$0		26	Other Unpaid Taxes & Interest		
7					27	Loans on Life Insurance Policies		
8					28	Contract Accounts Payable	Section H	
9	TOTAL CURRENT ASSETS				29	Cash Rent Owed	Section G	
10	Real Estate Owned	Section D			30	Other liabilities Due within 1 Yr. Itemize		
11	Real Estate Owned - Residence	Section D	$0		31			
12	Mortgages & Contracts Owned	Section E			32			
13	Notes & Accounts Receivable	Section C			33	TOTAL CURRENT LIABILITIES		
14	Due From Relatives & Friends	Section C			34	Real Estate Mortgages Payable	Section D	$0
15	Non-marketable Securities	Section B			35	Liens & Assessments Payable		
16	Personal Property & Vehicles	Section F	$0		36	Other Debts - Itemize		
17	Other Assets -Itemize				37			
18					38	Total Liabilities		
19					39	Net Worth (Total Assets minus liabilities)		
20	TOTAL ASSETS		$20,000		40	TOTAL LIABILITIES & NET WORTH		$0

ANNUAL INCOME			ESTIMATE OF ANNUAL EXPENSES	
Salary, Bonuses, & Commissions	$0		Income Taxes	$0
Dividends & Interest	$0		Other Taxes	$0
Rental & Lease Income (Net)	$		Insurance Premiums	$0
Alimony, child support, or separate maintenance income need not be revealed				
if you do not wish to have it considered as a basis for repaying this obligation.				
Other Income-Itemize	$		Mortgage Payments	$0
Provide the following information only if Joint Credit is checked above.				
Other Persons Salary, Bonuses & Commissions	$		Rent Payable	
Alimony, child support, or separate maintenance income need not be revealed				
if you do not wish to have it considered as a basis for repaying this obligation.				
Other Income of Other Person-Itemize	$		Other Expenses	$
TOTAL	$0		TOTAL	$0

GENERAL INFORMATION		CONTINGENT LIABILITIES	
Are any Assets Pledged? __x__No ____Yes		As Endorser, Co-maker or Guarantor	$
Are you a Defendant in any Suits or Legal Actions? __x__No ____Yes		On Leases or Contracts	$
(Explain):		Legal Claims	$
Have you ever been declared Bankrupt in the last 10 years? __x__No ____Yes		Federal - State Income Taxes	$
(Explain):		Other -	$

This statement represents the true, complete and accurate statement of my/our financial condition. I/we agree that if any change occurs that materially reduces the means or ability to pay any claims or demands I/we will immediately notify the bank in writing; and unless the bank is so notified, it may continue to rely upon the statement herein as a true, complete and accurate statement.

NOTE: Any willful misrepresentation could result in a fine and/or imprisonment under provisions of the U.S. criminal code.

Signed _____ Dated _____ Signed _____ Dated _____

Download the document above in the associated document via the QR code at the beginning of the book.

We really encourage people to update their PFS monthly or quarterly. This habit will keep you constantly aware of your financial standing and net worth. It will also be requested by financial institutions repeatedly throughout your business life, so keeping it updated will ensure that it is readily available when necessary.

There are several web applications that are widely used to keep track of all of your financial details automatically. One that we like is 'Mint' by Intuit. This is the same company that created QuickBooks, and their web-based software can tie into any other bank software and mortgage schedule to keep you with an updated PFS in real-time.

Loan Calculator

Once you start to become more successful, you will probably take out more debt for either personal or business items. This can sometimes become a complicated web of entities, timelines, and amounts of money. This spreadsheet is a helpful tool for tracking all of your loans in one place. So here's how to use it:

		Loan Balances	
		2019 Jun	
A	Practice Loan 1	$	325,975.66
B	Loan 2	$	244,016.94
C	Loan 3	$	196,993.34
D	Practice Loan 4	$	184,127.54
E	Loan 5	$	163,622.31
F	Buildout Loan	$	263,431.57
G	Property 1	$	98,294.64
H	Property 2	$	78,076.04
I	Property 2 Improvemen	$	13,336.19
J	Loan 6	$	294,433.66
K	Loan 6	$	139,268.76
L	Loan 6	$	7,227.26
	Total Loan Balances	$	2,008,804

1. Obtain the paperwork for each loan that you have for any business/personal entities

2. Start at Loan A

3. Place the Entity, Lendor, Loan Title, Term, Rate, and any other pertinent information

4. Make sure to put the monthly payments in the column as hard-coded

5. If the interest doesn't accrue correctly, you may have to type that amount in each month as well(Some banks do daily interest- which is hard to replicate)

6. Go through steps 2-5 for each loan

7. In Summary Cell L2- pick the matching correct number for the month

8. Zero out any unused sheets

_____

The sheet should be usable now!!

_____

9. Going forward, any month that you pay additional- put that added principal payment in the column on that loan

Here is the front page of the spreadsheet, which is compiled from the subsequent sheets in the spreadsheet.

Loan Balances

	2021	Jan	
A	Practice Loan 1	$	279,672.01
B	Loan 2	$	230,866.20
C	Loan 3	$	190,368.03
D	Practice Loan 4	$	131,170.87
E	Loan 5	$	108,979.97
F	Buildout Loan	$	225,200.52
G	Property 1	$	92,694.06
H	Property 2	$	71,823.23
I	Property 2 Improveme	$	7,842.84
J	Loan 6	$	279,198.60
K	Loan 6	$	103,465.17
L	Loan 6	$	(2,023.69)
	Total Loan Balances	$	**1,719,258**

Loan Balances By Corporation

%	Yrs	Personal LLC	$	700,906		Monthly	
4.000%	15	Practice Loan 1	$	279,672	Bank #1	$	3,451.32
4.000%	15	Loan 2	$	230,866	Bank #1	$	1,485.00
4.000%	15	Loan 3	$	190,368	Bank #1	$	995.00
%	Yrs	**Practice LLC 1**	$	465,351		Monthly	
5.000%	10	Practice Loan 4	$	131,171	Bank #2	$	3,451.32
5.000%	10	Loan 5	$	108,980	Bank #2	$	3,451.32
4.090%	10	Buildout Loan	$	225,201	Bank #2	$	2,849.00
%	Yrs	**Property LLC**	$	172,360		Monthly	
3.490%	10	Property 1	$	92,694	Bank #2	$	573.00
2.490%	10	Property 2	$	71,823	Bank #2	$	485.00
4.000%	10	Property 2 Improvements	$	7,843	Bank #2	$	325.00
%	Yrs	**Personal Debt**	$	380,640		Monthly	
5.000%	10	Loan 6	$	279,199	Bank #2	$	1,999.00
5.000%	10	Loan 6	$	103,465	Bank #2	$	2,395.00
5.000%	10	Loan 6	$	(2,024)	Bank #2	$	499.00

Total   **$ 1,719,258** $ 21,958.96

Here is an example from the first 'Loan' tab. For each loan that you have, fill out the table below, which is normally called an amortization schedule. Make sure the payments are accurate for each month, as well as interest rate, and the ending balance for each month going forward. Typically the Excel spreadsheet will calculate this accurately, unless your bank has a different method of executing their interest rate.

	Borrower	Personal LLC				Loan #>>		
	Asset	Practice Loan 1				When is payment made?		
	Lender	Bank #1				Bank Address:		
	Term	15	Years					
	Rate	4.000%	%			Autopay?		

			Principal Balance	Monthly Interest	Monthly Principle	Mtg Payments	Additional Payments	Interest Rate	End Balance
	2018	Dec				Copy Monthly Payments bel		4.000%	340,000.00
1	2019	Jan	340000.00	1,133.33	2,317.99	3,451.32			337,682.01
2	2019	Feb	337682.01	1,125.61	2,325.71	3,451.32			335,356.30
3	2019	Mar	335356.30	1,117.85	2,333.47	3,451.32			333,022.83
4	2019	Apr	333022.83	1,110.08	2,341.24	3,451.32			330,681.59
5	2019	May	330681.59	1,102.27	2,349.05	3,451.32			328,332.54
6	2019	Jun	328332.54	1,094.44	2,356.88	3,451.32			325,975.66
7	2019	Jul	325975.66	1,086.59	2,364.73	3,451.32			323,610.93
8	2019	Aug	323610.93	1,078.70	2,372.62	3,451.32			321,238.31
9	2019	Sep	321238.31	1,070.79	2,380.53	3,451.32			318,857.79
10	2019	Oct	318857.79	1,062.86	2,388.46	3,451.32			316,469.33
11	2019	Nov	316469.33	1,054.90	2,396.42	3,451.32			314,072.90
12	2019	Dec	314072.90	1,046.91	2,404.41	3,451.32			311,668.49
13	2020	Jan	311668.49	1,038.89	2,412.43	3,451.32			309,256.07
14	2020	Feb	309256.07	1,030.85	2,420.47	3,451.32			306,835.60
15	2020	Mar	306835.60	1,022.79	2,428.53	3,451.32			304,407.07
16	2020	Apr	304407.07	1,014.69	2,436.63	3,451.32			301,970.44
17	2020	May	301970.44	1,006.57	2,444.75	3,451.32			299,525.69
18	2020	Jun	299525.69	998.42	2,452.90	3,451.32			297,072.79
19	2020	Jul	297072.79	990.24	2,461.08	3,451.32			294,611.71
20	2020	Aug	294611.71	982.04	2,469.28	3,451.32			292,142.43
21	2020	Sep	292142.43	973.81	2,477.51	3,451.32			289,664.91
22	2020	Oct	289664.91	965.55	2,485.77	3,451.32			287,179.14
23	2020	Nov	287179.14	957.26	2,494.06	3,451.32			284,685.09

Pro Forma Spreadsheet

The Pro Forma Spreadsheet is the next document that will be requested. This is specifically a document that outlines what the practice expects to profit or lose over the first couple of years. After going through the exercise, you will get to see exactly how much money you will need from the bank in the form of 'working capital'. (Working capital is a short-term loan from the bank that covers operational expenses for the first few months then is paid back quickly because it is usually at a higher interest rate. Sometimes working capital is also called a line of credit.) If throughout negotiations you decide to purchase the accounts receivable (AR) from the seller, then you might not need much working capital. If you buy the AR, this means that the collections coming in from the first day are 100% yours to keep. This can surely help cash flow and make things go smoother from day 1, however there's some calculations to be done before deciding whether this is the best course of action. We will address that in the next chapter. However, if you decide not to purchase the AR, you will surely need some working capital to run the business before collections ramp up to a level where it will cover all necessary expenses.

The Pro Forma is also extremely useful to plot out how much you think you'll want to spend in different departments in order to hit the growth goals you have set out for yourself.

- ProForma Spreadsheet Key Points:
  - Tells you how much you would need from a bank in a line of credit
  - Use as a projected budget for the future
  - Overestimate for unexpected expenses
  - Borrow aggressively and spend conservatively

To start the Pro Forma, download the document and follow these steps.
1. Along the top, enter the months in text boxes. The mock sheet has you purchasing and taking over your practice starting in July. However, remember that there are some expenses to expect before you start, including legal, accounting, and any other miscellaneous expenses. (If you are sending out a mailing, informing the patient base of the transition, you might split the cost with the seller and that expense might actually be in the month or days before you actually start seeing any revenues from the practice.)
2. Begin entering how much revenue you will plan on receiving each month. This is not 'production', it is only collections. Keep in mind that collections always trails production by at least 30-60 days, especially at the beginning of your acquisition. This is typically due to insurance negotiations, payment plans, and the slower flow of patients. However, if you do decide to purchase the Accounts Receivable (AR), then you can expect a better immediate cash flow.
3. Enter all cost categories and their expected monthly cost
   a. Some are based on a percentage of revenues - like supplies or lab costs. These are the "variable expenses".
   b. Some are more stable costs like rent, utilities, or insurance. These are considered the fixed costs and do not change with increases in revenues.
4. The staff payroll line is calculated off of the second tab, and is a computed number based on the hours of an employee each month, as well as their pay rate. Enter each

employee's start date, pay rate, and expected hours. If you already have this number from the seller, enter the payroll that they have seen over the past few months.

5. At the bottom of the sheet, you will see that the costs start to add up and then culminate into the 'EBITDA' line. This is your overall profitability line. The line below the EBITDA line is then the Net Negative financial number. If you buy the AR, then you probably will not dip into a negative number at all. However, if you decide to pass on the AR, then you will most likely need to prepare to go negative. This negative number is how 'low' your bank account will go during the first phase of your startup. This is also the number you should tell your bank you will require in a working capital loan.

Keys to the Pro Forma:
- Always overestimate expenses and underestimate revenues
- Always tell the bank a higher working capital loan if you will be using one
  - No matter whether you buy the AR or not, you should plan on getting a working capital loan or line of credit from the bank.

See the next two pages for examples of the Pro Forma:

Here is the front page of the pro forma statement:

Pro Forma Statement

	T-3 April	T-2 May	T-1 June	1 July	2 August	3 September	4 October	5 November	6 December	Year 1
Sales										
Total Cost of Goods Sold	$ -	$ -	$ -	$ -	$ -	$ -	$ -	$ -	$ -	$ -
Staff Salary	$ -	$ -	$ -	$ -	$ -	$ -	$ -	$ -	$ -	$ -
Doctor 1 Disbursement										$ -
Doctor 2 Disbursement										$ -
Salaries & Wages	$ -	$ -	$ -	$ -	$ -	$ -	$ -	$ -	$ -	$ -
Payroll Taxes										$ -
Group Insurance										$ -
Employee Benefits										$ -
Workman's Comp										$ -
Employee Benefits	$ -	$ -	$ -	$ -	$ -	$ -	$ -	$ -	$ -	$ -
Malpractice Insurance (Harold Diers)2 docs										$ -
Janitorial Services										$ -
Sedation - under Direct Operating										
Dental Supplies										$ -
Misc.										$ -
Dues, License, Fees										$ -
Fixed Equipment Rental	$ -	$ -					$ -	$ -	$ -	$ -
Practice Software Lease										$ -
Pitney Bowes Postage Machine Rental										$ -
Direct Operating										$ -
Monthly Marketing / Promotion										$ -
Advertising										$ -
Marketing/Promotion	$ -	$ -	$ -	$ -	$ -	$ -	$ -	$ -	$ -	$ -
Electric										$ -
Gas										$ -
Water										$ -
Garbage										$ -
Utility Services	$ -	$ -	$ -	$ -	$ -	$ -	$ -	$ -	$ -	$ -
Credit Card Fee										$ -
Bank Charges										$ -
Professional Fees										$ -
Office Supplies & Postage										$ -
Telephone & Datacom										$ -
Dues/Subscription										$ -
Personnel Expense(Scrubs, etc.)										$ -
Training Expense										$ -
General/Administrative	$ -	$ -	$ -	$ -	$ -	$ -	$ -	$ -	$ -	$ -
Repairs & Maintenance										$ -
Repairs & Maintenance	$ -	$ -	$ -	$ -	$ -	$ -	$ -	$ -	$ -	$ -
Property/Liability Insurance										$ -
Rent										$ -
CAM Charge				$ -	$ -	$ -	$ -	$ -		$ -
Taxes/Licenses										$ -
Occupancy Costs	$ -	$ -	$ -	$ -	$ -	$ -	$ -	$ -	$ -	$ -
Operating Expenses	$ -	$ -	$ -	$ -	$ -	$ -	$ -	$ -	$ -	$ -
EBITDA	$ -	$ -	$ -	$ -	$ -	$ -	$ -	$ -	$ -	$ -
Total Negative Cash Flow	$ -	$ -	$ -	$ -	$ -	$ -	$ -	$ -	$ -	

Here is the hours worked and wage planning sheet:

Pro Forma Statement	T-3 April	T-2 May	T-1 June	1 July	2 August	3 September	4 October	5 November	6 December
Sales									
Revenue									
Patient Refund									
Other	-	-	-	-	-	-	-	-	-
Total Sales	$	$	$	$	$	$	$	$	$
Cost of Goods Sold									
Dental Supplies									
Lab Fees	-	-	$	$	$	$	$	$	$
Total Cost of Goods Sold	$	$	$	$	$	$	$	$	$
Staff Salary	$	$	$	$	$	$	$	$	$
Doctor 1 Disbursement									
Doctor 2 Disbursement									
Salaries & Wages	$	$	$	$	$	$	$	$	$
Payroll Taxes									
Group Insurance									
Employee Benefits									
Workman's Comp									
Employee Benefits	$	$	$	$	$	$	$	$	$

Budget + Gameplan

Once you're up and running, the Pro Forma Spreadsheet no longer works to track real-time expenses. While the Pro Forma is great for setting out a plan in the future to get financing, you need a dynamic sheet to help in the operational aspects of your new business. That's why we created the Budget + Gameplan sheet. This Budget is only for your internal use, however the financing institution might be interested to see this spreadsheet every few years to see how the practice has been producing and where they expect it to grow. See the spreadsheet here:

Example Dental 2021	End-of-Year		Jan-21	Feb-21	Mar-21	Apr-21	May-21	Jun-21	Jul-21	Aug-21	Sep-21	Oct-21	Nov-21	Dec-21	
Ordinary Income	$ 996,290	100.0%	$ 79,000	$ 80,580	$ 82,192	$ 83,835	$ 83,835	$ 83,835	$ 83,835	$ 83,835	$ 83,835	$ 83,835	$ 83,835	$ 83,835	$ 83,024
Refunds	$ (12,000)	-1.2%	$ (1,000)	$ (1,000)	$ (1,000)	$ (1,000)	$ (1,000)	$ (1,000)	$ (1,000)	$ (1,000)	$ (1,000)	$ (1,000)	$ (1,000)	$ (1,000)	
Other	$ -		$ -	$ -	$ -	$ -	$ -	$ -	$ -						
Total Income	$ 984,290		$ 78,000	$ 79,580	$ 81,192	$ 82,835	$ 82,835	$ 82,835	$ 82,835	$ 82,835	$ 82,835	$ 82,835	$ 82,835	$ 82,835	
Lab Fees	$ 59,057	6.0%	$ 4,921	$ 4,921	$ 4,921	$ 4,921	$ 4,921	$ 4,921	$ 4,921	$ 4,921	$ 4,921	$ 4,921	$ 4,921	$ 4,921	$ 59,057
Dental Supplies	$ 39,372	4.0%	$ 3,281	$ 3,281	$ 3,281	$ 3,281	$ 3,281	$ 3,281	$ 3,281	$ 3,281	$ 3,281	$ 3,281	$ 3,281	$ 3,281	$ 39,372
Combined Supplies/Lab	$ 98,429	10.0%	$ 8,202	$ 8,202	$ 8,202	$ 8,202	$ 8,202	$ 8,202	$ 8,202	$ 8,202	$ 8,202	$ 8,202	$ 8,202	$ 8,202	
Office and Postage	$ 12,000	1.2%	$ 1,000	$ 1,000	$ 1,000	$ 1,000	$ 1,000	$ 1,000	$ 1,000	$ 1,000	$ 1,000	$ 1,000	$ 1,000	$ 1,000	
Vehicles	$ 12,000	1.2%	$ 1,000	$ 1,000	$ 1,000	$ 1,000	$ 1,000	$ 1,000	$ 1,000	$ 1,000	$ 1,000	$ 1,000	$ 1,000	$ 1,000	
Doctor Vehicle	$ 12,000		$ 1,000	$ 1,000	$ 1,000	$ 1,000	$ 1,000	$ 1,000	$ 1,000	$ 1,000	$ 1,000	$ 1,000	$ 1,000	$ 1,000	
Other	$ -		$ -	$ -	$ -	$ -	$ -	$ -	$ -	$ -	$ -	$ -	$ -	$ -	
Other	$ -		$ -	$ -	$ -	$ -	$ -	$ -	$ -	$ -	$ -	$ -	$ -	$ -	
Professional Fees	$ -	0.0%	$ -	$ -	$ -	$ -	$ -	$ -	$ -	$ -	$ -	$ -	$ -	$ -	
Licenses and Permits	$ 1,320	0.1%	$ 110	$ 110	$ 110	$ 110	$ 110	$ 110	$ 110	$ 110	$ 110	$ 110	$ 110	$ 110	
Dues and Subscriptions	$ 600	0.1%	$ 50	$ 50	$ 50	$ 50	$ 50	$ 50	$ 50	$ 50	$ 50	$ 50	$ 50	$ 50	
Telephone	$ 6,828	0.7%	$ 569	$ 569	$ 569	$ 569	$ 569	$ 569	$ 569	$ 569	$ 569	$ 569	$ 569	$ 569	
Rent	$ 36,000	3.7%	$ 3,000	$ 3,000	$ 3,000	$ 3,000	$ 3,000	$ 3,000	$ 3,000	$ 3,000	$ 3,000	$ 3,000	$ 3,000	$ 3,000	
Repairs and Maintenance	$ 6,000	0.6%	$ 500	$ 500	$ 500	$ 500	$ 500	$ 500	$ 500	$ 500	$ 500	$ 500	$ 500	$ 500	
Insurance Expense	$ 6,000	0.6%	$ 500	$ 500	$ 500	$ 500	$ 500	$ 500	$ 500	$ 500	$ 500	$ 500	$ 500	$ 500	
Real Estate Taxes	$ -	0.0%	$ -	$ -	$ -	$ -	$ -	$ -	$ -	$ -	$ -	$ -	$ -	$ -	
Salaries and Wages	$ 480,000	48.8%	$ 40,000	$ 40,000	$ 40,000	$ 40,000	$ 40,000	$ 40,000	$ 40,000	$ 40,000	$ 40,000	$ 40,000	$ 40,000	$ 40,000	$ 40,000
Owner Dr. Salary	$ 156,000	15.8%	$ 13,000	$ 13,000	$ 13,000	$ 13,000	$ 13,000	$ 13,000	$ 13,000	$ 13,000	$ 13,000	$ 13,000	$ 13,000	$ 13,000	
Other Salar	$ -	0.0%	$ -	$ -	$ -	$ -	$ -	$ -	$ -	$ -	$ -	$ -	$ -	$ -	
Other Salary	$ -	0.0%	$ -	$ -	$ -	$ -	$ -	$ -	$ -	$ -	$ -	$ -	$ -	$ -	
Associate Salary	$ -	0.0%	$ -	$ -	$ -	$ -	$ -	$ -	$ -	$ -	$ -	$ -	$ -	$ -	

In this sheet, it gives you a 12 month picture of your practice and all expenses. This sheet is organized in a similar fashion as the Pro Forma, but can also be changeable to the specific areas of your practice where you'll have expenses. There are 3 main tabs in this spreadsheet:

1. Gameplan
2. Actual
3. Comparison

The Gameplan can also be referred to as the 'Budget'. It is the expected revenues and costs of the practice over the next 12 months. All the revenues drop down into the 'Total Income' column, and all expenses are below. Each category of expenses is a computed total line for the category, it is then all added up into the total net revenues at the bottom.

For setting up the Gameplan, we usually suggest that you do this exercise in November of the previous year. During this time, you should review all expenses of the practice, see where you're above normal percentages, see where you're doing well, and then plot out the next full year. Going through this exercise can take some effort, but it is valuable for helping to plan for both staffing levels, expected profit, and taxes.

When putting in the Gameplan numbers, remember that some columns are going to be variable expenses, and we suggest trying to tie those costs to a percentage basis of the revenues. For example, your goal might be to keep dental supplies at 4.5% of revenues. In this case, you should put 4.5% X Revenues for this cost category. However, some are fixed expenses, and in this case you should put those as flat-line numbers across the sheet. For example, rent will not fluctuate month-to-month, so you can enter the costs and you won't need to correlate this number with production at all.

The "Actual" tab is the costs that you will put in each month as you go through the year. It will start out empty and then you will add your costs each month as you go through the year. One thing to remember is that as you change anything on the 'Gameplan' tab, that you'll want to change it on the 'Actual' and 'Comparison' tabs as well in the exact same place.

| Example Dental | | 2 | 2 |
2021	End-of-Year	Jan-21	Feb-21
Ordinary Income	$ -	$ -	$ -
Refunds	$ -	$ -	$ -
Other	$ -	$ -	$ -
Total Income	$ -	$ -	$ -
Lab Fees	$ -	$ -	$ -
Dental Supplies	$ -	$ -	$ -
Combined Supples/Lab	$ -	$ -	$ -
Office and Postage	$ -	$ -	$ -
Vehicles	$ -	$ -	$ -
Doctor Vehicle	$ -	$ -	$ -
Other	$ -	$ -	$ -
Other	$ -	$ -	$ -
Professional Fees	$ -	$ -	$ -
Licenses and Permits	$ -	$ -	$ -

The final tab, and the aspect where this spreadsheet truly helps- is the 'Comparison' tab. On this page, it will show you the dynamic Month comparison, year to date comparison, and end of year comparison. The only box to be changed on this page is to do the pull-down menu picking which month you're at so far. After you pick that, it will decide which columns to add up on the other tabs, and then you can then start to do an analysis of what is going well and what is not.

| Example Dental | For the Month of: | January | Year-to-Date | | End-of-Year | |
2021	Gameplan	Actual 2021	Gameplan	Actual 2021	Gameplan	Actual 2021
Ordinary Income	$ - #DIV/0!	$ - #DIV/0!	$ - #DIV/0!	$ - #DIV/0!	$ 996,290 100.0%	$ - #DIV/0!
Refunds	$ - #DIV/0!	$ - #DIV/0!	$ - #DIV/0!	$ - #DIV/0!	$ (12,000) -1.2%	$ - #DIV/0!
Other	$ - #DIV/0!	$ - #DIV/0!	$ - #DIV/0!	$ - #DIV/0!	$ - 0.0%	$ - #DIV/0!
Total Income	$ -	$ -	$ -	$ -	$ 984,290	$ -
Lab Fees	$ - #DIV/0!	$ - #DIV/0!	$ - #DIV/0!	$ - #DIV/0!	$ 59,057 6.0%	$ - #DIV/0!
Dental Supplies	$ - #DIV/0!	$ - #DIV/0!	$ - #DIV/0!	$ - #DIV/0!	$ 39,372 4.0%	$ - #DIV/0!
Combined Supples/Lab	$ - #DIV/0!	$ - #DIV/0!	$ - #DIV/0!	$ - #DIV/0!	$ 98,429 10.0%	$ - #DIV/0!
Office and Postage	$ - #DIV/0!	$ - #DIV/0!	$ - #DIV/0!	$ - #DIV/0!	$ 12,000 1.2%	$ - #DIV/0!
Vehicles	$ - #DIV/0!	$ - #DIV/0!	$ - #DIV/0!	$ - #DIV/0!	$ 12,000 1.2%	$ - #DIV/0!
Doctor Vehicle	$ - #DIV/0!	$ - #DIV/0!	$ - #DIV/0!	$ - #DIV/0!	$ 12,000 1.2%	$ - #DIV/0!
Other	$ - #DIV/0!	$ - #DIV/0!	$ - #DIV/0!	$ - #DIV/0!	$ - 0.0%	$ - #DIV/0!
Other	$ - #DIV/0!	$ - #DIV/0!	$ - #DIV/0!	$ - #DIV/0!	$ - 0.0%	$ - #DIV/0!
Professional Fees	$ - #DIV/0!	$ - #DIV/0!	$ - #DIV/0!	$ - #DIV/0!	$ - 0.0%	$ - #DIV/0!
Licenses and Permits	$ - #DIV/0!	$ - #DIV/0!	$ - #DIV/0!	$ - #DIV/0!	$ 1,320 0.1%	$ - #DIV/0!
Dues and Subscriptions	$ - #DIV/0!	$ - #DIV/0!	$ - #DIV/0!	$ - #DIV/0!	$ 600 0.1%	$ - #DIV/0!

While the Budget + Gameplan is a complicated sheet with a lot going on, we highly suggest using this or some other software to track.

Master Formulary

The best way to control dental supply costs is to keep a master formulary for all supplies. This will be the top 400 items that you order on a semi-regular basis. All of your composite, impression materials, stone, personal protective equipment, and so on.

SKU	Discription		QUANTITY in PK
	ANESTHETICS		
8053006	Accuject 27g Short Needles		100
8871416	Monoject 30g Short Needles		100
8871418	Monoject 30g X-Short Needles		100
8200360	Carbocaine 3% Plain		50
8050215	Citanest Forte 4% w/epi		50
9515510	Lidocaine HCL 2% w/epi		50
8053850	Polocaine 3% Plain		50
9533808	Protector Needle Sheaths		500
9515480	Septocaine Gold 4% 1:100		50
9515482	Septocaine Silver 4% 1:200		50
3414070	Sharps Container 1.5qt		1
9521621	Topex Topical Gel Cherry (Sultan)	1oz	
9521658	Topex Topical Gel Strawberry (Sultan)	1oz	
	Stabident	20/pk	

The first step in the process of creating your own master formulary is to assemble the list of all the supplies that you will ever order. When we say *all*, we truly do mean *all*. This is going to seem like an insanely tall order, however it is vital to keep costs down. You will not want anyone on your team ordering random supplies from different places. You know what you want, so set the ground rules from day 1 that these are the preferred supplies. With taking over an acquisition, there might be things you don't *like* to order, but are necessary to match the items or equipment that the facility uses. We have definitely had that experience with radiological film developing liquids. There have been offices we have purchased that still used film, and we haven't been able to switch away fast enough, so we had to purchase the expensive bottles of liquids!

After you have the supply list, go through and find the best cost for each supply. In the past, we've had an assistant do this. However, there are now softwares that are much more adept at giving real-time pricing and availability for products. Our favorite is called Dentira. It is a real-time calculated software that will help you keep your supplies at the lowest cost possible, while actually being quite user friendly.

Discription	QUANTITY in PK	HS SKU	HS $	DARBY SKU	DARBY $	NET32 $
ANESTHETICS						
Accuject 27g Short Needles	100	1504183	$15.74	8053006	$13.07	
Monoject 30g Short Needles	100	1945141	$10.39	8871416	$9.74	
Monoject 30g X-Short Needles	100	1941753	$10.39	8871418	$9.74	
Carbocaine 3% Plain	50	8567167	$37.85	8200360	$47.97	
Citanest Forte 4% w/epi	50	1500059	$42.25	8050215	$39.75	
Lidocaine HCL 2% w/epi	50	4651205	$26.15	9515510	$27.16	
Polocaine 3% Plain	50	1500004	$47.51	8053850	$43.75	
Protector Needle Sheaths	500	9911756	$56.06	9533808	$45.77	
Septocaine Gold 4% 1:100	50	2288210	$43.30	9515482	$42.57	
Septocaine Silver 4% 1:200	50	2280944	$43.30	9515480	$42.57	
Sharps Container 1.5qt	1	9875812	$3.50	9414070	$4.10	
Topex Topical Gel Cherry (Sultan)	1oz	3125235	$10.79	9521621	$8.13	
Topex Topical Gel Strawberry (Sultan)	1oz	3127938	$10.79	9521658	$8.13	
Stabident	20/pk					$44.95

After you have entered the costs into the spreadsheet, if you choose to do it manually, you can then create orders as often as necessary, and then you will be able to go to wherever you can purchase that supply the cheapest. This allows you to keep your supply budget at the lowest possible amount.

Supply Budget

The biggest cost overrun for most practices is the supply budget. We have found that time and time again in small practices, and even groups that have revenues upwards of $8 Million per year. Sometimes it's "percentage creep", where at one point the practice was spending only 4.5%, and then eventually it rises to 6% or 7%. Spread out over time, this can add up to hundreds of thousands, even millions of dollars.

The best way to combat this is to track your supply spending in a detailed manner. This spreadsheet will help. To start, you will want to put in your historical revenues into the first page shown below. In this example, it starts with April 2021 with $20,000. Then $50,000 in May and going forward. Basically your target supply spend should be anywhere between 4 and 5% of the last 3 months averaged revenues. So if you're consistently collecting $50,000 in revenues, then 4% times that number is $2,000 a month to spend on supplies.

All Smiles Dentistry	Jan , 2021	Feb , 2021	Mar , 2021	Apr , 2021	May , 2021	Jun , 2021	Jul , 2021	Aug , 2021	Sep , 2021	Oct , 2021
Revenues				$20,000	$50,000	$50,000	$50,000	$50,000	$50,000	$50,000
Percentage Target	4%	4%	4%	4%	4%	4%	4%	4%	4%	4%
Budget					$1,400	$1,400	$1,600	$2,000	$2,000	$2,000
Actual Spend										
Actual %				0.00%	0.00%	0.00%	0.00%	0.00%	0.00%	0.00%
Office #2										
Revenues										
Percentage Target										
Budget										
Actual										
Actual %										

Remember that in growth mode it is not wise to try to squeeze expenses too much. This will increase the risk that you could run out of materials and not be able to finish a procedure. Especially after the COVID supply chain problems following 2020, it is dangerous to keep a low stock on items. For this reason, you'll need to always maintain moderate quantities of supplies while simultaneously keeping an eye on the budget. As you approach your predetermined spending limit, you'll need to start making tougher decisions on where to cut costs.

As you start tracking your orders, use the second tab in the spreadsheet. The top line of the spreadsheet will have you enter

All Smiles Dental			$2,000	
Date Order	Vendor	Supplies	Dental Supplies	Small Equip
April 2021		Details		
		Total Spent	$518.32	$1,449.00
4/2/21	Ultradent	desensitizing gel, microbrush tips	$135.06	
4/6/21	Ebay	coupler/handpieces		$1,449.00
4/6/21	Darby	saliva ejectors, small/medium gloves, chlorhexidine, 256	$383.26	

your budget in large numbers. This is the number copied over from the first sheet. Then, in each line below that, you'll enter the date you ordered, the vendor, the supplies you ordered, and the cost. With each order, you will receive an invoice at a later date and you'll want to double check it for accuracy, as there are often discrepancies.

After each month ends, you will then move all those cells downward, and add in enough space to put a new month in. This way you can always keep your supplies on a running tab, be able to verify that you received the order, and keep costs within the budget for each month.

We hope that these documents in this section have been helpful and will allow you to execute the acquisition process with more clarity around the financial sides. While it might seem like a lot of work up-front, we often think back to the quote from Jocko Willink about execution. He says, "We do not rise to the occasion, we fall to the highest level of preparation." We know that going through this level of financial preparation will allow you to be absolutely prepared for executing an acquisition and transition with financial stability.

After finishing these documents in this chapter, you are now fully prepared to start negotiating and working towards acquiring a practice.

Notes:

_____

_____

_____

_____

_____

_____

_____

_____

_____

_____

_____

_____

_____

_____

_____

_____

_____

_____

_____

_____

_____

_____

_____

_____

_____

_____

Chapter 4

Valuation and Negotiation

The next stage in the acquisition journey is to establish a real value for a practice and begin the negotiation process. By this stage, you have researched and visited the practice. Hopefully the broker or seller has now furnished the accurate numbers and documentation in order for you to come to an appropriate valuation on the office. As stated in the earlier chapter, the minimum documents that you need are the following:

1. Last 3 years Profit and Loss Statements
2. Last 3 years Tax Returns
3. Codes and Production over the last 3 years
4. Everything in the 'Acquisition Analysis Spreadsheet' for general information

After you have obtained these documents, you will be able to begin the valuation process. While doing this exercise, keep in mind that the value that you put on the practice is all part of the negotiations process and also provides you with a deeper understanding of the economics of the practice you wish to purchase. It is important to realize that no valuation method is perfect.

A valuation is truly just used as a *tool* utilized by both sides of a negotiation table to give each party a starting point. The seller could have a valuation that they use to increase the price. Similarly, you could find your own valuation that you use to decrease the price. Methods differ, price differs, and it's all part of the game.

The final value of the practice will really come down on whatever price the buyer is willing to pay, and whatever the seller is willing to accept. This is the way a free market works, and of course there are a myriad of variables that either tilt the tables in your direction or your sellers! To gain a further understanding on all the intricate pieces at play during an acquisition process, we recommend *'The Art of Selling your Business'* by John Warrillow. This will help you understand the seller's attitude, and thereby allow you to gain a better picture of how you can negotiate strategically.

Valuation

There are a couple of reliable methods that are used to determine the value of a dental practice if you will be the sole practitioner of the entity. Some selling doctors think it is a percentage of historical revenues, or some other measure similar to this. However, we should look at the bigger picture, and the important, relevant data. Rather than using methods that were created in an antiquated dental practice industry, we need to treat this like a real business. When looking at a practice, some methods leave out many important variables. For us to come to the most accurate method that allows you to have long-term financial success, we need to include all these variables. In the dental market, we will describe the three major methods of valuing a practice, and then we will go in depth on the one we think is most accurate. Here are the three major ways to value a dental practice:

1. Percentage of Historical Revenues
2. Multiple of EBITDA (Earnings Before Interest Taxes Depreciation and Amortization)
3. Value of Equipment and Hard Assets

Percentage of Historical Revenues

This is one of the most common ways that practice brokers will try to value a practice before they put it on the market. It has a history that is as old as dentistry, but one that should probably be left in the prehistoric, 'wooden dentures' era. While we still see it utilized often, the flaws in this methodology outweigh the advantages and in most cases there are better ways to arrive at an accurate value.

Practice brokers will often value a practice at 60%-100% of the previous year's revenues. Typically the range is even narrower at 60%-80%, but for certain areas of the country it can be higher. If the practice is older or has more undesirable properties, then the price will most likely fall into the lower percentage range. However, if the practice is newer, with more desirable qualities, the value will move towards a higher percentage.

Here's an example:

Prior Years Revenues	$440,000	
60%	$264,000	Low End
100%	$440,000	High End

In the example above, the valuation on this practice would fall somewhere between $264,000 and $440,000 depending on health of the business, quality of fixed assets, and other contributing factors. While we do not necessarily encourage buyers to use this method, we recommend multiple methods of valuation applied in order to get a range of price points.

A few key advantages to this methodology:
- Easy to execute quickly
- No need for high level financial analysis

And a few key disadvantages:
- Valuation is not based on the profitability of the practice

- A valuation is calculated without analyzing the health of the business

In summary, the percentage of prior years revenues methodology is a measuring stick, but can be an inaccurate method to calculate the true value of the business. Without taking a thorough analysis of multiple aspects of the business into account, an accurate valuation cannot be calculated. We would describe this method as trying to value a car by only looking only at the exterior. It might esthetically look pleasing in paint color and interior leather, but if the engine and mechanicals are broken, then the car should not be worth much.

EBITDA

EBITDA stands for 'earnings before interest, taxes, depreciation, and amortization'. Basically, EBITDA is the cash earnings of the business without all of the tax implications, which really only happen after you make money. When you start any valuation, it is always good to get the prior 3 years tax returns from the seller's business. Three years gives a decent picture of the average collections of the business, and since it is reported to the IRS, usually you can trust that it is true. Of course some people rob the IRS of due taxes, but hopefully that's not the person selling to you! The other more detailed way to get these numbers is to get the actual Profit and Loss statements from the seller or their accountant. The P&L as we call it, will give you a proper look at all of the collections and expense categories that can be lost on the IRS forms. These P&L statements will help you to understand what cost categories may be high or low based on the type of procedures the seller is performing. These reports may even give you an idea of ways to improve the profitability of the practice once you take ownership.

Step 1: Normalize
Once you have 3 years of tax returns or P&L statements, you then need to normalize each year. Often dentists will run certain expenses through the business that may not be necessary when a new owner takes over. This may include the doctor's entire family cell phone bill, their home internet (for home office use of course), their car, and occasionally their boat, lake house, or plane. Some doctors like to fly their plane to their weekend CE courses!

Many expenses can legally be run through your business. Meals with people when you meet with them on business related topics are quite common. Vehicle expenses are common as well. To this rule: vehicle expenses should be kept at a moderate level unless the car is used for business purposes a majority of the time. In case you possibly use your personal car for a majority of the time, there is a document called an Agency Agreement, which allows your business to pay for a majority of the costs of your personal car if certain requirements are met.

The best way to normalize the income is to copy the most recent P&L into a spreadsheet. In column A, list the P&L categories. In column B, put the costs from the dental practice as it is currently being run. In column C,remove the expenses that will be eliminated with new ownership. These expenses include travel, CE, and other items that aren't critical to the running of the business. They can also include donations, or advertising expenses that are really just set up as donations. For example, perhaps the previous dentist sponsored his child's baseball team. Will that continue? They gave $2,000 to the Save the Beetles campaign, but is this expense critical to the business success? After removing those expenses, the cost of these perks should be added into the profitability of the practice. See the simple example below. Column D is the 'normalized' P&L from the practice, and this column will give you the most accurate 'profit' from the practice.

The current dentist is taking home $104,360 as 'profit' from his business. After taking out the car, donations, and other expenses that the new owner will not incur, the profit jumps to $123,000. This new 'normalized profit' is the first starting number for the next calculation.

	2020 P&L	Normalized	New P&L
A	B	C	D
Income	600,000		600,000
Staff costs	180,000		180,000
Dentist Salary	150,000		150,000
Supplies	36,000		36,000
Lab Fees	48,000		48,000
Vehicle	7,640	-7640	0
Office Costs	17,800		17,800
Rent	24,700		24,700
Donations	2,000	-2000	0
Advertising	15,000		15,000
Travel and CE	9,000	-9000	0
Other	5,500		5,500
Profit	$104,360		Normalized: $123,000

Important to this exercise is assigning salary levels for the owner or associate dentists. This can be something from $80,000 to $180,000. This impacts taxes for the seller as they take income, but also impacts valuation. For a practice, try to use a calculation that is typical for an associate or senior dentist working in the area. If the practice is producing $600,000, it is not realistic to pay the dentist $60,000, or 10%. First and foremost, if the IRS notices this, they will probably perform an audit and back taxes might be owed. Secondly, it's unlikely that you would be able to become an associate and take home only 10% of collections. Finding good associates is challenging, and finding ones that will work for 10% is impossible. In this scenario, and in general, you should make the dentist's salary as much as 25% of collections. Typically it is closer to 30% of collections, but may be as high as 35% of collections in certain areas of the country.

Also make sure to watch for a selling dentist to try to normalize the profit as high as possible. It is in their interest to get that profit number up, thereby increasing the value of the practice. At this point all normalization becomes a negotiation. Hopefully all parties involved in the transaction understand what makes true business expenses. This will make a fairly easy agreement on the actual profit calculation of the practice.

Step 2: Once you perform this 'normalization' exercise for each of the previous 3 years, you can then perform the EBITDA calculation. The table below shows the calculations.

			Most Recent Year
	2018	2019	2020
EBITDA	$113,000	$117,500	$123,000
Weighted Multiple	1	2	3
	$113,000	$235,000	$369,000
Total	$717,000		
Multiple	6		
Total divided by Multiple =	$119,500	Average Weighted EBITDA	

As you can see, the previous 2 years weren't as profitable as the most recent. It is prudent to give more weight to the most recent year, because the new dentist will hopefully be able to match that production and income. Previous years have less weight due to various factors including different rents, costs, and the overall economy.

After multiplying the EBITDA by the weight, you then add all of the totals together for a large sum. In this scenario, it is $717,000. Since you multiplied all the previous numbers by 1, 2 and 3, then you add those together for a total of 6. Then divide $717,000 by 6 to get your annualized average weighted EBITDA.

If you were to look at 4 years of returns, you would take the weights of 1, 2, 3, and 4, and then divide by 10.

In this scenario, you arrive at $119,500 for the average weighted EBITDA. This is the number that is used as the benchmark by most corporate brokerage firms. They all take this number and apply a multiple to it. In the dental industry, it is common to have multiples of anywhere from 3 to 6. A multiple of 3 would indicate a practice that needs some updating in either equipment, technology, or both. This indicates the practice will need some investment from the buyer right at the time of the sale. As you move towards 4, this indicates the practice is already producing and collecting at a good rate. A practice with a multiple of 4 would need no major investment from the buyer. Typically a '4' practice is a very good practice that many potential buyers would be eager to purchase. There have been sales of EBITDA multiples in the 4.5 to 6.5 range, but those are typically paid for by investors or corporate groups who have a plethora of free cash that needs to be invested quickly. They tend to have private equity backing, and are willing to pay more to enter a market they think is good. Above 4 is not a typical dental practice multiple in the single doctor practice category. See the table below for potential values for our example practice.

Multiple	3	3.5	4	5	6
Price	$358,500	$418,250	$478,000	$597,500	$717,000

After plugging the numbers into this table, we see that the value of this dental practice is anywhere between $358,000 and $717,000. This is definitely a large range, but can point to the wide range that valuations can occur in valuing a practice. This is also just the starting point for the valuation. After assigning this valuation multiple, you begin to assess things that are not included in the calculation. Use the factors in the next section to determine whether the multiple should be closer to the lower end of the range, or the higher. Also, it might allow you room to negotiate if some other variables are in play.

Value of Equipment and Hard Assets

In some cases, the value of the business cannot be calculated from either a percentage of historical collections or the EBITDA method. In these cases, you will have to come up with a third method. The third way to value a practice is whatever it would cost you to build this exact practice in today's dollars, and then 'discount' it back based on age of the practice and equipment.

Let us assume that to build a brand new practice, it will cost $500,000 in construction of the build-out, equipment, supplies, and technology. Here is a list of a 'startup' budget and the approximate costs for each piece of equipment. Each of these is an approximate value for the equipment and costs that you would incur to do a startup in the area.

Name	Value
Buildout	$345,000
Server	$3,000
Xray Sensors	$7,000
CBCT	$47,000
Phones	$4,000
Supplies	$15,000
Chairs	$38,000
Dental Units	$14,000
Cabinetry	$12,000
Suction	$4,000
Compressor	$5,000
Xray tubes	$6,000
TOTAL	$500,000

Of course it is important to remember that if you actually did the startup, then all of the equipment would be brand new and everything would be exactly the way you want it. However, you would also have no patients, income, or team members to help you start the practice.

The next step is to then factor in some of the age of the equipment.

In order to factor in the age of the equipment, we must take into account its lifespan. For example, the server we purchased for $3,000 will only last about 5 years. If the server is 3 years old, then we have already 'used up' 60% of the value of that server. This only leaves the remaining 40% of value in the server, which is $1,200. When we start to do that for each subsection of the possible practice acquisition, we come up with a spreadsheet like this:

Valuation of Equipment and Hard Assets

Name	Age	Lifespan	Remaining Age	%	Value	Discounted Value
Buildout	7	40	33	83%	$345,000	$284,625
Server	3	5	2	40%	$3,000	$1,200
Xray Sensors	3	10	7	70%	$7,000	$4,900
CBCT	3	10	7	70%	$47,000	$32,900
Phones	3	10	7	70%	$4,000	$2,800
Supplies	0	100	100	100%	$15,000	$15,000
Chairs	7	25	18	72%	$38,000	$27,360
Dental Units	7	25	18	72%	$14,000	$10,080
Cabinetry	7	40	33	83%	$12,000	$9,900
Suction	7	15	8	53%	$4,000	$2,133
Compressor	7	15	8	53%	$5,000	$2,667
Xray tubes	7	25	18	72%	$6,000	$4,320

New Value	**Today's Value**
$500,000	$397,885

In this example, the brand new practice would cost $500,000, however since some of the equipment is 7 and 3 years old, the practice value of the equipment is only $397,885. When you are doing this calculation, you must use this as an anchor to consider that if you were to purchase the practice for $397,885, you would essentially be getting the existing patients, team and systems for free. This method is useful for vacant practices, and for internal calculations or quick sale of practices where there might not be any patient charts.

Other Factors in Practice Valuation

Here are some other factors in determining the value of a practice that might help in determining the appropriate EBITDA multiple, or the appropriate percentage of revenue for valuation purposes.

- Location:
    - Is the practice in a prime location?
    - What's the strength of the competition in the surrounding areas?
    - What are daily traffic numbers on the street outside the front door?

- What is the number of rooftops in the 1-mile, 3-mile, and 5-mile radius?
- What is the growth plan for the city around this location? Growing or stagnant?
- PPO participation:
  - How many PPO plans does the office take?
  - What percentage of patients are covered by which PPO plans?
  - What percentage of write-off do the PPO plans take off the usual and customary fees?
- Physical location:
  - Are you buying the building/space?
  - Are the lease or sale terms favorable for the buyer?
  - Number of operatories- Is there room for growth?
  - Age of building- Will there be higher repair costs in the future?
  - Are there enough parking spots for the practice?
  - Is parking directly in front of the space or is it often occupied by an adjacent tenant?
- Equipment:
  - Age and quality of equipment?
    - Use Acquisition Analysis Spreadsheet for equipment list
  - Will any equipment need to be updated?
  - Will there be any technology that needs updating?
- Staff Retention:
  - How many staff will be staying on?
  - What is the current compensation for the staff- above or below market rate?
- Procedures performed:
  - Does the doctor perform many procedures that are specialized in nature? Implants, full mouth reconstruction, molar root canals
  - Does the doctor do all their own hygiene?
  - Does the doctor already do a high volume of crowns? (Will all teeth be crowned prior to your arrival?)
- Patients
  - What is the number of active patients? (Seen in the last 18 months)
  - How many patients have had 2-3 prophy/perio maintenance in the last 18 months?
  - How many new patients per month?
  - Has the practice been net positive or negative on active patients? (Growing or shrinking practice?)
- Legal Issues
  - Is the seller set up as a PC, LLC, or C-Corp?
  - Are there any existing liens against the business?
  - Any liens against the building?
  - Any pending malpractice lawsuits?
  - Any other legal liabilities?

Valuations Recap and Final Points

After reviewing all three valuation methods, it is important to recap the methodology and go through the thinking behind how the appropriate value was derived. For most practices, the EBITDA method will work and give you an approximate value that will be a good starting point for negotiations. This will be based on the dental practices effectiveness as a business, and will give you assurance that you will be able to provide the necessary cash flow to pay the debt even after paying yourself. When the EBITDA method comes up with a valuation that seems extremely irregular, however, then you must also calculate the valuation from one of these other two methods to come up with an amalgamated value based on multiple methods.

As you start to come to the final valuation of the practice, remember two important points about purchasing a business. First is that you should only pay for the business as it is situated right now, not based on the *potential* that the business has. For example, a broker might say, "The area is really growing and we know that once you step in you'll be able to really hit it out of the park." While this might be true, you cannot pay more for an asset because it *might* be worth more in your hands. You should only pay what it is worth today, and for how the business was operated in the seller's possession.

Secondly, you will always need to do some improvements once you take ownership. That could be something small like just some paint on the walls, or it could be a major equipment upgrade like a server, digital x-rays, and CBCT. In either case, you will want to use this 'upgrade cost' as a tool to try to lower the price of the practice. As negotiations proceed, you must continually point out, both in your mind and the sellers, that the practice isn't usable by you until you get certain aspects fixed.

In the end, remember that your valuation method is just a starting point for negotiations. The seller's valuation is also their starting point. The valuation you put together at this stage is not a locked number, and the seller may push against your value and try to bring it closer to what they have the practice offered at. In these cases, you must be confident in your methodology and support your calculated value with as much data as possible. In many negotiations that we have seen, a valuation is much more likely to be acceptable to a seller when the value is backed by strong data and less based on a potential or emotional attachment.

Negotiation

Negotiating the sale of a business that has been the lifeblood of a dentist for years or decades can be an emotional decision and one that is not based on numbers.

The picture of the ideal buyer in their mind may be someone who is just like them and wants to run the practice just like they have over the past 35 years. Since this is not likely to happen, no matter how the negotiation plays out, some level of calibration of expectations may need to be facilitated by the broker to the seller, or from the buyer to the seller.

This complicated process can be short, or extremely drawn out, depending on the circumstances. Remember however, that if this is a practice you want to purchase, that there are a few rules in relationships to keep in mind that might help the seller feel more comfortable with you, even if your price is not what they had hoped for. Just as with any friendship, most positive seller-buyer relationships are based on a formula that has been written about called the 'Friendship Formula'.

Friendship = **Proximity** x (**Frequency** + **Duration**) x **Intensity**

In the case of negotiations with a seller, it's a good idea to be as much their friend as their buyer. Looking at this formula, it is important to remember that you will want to play off the major factors in the formula to make sure they feel good about selling to you, rather than someone else. If they 'like' you, then they are likely to be more willing to reduce their asking price in order to come to an agreement with you, rather than hold out and sell for a bit more money to someone they have no relationship with, or possibly even dislike.

After you have developed a relationship with them and have gotten a firm handle on the value of the practice, then you are ready to make an offer. During this process it is best to physically sit in the same room with the seller, or at a minimum have a phone call with their representative and discuss factors that went into your valuation. Try to deliver the offer in both written and verbal format, because the broker or representative might not convey your exact statements to the seller unless it is specifically laid out in the most detailed format possible.

It is not a good idea to approach the negotiation by disparaging the seller's practice. Even if the walls are orange and they use silver points for endodontics, you have to find many things to compliment about the business. Remember, the end goal is to come to a mutual agreement on a price that works for both parties. It cannot be said strongly enough- there will likely be a great deal of emotion for the seller. If an offer comes in substantially lower than the list price, the seller may come to the conclusion that, "this buyer is trying to low-ball me and doesn't respect the business I've built." This is a common reaction among sellers, and to be honest, we have been on both sides of the table. We have sold practices and were insulted by the initial offer from a potential buyer. If you do this for long enough, this is bound to happen. For this reason, we suggest that any time an offer is made in writing, and verbally, that you include the following:

- Recap of their asking price and **thank them** for giving you the opportunity to make an offer, and for providing thorough data
- Your methodology and your data to support it
- Possible communications with your banker/financing institution to back up your position
- Positives about their practice which you love
- **Apologize** that this offer isn't what they were expecting, but express the hope that you and the seller can come to an agreement

Here is a sample letter from a buyer trying to negotiate down a practice from $625,000 to a lower price:

John (the broker),

Thank you for getting me the prospectus packet of information, it looks like Dr. Seller has built up a loyal patient base over the past 35 years.

I wanted to keep this process moving forward quickly, and so I spoke with Susie at ABC Bank today, she was very informative. Her and I both shared concerns over the cash flow and debt service after normalizing the P&Ls.

I have been running the analytics and I'm not coming up with the same value as you propose. The EBITDA on the office is too low to use a multiple that would allow me to use that as a proper valuation method. Even after normalization, I couldn't arrive at the number that Dr. Seller is hoping for. For this reason, I moved onto a mixture of a few other widely utilized methodologies. Using a mix of fixed assets and percentage of revenues, I came up with a valuation range for the practice between $449k and $517k. I understand the asking price is higher and my goal is NOT to insult Dr. Seller. I respect what he has built and I believe there is great opportunity in his practice. However, after speaking with Lori at the bank and my own valuation methods, I believe that the practice numbers support this valuation pricing range.

I would love to discuss this further with you and receive your feedback.

Best,

Dr. Buyer

Hopefully the seller and broker respond favorably to this start of the negotiation, but do not be put off if the seller takes offense and decides to stop communicating for a few days. Oftentimes the role of the broker in this scenario is to have the price be as high as possible. Therefore, the broker will most often try to solicit purchase offers from interested parties before coming back to negotiate with you.

Depending on whether it is a buyer's market or seller's market, the process timeline can vary greatly. An agreement can be reached in an hour, or the negotiation could drag on for months. Remember, once the price is agreed upon, this is only the first step. As the negotiation continues to play out, remember the friendship formula as well as the fact that many deals just do not work out for one reason or another.

As negotiations proceed, remember that a broker will usually ask you to sign a letter of intent (LOI). This is a non-binding letter that provides the buyer a chance to fully do any due diligence on the practice prior to signing a 'purchase agreement' which will then close at a certain point in the future. The letter of intent usually binds the seller to not accept or entertain any other offers, while it gives the buyer a chance to look for any factors that might significantly impact the practice valuation or sale timeline. This period of time also gives the buyer the ability to finalize financing and get all the paperwork together.

Here's an interesting psychological factor to consider. After the time when an LOI is signed, a buyer will often unconsciously begin to believe that their business is 'sold'. Having even the smallest amount of evidence that someone is interested in buying their business often creates a belief that they are close to the finish line. It is during this due diligence period that you, as the buyer, should be looking for any odd facts or mitigating factors that might cause you to change your offer to a lower amount. It also gives you a chance to start to negotiate some of the other factors that go into a practice sale including the allocation of assets, non-compete clause, and the accounts receivable. While changing the deal at the '11th hour' is typically frowned upon in negotiations, remember that the closer you are to the finish line, the more willing the seller might be to accept something that they would have considered impossible at the beginning of negotiations.

Taxes, Depreciation and Allocation of Assets

The next step in the sale is the negotiation of the percentage of the sales price allocated to fixed assets, 'blue sky', and the non-compete clause. This is important to discuss because it has different tax implications for the buyer and seller. Fixed assets are often called FF&E; for furniture, fixtures, and equipment. These are the things that could be carried out the door to a new location if you left a space. They can often be depreciated very quickly for tax purposes under current tax law. 'Blue Sky', or 'Goodwill' of the business is typically the patient charts and intangibles of the business. The Non-compete is usually also assigned a value in the business operations. Each of these categories has different tax implications.

The buyer and seller should come to an agreement on which percentage allocation is given to equipment, which can usually be between 10-40% of the practice price. In certain situations, if for instance, a practice is distressed, or has been unoccupied for several months, this percentage can approach 90%. FF&E also includes all the dental supplies and office supplies as well. If there are many computers or digital sensors, this would increase the percentage allocated to this.

It is advantageous for the seller to keep this amount as low as possible since the previous owner most likely already depreciated this asset down in value. They will have to pay a higher tax rate on this amount. For the buyer, it is desirable to set this as high as reasonably possible.

At the time of sale there should be two addenda to the contract. Addendum A should include all FF&E that is included in the sale. This list of included assets should be relatively exhaustive, but it doesn't need to go down to the serial numbers on each chair or handpiece. Addendum B should list anything that is not included in the sale. Some selling doctors want to take artwork or items that may have sentimental value to them. Identifying items like this can avoid having problems at the time of sale or immediately thereafter.

'Blue Sky', or goodwill, is the value of the active patients within the practice. This is often the largest allocation of the purchase price, as this is really where much of the value resides. For a seller, it is always better to have most of the value allocated to blue sky, as this is taxed at a lower rate for the seller. The buyer then has to amortize this cost over many years, which is not advantageous for the buyer. Arriving at this figure is a negotiation and there is no mathematical way to prove the value of 'Blue Sky'.

The last portion of the allocation price is the value to be assigned to a non-compete clause. Usually this is $5,000 to $15,000. If you are worried about a selling doctor going back into practice, it is a good idea to have a lawyer write up a good non-compete clause. This clause can be very lenient or more stringent. One common type of non-compete clauses assigns a value of $4,000 to each patient of record. "Patient of record" is usually defined as someone who has been seen in the last 18 to 24 months. If the selling doctor was to move down the street and see that patient, the selling doctor would have to pay the buyer $4,000 each time a former patient was seen. The value of the clause is tax favorable for the buyer, not the seller.

Below are a few examples of the allocations in recent sales:

Ex. 1	Total Price	$675,000	Annual Revenue $900k
	FF&E- $170,000	Goodwill- $500,000	Non-Compete- $5,000
Ex. 2	Total Price	$175,000	Annual Revenue $320k
	FF&E- $25,000	Goodwill- $150,000	Non-Compete- $0 (Doctor continued working)
Ex. 3	Total Price	$190,000	Annual Revenue $360k
	FF&E- $70,000	Goodwill- $110,000	Non-Compete- $10,000

Once the allocations have been negotiated and agreed upon, they should be explicitly stated in the contract in a table. This is very important because when closing occurs, both parties will have to sign the IRS Form 8594 to let the IRS know that everyone was in agreement. This allows the IRS to appropriate deductions per party.

Key Points on Taxes and Depreciation

Remember, the role of a good accountant is to make sure that you pay the taxes for which you are responsible, and not more. Finding the right mix of asset allocation is extremely important and can make a significant difference in the taxes that you will pay in the coming years. Make sure to discuss all these aspects with your accountant prior to finalizing the paperwork.

Maximize Depreciation

Depreciation is the *"reduction in the value of an asset with the passage of time, due in particular to wear and tear."* This can either be in reference to the tax side of depreciation or the actual operational wear and tear on any asset. After you purchase an asset, you can usually use a depreciation table to figure out how much value the asset lost in any given year. Remember that this depreciation amount reduces net income, and thereby reduces tax liability. It is not real money, only a line item that helps with taxes.

Let's assume you buy a piece of equipment, a Cone Beam-CT machine, for $47,000. A high-tech piece of equipment like this is usually almost obsolete in 3 to 5 years. Due to this fact, the IRS will usually allow you to say that the asset lost value over the course of either 3 or 5 years. Your accountant will be able to help classify this cost, but in general, you want to depreciate it as fast as possible. This table shows the percentages of depreciation that an asset can experience during each year of its lifespan.

Year	Depreciation Rate- Property Half-year Convention					
	3 -Year	5-Year	7-Year	10-Year	15-Year	20-year
1	33.33%	20.00%	14.29%	10.00%	5.00%	3.750%
2	44.45	32.00	24.4	18.00	9.50	7.219
3	14.81	19.20	17.49	14.40	8.55	6.667
4	7.41	11.52	12.49	11.52	7.70	6.177
5		11.52	8.93	9.22	6.93	5.713
6		5.76	8.92	7.37	6.23	5.285
7			8.93	6.55	5.90	4.88
8			4.46	6.55	5.90	4.522
9				6.56	5.91	4.462
10				6.55	5.90	4.461
11				3.28	5.91	4.462
12					5.90	4.461

13					5.91	4.462
14					5.90	4.461
15					5.91	4.462
16					2.95	4.461
17						4.462
18						4.461
19						4.462
20						4.461
21						2.231

Internal Revenue Service, 2021

In recent years, Congress has almost always instituted Section 179. Sec. 179 of the tax code allows for any purchase up to $250,000 to be depreciated all in one year. Typically, if you buy a piece of equipment with the profits from a given year, you then have to pay your normal tax rate on those profits first. So, let's say you made $100,000 in profits in a given year. After taxes take 38%, you then have only $62,000 to potentially buy any assets.

However, if Sec. 179 is in place during that particular tax year, you will be able to claim any depreciation, totaling up to $250,000, all in one year. So if you purchased a CBCT, and you depreciate the entire amount in a single year, you avoid paying the $17,860 in taxes on that $47,000. It is as if the US Federal Government will purchase for you about 40% of any new equipment up to $250,000 during a single year.

So, in general, if you spend less than $250,000 on equipment during a single year, then you will be able to take the entire cost of the equipment as a tax 'loss'. If you spend more than $250,000, then you will have to refer to the original percentage on the depreciation schedule in the table noted previously.

Real Estate Depreciation

Many times dentists will own their real estate as well as their practice. Most tax planning professionals will say that a piece of commercial real estate will depreciate over 39.5 years. To calculate this depreciation, make sure you separate the value of the building from the value of the land. The IRS legally says that the land is not depreciable, but that the building will depreciate fully over 39.5 years. That means that every year, you will take 2.53% depreciation over the course of 39.5 years.

Let's say that a property was purchased for $250,000. The land is worth $100,000 and the building is worth $150,000. For every year for the life of the building, you can take a 2.53% loss on the building portion, or $3,795 per year.

A method to accelerate depreciation is to ask your accountant for a segregation study. In a segregation study, your accountant or tax advisor will take your building and divide its value into sub-categories like:

- Site Work
- Concrete & Masonry: Sidewalks, foundation, flooring
- Steel: Shell of the building
- Woods & Plastics: Finish woodwork, cabinetry, rough carpentry
- Thermal & Moisture Protection: Roofing, insulation,
- Doors & Windows
- Specialties: Dental cabinetry, dental lighting, restrooms, lockers
- Finish: Carpet, paint
- Mechanical
- Electrical

After you have a segregation study completed, you can then depreciate some of these areas faster than the 39.5 years. Items like the Electrical can potentially be depreciated in 15 years. Carpet and paint will wear out in 5 to 7 years. In this scenario, you can accelerate the depreciation schedule to get more depreciation in the early years of property ownership. This means more money in your pocket in the early years of property ownership.

Accounts Receivable

A common question when a selling doctor leaves a practice is whether they should hold onto any monies owed to them. Accounts Receivable (AR) are the totality of debts owed to the previous business by patients and insurers who are in the process of paying. There are three options for the AR:
- Purchase the AR
- Seller retains AR and buyer services it
- Seller retains AR and either services it themselves, or hires a 3rd party to do so

Purchase the AR

If the buyer purchases the AR, there should be a 'discount' applied to the amount due. Obviously many patients who felt obligated to pay their retiring doctor, may not feel the same way towards the new owner. This change in ownership may give that patient the impression that they can stop paying. The other reason to pay a reduced fee on the AR is that it is going to cost the new owner time, postage, and energy to go after these people who, for one reason or another, were slow to pay the retiring/selling doctor.

If you do purchase the AR, look closely at as many of the accounts as possible to know which discount percentages to assign to them. In general, here is a rule:

- 0-30 Days: Pay 85%
- 31-60 Days: Pay 80%

- 61-90 Days: Pay 50%
- Over 90 Days: Pay 30%

This is an average allocation of percentages and can be modulated depending on the circumstances and the goodwill that you think patients owe the selling doctor. When servicing this debt, it should appear that all debts are still being paid to the selling doctor. Letters should continue to come from the former dental practice, and patients should feel as though they are still paying the selling doctor monies owed to him or her.

You can modulate the percentages based on historical trends, if they are available from the selling doctor. If the doctor has a very tight collections policy, maybe these percentages rise up towards 90% or 93% on the 0-30 Day AR. If the seller has a poor collections policy, with it taking more than 45 days to collect any money, it might be better to move towards 80% or less.

The only advantage to this option is that all the collections that come in the door from day one go into the buyer's pocket. While there is an upfront cost to purchasing the AR, the ease of having cash-flow from the beginning is a good place to start. When financing, the bank will usually help with the entire cost, so the entire loan amount will include this AR. So even though you are paying interest on this, it can sometimes decrease the headaches that come with slow cash-flow and transitions.

In some cases, selling doctors may feel slighted if they feel this is a 'low-ball' number. If this is the case, you might consider the next option.

Seller Retains AR and Buyer Services It

In this option, the selling doctor maintains control and ownership of the AR. The Buyer then services it under the control of the purchased dental practice. In this case, it still appears that all debts are being paid to the dental practice and the selling doctor. The only difference is that after the money comes in, the purchaser transfers the payments to the seller.

If you choose to go this route, it is important to include in the selling document a few 'rules of engagement'.

1. Limits on Actions: The buyer and seller should maintain and limit how aggressive they want to be in pursuing these accounts. There should be agreement that if an account is sent to a collection agency, that both parties are aware and informed of this fact.
2. First-In Money: If a patient owes money to a selling doctor and then gets service done with the new doctor, where does the first-in money go? Buyer and seller should agree on this scenario, but it usually means that the seller gets paid for what is owed to them first.
3. Collections Fee: After a certain number of days, either 30 or 45, a 10-20% fee is assessed on all collections for the selling doctor. This way, the money that is already in the pipeline, either from insurance or checks in the mail, will go 100% to the selling doctor. Any money that comes in after that date requires some work by the buyer. In

this case, the buyer should get paid a reasonable percentage for the work to collect that money.

4. End Date: After a certain date it will become a nuisance to continue to maintain the seller's accounts. The remaining amount is typically very small. The buyer and seller should agree on an endpoint to the collections, so that there isn't an infinite timeline. Usually 6 months is appropriate. At that point, any accounts could be purchased out for a large discount, maybe 10-15% of the amount.

The only downside to collecting for a selling doctor is that there is a lot of energy associated with collecting and splitting out payments if you have a busy practice. Sometimes this can eat up a lot of energy from a staff that is already stressed by the change in ownership. Setting the ground rules from the beginning can ease a lot of the stress, and ensure that there isn't any ill will between the parties after the sale.

Seller Retains AR and Services it

In this case, the seller will retain the AR. Sometimes a retiring dentist will take their book of accounts home and do it themselves, but more often their accountant will take care of it for them. Usually many patients will still mail checks to the practice or come to the practice to pay. In this case, you can keep a separate box for all payments, and then send this to the seller, or their accountant, as warranted.

There are many other small, but important, details to address in the sale or purchase of a practice. It is always a good idea to engage a knowledgeable legal team to help you address these issues.

Real Estate & Leases

In many cases the real estate comes with the practice, or is at least possibly part of the sale of the business. In these cases, the negotiations are for both entities simultaneously. Usually the seller will have a rough valuation, or possibly an appraisal of the building.

Appraisals are usually done by a certified appraiser, who has to show their work and come up with a valuation based on real math without any emotion involved. This can be good in many cases for a bank loan or tax valuation, however when a seller gets an appraisal, they may ask the appraiser to find the highest possible value that has data to back it up. In these cases, the value may come back higher than expected due the appraiser using comparables and justifications that are on the high end of the spectrum. If this occurs, it's important to counter with your own data showing more accurate comparables and data. This can be one way to bring the value to a more reasonable level.

It is also important to remember that when packaging the entire sale together into one lump sum, it can be more psychologically fulfilling for the seller. Look at the example below:

- $400,000 for the Dental Practice, $700,000 for the Real Estate

Vs.

- $1.1 Million for your business

Even though they are mathematically the same, there is a psychological effect that has been described by Nobel winner Daniel Khaneman and his partner Amos Tversky that state that the larger number will have a greater effect on your brain, even though they are mathematically the exact same. Taking advantage of this psychological bias might help you when you make an offer. So, make sure to always talk in 'big' numbers.

Evaluating Real Estate

When purchasing real estate it is important to have a firm understanding of what you are buying. During a house purchase, most banks will want an inspection of the property to verify the structural integrity, electrical integrity, plumbing quality and general state of the house. In some cases when they find severe deficiencies, the bank will make sure all problems are fixed prior to closing so that they are not lending on a house that might turn out to be a 'lemon'.

In commercial real estate, it is also a good idea to go through a similar process, albeit sometimes more complicated. One of the first inspections that can be performed is a general inspection from a home inspection company. You might need to call a few inspectors to find one comfortable doing a commercial inspection, but it is not typically very difficult. In these cases an inspection can cost a few hundred dollars and they will identify any simple to moderate issues with a building.

In some cases when an inspector finds an issue, additional experts might need to be called in to review the findings. This might include structural engineers or contractors to see what might need to be fixed, the process necessary and the cost.

The next few items are inspections that may or may not be needed depending on how detailed you want to be in your research. The first is a Phase I Environmental Site Assessment, commonly referred to as an ESA, or Phase I ESA. This is completed to research the current and historical uses of a property as part of a commercial real estate transaction. The intent of the report is to assess if current or historical property uses have impacted the soil or groundwater beneath the property and could pose a threat to the environment and/or human health. If these issues are found, it presents a potential liability for the lender and/or owner, as well as affecting the value of the property. In the past some issues that we have seen are if the property had historical uses such as dry cleaners, gas stations, auto/vehicle repair, printing operations, and manufacturing.

A Phase I ESA typically includes the following:
- A site visit to observe current and past conditions and uses of the property and adjacent properties

- A review of federal, state, tribal, and local regulatory databases including, but not limited to, underground storage tanks, aboveground storage tanks, known or suspected release cases, the storage of hazardous substances and disposal of hazardous wastes including petroleum products, and institutional and engineering controls
- A review of historical records, such as historical aerial photographs, fire insurance maps, historical city directories, and historical topographic maps
- A review of state and local agency records, including but not limited to state environmental agencies, Building Departments, Fire Departments, and Health Departments.
- Sometimes it includes interviews with current and past property owners, operators, and occupants, or others familiar with the property
- Sometimes it also includes interviews with the Report User for title or judicial records for environmental liens and activity and use limitations

This research is evaluated by the Environmental Professional to identify potential environmental risks to the property such as current or historic operations that are known or suspected to have used hazardous substances or petroleum products during onsite operations.

While not part of ASTM requirements, Phase I ESA reports typically include a discussion of observed suspected asbestos, potential lead-based paint, and mold growth; as well as the potential for lead in drinking water and radon. Sampling for these non-ASTM concerns is beyond the scope of a standard Phase I ESA, but can be included upon request.

A recognized environmental condition, some sort of problem, indicates known contamination or the potential for the subsurface to have been impacted by contamination (either from the subject property or possibly from an offsite source). The identification of any of these problems will often include a recommendation for a Phase II Environmental Site Assessment to collect soil, groundwater, and/or soil vapor samples from the subsurface to analyze for the presence of contamination.

A Phase II ESA will often cost a bit more, typically between $5,000 and $10,000 depending on what needs to be assessed and the size of the property. Typically this is only done if problems are found in a Phase I study.

Once you are sure your property is free of any problems and passes both an inspection and your gut test, then you should be good to purchase the property with some assurances that it will be a good deal for you in the long term.

Taking over a Lease

In some cases, you will be taking over a lease from the selling doctor. In this scenario you will want to have your legal counsel look over the lease contract very closely.

Here are some important points to consider when reviewing a lease:

Types of Leases-

- Gross Rent Lease: one amount for all rent and incidentals, single monthly amount
- Modified Gross Rent: landlord and tenant share a portion of all expenses
- Net Leases: rent goes to landlord, then tenant pays all other incidentals
  - Triple Net (NNN) = tenant pays all taxes, insurance, and maintenance on building
- Percentage Rent Lease: tenant pays base rent and then a percentage of sales over time (common in mall scenarios)

Lease Notes for Acquisitions:

- Know exactly what the existing rent was, impacting the profitability of the practice
- Know what future rents will be - **this can have a huge impact on business valuation**
- Have a clause for 'First Right-of-refusal' to purchase the building, or try to include one when signing a longer lease
  - Sometimes the seller can get this from a landlord before they then sell it to you
- Probably want to try to negotiate a new lease if possible
  - Seller might be able to negotiate a better lease before sale, which then goes to your benefit. You can always suggest a good lease negotiator that costs the seller nothing.
- Triple Net costs are usually not negotiable
- Will make sure tenant has ability to audit the costs on the 'common fees'

Biggest Negotiation Failures:

- If there's a relocation clause - landlord with 30 days notice can move a tenant into a 'similar space' within the shopping center
- Landlord require certain working hours
- Mechanics liens….tenant has a right to work around any liens from contractors (Bonding around a lien)

Negotiating other points:

- When to return a security deposit?
- Ask for specific inflator on the % - so that you can know the exact cost over the life of the lease
- Try to get a 10 year with 2 x (5 year options)...so that you can amortize your investment over 20 years, even to have the option for more is a good idea
- Ask for Latent Defect protection- landlord would pay for any defects that come to light in the building after tenant already moved in (ie. foundation, roof, etc)
- Even mid-lease you can hire a re-negotiator to help
- When re-negotiating….you'll need about 12 months lead time prior to termination to fully negotiate the lease
- Just because neighbor is paying $20/NNN doesn't mean you should be paying that….each tenant is individual
- You need your own broker in any project, do not just call up the name on the sign, it is NOT a do-it-yourself project

Top Items you NEED in your Lease:

1. Always negotiate a 'cap' on lease net costs (maintenance and insurance)
2. Never let a landlord require/limit certain working hours
3. Always get Latent Defect protection- make sure any structural issues won't be your responsibility to fix
4. Know the exact inflators over the life of the lease
5. Get your security deposit back after a few years
6. Always maintain the ability to audit the Triple Net Costs
7. If you sell the practice, make sure your lease holds over to the next person
8. Make sure your landlord can't move you to another 'similar' spot
9. Review lease termination/renegotiation conditions if your strip center or location goes into foreclosure (Security Non-Disturbance Clause)
   a. Ownership change of building doesn't break the lease

One of the biggest keys we can encourage at this point is to have professional representation when negotiating leases. There are many real estate professionals across the country who specialize in lease negotiations. They will help you navigate the waters from start to finish, and hopefully avoid a potentially disastrous situation down the road. They can also lessen your legal bill as they will work through any lease contracts on your behalf.

It might be tempting to avoid this, but remember that lease negotiators actually do not cost *you* any money. In almost all situations they get a cut from the landlord or the landlord's leasing agent- which is typical of the real estate industry. So, they are free to you, and help you get better terms in the end.

Wrapping up Valuation and Negotiations

By this point in the process, you have identified a good market, prepared all the financial statements, found a seller, audited their charts and office equipment, negotiated many of the points of the deal. It might feel very satisfying, but we will warn you that you still have a ways to go before the office keys get handed to you.

As you continue in the process, the next stage is finalizing all the contracts. Remember that this is still an extension of the negotiation process, which could possibly take months.

The next pages will give you all the legal documents and advice to come up with the most advantageous ways to set up your new business to take over this seller's business in a legal, safe and efficient manner.

Chapter 5

Legal and Contracts

The next stage in the journey includes all of the legal questions that arise when buying a business. Whether you are buying or starting a dental practice from scratch, you will need the very best professional advice. The importance of having good lawyers and accountants cannot be understated. Finding a team that specializes in dental transactions can be difficult or time-consuming, but the special knowledge they bring can save hundreds of thousands of dollars down the road. Check with a local attorney for regulations in your state, as many state laws dictate the best course strategy.

After the preliminary negotiations are in full force, the next stage starts when the buyer and seller tentatively agree to work together to come to a sale agreement. This agreement is referred to in document form as a Letter of Intent, or LOI. The LOI is usually very short and simple, and basically only refers to the willingness of the parties to negotiate with each other. It will normally include parts that stipulate that the seller should not try to deal with anyone else. Once the seller 'accepts' or signs the LOI, that usually gives 30-60 days of negotiation and due diligence. During that period, hopefully the parties can come to agreements on all the terms of the deal. For that, sometimes the seller will actually require an 'earnest money deposit', but that is more common in the general business world than in the dental industry.

In an LOI, there are usually contingencies as well. Contingencies are things that have to happen in order for the LOI to remain valid while leading to a purchase agreement. The most common contingency is that the buyer can get financing for the business acquisition. In the case where a bank says, 'We will not lend you the money", the buyer is relinquished from the agreement and does not have to go through with any purchase. This can happen sometimes, but if you have gone through the steps listed earlier in the book, then you will not usually have this contingency to worry about.

Here's an example Letter of Intent (LOI):

Effective Date: May 1, 2021

RE: Purchase of a Grain Acres Dental Practice

I. The Buyer: Dr. John Buyer (the "Buyer")

II. The Seller: Dr. Bob Seller (the "Seller").

III. The Business: Grain Acres Dental, LLC (the "Business").

IV. Purchase Price: The Buyer will enter into an agreement with the Seller for four hundred thousand dollars ($400,000.00) for 100% ownership interest in the Business.

V. Real Estate: This Letter of Intent includes real estate located at _____. (You may choose to either include or exclude the real estate. If excluded, then you may want to stipulate that you are buying the leasehold improvements.)

    Legal Description: _____

    Real Estate Purchase Price: One Million Dollars ($1,000,000)

VI. Payment: The Purchase Price for the real estate and the Business will be paid with _____ at the closing.

VII. Financing: The Buyer has made it known that this Letter of Intent is not conditional on their ability to obtain financing.

VIII. Binding Effect: This Letter of intent that shall be considered binding. Therefore, the parties acknowledge that remedies at law will be inadequate for any breach of this Agreement and consequently agree that this Agreement shall be enforceable by specific performance. The remedy of specific performance shall be cumulative of all of the rights at law or in equity of the parties under this Agreement.

IX. Bank Accounts: The accounts of the seller are (included or excluded) as part of the sale of the business.

X. Formal Agreement: There shall be no formal agreement (the "Formal Agreement") created as this Letter of Intent is binding.

XI. Seller's Conduct: The Seller agrees that during the purchase process to hold a fiduciary duty in the best interests of the Business. The Seller shall in no way conduct any action that would disrupt the on-going status of the Business's day-to-day operations. This obligation shall continue until the closing date.

XII. Closing: The closing (the "Closing") is the act of closing the transaction where the Seller exchanges the Business for the Purchase Price. The Closing shall be agreed

---

upon between the Buyer and Seller following a formal agreement, later to be signed, or after the terms are met in this Letter of Intent.

XIII. Closing Costs: All costs associated with the Closing shall be the responsibility of the Buyer.

XIV. Termination: This Letter of Intent will terminate if there has not been a formal agreement signed or a closing within 180 days from the Effective Date.

XV. Access to Information: After the execution of this Letter of Intent the Buyer, and its advisors, shall have full access to any and all information about the Business. The Buyer shall maintain a fiduciary duty to keep the information that it obtains confidential and agrees to not share with any third (3rd) party unless the Seller gives their written consent.

XVI. Return of Materials: Any information that is obtained by the Buyer through the Seller shall be returned if a Formal Agreement or Closing cannot be completed.

XVII. Conditions: It shall be the obligation of the Buyer to review all materials provided and, subject to the satisfaction of the Buyer, enter into a formal agreement within the specified time-period as outlined in Section XI.

The conditions of this Letter of Intent include:

The review and approval of all materials in the possession and control of the Seller;

The Buyer and its advisors having had a reasonable opportunity to perform any searches and due diligence to their satisfaction; and

The Buyer being able to communicate with necessary clients, employees, customers, vendors, tenants, or other third (3rd) party necessary.

XVIII. Confidentiality: All negotiations regarding the Business between the Buyer and Seller shall be confidential and not to be disclosed with anyone other than respective advisors and internal staff of the parties and necessary third (3rd) parties. No press or other public releases will be issued to the general public concerning the Business without the mutual consent or as required by law, and then only upon prior written notice to the other party unless otherwise not allowed.

XIX. Good Faith Negotiations: The Buyer and the Seller agree to act honestly and diligently to enter into "good faith" negotiations to execute a formal agreement and/or enter into a Closing.

XX. Exclusive Opportunity: Following the execution of this Letter of Intent, the parties agree to not negotiate or enter into discussions with any other party unless there are any existing agreements in place (e.g. option to purchase, first right of refusal, etc.).

XXI. Standstill Agreement: Following the execution of this Letter of Intent, and until the Closing, the Seller agrees not to sell any portion of the Business.

XXII. Currency: All mentions of money or the usage of the "$" icon shall be known as referring to the US Dollar.

XXIII. Governing Law: This Letter of Intent shall be governed under the laws by the State of _____.

XXIV. Severability: In case any provision or wording in this Letter of Intent shall be held invalid, illegal or unenforceable, the validity, legality, and enforceability of the remaining provisions shall not in any way be affected or impaired thereby.

XXV. Counterparts and Electronic Means: This Letter of Intent may be executed in several counterparts, each of which will be deemed to be an original and all of which will together constitute one and the same instrument. Delivery to us of an executed copy of this Letter of Intent by electronic facsimile transmission or other means of electronic communication capable of producing a printed copy will be deemed to be execution and delivery to us of this Letter of Intent as of the date of successful transmission to us.

SELLER

Seller's Signature _____ Date _____

Print Name _____

BUYER

Buyer's Signature _____ Date _____

Print Name _____

After the LOI is signed, the clock starts ticking for you to negotiate the final points of the deal, and to get your own business operations set up. It is at this stage that you should get your own attorney involved with the process to both help you set up your own entity, and negotiate the final purchase agreements. At this point, we will go through setting up your own entity.

Setting Up Your Corporation

Limited Liability Corporation

Most dental offices should be established as a Limited Liability Corporation (LLC), filing taxes as an S Corporation. While this is normally the case, some states will require a Professional Corporation, or PC. California is specifically this way, so in this case you will be a PC filing taxes as an S-Corp. In both of these cases, this means that the practice is formed as a closely held corporation that passes through all income, or losses, to its shareholders. In both scenarios, the owners claim the income on their personal income tax forms and pay tax at the personal income rate. To be an S Corporation, you must:
- Have no more than 100 shareholders
- All Shareholders are individual persons
- Have only one class of stock.

When forming an LLC or PC, you will need a legal team to apply for a name, draft all documents, and assign stock membership to any owners. If it is just a one-person company, then that one owner owns 100% of the stock.

Your first PC or LLC will own the dental business. This can be named the same as your dental practice, and it is basically your main company.

You may also want a second LLC for any real estate you own. You will want to form this LLC, and pay yourself market-rate rent from your dental business into this LLC. This structure provides a firewall against any unwanted legal troubles. If someone slips and hurts themselves on the sidewalk, they can sue the property LLC, but it will be harder to sue the dental business. It also serves as protection the other way: if someone sues your dental practice, they will have a harder time gaining access to any of your property income when the property is in a different LLC. Another advantage is that tax law is favorable towards property, which you should discuss with your CPA.

C Corporation

A C-Corporation is an entity where the income is taxed at the corporation level, and not passed through to the personal level. So after the business makes or loses money, it is taxed before being distributed as dividends.

This usually presents a poor value proposition for any dental practices, as you will pay taxes twice before getting to take any money home. The first tax is the corporate profit tax, and if you pay out dividends to shareholders, it is taxed a second time at a different rate. It is for this reason that the C-Corp is almost never used and should be avoided in dentistry. Check with your tax advisor however, as tax laws change frequently.

Getting Close to the Finish Line

If it looks like your due diligence period is promising and both parties are working towards an agreement, you will most likely start to work on a contract that fulfills all of the specifics of the deal that you are anticipating. All of the details regarding the practice are then put into a purchase agreement. The purchase agreement is sometimes signed earlier in the process, with a closing date further down the line. The closing date is the day when the money actually changes hands and the business entity is transferred to the new owner. However, sometimes all of the final paperwork is signed at the same time when money exchanges occur on closing day. Either process is acceptable.

The next documents we will share are sample purchase agreements. They vary in length significantly. While both do the job, using one versus the other depends on the preference of your legal team.

Here are the documents we will share next, all of which can be found in the Document Vault found in the QR code folder:

1. Short Asset Purchase Agreement
2. IRS Form 8594 Example
3. Long Asset Purchase Agreement
4. Stock Purchase Agreement
5. Real Estate Purchase Agreement
6. Termination and Rehire Letter
7. Closing Statement
8. Associate Dentist Employment Agreement
    a. If you're keeping retiring dentist on for a specific amount of time
9. Real Estate Purchase Agreements
    a. See Prior Chapter on Environmental Assessments if needed
10. Employment Agreement with Associate Doctors
11. Termination and Rehire Agreements with Team

In all of the following documents we want to stress the importance of reading and thoroughly understanding every document you decide to use. We are not attorneys, and we are not dispensing legal advice. Attorneys are well trained at understanding all of the specifics of documents and the purchase of each, and it is *extremely* prudent not to try to do this without legal representation. Our advice is to read through all documents carefully, highlight areas that you do not completely understand, and then jump on a call with your attorney to discuss each of the points. Contracts are not meant to be a foreign language, but they can seem like it. Generally, they are designed to be a rulebook and guidebook for how the transaction should happen. If one or both parties do not understand the rules, contracts can be broken and expensive lawsuits can occur. The best practice is to avoid misunderstandings from the very beginning.

The first document is the Short Asset Purchase Agreement. This agreement is slightly shorter and more simplified than the other example. It is quick and easily understandable and will work in most scenarios as a good starting point. See the next pages for the example:

SHORT ASSET PURCHASE AGREEMENT

THIS AGREEMENT, entered into this XXXXXXXXXX, between Seller, XXXXXXXXXX, a STATE XX professional corporation, and XXXXXXXXXX (jointly and severally hereinafter referred to as "Seller" and/or "XXXXXXXXXX" whichever reference is appropriate), ("Seller"), and Grain Acres Dental, LLC, a STATEXX Limited Liability Company, or its nominee ("Buyer").

RECITALS:

A. Seller leases the premises at _____

B. Seller desires to sell and Buyer desires to purchase the dental practice as a going concern and the assets of the practice but not the liabilities, sometimes referred to herein as the "Dental Practice".

AGREEMENTS:

NOW, THEREFORE, in consideration of the mutual promises set forth herein, the parties agree as follows:

1. SALE OF ASSETS

Seller agrees to sell, transfer and assign to Buyer, and Buyer agrees to purchase from Seller at the closing and on the closing date all right, title and interest in and to all of the assets, except real estate, owned and/or used by Seller in the operation of the Dental Practice, including without limitation the following assets and Dental Practice as a going concern, collectively referred to herein as the "Assets":

1.1 Equipment and Fixtures. All of the equipment, furniture and fixtures used in the Dental Practice at ADDRESS XXXX, including but not limited to the items described on Schedule 1.1 attached hereto (the "Equipment").

1.2 Goodwill. Except as otherwise set forth herein, all of the Goodwill and going concern of the Dental Practice, including all patient records and files, x-rays, computer and digital records, books, data, phone numbers, web page, domain name and information which are maintained by Seller at the Dental Practice to the extent the same relate to the Assets which are the subject of this Agreement or the operation of the Dental Practice (the "Goodwill").

1.3 Inventory and Supplies. All pharmaceutical, dental and office inventory and supplies which are located at the Dental Practice, ADDRESS XXXX, or which have been ordered and invoiced to Seller on or before the

Closing Date as also shown on Schedule 1.1 attached hereto ("Inventory").

1.4 Work-in-Process and Accounts Receivable. All work-in-progress and/or fees for services rendered by the Dental Practice which are owed to the Dental Practice and which have not been billed or invoiced by Seller as of the Closing date shall and at upon completion of Closing are hereby deemed be assigned to Buyer without further compensation, with or without additional documentation. Seller shall identify such customer accounts and unbilled work-in-progress amounts on Schedule 1.4, attached hereto. The parties acknowledge that the Assets being purchased include none of Seller's accounts receivable as of the Practice Closing Date. The parties acknowledge that for purposes of this Asset Purchase Agreement, accounts receivable shall be defined as all accounts or amounts which have been billed or invoiced by Seller (including without limitation amounts for goods and/or services rendered prior to the Practice Closing Date) to patients or any third-party insurer and/or government reimbursement for services rendered either partially pro-rata or in full on or before the Practice Closing Date. Patient services waiting for pre-treatment determination by a third party shall not be considered an account receivable of Seller.

A. Buyer does not purchase any Accounts Receivable. However, the buyer will continue to collect accounts receivable for the Seller. During the first 30 days, the Buyer will collect and give all monies to the seller at 100%. After the first 30 days, the buyer will collect all monies, take a 10% fee, and then remit the remaining 90% to the Seller.

B. Except for payments for accounts receivable as provided herein all monies received from patients or others for goods or services after the Practice Closing Date shall be owned by and the property of Buyer.

C. Buyer shall have the right to use any legal method of collection available for purchased accounts receivable. Buyer agrees to comply with all federal and state fair debt collection practice laws (if applicable).

1.5 Miscellaneous Assets. All soft and hard-copy and electronic financial records of the Dental Practice, the transfer of all computer software used for the operation of the Dental Practice (to the extent assignable and/or transferable as required by the software company owner, if applicable) and all related passwords and software keys, all managed care contracts in effect between Seller and any third party (to the extent assignable), and all other miscellaneous tangible and intangible non-cash assets of the Dental Practice that have not been specifically excluded from this sale and listed on the attached Schedule 1.1 shall be transferred to Buyer.

1.6 Excluded Assets. Seller shall retain all cash on hand and cash in banks

as of the date of Closing.

1.7 Liabilities Excluded. Except for the liabilities and obligations expressly assumed by Buyer herein, the Buyer does not assume, shall not be deemed or construed by the terms or provisions of this Agreement to have assumed, and hereby expressly disclaims any intent to assume any other liabilities or obligations of any kind of Seller or the Dental Practice.

1.8 Except for the aforementioned Excluded Assets, the Assets and Seller's interest in all other items used for the operation of the Dental Practice located at ADDRESS XXXX, on or after the Closing date shall be and are deemed conveyed to Buyer through this Agreement whether or not by Bill of Sale.

2. PURCHASE PRICE

2.1 Purchase Price. Buyer agrees to pay to Seller the sum of $265,000 for the Assets referenced in paragraph 1 above.

2.2 Allocation of Purchase Price. The Purchase Price for the Assets shall

be allocated as set forth below, and each party agrees that it shall treat the Purchase Price in accordance with such allocation for all purposes, including, but not limited to, federal and state income tax purposes, and shall comply with Internal Revenue Code § 1060:

All Physical Assets, Dental Equipment, Furniture, Fixtures, Complete inventory and other supplies $60,000

Patients/Goodwill (including all patient lists, records, etc.) $205,000.00

Total $265,000

3. Payment of Purchase Price.

The Purchase Price shall be paid in cash or certified funds on the Closing Date.

4. ACCOUNTS PAYABLE

4.1 Recurring Accounts. Seller shall pay for all outstanding contractual obligations, including but not limited to rents, taxes, insurance, telephone, contracted advertisements (such as yellow page ads), water, sewer and other utility charges and expenses for the Dental Practice accruing up to the Closing date, regardless of when due; Buyer shall be solely responsible for such expenses incurred on and after the Closing date.

4.2 Existing Contracts. Seller has no existing continuing contracts on any items being purchased.

4.3 Personal Property Tax. Seller will pay the personal property tax, if any,

on the Assets for the period up to the Closing Date.

5. CLOSING

5.1 Closing Date and Location. The execution and delivery of the agreements, instruments, documents and consideration contemplated under this Agreement (the "CLOSING") will take place on a date mutually agreeable to both parties but no later than April 20th at the offices of Jim Watts. (the "CLOSING DATE").

5.2 Seller's Deliveries. At the Closing, Seller shall deliver the following to

Buyer: Keys,

a. A Warranty Bill of Sale for the Assets in the form attached hereto as

Schedule 5.2.

b. Possession of all of the Assets including Unemployment

Compensation Insurance reserve accounts, funds, and documents.

c. Executed and properly completed Form 8594 to be filed in accordance with Internal Revenue Code § 1060 regarding the allocation of the Purchase Price hereunder;

d. Releases from any lienholders related to any of the Assets.

e. Assignments or other appropriate instruments of conveyance, assigning and transferring to Buyer all of the existing contracts being assumed by Buyer under this Agreement.

f. All documents, instruments and certificates of title reasonably required by Buyer to carry out the terms of this Agreement.

g. A Schedule of unbilled work-in-progress and accounts receivable in the form attached hereto as Schedule 1.4.

h. A UCC lien search dated as of the Closing date showing no liens, claims or encumbrances against the Assets or the Dental Practice.

i. A Consent Resolution of Seller with respect to resolutions adopted by all the Members of Seller authorizing the transactions contemplated herein.

5.3 Buyer's Deliveries. At the Closing, Buyer shall deliver the following to Seller:

a. The Purchase Price in cash or certified funds.

b. A Consent Resolution of Buyer with respect to resolutions adopted by all the Members of Buyer authorizing the transactions contemplated herein.

c. All other documents and instruments reasonably required by this Agreement to carry out the terms hereof.

5.4 Contingencies.

5.5 Inspection of Assets. At any time mutually acceptable by the parties hereto, Buyer may inspect the Premises and all the Assets of the Dental Practice and any of the financial books of the Dental Practice on or before the Closing date. If prior to Closing date examination of the Premises or Assets reveals any legal defect to title (including any encumbrances) or any other defective condition to the Premises or any Asset being purchased herein that is not specifically noted and listed on the attached Schedules or otherwise, Buyer may declare this Agreement null and void or provide that the Seller shall have thirty (30) calendar days after written notice from Buyer in which to negotiate an acceptable resolution to Buyer's satisfaction or correct such defect or condition and, if necessary, extend the Closing date accordingly. In the event, the Seller is unable to correct such defect within thirty (30) days, unless the parties otherwise agree, Buyer may declare this Agreement null and void.

5.6 Possession of the Dental Practice. Unless otherwise specifically set forth herein or otherwise mutually agreed, Seller shall deliver and Buyer shall assume possession of the Dental Practice on the Closing date.

6. REPRESENTATIONS AND WARRANTIES OF SELLER

Seller represents and warrants to Buyer that at the date hereof and on the Closing Date:

6.1 Tax Matters.

a. All federal, state, local and foreign tax returns (including, without limitation, estimated tax returns, withholding tax returns with respect to employees, and FICA and FUTA returns) required to be filed by or on behalf of Seller or for which Seller has any liability have been accurately prepared and timely filed. All taxes due for tax years or periods ending on or before the date of Closing have been paid, other than those not yet due and payable or those which are being contested on a timely basis. As of the date hereof, there is no deficiency or refund litigation or matter in controversy with respect to any taxes that might result in determinations adverse to the transactions contemplated herein. All taxes due with respect to completed and settled examinations or concluded litigation have been paid.

b. There are no claims or assessments pending against Seller for any alleged deficiency in any tax which could have a material adverse effect on the transactions contemplated herein, nor (1) audit or investigation of Seller with respect to any liability for taxes for which Seller may be liable; or (2) to the Seller's knowledge any threatened claims or assessments for taxes against Seller.

6.2 Title to Assets. Seller has good and marketable title to all of the Assets, free and clear of any mortgage, lien, pledge, charge, claim or encumbrances. Seller shall transfer all right, title and interest in and to the Assets to Buyer, without reservation or encumbrance.

6.3 Litigation. Except as disclosed to Buyer in writing:

a. Seller is not engaged in nor is it a party to nor threatened with any legal action or other proceeding or investigation before any court, arbitrator or governmental agency, nor is Seller aware of any potential adverse claim, the outcome of which could involve the payment by Seller of any amount, or which could result in a non- monetary judgment, order or award that (singly or in the aggregate) could adversely affect the Practice, Assets or condition of Seller; and

b. There are no outstanding orders, rulings, decrees, judgments or stipulations to which Seller is a party or by which the Practice or Assets are bound or affected (1) involving any amount, or (2) which could result in a non-monetary judgment, order or award that singly or in the aggregate could materially adversely affect the Practice or the Assets.

6.4 Brokers or Finders. This Agreement and the transaction contemplated hereby have been carried on directly by Seller with Buyer without the intervention of any finder, broker or third party.

6.5 Books and Records. Seller shall present such books and records Buyer may request which are maintained in the operation of the Dental Practice to Buyer for examination and review prior to closing including, but not limited to, accounts receivable lists, patient information, balance sheets, operating statements, and tax returns, and all such books and records shall, for the periods shown, be true and correct in all material respects, accurately reflect the financial condition and operating results of Seller's Dental Practice, and be free of material omissions.

6.6 Employees. None of Seller's employees are employed pursuant to a written employment agreement or have been given any representations, either written or oral, that their employment is for a term of definite duration. Thus, all Sellers' employees are "at-will" employees who may be terminated at any time without cause. Further, Seller has no knowledge, after reasonable investigation, of any claim, demand, or cause of action that any current employee of Seller may have against Seller. Seller agrees to be responsible for the payment to all such employees of all wages and benefits due and owing to them up to the Closing Date. Seller shall pay all benefit costs for the employees including vacation and sick or any other leave days accrued prior to and up to the Closing Date. Prior to Closing, the Seller shall prepare and provide to Buyer for review a schedule and certificate, in the form substantially similar to Schedule 6.6 attached hereto, representing that Seller has fully taken care of and completed the above items. In addition, Seller will legally terminate each of its employees and contractors as of the Closing date and will withhold and pay all related employment and social security taxes, benefits, and insurance premiums accrued as of the Closing date. Buyer shall not have any responsibility or obligation to hire any such employees of the Dental Practice nor does Buyer assume any liability or responsibility for any obligation owed to such employees whatsoever, including, without limitation, any compensation, pension, retirement, severance or other benefit of any kind or nature, and/or any employment taxes due with respect to any individuals employed in the Dental Practice prior to the Closing date and Seller hereby agrees to indemnify and hold Buyer harmless from same.

6.7 Condition of Assets. The Assets, whether owned or leased, are and as of the Closing Date will be in good and working condition unless otherwise specifically approved by Buyer in writing.

6.8 Financial Matters. All financial data, certificates, schedules, practice profiles, contracts, exhibits or other instruments and/or written information concerning the Dental Practice furnished by Seller to Buyer are materially true and correct in all material respects and are an accurate representation of the Dental Practice on the signature date and on the Closing date, and contain no obligation that is not in the ordinary course of the business of the Dental Practice. Seller specifically understands that Buyer is relying upon the accuracy of the information and documentation provided by Seller as a material factor for determining the Dental Practice value and is a material inducement for Buyer to acquire the Dental Practice.

6.9 Disclosures. Seller has disclosed to Buyer any known material information and/or changes that have occurred in the Dental Practice (including, but not limited to any past occurrence within a period of 36 months prior to the signature date and/or any litigation, disciplinary actions or threatened actions by any person or governmental agency against Seller and/or the Dental Practice, pending or otherwise) or other actions that could reasonably be expected to materially and adversely affect the desirability or economic potential of the Dental Practice or the value of the Assets prior to the Closing date.

6.10 Authority. Seller has the necessary power, authority and capacity to enter into this Agreement carry out Seller's obligations contemplated hereby, without the necessity of any act or consent of any other person or entity (except with respect to those leases and other contractual arrangements that are not assignable or transferable without the consent of the counterparty, if any, copies and/or an acceptable verified list of which shall be provided to Buyer within 10-days of Buyer's signing this Agreement), and that this Agreement constitutes a legal, valid and binding obligation of Seller, enforceable against Seller in accordance with its terms. Seller warrants that the execution and delivery by Seller of this Agreement and the documents contemplated herein, as well as the consummation by Seller of the transactions contemplated thereby, do not and will not (i) violate the terms of any instrument, document or agreement of which Seller is a party, or by which Seller or the property of Seller is bound, or be in conflict with, result in a breach of or constitute (upon the giving of notice, lapse of time or both) a default under any such instrument, document or agreement, or result in the creation of any lien upon any of the Assets, or (ii) violate any order, writ, injunction, decree, judgment, ruling, law, rule or regulation of any federal, state, county or foreign court or governmental authority applicable to Seller relating to the Dental Practice.

6.11 Compliance with Law. To the best of Seller's knowledge Seller has complied with all applicable local, state and federal regulations, statutes, laws, ordinances, rules, regulations, orders or directives relating to the operation of the Dental Practice.

7. INDEMNIFICATION

7.1 Buyer's Indemnification. Buyer agrees to assume all obligations pertaining to the patients of the Dental Practice being transferred to Buyer under this Agreement which arise on or after the Closing Date, including all obligations, rights and privileges pertaining to payments made, received or due to such patients, Medicare, Medicaid or insurers.

7.2 Seller's Indemnification. Seller shall indemnify, defend and hold Buyer harmless against and in respect of:

a. Any and all losses, damages or deficiencies arising as a result of or relating in any manner to any breach of a warranty, misrepresentation or non-performance of any material provision of this Agreement by Seller;

b. Any and all obligations, losses, damages or deficiencies resulting from any obligations, contracts or agreements to which Seller is a party where such obligations were assumed by Buyer;

c. Any and all obligations, losses, damages or deficiencies resulting from any obligations, contracts or agreements relating to the Dental Practice to which Seller is a party where such obligation, contract, or agreement was not assumed by Buyer;

d. The ownership of the Assets and the operation of the Dental Practice before the Closing Date, including environmental liabilities relating to the operation of the Dental Practice to the extent such liabilities exist at the Closing Date;

f. Any and all actions, suits, proceedings, demands, assessments, judgments, costs, and expenses (including reasonable attorneys' fees) incident to any of the foregoing.

8. DENTAL PRACTICE RECORDS

8.1 Patient Records. Buyer shall retain all patient records of the Dental Practice existing at the time of Closing in accordance with laws, confidentiality requirements and Buyer's record retention practice ("Existing Records"). Only as required or allowed by law and in the event of a malpractice action or claim against Seller, Buyer will provide reasonable access to such Existing Records to Dr. Fisher., his agents and professional liability insurer and its agents, upon written request. Seller warrants, covenants, and agrees that it, and its agents, shall comply with all statutes, regulations, ordinances, rules, court orders and agency determinations relating to the Existing Records, including but not limited to complying with the Health Insurance Portability and Accountability Act, as amended, and all implementing regulations. Seller agrees to indemnify, defend and hold harmless Buyer, its members, officers and agents, from any and all claims, damages and liabilities resulting from or arising out of Buyer granting access to the Existing Records to Seller.

8.2 Business Records. Following Closing and for a period of one (1) year after Closing, Buyer agrees to permit Seller to have reasonable access to and the right to copy the books and records containing information about the Dental Practice prior to the Closing date acquired by Buyer in connection with this transaction for purposes of preparing and filing tax returns, prosecuting or defending any claim, suit investigation or proceeding relating to any governmental entity or any third party and for tax and regulatory purposes. Before providing access to any such books and/or records, Seller must submit a written request to Buyer, which described with reasonable sufficiency the books and/or records Seller wishes to inspect and copy and the reason Seller wishes to inspect and copy such books and/or records. Seller shall reimburse Buyer the reasonable costs associated with allowing Seller access to such historical books and/records.

9. MISCELLANEOUS

9.1 Survival. All representations and warranties set forth in this Agreement, and all rights, remedies, obligations, and all covenants and agreements in this Agreement, or in any ancillary agreement and/or in each of the transactions contemplated hereby, which, by their terms contemplate performance which is to extend beyond or occur after execution and/or Closing, shall survive Closing and shall remain in effect and be enforceable as between the parties hereto in accordance with their terms.

9.2 Waivers. The waiver by or on behalf of any party hereto of a breach of any provision of this Agreement shall not operate or be construed as a waiver of any subsequent breach. At any time prior to the Closing, Seller and Buyer may waive in writing any conditions to their respective obligations hereunder which have not been satisfied.

9.3 Expenses and Post Closing Dental Services.

(a) Except as provided elsewhere in this Agreement, whether or not the Closing occurs, each of the parties hereto shall bear and pay all costs and expenses incurred by it or on its behalf in connection with this transaction, including fees and expenses of its own financial or other consultants, accountants and counsel.

9.4 Entire Agreement. Except as otherwise expressly provided herein, this Agreement (including the Schedules and Exhibits hereto) contains the entire agreement between the parties with respect to this transaction and supersedes all prior arrangements or understandings with respect thereto, written or oral. This agreement may not be modified or changed except by an instrument or instruments in writing, signed by both Buyer and Seller.

9.5 Benefit. The terms and conditions of this Agreement shall inure to the benefit of and be binding upon the parties hereto and their respective successors, assigns, executors, administrators or other personal representatives. Nothing in this Agreement, expressed or implied, is intended to confer upon any party, other than the parties and their respective successors-in-interest, any rights, remedies, obligations or liabilities under or by reason of this Agreement, except as expressly provided herein.

9.6 Notices. All notices or other communications which are required or permitted hereunder shall be in writing and will be deemed to be sufficient if delivered personally or sent by registered or certified mail, postage prepaid, or telecopied, with confirmation of receipt (provided that a copy is simultaneously sent by regular mail) or sent by nationally recognized overnight courier, to the following persons and addresses, or to such other persons and addresses as may be designated from time to time by the receiving party:

If to Buyer: and Grain Acres Dental

Address here:

If to Seller: Dr. John Seller

Address here:

Any such notices shall be deemed to have been given as of the date so personally delivered, or faxed one (1) day after sent by overnight courier and five (5) days after mailed.

9.7 Further Assurances. After the Closing, the parties agree to execute all additional documents and take all actions reasonably needed to accomplish the purposes of this Agreement and to carry out the terms hereof.

9.8 Governing Law. This Agreement shall be interpreted under and governed

by the internal laws of the State of STATE XX.

9.9 Severability. Invalidity of any provision of this Agreement shall not render invalid any of the other provisions of this Agreement. It is the intention of the parties that this Agreement shall constitute a binding and legally enforceable agreement. In the event a court of competent jurisdiction shall for any reason determine that any one or all of any combination of the restrictions and limitations placed upon and agreed to by Seller hereunder are not adequately limited as to time, scope or geographic location, or are for any other reason unenforceable, then in that event, the parties expressly authorize and do hereby jointly request the court to exercise its equitable power and to reform this Agreement to the extent and in the manner necessary and/or appropriate under the circumstances, so as to render the covenants enforceable to the maximum extent possible and thereby effectuate the intention of the parties.

9.10 Non-Assignability. This Agreement shall not be assignable by either party without the prior written consent of the other party. Any attempted assignment or transfer hereof shall be in breach of this Agreement and shall be null and void and of no force or effect.

9.11 Counterparts. This Agreement may be executed in any number of counterparts, each of which, when executed, shall be deemed to be an original and all of which together shall be deemed to be one and the same instrument.

9.12 Incorporation by Reference. Each Exhibit or Schedule which is referred to herein and which is attached hereto shall be deemed to be incorporated herein and made a part hereof by such reference to the same extent and with the same effect as if the same were set forth herein in their entirety.

9.13 Interpretations. Any uncertainty or ambiguity existing herein shall not be interpreted against either party because such party prepared any portion of this Agreement, but shall be interpreted according to the application of rules of interpretation of contracts generally. The headings and table of contents (if any) used in this Agreement are inserted for convenience and reference only and are not intended to be an integral part of or to affect the meaning or interpretation of this Agreement.

9.14 Time is of the Essence, Computation of Time. Time is of the essence with respect to every covenant, condition to be satisfied, and action to be taken hereunder, and the parties shall proceed accordingly with respect to every action necessary, proper or advisable to make effective the transaction contemplated by this Agreement. Whenever the last day for the exercise of any privilege or the discharge of any duty hereunder shall fall upon any day which is not a business day, the party having such privilege or duty may exercise such privilege or discharge such duty on the next succeeding business day.

IN WITNESS WHEREOF, the parties hereto have executed this Agreement or have caused this Agreement to be executed in their behalf by an officer thereunto duly authorized, on the date first above written.

XXXXX DENTAL OFFICE, a STATE XX professional corporation, Seller By

_____

Authorized Official

Dr. John Seller , D.D.S., Seller

_____

Individually

Grain Acres Dental, LLC, a STATEXX Limited Liability Company, Buyer By

_____

Authorized Official

Dr. John Buyer, D.D.S., Buyer

_____

Individually

INDEX OF SCHEDULES

Schedule 1.1 Dental Equipment, Furniture, Fixtures, Inventory and Supplies

Schedule 1.4 Unbilled Work-in-Progress Accounts

Schedule 5.2 Bill of Sale

Schedule 6.6 Certification and List of Employees / Independent Contractors

SCHEDULE 1.1

LIST DENTAL EQUIPMENT, FURNITURE, FIXTURES, INVENTORY AND SUPPLIES INCLUDED

LIST ANY EXCLUDED ASSETS

SCHEDULE 1.4

LIST UNBILLED WORK-IN-PROGRESS ACCOUNT

SCHEDULE 5.2

WARRANTY BILL OF SALE

In consideration of the sum of $265,000, XXXXX DENTAL OFFICE, a STATEXX professional corporation, and Selling Dentist D.D.S., (whether one or more herein after "Grantor"), hereby sells, assigns, transfers and conveys to Grain Acres Dental, LLC, a STATEXX Limited Liability Company ("Grantee"), its successor-in- interest and assigns forever, the following assets:

1. All of the equipment, furniture and fixtures located at Grantor's dental practice at address ADDRESS XXXX, including but not limited to the items set forth in any Exhibit "A" or SCHEDULE 1.1 as attached hereto.

2. All of the goodwill and going concern value of Grantor's dental practice, including all patient records and files, x-rays, computer and digital books, records, data, phone numbers, Yellow Page ads, web page, domain name, and information maintained by Grantor at the dental practice.

3. All pharmaceutical, dental and office inventory and supplies located at the dental practice as of the date hereof and all Unemployment Compensation Insurance reserve accounts, funds, and documents.

Grantor covenants and agrees with Grantee that Grantor is the lawful owner of the foregoing assets; that the same are free from all encumbrance whatsoever; that Grantor has good right to sell the same; and that Grantor will warrant and defend the same against the lawful claims and demands of all persons and entities.

IN WITNESS WHEREOF, Grantor has executed this Warranty Bill of Sale as of the day of , 2017.

XXXXX DENTAL OFFICE PC, a STATEXX professional corporation, Seller, Grantor By

_____

Authorized Official

John Seller DDS, Seller, Grantor, individually

_____

Exhibit "A" (Equipment, furniture and fixtures List Located at Grantor's dental practice at address ADDRESS XXXX

SCHEDULE 6.6

CERTIFICATION AND LIST OF EMPLOYEES / INDEPENDENT CONTRACTORS XXXXX DENTAL OFFICE (as of DATE)

The undersigned, as the current president or authorized officer of XXXXX DENTAL OFFICE, PC, ("Dental Practice") does hereby authenticate, warrant, and certify on behalf of the Dental Practice that (a) the below list of employees and independent contractors of Dental Practice is true, complete, and accurate as of the listed date, (b) no additional employees and/or independent contractors will be hired or retained between such date and the Closing date of the parties Asset Purchase Agreement, and (c) the listed employees have no employment agreements or contracts as they are all oral, (d) I have validly terminated the employment of each employee effective as of the Closing date, and (e) I have paid or made arrangements to pay all employee salaries and benefits due and owing to them, including cashing out and paying them for any accrued and unused sick, vacation or other leave which such employees had through the Closing date and hereby agree to indemnify and hold Grain Acres Dental, LLC, harmless from same..

Name	Position	Benefits	Salary	Yrs of Service	Written Agreement	Want to Stay
Jessica Davison	Dental Assistant		$19/hr	3	N	Y
Lori Mayfield	Front Desk/DA		$17/hr	1	N	Y
Cheryl Stubble	Office Manager		$52,000/yr	2	N	Y
Kim Westin	Hyg.		$37/hr	3	N	Y

DATED _____, 2021.

XXXXX DENTAL OFFICE, PC, a STATEXX professional corporation By

_____

Dr. John Seller, D.D.S., President

Example 8594

Form **8594** (Rev. December 2012) Department of the Treasury Internal Revenue Service	**Asset Acquisition Statement** **Under Section 1060** Attach to your income tax return. Information about Form 8594 and its separate instructions is at www.irs.gov/form8594	OMB No. 1545-1021 Attachment Sequence No. **169**

Name as shown on return	Identifying number as shown on return

Check the box that identifies you:
☐ Purchaser   ☒ Seller

Part I   General Information

1 Name of other party to the transaction	Other party's identifying number

Address (number, street, and room or suite no.)

City or town, state, and ZIP code

2 Date of sale	3 Total sales price (consideration) 265,000

Part II   Original Statement of Assets Transferred

4 Assets	Aggregate fair market value (actual amount for Class I)	Allocation of sales price
Class I	$	$
Class II	$	$
Class III	$	$
Classes IV	$	$
Class V	$ 60,000	$ 60,000
Class VI and VII	$ 205,000	$ 205,000
Total	$ 265,000	$ 265,000

5   Did the purchaser and seller provide for an allocation of the sales price in the sales contract or in another written document signed by both parties? .... ☒ Yes ☐ No

If "Yes," are the aggregate fair market values (FMV) listed for each of asset Classes I, II, III, IV, V, VI, and VII the amounts agreed upon in your sales contract or in a separate written document? .... ☒ Yes ☐ No

6   In the purchase of the group of assets (or stock), did the purchaser also purchase a license or a covenant not to compete, or enter into a lease agreement, employment contract, management contract, or similar arrangement with the seller (or managers, directors, owners, or employees of the seller)? .... ☐ Yes ☒ No

If "Yes," attach a statement that specifies **(a)** the type of agreement and **(b)** the maximum amount of consideration (not including interest) paid or to be paid under the agreement. See instructions.

For Paperwork Reduction Act Notice, see separate instructions.

DAA

Form **8594** (Rev. 12-2012)

ASSET PURCHASE AGREEMENT
TABLE OF CONTENTS

SECTION

EXHIBIT"C"	
RESTRICTIVE COVENANT AGREEMENT	
1. RESTRICTIVE COVENANT	
2. NON-SOLICITATION	
3. PATIENT REVENUE REIMBURSEMENT	
4. WAIVER OF RIGHT TO PROTEST	
5. SPECIFIC PERFORMANCE	
EXHIBIT "D"	
REAL ESTATE PURCHASE AGREEMENT	
EXHIBIT "E"	
ADDITIONAL PROVISIONS AND MODIFICATIONS	
EXHIBIT "F"	
CORPORATE RESOLUTION	

ASSET PURCHASE AGREEMENT

THIS ASSET PURCHASE AGREEMENT (the "Asset Purchase Agreement") is entered into on _____,201_, (the "Signature Date") by and between Village Dental, P.C., a STATE***** professional corporation, and Dennis Seller, D.D.S. (jointly and severally hereinafter referred to as "Seller" and/or "Dr. Seller" whichever reference is appropriate), and Grain Acres Dental, LLC , a STATE***** Limited Liability Company (hereinafter referred to as "Purchaser"). Dennis Seller and Judy Seller are husband and wife.

WHEREAS, Seller operates a dental practice (the "Practice") located at ADDRESS***** (which, for purposes of this Asset Purchase Agreement, shall hereinafter be referred to as the "Premises"); and

WHEREAS, Seller also owns the real estate at the Premises known at Village North 8th, Lot 6 located in Lincoln, COUNTY***** County, STATE***** (which is hereinafter be referred to as the "Real Estate" or "Property"; and

WHEREAS, Seller, in furtherance of this Asset Purchase Agreement, desires to sell to Purchaser all of Seller's right, title and interest in and to all of the assets of the Practice (as described in more detail in Section 1 below, collectively hereinafter referred to as the "Assets"); and

WHEREAS, Purchaser desires to purchase and acquire all of Seller's rights, title and interest in the Assets in accordance with the terms and conditions set forth in this Asset Purchase Agreement.

NOW, THEREFORE, in consideration of the premises as well as the parties' respective promises, representations, covenants and warranties herein, the performance of each unto the other, and other good and valuable consideration, the receipt and sufficiency of which are hereby acknowledged, the parties agree as follows:

1. SALE OF ASSETS: Subject to the terms and conditions described herein, Seller agrees to sell assign, transfer, convey and deliver to Purchaser, and Purchaser agrees to purchase, accept, assume and receive all of Seller's right, title and interest in and to all of the Assets owned and/or used by Seller in the operation of the Practice (other than those specifically excluded and identified on the attached Exhibit "A-1" the "Excluded Assets") including without limitation the following:

    EQUIPMENT: Except for the hereinafter described Excluded Assets (if any), all clinical, lab and office equipment located on the Premises on the Signature Date, including but not limited to those listed on the attached Exhibit "A".

    OFFICE FURNITURE AND FIXTURES: Except for the hereinafter described Excluded Assets (if any), all office furniture, furnishings and trade fixtures located on the Premises on the Signature Date, including but not limited to those listed on the attached Exhibit "A".

    OFFICE AND CLINICAL SUPPLIES: All clinical supplies and instruments, all paper goods and the office supplies located on the Premises on the Date of Possession (as hereinafter defined); Seller agrees to have a usual and customary inventory of supplies used for the operation of the Practice to be on hand on the Date of Possession.

REAL ESTATE AND MISCELLANEOUS ASSETS: Seller has agreed to sell the Premises and the Real Estate to Purchaser (the Purchase Agreement for the Real Estate is attached hereto as Exhibit "D"), all soft and hard-copy and electronic clinical and financial records related to all patients of the Practice ("Patient Records"), all work in progress (including all work partially completed as of the Date of Possession), the transfer of all computer software used for the operation of the Practice (to the extent assignable and/or transferable as required by the software company owner, if applicable) and all related passwords and software keys, transfer of all telephone numbers and any related yellow page ads to Purchaser, any generic name used in the operation of the Practice if applicable (whether used as a corporate designation or not), any Practice related websites and email addresses in use by the Practice, all professional employee contracts (if any), all managed care contracts in effect between Seller and any third party (if any), and all other miscellaneous tangible and intangible non-cash assets of the Practice that have not been specifically excluded from this sale and listed on the attached Exhibit "A-1" shall be transferred to Purchaser. Within 5-days of the signing of this Asset Purchase Agreement, Seller shall provide to Purchaser for review prior to closing, written documentation in a form acceptable to Purchaser: (1) a list of all computer software and the transfer restrictions, requirements or terms for continuation for the Practice, if any; (2) copies of all Practice policies, regulation and bylaws; (3) copies of all Practice contracts leases, and other outstanding obligations; (4) all professional or other employee contracts, policies, handbooks and/or the specific terms and conditions of all Practice employee salaries and benefits; (5) copies of all managed care contracts of the Practice in effect between Seller and any third party, if any; and (6) copies of any leases of any third party on the Property and 2 years' worth of utility expenses on the Property and Premises.

GOODWILL: Seller's personal goodwill of the Practice that has been established by Dr. Seller, to include the preparation, execution and mailing of a letter of introduction and recommendation to the patients of the Practice. Purchaser shall review and approve such letter of introduction and recommendation. Following the Closing Date (as hereinafter described) and as a specific condition of this sale, Seller agrees to put forth Seller's reasonable best efforts to transfer Seller's personal goodwill to Purchaser. The parties acknowledge and agree that this goodwill is based on the relationship between Dr. Seller and the patients and referral sources of the Practice and represents both a personal, non-corporate and corporate asset that is being conveyed individually by Dr. Seller and jointly and severally by Seller through this Asset Purchase Agreement.

EXCLUDED ASSETS: All cash assets of the Practice such as checking and savings accounts, petty cash, cash on hand, cash deposits for the lease and utilities (if any), retained earnings, accounts receivable, pension and/or profit sharing plans, insurance premium refunds, all automobiles, personal items such as professional plaques, books and personal stationery, malpractice insurance policies, casualty insurance, liability insurance and any and all other insurance policies maintained in connection with the Practice are and will remain the sole property of Seller following the Closing Date and are specifically excluded from this sale; in addition, the assets of the Practice described on the attached Exhibit "A-1" are also excluded from this sale (all of the aforementioned excluded items shall collectively be referred to as the "Excluded Assets").

A.   Unless otherwise specifically set forth herein, Seller's interest in the Assets shall be absolute ownership, free and clear of any liens, debts and encumbrances of any kind. In addition, should there be any charge for transferring the telephone number and yellow page ads for the Practice, and/or transferring the dental software license to Purchaser (if applicable), and/or monthly payments payable to a third party software supplier for maintenance and support, then such expense and or payments shall be paid and/or assumed by Seller prior to the Closing Date and the Purchaser following the Closing Date.

B.   Except for the aforementioned Excluded Assets, the Assets and Seller's interest in all other items used for the operation of the Practice and located on the Premises on or after the Closing Date shall be conveyed to Purchaser through this Asset Purchase Agreement by Bill of Sale or appropriate conveyance instrument at the Closing, whether Seller's interest is joint or several, corporate or individual, proprietary or leased (to the extent assignable).

C.   In addition to the sale of the Assets, and as a specific condition of the purchase of the aforementioned personal goodwill, Dr. Seller agrees to be bound by the terms of the Restrictive Covenant as described in the attached Exhibit "C".

1   PURCHASE PRICE: In consideration of the sale, transfer, conveyance, assignment and delivery of the Assets and in reliance upon the representations and warranties made herein by Seller, Purchaser shall pay to Seller at Closing the sum of SIX HUNDRED SEVENTY-FIVE THOUSAND AND 00/100 DOLLARS ($675,000.00) (the "Purchase Price"), paid and allocated pursuant to the terms as hereinafter described.

2   ALLOCATION OF THE PURCHASE PRICE: The Purchase Price shall be allocated as follows:

ASSET		ALLOCATION
Furniture, Fixtures and Equipment	$	128,000
Office Inventory and Clinical and Other Supplies	$	42,000
Goodwill	$	500,000
Restrictive Covenant	$	5,000

Purchaser and Seller each agree to report in accordance with and be governed and bound by the allocations set forth in this Section 3 with respect to any state or federal tax returns. Each party acknowledges and agrees to comply with Section 1060 of the Internal Revenue Code of 1986, as amended (the "Code"), and any Treasury Regulations issued thereunder. The parties shall file Form 8594 with their respective federal income tax returns in a manner consistent with said allocations for the tax year in which the Closing occurs.

4.   METHOD OF PAYMENT: The Purchase Price shall be paid to Seller by Purchaser in cash (or cash equivalent) in full on the hereinafter defined Closing Date.

5.   SIGNATURE DATE AND CLOSING: The parties shall initial and sign this Asset Purchase Agreement on the Signature Date. The Practice and the Assets (not including the aforementioned Excluded Assets) shall be conveyed to Purchaser (the "Closing")

only upon completion of the following three conditions: (i) Purchaser has the required license to practice dentistry in STATE*****; (ii) this Asset Purchase Agreement and the attached exhibits are initialed and signed by all the parties hereto; (iii) the Purchase Price is paid in full by the Purchaser. The actual date and time the aforementioned terms of the Closing are completed by Purchaser shall hereinafter be referred to as the "Closing Date".

6.   DATE OF POSSESSION AND CLOSING DATE: Unless otherwise specifically set forth herein or otherwise mutually agreed, Seller shall deliver and Purchaser shall assume possession of the Practice (the "Date of Possession") on or before December 31 , 2021. The Closing Date shall also be the Date of Possession.

7.   INSPECTION OF ASSETS AND EXAMINATION OF TITLE: At any time mutually acceptable by the parties hereto, Purchaser may inspect all the Assets of the Practice on or before the Closing Date. Subject to Seller's representations and warranties relating to the condition of the Assets as of the Closing Date (as hereinafter described), completion of the Closing indicates Purchaser's satisfactory acceptance of the Assets as is and where is. However, if prior to Closing Date examination of title reveals any legal defect to title (including any encumbrances) that is not specifically noted and listed on the attached Exhibit "E", Purchaser may declare this Asset Purchase Agreement null and void or provide that the Seller shall have thirty (30) calendar days after written notice from Purchaser in which to correct such defect and, if necessary, extend the Closing Date accordingly. In the event, the Seller is unable to correct such defect within thirty (30) days, unless the parties otherwise agree, Purchaser may declare this Asset Purchase Agreement null and void.

8.   BILL OF SALE: Seller shall execute and deliver to Purchaser on the Closing Date, a Bill of Sale for the Assets substantially in the form of Exhibit "B", attached hereto and made a part hereof. **Seller** disclaims **all implied warranties including the implied warranties of fitness for a particular purpose and merchantability of the Assets. The disclaimer of implied warranties, however, does not negate the express warranties as described herein.**

9.   TAXES: If any tax, including but not limited to state or local sales tax, transfer or use tax or documentary stamp tax is or becomes due as a result of the sale of the Assets, then all such taxes (including for any bulk sales tax, income taxes resulting from this sale, and any other sales and/or transfer taxes owed by Seller resulting from any applicable statutes for this sale, if any) shall be the responsibility of and be paid by Seller as and when required.

10. PRACTICE PRO-RATED EXPENSES AND LIABILITIES: Seller shall pay for all outstanding contractual obligations, including but not limited to rents, taxes, telephone, contracted advertisements (such as yellow page ads), water, sewer and other utility charges and expenses for the Practice accruing up to the Date of Possession, regardless of when due; Purchaser shall be solely responsible for such expenses incurred on and after the Date of Possession.

   A.   If applicable, any ad valorem and personal property taxes shall be pro-rated between Seller and Purchaser as of the Date of Possession. All taxes and expenses due and payable up to the Date of Possession shall be borne and paid solely by Seller. In addition, the Purchaser shall pay any expenses incurred for changing the office sign, if applicable.

B. Seller shall compensate at Purchaser's option either the Purchaser or the current employees of the Practice for all salary and benefits, including but not limited to accrued salaries, vacation and sick pay, maternity leave and any other employee benefits and/or bonuses due them for that or any prior employment periods prior to the Date of Possession. Prior to Closing, the Seller shall prepare and provide to Purchaser for review and Seller and Purchaser shall agree on a written schedule of the above items. In addition, Seller will terminate each of its employees and contractors as of the Date of Possession and will pay all related employment and social security taxes and insurance premiums accrued as of the Date of Possession. Purchaser shall not have any responsibility or obligation to hire any such employees of the Practice nor does Purchaser assume any liability or responsibility for any obligation owed to such employees whatsoever, including, without limitation, any compensation, severance or other benefit, and/or any employment taxes due with respect to any individuals employed in the Practice prior to the Date of Possession.

C. The parties understand and agree that the work-in-progress is an Asset of the Practice that is being conveyed to the Purchaser through this Asset Purchase Agreement. Therefore, Purchaser shall be reimbursed by Seller (on the Date of Possession) for any full or partial patient pre-paid fees (paid to Seller prior to the Date of Possession) for services scheduled to be rendered following the Date of Possession. Should Seller complete any portion of that work-in-progress following the Date of Possession, then the fees for such services shall be collected by Purchaser and Seller shall be compensated according to the terms mutually agreed to by the parties at that time. Seller shall be obligated to pay any and all patient credits and/or patient refunds due as of the Date of Possession or as requested by the patient after the Date of Possession for work or activities occurring prior thereto to the appropriate patient, as and when requested by either the patient or Purchaser.

11. ACCOUNTS RECEIVABLE: The parties acknowledge that the Assets being purchased do not include Seller's accounts receivable as of the Date of Possession, which shall remain the property of Seller. For purposes of this Asset Purchase Agreement, accounts receivable shall be defined as all amounts or fees billed by Seller (including without limitation amounts for goods and/or services rendered prior to the Date of Possession) to patients or any third-party insurer and/or government reimbursement for services rendered either partially pro rata or in full on or before the Date of Possession. Patient services waiting for pre-treatment determination by a third party shall not be considered an account receivable of Seller. Seller and Purchaser shall agree on the list and amount of accounts receivable subject to this paragraph at Closing. In addition:

A. Purchaser agrees to bill (monthly), collect payments on Seller's behalf and allow Purchaser's staff to put forth a reasonable effort to collect Seller's outstanding accounts receivable following the Date of Possession. In return, Seller agrees to pay Purchaser a 10% collection fee for each dollar collected. Purchaser shall on a monthly basis, remit to Seller any such payments received. The parties agree that Purchaser is not in any way assuming ultimate responsibility for collecting those Seller receivables and Seller agrees to indemnify and hold harmless Purchaser from and against any and all claims, threatened claims, costs or expense arising out of or related to Purchaser's efforts to collect Seller's accounts receivable.

B.   Except for accounts receivable and amounts on the agreed upon list, all monies received from patients or others for goods or services after the Date of Possession shall be owned by and the property of Purchaser.

C.   Seller agrees that no extraordinary method of collection will be utilized for any of Seller's accounts receivable without first giving advance written notice to Purchaser. After notice to the Purchaser, Sellershall have the right to use any legal method of collection available to Seller for listed accounts receivable. In all collection efforts undertaken by Seller, or on Seller's behalf, Seller agrees to clearly notify the patient or debtor that Seller is acting for Seller's own account and not that of Purchaser. Seller and Purchaser agree to comply with all federal and state fair debt collection practice laws (if applicable).

D.   The parties acknowledge and agree that Purchaser is not assuming responsibility for any liability, contingent or otherwise, resulting from the accounts receivable or any disputed billings involving same and Seller agrees to and does hereby indemnify and hold Purchaser and Purchaser's dentists, employees and agents harmless from any and all claims, damages or causes of action related to same under any law. Upon appropriate release or consent by the patient, the Seller or Seller's designee shall, during normal business hours and upon reasonable notice, have reasonable access to and/or be provided copies of the clinical and financial records related to Seller's outstanding accounts receivable; Seller shall pay all actual cost and time expense of said copies or for any specific financial reports requested by Seller.

12.   SELLER WARRANTIES: Except where otherwise provided to the contrary in this Asset Purchase Agreement or any of the attached exhibits, Seller acknowledges that Purchaser is not assuming any liability and/or obligation of Seller or the Practice or the Assets. All outstanding liabilities of the Practice prior to the Date of Possession (including office rent and/or equipment lease(s), if any) not expressly assumed by Purchaser hereunder shall be timely paid in full and discharged by Seller on or before the Date of Possession. In addition:

A.   **SELLER WARRANTS THAT, TO THE BEST OF SELLER'S ACTUAL KNOWLEDGE, ALL FINANCIAL DATA, FEDERAL INCOME TAX RETURNS, CERTIFICATES, SCHEDULES, PRACTICE PROFILES, CONTRACTS, EXHIBITS OR OTHER INSTRUMENTS AND/OR WRITTEN INFORMATION CONCERNING THE PRACTICE FURNISHED BY SELLER TO PURCHASER ARE MATERIALLY TRUE AND CORRECT IN ALL MATERIAL RESPECTS AND ARE AN ACCURATE REPRESENTATION OF THE PRACTICE ON THE SIGNATURE DATE, AND CONTAIN NO INCOME OR TAX OBLIGATION THAT IS NOT IN THE ORDINARY COURSE OF THE BUSINESS OF THE PRACTICE. SELLER SPECIFICALLY UNDERSTANDS THAT PURCHASER IS RELYING UPON THE ACCURACY OF THE INFORMATION AND DOCUMENTATION PROVIDED BY SELLER AS A MATERIAL FACTOR FOR DETERMINING THE PRACTICE VALUE AND IS A MATERIAL INDUCEMENT FOR PURCHASER TO ACQUIRE THE PRACTICE.**

B.	**SELLER WARRANTS THAT, PRIOR TO THE SIGNATURE DATE, SELLER HAS INVESTIGATED AND INDEPENDENTLY EXAMINED, TO SELLER'S COMPLETE SATISFACTION, THE PERSONAL, PROFESSIONAL AND FINANCIAL BACKGROUND OF THE PURCHASER AND THAT SELLER HAS NOT RELIED ON ANY STATEMENTS, WARRANTIES OR REPRESENTATIONS, EXPRESSED OR IMPLIED, FROM PURCHASER OR ANY THIRD PARTY CONCERNING PURCHASER'S SUITABILITY FOR THIS ACQUISITION.**

C.	**SELLER WARRANTS THAT SELLER HAS INDEPENDENTLY CONSULTED WITH SELLER'S OWN ATTORNEY AND ACCOUNTANT AND IS RELYING SOLELY UPON THEIR RESPECTIVE LEGAL, FINANCIAL, TAX AND/OR ACCOUNTING ADVICE FOR ALL ISSUES RELATED TO THIS TRANSACTION.**

D.	Seller has disclosed to Purchaser any known material information and/or changes that have occurred in the Practice (including, but not limited to any past occurrence within a period of 36 months prior to the Signature Date and/or any litigation, disciplinary actions or threatened actions by any person or governmental agency against Seller and/or the Practice, pending or otherwise) or other actions that could reasonably be expected to materially and adversely affect the desirability or economic potential of the Practice or the value of the Assets prior to the Signature Date; such previous or pending actions or changes, if any, shall be in writing and included in Exhibit "E".

E.	Seller warrants that Seller has no known and/or diagnosed condition, including drug or alcohol dependency, disease, disorder and/or disability (if any) that could materially and adversely affect the value of the Practice.

F.	Seller warrants that, to the best of Seller's actual knowledge, all equipment, furniture and fixtures being transferred through this Asset Purchase Agreement meets applicable state and federal regulations and shall be free from known defects, liens of any nature, in good repair and working order (normal wear and tear excepted) on the Date of Possession unless otherwise specified on the attached Exhibit "A".

G.	Seller further warrants that on the Signature Date:

	(i)	Seller has the necessary power, authority and capacity to enter into this Asset Purchase Agreement and carry out Seller's obligations contemplated hereby, without the necessity of any act or consent of any other person or entity, and that this Asset Purchase Agreement constitutes a legal, valid and binding obligation of Seller, enforceable against Seller in accordance with its terms;

	(ii)	there are no contracts with any employee or independent contractor of the Practice that cannot be terminated at will by Seller, and that there have been no extraordinary increases in the compensation payable to any of the employees of the Practice and no provisions for any awards, bonuses, stock options, loans, profit sharing, pension, retirement or welfare plans or similar or other disbursements or arrangements for or on behalf of such employees that would become payable by Purchaser following the Closing Date, and, to Seller's actual knowledge, that no such claim is pending or could be asserted by any current or former employee of the Practice;

(iii)   that to the best of Seller's knowledge, the office is properly zoned for its intended use by Purchaser and that the lease for the Premises is not in default nor has been in default without being promptly cured by Seller (if applicable) as a result of Seller's act or omission;

(iv)   Seller is the sole lawful owner of the Practice and Assets and that Seller has good, valid and marketable title to the Assets, and subject to the terms of Section 1 in this Asset Purchase Agreement, the Practice and Assets will be free and clear of any liens, claims, equities, charges, options, security interests or encumbrances of any nature whatsoever with no defects of title as of the Closing Date, unless indicated to the contrary on Exhibit "E" (if applicable);

(v)   Seller shall not be in material default under any contract, lease or any other commitment whatsoever which might reasonably be expected to result in a material and adverse effect, either directly or indirectly, Purchaser, the Assets and/or the operation of the Practice following the Date of Possession;

(vi)   except for any current operating obligations of the Practice outstanding as of the Closing Date, there will be no Practice-related, current or past-due obligations to creditors of Seller (including brokerage fees, patient refunds or allowances, if any) outstanding as of the Closing Date, and Seller will pay in full all obligations related to the operation of the Practice prior to the Date of Possession and any obligations related to its sale in accordance with the terms of such obligations, unless and only to the extent contested in good faith as long as no claim on Purchaser is made for any such obligation;

(vii)   that there has been no work performed at the Premises by any third party which has not been timely paid in full or would otherwise give rise to any form of lien if not timely paid;

(viii)   Seller agrees to comply with all applicable state and federal laws applicable to this transaction or Seller's actions necessary to accomplish this transaction, including but not limited to those laws related to unemployment, workers' compensation and COBRA requirements (if any);

(ix)   to the best of Seller's knowledge Seller has complied with all applicable local, state and federal regulations, statutes, laws, ordinances, rules, regulations, orders or directives relating to the operation of the Practice;

(x)   Seller and all clinical practitioners employed in the Practice, if any, are currently licensed to practice dentistry in STATE***** and are in material compliance with all applicable federal, state and local laws, rules and regulations relating to such professional licensure.

H. Seller warrants that the execution and delivery by Seller of this Agreement and the documents contemplated herein, as well as the consummation by Seller of the transactions contemplated thereby, do not and will not (i) violate the terms of any instrument, document or agreement of which Seller is a party, or by which Seller or the property of Seller is bound, or be in conflict with, result in a breach of or constitute (upon the giving of notice, lapse of time or both) a default under any such instrument, document or agreement, or result in the creation of any lien upon any of the Assets, or (ii) violate any order, writ, injunction, decree, judgment, ruling, law, rule or regulation of any federal, state, county or foreign court or governmental authority applicable to Seller relating to the Practice.

I. Seller warrants that there are no taxes or present disputes as to taxes of any nature payable by Seller which will impair the consummation of the transaction contemplated by this Agreement, result in any lien upon the Assets, or impose on Purchaser any burden or obligation to assume or pay any taxes of any nature (except for any taxes due as a result of the sale of the Assets, if any). Except for employee withholding taxes which will be deposited and/or paid according to the payment schedules required by law and prorated between Seller and Purchaser as appropriate at closing, to the best of Seller's knowledge and belief, all tax returns of Seller (federal, state, city or otherwise) required by law to be filed on or before the Date of Possession have been duly filed in an accurate and correct manner and all corresponding taxes have been paid.

J. Seller warrants that to the best of Seller's knowledge and belief, Seller is not in violation of, under any investigation with respect to, threatened to be charged with or been given notice of any non-compliance with, enforcement action under or violation of any applicable law, statute, order, rule, regulation, agency agreement, judgment, decree, penalty or fine entered by any federal, state, local or foreign court or governmental authority relating to the Practice or the Assets; and that, to the best of Seller's knowledge, there are otherwise no facts relating to the Assets or Seller's operation of the Practice which, if known by a potential claimant or governmental authority, would give rise to a claim or proceeding to which the Practice or the Assets would be subject after the Date of Possession.

K. Seller warrants that there is no suit, action, arbitration, or legal, administrative, or other proceeding, or governmental investigation, pending or, to the best of Seller's knowledge and belief, threatened, against or affecting the Practice, Seller or the financial condition of Seller, nor is Seller in default with respect to any order, writ, injunction, or decree of any federal, state, local or foreign court, department, agency or instrumentality; and that there are no facts or circumstances that might lead to a claim nor has any claim been made by any third party relating to the Practice, Seller or Seller's financial condition which would give rise to a claim or proceeding to which Purchaser or the Assets would be subject after the Date of Possession.

L. Seller warrants that Village Dental, P.C. is a professional corporation duly organized, validly existing and in good standing under the laws of the State of STATE*****, that Dr. Seller is the sole owner of stock in such corporation and has all necessary corporate power and authority to execute, deliver and perform this

Asset Purchase Agreement and all other agreements and instruments to be delivered in connection with this Agreement. Upon completion of this Asset Purchase Agreement, Village Dental, P.C. will be a shell corporation.

13. PURCHASER WARRANTIES: Except to the extent otherwise set forth in this Asset Purchase Agreement, Purchaser acknowledges, warrants and agrees:

A. THAT ANY PRACTICE RELATED INCOME AND EXPENSE PROJECTIONS PROVIDED TO PURCHASER ARE PROJECTIONS ONLY AND ARE NOT TO BE CONSTRUED AS A REPRESENTATION OR WARRANTY RELATING TO THE FUTURE BUSINESS POTENTIAL OR INCOME AND EXPENSES OF THE PRACTICE, AND THAT SELLER'S PAST RESULTS DO NOT GUARANTEE FUTURE PERFORMANCE, AND THAT ANY FLUCTUATIONS OF INCOME AND EXPENSES FOLLOWING THE DATE OF POSSESSION ARE BEYOND THE CONTROL OF SELLER.

B. THAT PURCHASER (I) HAS INDEPENDENTLY CONSULTED WITH PURCHASER'S OWN ATTORNEY AND ACCOUNTANT AND IS RELYING SOLELY UPON THEIR RESPECTIVE LEGAL, TAX AND/OR ACCOUNTING ADVICE FOR ALL ISSUES RELATED TO THIS TRANSACTION, AND (II) HAS INDEPENDENTLY INVESTIGATED AND EXAMINED TO PURCHASER'S COMPLETE SATISFACTION, THE CLINICAL, FINANCIAL AND ALL OTHER RECORDS OF THE PRACTICE (INCLUDING THIRD PARTY MANAGED CARE CONTRACTS, IF ANY), AND (III) IS PURCHASING THE PRACTICE WITHOUT ANY STATEMENT, REPRESENTATION OR WARRANTY, EXPRESSED OR IMPLIED, FROM SELLER AND/OR FROM ANY OTHER THIRD PARTY INCIDENTAL TO THIS TRANSACTION, EXCEPT FOR THOSE SPECIFICALLY WRITTEN IN THIS AGREEMENT.

C. THAT, PRIOR TO THE SIGNATURE DATE, PURCHASER HAS INDEPENDENTLY EXAMINED AND DETERMINED TO PURCHASER'S COMPLETE SATISFACTION, ALL THE ASSETS AND THEIR RESPECTIVE VALUE, AND, EXCEPT FOR SELLER'S WARRANTIES SET FORTH IN THIS ASSET PURCHASE AGREEMENT RELATING TO THE WORKING CONDITION AND TITLE OF THE ASSETS, IS PURCHASING SAID ASSETS "WHERE AND AS IS" ON THE CLOSING DATE, SOLELY UPON PURCHASER'S INDEPENDENT EXAMINATION AT THAT TIME, WITHOUT ANY REPRESENTATION OR WARRANTY, EXPRESSED OR IMPLIED, FROM SELLER AS TO THE VALUE, CONDITION AND/OR MERCHANTABILITY OF THE ASSETS AND THE PRACTICE, OTHER THAN THOSE REPRESENTATIONS SET FORTH BY SELLER IN SECTION 12 ABOVE. PURCHASER AGREES THAT, FOLLOWING THE DATE OF POSSESSION, SELLER SHALL HAVE NO FURTHER RESPONSIBILITY OR LIABILITY TO PURCHASER RELATED TO THE CONDITION OF THE ASSETS EXCEPT FOR A BREACH OF SELLER'S WARRANTIES OF TITLE AND/OR ANY OTHER WARRANTIES SPECIFIED IN THIS ASSET PURCHASE AGREEMENT.

D. That Purchaser has the necessary capacity to enter into this Asset Purchase Agreement and carry out its obligations contemplated hereby, without the necessity of any act or consent of any other person or entity, and that this Asset Purchase Agreement constitutes a legal, *valid* and binding obligation of Purchaser, enforceable against Purchaser in accordance with its terms and; Purchaser is licensed to practice dentistry in STATE***** on the Closing Date.

E. That the execution and delivery by Purchaser of this Agreement and the documents contemplated herein, as well as the consummation by Purchaser of this acquisition, do not and will not (i) violate the terms of any instrument, document or agreement of which Purchaser is a party, or by which Purchaser or the property of Purchaser is bound, or be in conflict with, result in a breach of or constitute (upon the giving of notice, lapse of time or both) a default under any such instrument, document or agreement, or (li) violate any order, writ, injunction, decree, judgment, ruling, law, rule or regulation of any federal, state, county or foreign court or governmental authority applicable to Purchaser relating to the Practice.

F. Purchaser acknowledges the difficulty in making judgments relating to any clinical services rendered by Seller (or any professional employee of Seller) without knowledge of the facts and conditions that existed at the time the services were rendered. Therefore following the date Seller discontinues practicing dentistry on the Premises and Purchaser agrees to promptly notify Seller of any patient of the Practice who maintains that Seller (or any professional employee of Seller) warranted a service, and/or rendered an alleged defective service; and/or that a patient requests Purchaser to provide, free of charge or at a reduced fee, either corrective or replacement treatment and/or a partial or full refund for services rendered by Seller (or any professional employee of Seller). At that point, Purchaser and Seller shall agree on appropriate procedures for handling any such circumstances.;

G. That Grain Acres Dental, LLC is a Limited Liability Company duly organized, validly existing and in good standing under the laws of the State of STATE*****, and has all necessary power and authority to execute, deliver and perform this Asset Purchase Agreement and all other agreements and instruments to be delivered in connection with this Agreement.

14. USE OF SELLER'S NAME: Purchaser shall be allowed to use Seller's personal name when answering the Practice telephone for a period of up to 12 months following the date Seller discontinues practicing dentistry on the Premises. Such use of Seller's personal name shall not be construed as creating any association, partnership or joint venture between the parties. However, all rights to any generic name that may be used in the operation of the Practice (whether such name is a corporate or trade name) shall be permanently transferred to Purchaser on the Date of Possession.

15. ANNOUNCEMENTS: Seller and Purchaser agree to notify, in writing, all active

patients (the "Patients") of the Practice (or the head of household for families) whose treatment has been rendered within three (3) years prior to the Closing Date, and to all professional or other active referral sources of the Practice, a mutually approved, appropriate announcement of this transaction containing an introduction and recommendation signed by Seller (or Seller's estate, if applicable). The expense of such announcements shall be mutually agreed upon and shared equally by the parties hereto.

A. Both parties agree not to disclose or release any information concerning the negotiations and discussions pertaining to this transaction to any other person or entity other than each party's respective legal and tax advisors, without the prior written consent of the other party; provided however this limitation shall not apply to the extent necessary or appropriate to fully comply with any applicable law regulation, Purchaser financing, or the order of any court of competent jurisdiction.

B. Seller's announcement to the patients of the Practice shall be made exclusively for the benefit of Purchaser only. Seller agrees not to take any action that is designed or intended to have the effect of discouraging patients or others from using the Practice or otherwise from maintaining the same business relationships with Purchaser after the Date of Possession. Seller further agrees not to make any statement, orally or in writing, or take any other action that might damage the business of the Practice or the business and professional reputation of Purchaser or interfere with or adversely affect the relations of Purchaser and any of Purchaser's suppliers or employees.

C. Purchaser agrees not to make any statement, orally or in writing, or take any other action that might damage the business and professional reputation of Seller or interfere with or adversely affect the relations of Seller and any of Seller's suppliers or employees (if applicable).

16. PATIENT RECORDS: The parties agree that to ensure continuity of care for the aforementioned Patients of the Practice, Seller's custodial interest in, and responsibility for, all patient records shall transfer to Purchaser on the Closing Date, to the extent permitted by applicable law. Purchaser and Seller agree to comply with any applicable State and Federal regulations relating to the transferability and confidentiality of the clinical and financial content of the Patient Records, including but not limited to all applicable HIPAA privacy regulations. Purchaser agrees to retain the Patient Records according to law.

A. In the event of a malpractice action or claim against Seller, upon reasonable request, Purchaser will make all relevant original Patient Records available to Seller, to Seller's estate, and/or any former professional employee of the Practice (at Seller's expense), in accordance with the confidentiality requirements of any applicable Federal or State law, rules and regulations. Unless otherwise determined by the courts having jurisdiction over the matter, upon completion of such action, the original Patient Records shall be returned to Purchaser. Purchaser shall make copies of such Patient Records and maintain those copies until such time as the original Patient Records are returned.

B.   Purchaser may discard or destroy any Patient Records in accordance with laws, confidentiality requirements, and Purchaser's documents retention rules.

C.   Following the Date of Closing, with respect to any appliance for patients treated by Seller and held by Purchaser pending receipt of the final payment, such appliance shall not be disposed of by Purchaser without first notifying Seller and the patient, in writing, at least 30 days in advance of disposing of any such appliance.

17.   EXPENSES: Each party shall pay all their respective broker, consultant, attorney or accountant fees and expenses incurred by such party with respect to this Asset Purchase Agreement and the transaction contemplated hereby.

18.   ATTORNEYS AND DOCUMENTS: The parties acknowledge that each have been represented by independent legal counsel in this transaction, and/or have been advised to use their own independent legal counsel.

19.   INDEMNIFICATION: Each party (the "Indemnifying Party") hereby agrees to defend, hold harmless and expeditiously indemnify the other party (the "Indemnified Party") from, against and with respect to any and all liability, claim, loss, damage, obligation, cost or expense arising out of the Indemnifying Party's breach or violation of any representation, provision, warranty or covenant contained in this Asset Purchase Agreement or its exhibits (if such breach of covenant is decided by a court of competent jurisdiction or by admission of either party), including reasonable attorneys' fees in the defense of any legal proceeding asserting such a claim.

A.   Seller and/or Seller's assigns and successors agree to defend, hold harmless, and expeditiously indemnify Purchaser from, against and with respect to any and all loss which, in any manner, arises or results from the operation of the Practice prior to the Date of Possession, and/or from any liability or obligation of Seller and/or Seller's employees, agents, suppliers, vendors and/or independent contractors not expressly assumed by Purchaser hereunder.

B.   Purchaser shall defend, hold harmless and expeditiously indemnify Seller from, against and with respect to any and all loss arising out of any conduct or practice of Purchaser and Purchaser's employees at anytime on or following the Date of Possession, and/or from any liabilities or obligations of Seller expressly assumed by Purchaser and specifically described in this Asset Purchase Agreement (if any).

C.   Upon receipt of a claim or demand for which a party is entitled to indemnification, the Indemnified Party shall promptly:

(i)   notify the Indemnifying Party in writing of the nature of the indemnifiable claim, and the names and addresses of the persons involved in or having an interest in such claim; and

(ii)   furnish the Indemnifying Party with all documents and information within the possession, custody or control of the Indemnified Party and relating to such claim; and

(iii)   cooperate with the Indemnifying Party and its counsel including but not limited to appearing as a witness as may be reasonably required and responding to all reasonable requests for documents and answering interrogatories.

D.   Upon receipt of written notice of an indemnifiable claim and all other documents and instruments required to be furnished to the Indemnifying Party, the Indemnifying Party shall be responsible for providing a defense in a manner and utilizing attorneys selected by the Indemnifying Party, for which the Indemnifying Party shall be solely responsible for payment of all costs and expense. The Indemnifying party shall not enter any negotiation or settlements with the person or entity asserting the claim without receiving the prior express written consent of the Indemnified Party, which may not be unreasonably withheld, delayed or conditioned.

E.   In the event the Indemnifying Party defends the indemnifiable claim, it may do so under a reservation of its rights to cease the defense of the indemnifiable claim at a later date (upon reasonable prior written notice to the Indemnified Party) in the event it is determined that the Indemnifying Party has no obligation to defend or indemnify.

F.   The amount payable by an Indemnifying Party to an Indemnified Party with respect to a loss shall be reduced by the amount of any proceeds received by the Indemnified Party from any third party, including, without limitation, insurance proceeds on account of such loss. The parties hereto agree to use their best efforts to collect any and all insurance proceeds to which it may be entitled.

G.   Notwithstanding the foregoing indemnity and hold harmless provisions of this Asset Purchase Agreement or any other provision which may provide or be deemed to provide to the contrary, none of the indemnity and hold harmless provisions hereof shall apply with respect to any actions of professional liability to the extent that such actions are insured against by either party unless the underwriter successfully denies coverage, or the underwriter refuses to pay under the policy. Such Exclusion shall also not apply to any portion of a claim which exceeds the professional liability coverage.

H.   Should either party not fulfill the terms of indemnification as described herein, then, in the other party shall have the remedies provided by law.

20.   INTEGRATION: This Asset Purchase Agreement includes the attached exhibits, and embodies the entire agreement and understanding among the parties hereto regarding the subject matter hereof, and replaces and supersedes any prior agreements between the parties, oral or written, related to the subject matter hereof.

21.   CHOICE OF LAW: This Asset Purchase Agreement and all the exhibits shall be governed, construed and enforced according to the laws of the State of

STATE*****.

22.   BINDING EFFECT, ASSIGNMENT: Except to the extent of any contrary provisions herein, all of the terms of this Asset Purchase Agreement, whether so expressed or not, shall be binding upon the respective successors and assigns of the parties hereto, and shall inure to the benefit of, and shall be enforceable by the parties hereto and their respective heirs, executors, personal representatives, successors and assigns.

23.   SEVERABILITY: In the event any section or part of this Asset Purchase Agreement or any of the attached exhibits or parts thereof should be adjudged invalid, such adjudication shall in no manner affect the other sections or exhibits, which shall remain in full force and effect as if the section or exhibit so declared or adjudged invalid were not originally a part hereof unless the section or exhibit so declared or adjudged invalid materially affects the consideration or obligation either party is entitled to receive or assume hereunder.

24.   NOTICE: Any notice or payment required or permitted in this Asset Purchase Agreement and the attached exhibits, shall be in writing and delivered personally or sent by certified U.S. Mail, return receipt requested, with all postage and other charges pre-paid. Any such notice or payment from Seller to Purchaser shall be addressed to the principal office of Purchaser. Any such notice or payment from Purchaser to Seller shall be personally hand delivered to Seller or addressed to the last known residential address of Seller.

A.   Either party may change its address, or the designation of its representative, by notifying the other party of such change in writing.

B.   Except where provided to the contrary elsewhere in this Asset Purchase Agreement and subject to the terms herein, each party agrees to give to the other party written notice of any alleged breach or violation of this Asset Purchase Agreement or the attached exhibits, or of an intention to pursue legal action against the other arising out of this Asset Purchase Agreement. The party receiving such notice shall have thirty (30) days to cure if the default before the other party may proceed with any legal action or exercise their right of offset against the other party.

C.   This requirement of notice and time to cure shall not prohibit a party from seeking injunctive relief immediately following an alleged breach of this Asset Purchase Agreement by the other party.

25.   WAIVER OF BREACH: No breach or violation of any provision hereof may be waived except by an agreement in writing signed by the waiving party.

26.   SURVIVAL: All representations, covenants, warranties, obligations, indemnification, rights and responsibilities made or undertaken in this Asset Purchase Agreement and its exhibits, or in any document or instrument executed and delivered pursuant hereto shall survive the Closing. Time is of the essence with respect to all provisions of this Agreement (and its exhibits) that specify a time for performance: provided, however, that the foregoing shall not be construed to limit or deprive a party of the benefits of any grace or use period

allowed in this Agreement.

27.   CONSTRUCTION: Neither this Asset Purchase Agreement nor any uncertainty or ambiguity herein shall be construed or resolved using any presumption against any party hereto, whether under any rule of construction or otherwise.

28.   NOMENCLATURE: The use of the male gender shall include the female, the individual shall include the corporate, and the singular shall include the plural, and vice versa, wherever such usage is appropriate to the context.

29.   DISPUTE RESOLUTION: The parties hereto, whether individual, joint in class, in nature, or otherwise, may resolve disputes between them through agreed upon mediation and arbitration.

30.   ITEM HEADINGS AND INTERPRETATION: The item headings contained in this Asset Purchase Agreement are for convenience only and shall in no manner be construed as a part of this Asset Purchase Agreement. Whenever the words "include", "includes" or "including" are used in this Asset Purchase Agreement, they shall be deemed to be followed by the words "without limitation". In addition, any other information, including articles and summaries shall not affect in any way the meaning or interpretation of the text of this Asset Purchase Agreement.

31.   PERSONAL GUARANTY: Seller acknowledges and agrees that Seller has read this Asset Purchase Agreement and the attached exhibits in their entirety and that understands and agrees to be bound by the terms and conditions as stated therein. The Seller expressly waives the right to protest the reasonableness of, and individually and personally guaranty's the performance of the respective obligations, warranties and covenants contained in this Asset Purchase Agreement and the attached exhibits, whether corporate or individual.

32.   ADDITIONAL PROVISIONS AND/OR MODIFICATIONS: Other provisions or modifications of this Asset Purchase Agreement, if any, are set forth in Exhibit "E".

33.   SELLER'S CERTIFICATION:
      Seller does hereby certify that:

      (i)   Seller has the exclusive right, power and authority to sell these Assets; this Asset Purchase Agreement constitutes a legal, valid and binding obligation of Seller enforceable against Seller in accordance with its terms; that neither the execution of this Asset Purchase Agreement nor the consummation of this transaction will result in the breach of any term or provision of any agreement with respect to which Seller is a party;

      (ii)   all of the acts of the corporation are accepted, approved, and by the undersigned signature hereon, ratified. It is further represented and warranted by the undersigned that each and every act of the corporation contained herein has been accepted, and the execution of this Asset Purchase Agreement has been duly authorized and approved by all necessary corporate action on its part and is not in conflict with its charter or bylaws and does not constitute a breach of or default under any indenture, judgment, decree, rule or regulation binding upon it. A resolution of the corporation's stockholders and Board of Directors is attached hereto as Exhibit "F";

(i) Seller is a validly existing corporation in good standing under the laws of the jurisdiction of its incorporation and has adequate corporate power to enter into this Asset Purchase Agreement.

Dr. Seller agrees to personally guarantee all Seller's obligations, warranties and covenants herein and to be liable, jointly and severally, with Seller for all such obligations. In the event of a breach of any such obligation of Seller specified herein or in connection with this Asset Purchase Agreement, then Purchaser, in addition to seeking remedy from the corporation, may look directly to Dr. Seller for the appropriate remedy.

34. PURCHASER'S CERTIFICATION:
Purchaser does hereby certify that:

(i) Purchaser has the exclusive right, power and authority to acquire these Assets; this Asset Purchase Agreement constitutes a legal, valid and binding obligation of Purchaser, enforceable against Purchaser in accordance with its terms; that neither the execution of this Asset Purchase Agreement nor the consummation of this transaction will result in the breach of any term or provision of any agreement with respect to which Purchaser is a party;

(ii) all of the acts of the company are accepted, approved, and by the undersigned signature hereon, ratified. It is further represented and warranted by the undersigned that each and every act of the company contained herein has been accepted, and the execution of this Asset Purchase Agreement has been duly authorized and approved by all necessary company action on its part and is not in conflict with its articles of organization and does not constitute a breach of or default under any indenture, judgment, decree, rule or regulation binding upon it;

(iii) Purchaser is a validly existing Limited Liability Company in good standing under the laws of its jurisdiction and has adequate power to enter into this Asset Purchase Agreement.

IN WITNESS WHEREOF, the undersigned parties acknowledge that they have read this Asset Purchase Agreement in its entirety and have executed this Asset Purchase Agreement and the attached exhibits on the aforementioned Signature Date.

_____ Witness	Village Dental, P.C. By _____ Seller
_____ Witness	Dennis Seller, D.D.S. _____ Seller
_____ Witness	Judy Seller _____ Seller and Wife of Dennis Seller
_____ Witness	Grain Acres Dental, LLC By _____ Purchaser

FORM OF SPOUSAL CONSENT

I, the spouse of Dennis Seller, D.D.S., hereby acknowledge that I have read the foregoing Asset Purchase Agreement (the "Agreement") and know its contents. In accordance with the Agreement, I hereby agree on behalf of myself and all my successors in interest that the Agreement shall bind my community interest, if any, in all assets or any other form of ownership interest in and to Village Dental, P.C. and any interests therein.

Dated: _____

_____
Judy Seller Wife of Dennis Seller

EXHIBIT "A"

[INVENTORY AND MORE DETAILED DESCRIPTION INITIALED BY ALL PARTIES PRIOR TO SIGNING ASSET PURCHASE AGREEMENT AND VERIFICATION PRIOR DAY OF CLOSING]

Attached to and made a part of that certain Asset Purchase Agreement by and between Village Dental, P.C. and Dennis Seller, D.D.S. and Grain Acres Dental, LLC, Ben Buyer, D.D.S. and John Buyer, D.D.S.

EQUIPMENT, FURNITURE AND FIXTURES

- Recessed ultrasonic cleaning -nit
- Midmark Mil automatic sterilizer

- Gendex GX 770 x-ray heads (2)
- Schick digital sensors
- Planmeca PM 2002 CC panoramic x-ray
- Biosonic 810 Basic film processor

- Airtechniques Airstar 50 compressor
- Matrix vacuum pump

- Matrix Medical Nitrous Oxide portable stand
- Discus ZOOM

Operatories (4)

- Adec 4400 wall mounted controls
- Adec Preference II modular cabinets
- Adec 1040 Cascade chairs
- Adec 6300 Lights
- Computer workstations

- Cavitron Jet
- Biosonic US100R ultrasonic scaler

- Model trimmer
- Lathe

- Server
- Front desk computer work stations (2)
- Copier
- Fax machine
- Mail station

EXHIBIT "A-1"

Attached to and made a part of that certain Asset Purchase Agreement by and between Village Dental, P.C. and Dennis Seller, D.D.S. and Grain Acres Dental, LLC, Ben Buyer, D.D.S. and John Buyer, D.D.S.

ITEMS EXCLUDED FROM SALE

In addition to the items specifically excluded in Section 1 of the Asset Purchase Agreement, the following items are also to be excluded from this sale: None.

EXHIBIT "B" BILL OF SALE

KNOW ALL MEN BY THESE PRESENTS, THAT Village Dental, P.C. and Dennis Seller, D.D.S. (jointly and severally hereinafter referred to as "Seller"), for good and valuable consideration, in hand paid at and before the sealing and delivery of these presents, the receipt and adequacy of which is hereby acknowledged, does hereby sell, set over, transfer, assign and convey unto Grain Acres Dental, LLC, ("Purchaser") and any successors or assigns, all Seller's right, title and interest in and to all of the Assets (as defined in the attached Asset Purchase Agreement) subject to the terms and conditions, warranties and covenants described in the Asset Purchase Agreement and all exhibits attached thereto, whether such interest is joint or several, individual or corporate.

And for the same consideration, Seller, and Seller's successors and assigns, covenants with and warrants unto Purchaser and Purchaser's successors and assigns, that Seller is the lawful owner of the property hereby conveyed, that Seller has good and marketable title to Seller's interest in said property, and, to the extent described in the Asset Purchase Agreement, that said property is free and clear of any liens and encumbrances of any kind, character or nature, and that Seller, and Seller's successors and assigns will forever warrant and defend the same unto Purchaser and Purchaser's heirs and assigns, against all lawful claims and demands whatsoever. Successors and assigns include heirs, executors, administrators and personal representatives.

IN WITNESS WHEREOF, Seller has executed and delivered this Bill of Sale, effective the Closing Date described in the aforementioned Asset Purchase Agreement.

_____ Witness	Village Dental, P.C. By _____ Seller
_____ Witness	Dennis Seller, D.D.S. _____ Seller
_____ Witness	Judy Seller _____ Seller and Wife of Dennis Seller

FORM OF SPOUSAL CONSENT

I, the spouse of Dennis Seller, D.D.S., hereby acknowledge that I have read the foregoing Bill of

Sale and know its contents. In accordance therewith I hereby agree on behalf of myself and all my successors in interest that the Bill of Sale shall bind my community interest, if any, in all assets or any other form of ownership interest in and to Village Dental, P.C. and any interests therein.

Dated: _____   Judy Seller Wife of Dennis Seller

EXHIBIT "C"

RESTRICTIVE COVENANT AGREEMENT

THIS RESTRICTIVE COVENANT AGREEMENT (the "Restrictive Covenant Agreement") is entered into by and between Dennis Seller, D.D.S. (hereinafter referred to as "Dr. Seller" and/or the "Covenantor") and Grain Acres Dental, LLC, Ben Buyer, D.D.S. and John Buyer, D.D.S. (jointly and severally, together hereinafter referred to as the "Purchaser").

WHEREAS, Purchaser and Covenantor have simultaneously executed the attached Asset Purchase Agreement through which Purchaser has acquired a dental practice (the "Practice") located at ADDRESS***** (the "Premises"): and

WHEREAS, Covenantor, as an incentive and as a specific condition for Purchaser entering into the Asset Purchase Agreement and acquiring and paying for the goodwill of the Practice, makes, gives and agrees to these covenants respecting competition and solicitation, all ancillary to the sale of the Practice, in favor of Purchaser.

NOW, THEREFORE, in consideration of the premises as well as the parties' respective promises, representations, covenants and warranties, the performance of each unto the other, and other good and valuable consideration, the receipt and sufficiency of which are hereby acknowledged, the parties agree as follows:

1.   RESTRICTIVE COVENANT: In consideration of and in conjunction with the sale of the Practice, Covenantor hereby grants the following restrictive covenant (the "Restrictive Covenant").

   A.   Covenantor hereby individually covenants and agrees not to practice dentistry, in any location other than the Premises, as a private practitioner, partner, associate, contractor, employee or as a stockholder, officer or director of any corporation or organization so engaged, or lend Covenantor's name to any business organization competitive with the Practice, within COUNTY***** County, (the "Restricted Area") for a period beginning from the Date of Possession and continuing until three (3) years from the date Covenantor discontinues practicing dentistry on the Premises (the "Restricted Period").

   B.   For the purpose of this Restrictive Covenant Agreement, the "Premises" shall mean ADDRESS*****.

   C.   To "practice dentistry" shall not include (i) locum tenens coverage in anyone office within the Restricted Area for a period not to exceed five (5) days (in that same office) during any twelve (12) month period, or (ii) government sponsored public health or other institutional or charitable practice that is limited to treatment of non-private patients, or (iii) any non-clinical academic position in any dental related teaching institution.

D. If a court should hold that the Restricted Period and/or the Restricted Area is unenforceable, then to the extent permitted by law the court may prescribe a duration for the Restricted Period and/or a radius or area for the Restricted Area that is reasonable and the parties agree to accept such determination subject to their rights of appeal. Nothing herein stated shall be construed as prohibiting Purchaser from pursuing any other equitable remedy or remedies available for such breach or threatened breach, including recovery of damages from Covenantor or injunctive relief.

E. This Restrictive Covenant Agreement shall be considered a personal service agreement between Covenantor and Purchaser. Should Covenantor be in violation of this Restrictive Covenant then the Restricted Period shall be extended for a period of time equal to the period during which said violation or violations occurred. If Purchaser seeks injunctive relief from said violation in court, then the running of the Restrictive Period shall be suspended during the pendency of said proceeding, including all appeals by Covenantor. This suspension shall cease upon the entry of a final judgment in the matter.

F. Covenantor agrees not to discuss any practice related policies and/or issues that may be considered a breach of professional standards by Purchaser with the staff, patients, and/or referral sources of the practice, either before, during or following the Restricted Period. Covenantor agrees that any differences that may arise relating to such policies and/or issues will be discussed only with Purchaser, or if necessary, with Covenantor's legal representative or as required by any legal and/or administrative procedure.

2. NON-SOLICITATION: As a further inducement to Purchaser to acquire the Practice, Covenantor hereby warrants and agrees that, during the term of the Restricted Period, Covenantor, and/or any agent of Covenantor, will not solicit any of Covenantor's former patients of the Practice (those who have received treatment at any time during the 36 month period immediately preceding the last day Covenantor discontinues practicing dentistry on the Premises) to seek dental treatment in any other office other than that owned by the Purchaser. In addition:

A. During the Restricted Period, Covenantor (and/or any agent of Covenantor) agrees not to solicit any professional referral sources of the Practice, for any business that could otherwise be referred to Purchaser.

B. During the Restricted Period, Covenantor (and/or any agent of Covenantor) agrees not to recommend to any patients of the Practice to patronize any other practitioner (in the same fields of dental practice as Purchaser) other than Purchaser regardless of the distance of that patient's domicile from the Premises (unless that patient is relocating to another area outside of the Restricted Area).

C. During the Restricted Period, Covenantor (and/or any agent of Covenantor) agrees not to solicit, employ or contract with any of the employees of the Practice who were employed by Purchaser during the Restricted Period, to work for anyone other than Purchaser.

D.   If Covenantor will continue to practice dentistry in another location other than the Premises (if applicable), then Covenantor's immediate family members (limited to grandparents, parents, siblings and children of both Covenantor and Covenantor's spouse) shall not be included as a patient for purposes of this patient non-solicitation.

3.   PATIENT REVENUE REIMBURSEMENT: Covenantor acknowledges that Purchaser has given Covenantor valuable consideration for the purchase of the Practice and Covenantor's goodwill, which is directly associated with, and dependent upon the doctor-patient relationship established by Covenantor with the patients of the Practice. Covenantor further acknowledges and agrees that, because of Covenantor's long-term relationship with the patients of the Practice, a significant number of these patients would very likely transfer to another office where Covenantor could elect to provide dental services to the public in the future (and/or any other dental practice where Covenantor is a principal), even if such office is located outside the Restricted Area and at a time beyond the Restricted Period; therefore:

A.   Since Purchaser has paid Covenantor valuable consideration for those patients, and such payment was made in anticipation of future revenues for the Practice, then Covenantor agrees that should Covenantor practice dentistry on any former patient of the Practice (or said patient was treated by another dentist associated with any other dental practice in which Convenantor is a principal), at any location other than the Premises, either within or outside of the Restricted Area, for a period of 84 months following the date Covenantor discontinues practicing dentistry on the Premises, then Covenantor agrees to immediately pay to Purchaser the sum of THIRTY-FIVE HUNDRED 00/100 DOLLARS ($3,500.00) for each former patient of the Practice so treated (except for immediate family members which are limited to grandparents, parents, siblings and children of both Covenantor and Covenantor's spouse, if applicable), as reimbursement for the loss of the potential future revenue that could have been paid to the Practice by that patient.

B.   In addition, Covenantor acknowledges that Purchaser has paid Covenantor valuable consideration for the trained staff currently employed in the Practice at the time of the Closing, and that such trained staff is of considerable value to Purchaser. Therefore, should Covenantor employ one or more of Purchaser's employees to work in another office, either within or outside of the Restricted Area, for a period of 84 months following the date Covenantor discontinues practicing dentistry on the Premises, then Covenantor agrees to immediately pay to Purchaser the sum of TWENTY THOUSAND AND 00/100 DOLLARS ($20,000.00) for each such former employee of the Practice hired by Covenantor, as reimbursement for the cost to Purchaser for hiring and training a suitable replacement employee.

C.   Covenantor agrees to pay the aforementioned reimbursement payment(s) to Purchaser within ten (10) days of the date (i) Covenantor practiced dentistry on a former patient of the Practice, or (ii) said patient was treated by another dentist associated with any other dental practice in which Convenantor is a principal, and/or (iii) Covenantor employed one or more of the aforementioned employees of the Practice. Failure by Covenantor to pay such required reimbursement payments within the aforementioned ten day period, shall result in the payment amount due being increased by one hundred percent (100%); however, the cumulative payments for reimbursement shall not exceed 100% of the total Purchase Price for the Practice (as described in the Asset Purchase Agreement).

D.   Covenantor acknowledges and agrees that the reimbursement payments are an incentive and are a specific condition for Purchaser acquiring and paying for the Practice. Both parties agree that the required reimbursement payments do not prohibit Covenantor from practicing dentistry on the former patients of the Practice or employing any of the employees of the Practice in another office, but merely reimburses Purchaser for any future lost revenues resulting from such patient transfers, and/or expenses associated with hiring and training replacement employees.

1   WAIVER OF RIGHT TO PROTEST: The restrictive covenants contained herein are ancillary to a sale of the Practice and are to be construed as cumulative with those set forth in any other agreements between the parties hereto. Covenantor expressly agrees that the duration, geographical limitations and description of the prohibited conduct described in this Restrictive Covenant Agreement are reasonable and that Covenantor has received valuable consideration for the warranties and covenants contained herein. Covenantor further expressly waives the right to protest the reasonableness of the limitations, warranties, geographical limitations and prohibited conduct specified in this Restrictive Covenant Agreement.

2   SPECIFIC PERFORMANCE: Any breach of the warranties and covenants contained herein shall be subject to specific performance by temporary as well as permanent injunction or other equitable remedies by a court of competent jurisdiction. The obtaining of any such injunction shall not prevent the obtaining party from also seeking and obtaining any damages incurred as a result of such breach, either prior to or after obtaining such injunction. If any court of competent jurisdiction determines that either party has breached any of the foregoing covenants, then that party shall pay all reasonable costs of enforcement of the foregoing covenants including, but not limited to, court costs and reasonable attorneys' fees, including such costs and fees through any appeals.

IN WITNESS WHEREOF, Covenantor has executed this Restrictive Covenant Agreement on the aforementioned Signature Date.

_____ Witness	Dennis Seller, D.D.S. _____ ____ Seller
_____ Witness	Grain Acres Dental, LLC By _____ Purchaser
_____ Witness	Ben Buyer, D.D.S. _____ ____ Purchaser

	John Buyer, D.D.S.
_____ Witness	_____ ___ Purchaser

EXHIBIT "D"
PURCHASE AGREEMENT

The undersigned Buyer agrees to purchase and the Seller agrees to sell and convey ADDRESS Drive, Lincoln, STATE*****, legally described as: Village North 8th, Lot 6, located in Lincoln, COUNTY***** County, STATE***** including all fixtures and equipment permanently attached to the property. The only personal property included is as set forth on the Asset Purchase Agreement of even date herewith as executed between the parties hereto. Dennis Seller and Judy Seller are husband and wife.

Subject, however, and on condition that the Seller thereof has a marketable title in fee simple. Seller agrees to obtain and furnish to Buyer a title insurance commitment and policy insuring marketability. Such title insurance shall be paid one-half by Buyer and one-half by Seller. Buyer agrees that should a valid title defect exist, Seller has a reasonable time to correct said defect not to exceed thirty (30) days from the date of Seller's receipt of the title insurance commitment. Seller agrees to convey to Buyer or Buyer's nominee by Warranty Deed, free and clear of all leases (except as noted), liens, encumbrances, special assessments levied or assessed, or special assessment districts that have been created and ordered constructed, as of date of acceptance of this Agreement to Purchase, except: [*Detail any leases, terms, etc., and/or attach written leases or certification of accuracy by tenant*].

1. Buyer agrees to pay $600,000.00 which shall be paid to Seller at closing in cash or certified funds.

2. Buyer, at Buyer's expense, will conduct an environmental site assessment in a form acceptable to Buyer. In the event the assessment reflects environmental problems, Buyer shall consult with Seller and Seller shall have a reasonable time to correct the same, not to exceed thirty (30) days from the date of notice by Buyer. If the Seller does not elect to correct the problems, Buyer shall have the option of declaring this Agreement null and void and of no force and effect. Following the date of closing, the Buyer agrees to indemnify and hold the Seller harmless for all obligations, losses, damages, penalties, claims, actions, costs and expenses levied against the property, the Buyer and/or the Seller as a result of a violation of local, state, or federal laws related to hazardous materials or other environmental hazards in existence, incurred or created prior to closing.

3. Buyer acknowledges that prior to the execution of this agreement, Buyer received a completed "Seller Property Condition Disclosure Statement" from the Seller. Buyer further acknowledges that Buyer received the pamphlet entitled "Protect Your Family from Lead in Your Home" and that a lead-based paint addendum is incorporated into this agreement. Buyer does not wish to conduct a termite and wood destroying insect inspection.

4. Seller shall pay all taxes to and including the year prior to the year of closing. Taxes for the year during which closing occurs shall be prorated to date of possession. Taxes shall be prorated on the basis of the prior year's taxes unless the current tax rate is available, in which case taxes shall be prorated on the basis of the current tax valuation and tax rate.

5. Buyer and Seller agree to close the purchase on or before the 31st day of December,

2021, unless another date is mutually agreed to by the parties. It is agreed that Union Title Company shall act as Escrow and Closing Agent with closing costs to be paid one-half by Buyer and one-half by Seller. The documentary stamp tax shall be paid by Seller. Possession of the property shall be given to the Buyer on the date of closing. At the time of closing, the Deed to be delivered by the Seller to the Buyer shall show the Buyer or Buyer's other nominee or assignee as Grantee.

6.   This agreement shall in no manner be construed to convey the property or to give any right of possession. Risk of loss or damage to the property, prior to closing date, shall rest with the Seller. If, prior to closing, the structures on the property are materially damaged by fire, explosion, or any other cause, Buyer shall have the right to rescind this agreement. There shall be no deposit by Buyer.

7.   If Buyer fails to consummate the purchase other than for the reasons provided herein, Seller may, at Seller's option, utilize such legal remedies as are available to Seller by reason of such failure.

IN WITNESS WHEREOF, the Buyer and Seller have agreed to the above and executed this Purchase Agreement this _____ day of _____, 20___.

Village Dental, P.C., Seller
By _____
            Authorized Official
	Grain Acres Dental, LLC, Buyer
	By
	_____
	            Authorized Official

Dennis Seller, D.D.S., Seller _____ Individually	
Judy Seller, Seller _____ Seller and Wife of Dennis Seller	

Dennis Seller, Revocable Living Trust Dated February 15, 1996, Seller
By _____
            Authorized Trustee
By _____
            Authorized Trustee	

STATE OF STATE*****   )
) SS.
COUNTY OF COUNTY*****   )

The   foregoing   instrument   was   acknowledged   before   me   this   _____   day   of
_____, 20__, by _____ owner of the real
estate.

_____
                                                    Notary Public

STATE OF STATE*****   )
) SS.
COUNTY OF COUNTY*****   )

The foregoing instrument was acknowledged before me this   day of
, 20__, by _____ owner of the real estate.

_____
                                                    Notary Public

STATE OF STATE*****   )
) SS.
COUNTY OF COUNTY*****   )

The foregoing instrument was acknowledged before me this   day of
, 20__, by _____ owner of the real estate.

_____
                                                    Notary Public

STATE OF STATE*****   )
) SS.
COUNTY OF COUNTY*****   )

The foregoing instrument was acknowledged before me this   day of
, 20__, by _____ owner of the real estate.

_____
                                                    Notary Public

EXHIBIT "E"

Attached to and made a part of that certain Asset Purchase Agreement by and between Village Dental, P.C. and Dennis Seller, D.D.S. and Grain Acres Dental, LLC, Ben Buyer, D.D.S. and John Buyer, D.D.S.

ADDITIONAL PROVISIONS ANDIOR MODIFICATIONS

Any provisions set forth in the attached Asset Purchase Agreement and/or its exhibits which are inconsistent or contrary to the provisions set forth in this exhibit shall be void and have no effect. All other terms shall remain in full force and effect.

NONE

EXHIBIT "F"

CORPORATE RESOLUTION

CONSENT IN LIEU OF MEETING OF THE BOARD OF DIRECTORS AND SHAREHOLDERS OF

Village Dental. P.C.

The undersigned, being all the director(s) and stockholder(s) of Village Dental, P.C., hereby consent the following action and adopt the following resolution pursuant to the By-Laws of the corporation and the applicable business corporation code of the State of STATE*****:

RESOLVED, that the President of the corporation is hereby authorized and directed to enter into and execute the attached Asset Purchase Agreement, Real Estate Purchase Agreement and all such other agreements which are necessary and proper for the sale of the practice, building and its assets owned by Village Dental, P.C.; a list of such assets are described in the Asset Purchase Agreement and its Exhibits.

Date	By
Date	By

(SAMPLE) STOCK PURCHASE AGREEMENT

This STOCK PURCHASE AGREEMENT (this "Agreement") dated effective as of 11:59 p.m. (Central) on February 28, 2021 (the "Closing Date"), is by and between _____, DMD, an individual also known as _____ ("Seller"), _____ (the "Practice"), and Dr._____, an individual ("Purchaser").

WHEREAS, Seller is a dentist licensed to practice dentistry in the State of STATE**** and is engaged in the practice of general dentistry with an office located at _____ (the "Premises");

WHEREAS, Seller owns 100% of the issued and outstanding shares of stock (collectively, the "Shares") of the Practice;

WHEREAS, the Practice operates the dental office located at the Premises;

WHEREAS, Purchaser is a dentist licensed to practice dentistry in the State of STATE****; and

WHEREAS, Seller desires to sell to Purchaser and Purchaser desires to purchase from Seller all of Seller's right, title, and interest in the Shares upon the terms and conditions hereinafter set forth.

NOW, THEREFORE, in consideration of the recitals, mutual promises, covenants, and conditions set forth and other good and valuable consideration, the receipt and sufficiency of which is hereby acknowledged, Seller and Purchaser agree as follows:

ARTICLE 1
PURCHASE OF SHARES

     1.1   **Sale of Shares.** Seller hereby sells, assigns, and transfers to Purchaser all of Seller's right, title, and interest in the Shares.

     1.2   **Acceptance of Shares.** Purchaser hereby accepts assignment and transfer of all of Seller's right, title, and interest in the Shares.

ARTICLE 2
PURCHASE PRICE AND PAYMENT

     2.1   **Purchase Price.** The total purchase price for the Shares shall be _____(the "Purchase Price").

     2.2   **Method of Payment.** Purchaser shall pay the Purchase Price to Seller on the Closing Date in cash or certified funds.

ARTICLE 3
REPRESENTATIONS AND WARRANTIES OF SELLER

Other than as disclosed on the schedules to this Agreement, which disclosures shall qualify the following representations and warranties in all respects, Seller makes the following representations and warranties to Purchaser as of the Closing Date:

3.1   **Organization and Standing.** The Practice is, on the Closing Date, a professional corporation duly organized, validly existing, and in good standing under the corporation and other laws of the State of STATE**** with the power to own its property and assets and to carry on its business as now being conducted.

3.2   **Binding Effect.** This Agreement, when executed and delivered by the parties thereto (assuming due execution and delivery by Purchaser), constitutes a valid and legally binding obligation of Seller, enforceable against Seller, as applicable, in accordance with its terms, except as enforceability may be limited by bankruptcy, insolvency, fraudulent conveyance, reorganization, or moratorium laws, other similar laws affecting creditors' rights, and general principles of equity affecting the availability of specific performance and other equitable remedies.

3.3   **Capitalization and Ownership.** The authorized capital stock of the Practice consists solely of 100 shares of common stock, of which 100 have been issued to Seller. Each of Seller's Shares has been duly authorized and validly issued, is fully paid and nonassessable, and was not issued in violation of the preemptive rights of any past or present shareholder. No option, right, subscription, warrant, call, conversion right, commitment, or other agreement of any kind exists which obligates the Practice to issue any of its authorized but unissued capital stock or would otherwise entitle any person or entity to acquire any stock or other securities of the Practice. All of the Shares are owned by Seller and are free and clear of all liens, encumbrances, and claims of any kind. Seller has good and marketable title to the Shares being sold to Purchaser. Upon their transfer to Purchaser at the Closing, the Shares shall be free and clear of all liens, charges, security interests, and restrictions.

3.4   **Subsidiaries.** The Practice has no subsidiary companies.

3.5   **Financial Statements.** Schedule 3.5 sets forth the unaudited financial statements for the Practice (collectively, the "Financial Statements"), and such Financial Statements fairly present the financial condition of the Practice as of the dates thereof; it being understood that such Financial Statements were not prepared in accordance with GAAP.

3.6   **Indebtedness.** Schedule 3.6 attached hereto sets forth all outstanding indebtedness to which the Practice is party or an obligor, including with respect to each item of indebtedness the lender and principal balance outstanding, in each case as of the Closing Date (such indebtedness, the "Practice Debt").

3.7   **No Breach.** Neither the execution nor the delivery of this Agreement nor the consummation of the transaction contemplated by this Agreement conflicts with or will conflict with, or results or will result in a breach of the Practice's Articles of Incorporation,

Bylaws, or the terms or provisions of any agreement to which Seller or the Practice is a party or by which Seller or the Practice is bound.

      3.8   **Patient Records.** The patient records maintained by the Practice are materially true, accurate and complete.

      3.9   **Taxes.** All federal, state, local and other taxes that the Practice is required to pay relating to any period prior to the Closing Date that were due and owing prior to the Closing Date have been paid in full. There are no tax returns under audit nor has the Practice been contacted by any revenue agency regarding additional tax liability.

      3.10   **Litigation and Proceedings.** Seller warrants that there is no suit, action, arbitration, mediation, administrative proceeding, investigation, peer review, or other proceeding pending or, to Seller's knowledge, threatened (a) against Seller and/or the Practice or (b) relating to Seller's right to sell the Shares to Purchaser.

      3.11   **Assets.** Seller warrants that the assets owned by the Practice are in working order on the Closing Date in all material respects, subject to ordinary wear and tear, but notwithstanding the foregoing Seller disclaims any express or implied warranties concerning performance or fitness of such assets. Purchaser has been given access to examine the assets and that Purchaser accepts the equipment "as is" on the Closing Date. The Practice has good and marketable title to, or has a leasehold interest in, all its property and assets, real and personal, including those reflected in the Financial Statements. Other than liens associated with the Practice Debt, the Practice's property and assets are not subject to any mortgage, pledge, lien, conditional sales agreement, encumbrance, or charge except as shown in the Financial Statements.

      3.12   **Contracts.** Neither Seller nor the Practice is a party to any material written or oral contract for the purchase of materials, supplies, equipment, fixtures, or any other agreement that will survive the Closing Date that has not been disclosed to Purchaser.

      3.13   **Material Adverse Change.** As of the Closing Date there has not been any material adverse effect on the business of the Practice.

      3.14   **No Default.** The Practice is not in material violation or breach of any contract or instrument to which it is party except to the extent such violation or breach would not have a material adverse effect on the Practice. To the actual knowledge of Seller, no counterparty to any written contract to which the Practice is subject or bound is, as of the date hereof, in material breach of any such agreement or commitment to which the Practice is subject, except to the extent such violation or breach would not have a material adverse effect on the Practice.

      3.15   **Employment Matters.** The Practice has materially complied with all applicable federal, state, and local laws and regulations relating to the employment of labor, including the provisions thereof relating to wages, hours, collective bargaining, and the payment of Social Security, and the Practice is not liable for any arrears of wages or any tax or penalties for failure to comply with any of the foregoing other than those of an immaterial nature, nor has it any material lawsuit pending or, to the actual knowledge of Seller, threatened by any employee of the Practice.

3.16   **Compliance with Laws.** The Practice has materially complied with all federal, state, and local statutes, ordinances, rules, regulations, and court or administrative orders applicable to the Practice.

3.17   **No Power of Attorney.** The Practice does not have outstanding any power of attorney to act on behalf of the Practice.

3.18   **Loans and Obligations.** There are no loans, liabilities, or other obligations payable to the officers, directors, employees or stockholders of the Practice, except salaries and wages and reimbursement of expenses incurred in the ordinary course of business.

3.19   **Bank Accounts.** The Practice maintains and has maintained all bank accounts of the Practice in material accordance with all applicable laws, rules, and regulations. There are no disputes with regard to such bank accounts or the balances thereof. All authorized signatories for all such bank accounts are set forth on Schedule 3.20 hereto.

3.20   **No Violations.** Seller's execution and delivery of this Agreement and performance hereunder will not (a) constitute a violation by Seller or the Practice of any existing provision of any law, rule, or regulation, (b) violate any existing term or provision of any order, writ, judgment, injunction, or decree applicable to Seller or the Practice, (c) conflict with or result in a breach or default (or give any party the right to declare a breach or default upon notice or passage of time or both) of any agreement or instrument to which Seller or the Practice is a party or by which either of them, or any of their material properties or assets, are bound or subject, or (d) otherwise result in the creation or imposition of any lien, charge, security interest, or encumbrance of any nature on the Practice or its assets.

3.21   **Fraud and Abuse.** Neither Seller nor the Practice has engaged in any activities which are prohibited under the federal Anti-kickback Statute (42 U.S.C. §1320a-7b), the Stark Law (42 U.S.C. §1395nn), or the regulations promulgated thereunder pursuant to such statutes or any other related state or local statutes and regulations, including, but not limited to, knowingly and willfully soliciting or receiving any remuneration, kickback, bribe, or rebate, directly or indirectly, overtly or covertly, in cash or in kind, or offering to pay or receive such remuneration (a) in return for referring an individual to a person for the furnishing or arranging for the furnishing or any item or service for which payment may be made in whole or in part by Medicare or Medicaid, or (b) in return for purchasing, leasing, or ordering or arranging for recommending purchasing, leasing, or ordering any good, facility, service, or item for which payment may be made in whole or in part by Medicare or Medicaid.

3.22   **Insurance.** Schedule 3.24 hereto sets forth all insurance policies currently maintained by the Practice. The Practice has not materially breached or otherwise failed to perform in any material respect its obligations under any of its insurance policies nor has the Practice received any adverse written notice or communication from any of the insurers party to the policies with respect to any such alleged breach or failure in connection with any of the policies.

3.23   **Power to Perform.** Seller has all requisite power to enter into this Agreement, to own and hold, and to transfer and sell to Purchaser the Shares as provided herein and to perform each of Seller's obligations hereunder.

3.24   **Approvals.** All actions and approvals required to authorize and consummate the valid execution, delivery, and performance by Seller and the Practice of the transactions contemplated herein have been, or will be at Closing, duly taken and obtained.

ARTICLE 4
REPRESENTATIVE AND WARRANTIES OF PURCHASER

4.1   **Authorization.** Purchaser has all requisite power and authority to execute and deliver this Agreement and the documents contemplated hereby and to perform Purchaser's obligations hereunder and thereunder.

4.2   **Binding Effect.** This Agreement, when executed and delivered by the parties thereto (assuming due execution and delivery by Seller), constitutes a valid and legally binding obligation of Purchaser, enforceable against Purchaser, as applicable, in accordance with its terms, except as enforceability may be limited by bankruptcy, insolvency, fraudulent conveyance, reorganization, or moratorium laws, other similar laws affecting creditors' rights, and general principles of equity affecting the availability of specific performance and other equitable remedies.

4.3   **Eligibility.** Purchaser is eligible to acquire the Shares under applicable law and pursuant to the Practice's organizational documents.

ARTICLE 5
SELLER'S CLOSING OBLIGATIONS

Seller shall deliver to Purchaser:

5.1   **Stock Certificate.** At or promptly following the Closing Date, a stock certificate reflecting the transfer of all of Seller's right, title, and interest in the Shares to Purchaser.

5.2   **Covenant.** On the Closing Date, the executed Restrictive Covenant Agreement in the form attached as **Exhibit 7.5**.

5.3   **Miscellaneous.** All other documents required by this Agreement to be delivered to Purchaser or reasonably necessary to carry out the intent of the parties.

ARTICLE 6
PURCHASER'S CLOSING OBLIGATIONS

At Closing, Purchaser shall deliver to Seller:

6.1   **Purchase Price.** The sum of $_____ in cash or certified funds.

6.2   **Miscellaneous.** All other documents required by this Agreement or reasonably necessary to carry out the intent of the parties shall be executed by Purchaser and delivered to Seller.

ARTICLE 7
SELLER'S OBLIGATIONS AFTER CLOSING

Following Closing, Seller shall have the following obligations:

7.1   **Practice Transition Letter.** At Purchaser's option, Seller will use her commercially reasonable efforts to cooperate in the preparation of a transition letter which will be mailed to the Practice's active patients. The cost of preparing and mailing the letter shall be paid by Purchaser.

7.2   **Limited Non-Exclusive Use of Name.** For one (1) years after the Closing Date, the Practice shall have the limited and exclusive right to use and maintain Seller's name on the building directory and office door and to answer the business phone in the name of both Seller and Purchaser, so long as such use is consistent with the rules and regulations governing the practice of dentistry in the State of STATE****.

7.3   **Professional Liability Insurance.** For the three-year period after the Closing Date, Seller agrees to obtain "tail" professional liability insurance when appropriate to cover any claim made after Closing arising from Seller's dental treatment prior to Closing. Seller shall provide Purchaser with evidence of insurance upon request.

7.4   **Non-Compete.** Seller shall comply with the terms of the Restrictive Covenant Agreement attached as **Exhibit 7.5** in accordance with its terms.

7.5   **Taxes.** Seller shall prepare and file all Practice tax returns and filings in respect of all periods ending on or prior to February 28, 2021 (a "Pre-Closing Tax Period"). Seller shall prepare and file all Practice tax returns and filings in respect of tax periods involving any period prior to February 28, 2021 (including any periods that end after February 28, 2021) (a "Straddle Period"); provided, that, Seller shall provide Purchaser an opportunity to review, comment on and approve such tax returns or filings, which approval shall not be unreasonably withheld, conditioned or delayed. Purchaser shall promptly notify Seller following receipt of any notice of any tax proceeding relating to any tax return or filing of the Practice filed with respect to any Pre-Closing Tax Period or Straddle Period. In the case of any tax proceeding that relates to any tax return or filing of the Practice for a Pre-Closing Tax Period or Straddle Period, Seller shall be permitted to control the conduct of such tax proceeding at Seller's sole cost and expense.

7.6   **Trade Name.** Seller hereby assigns to Purchaser all right, title, and interest Seller may hold in the trade name _____ and all derivatives thereof. Seller warrants and represents to Purchaser that no other person or entity, other than the Practice, has any rights in such trade name.

7.7   **Delivery of Documents, Keys, Passwords, Etc.** Promptly following the Closing, Seller will deliver to Purchaser (a) all of the books and records of the Practice (to the extent not physically located at the Premises), (b) all keys used by the Practice in Seller's possession (including for the Premises), and (c) all passwords and other administrative credentials used by the Practice.

ARTICLE 8
PURCHASER'S AND THE PRACTICE's OBLIGATIONS AFTER CLOSING

Following Closing, Purchaser and the Practice shall have the following obligations:

8.1   **Operation of Business.** Following the Closing, Purchaser shall operate and conduct the Practice in a good and professional manner.

8.2   **Purchaser's Limited Usage of Seller's Name.** Purchaser will cause the Practice to only use Seller's name as described and for the time periods stated in Section 7.3. The Practice shall pay all costs incurred relative to said usage. The Practice's limited and non-exclusive use of Seller's name shall not be construed as creating any association, partnership, or joint venture between the parties. Following the expiration of the applicable time period as set forth in Section 7.3, Purchaser and the Practice will cease using the legal name of Seller on any signage or new marketing materials, and shall also promptly thereafter change the legal name of the Practice to a name that does not use the name of Seller or any portion thereof.

8.3   **Employee and Patient Records.** Purchaser shall cause the Practice to maintain appropriate patient records with adequate documentation in accordance with guidelines and community standards for the practice of dentistry in the State of STATE****. Purchaser will cause the Practice to maintain employee files and abide by all applicable employment laws, including but not limited to, OSHA rules and regulations, and federal, state, and local laws.

8.4   **Assumption of Liabilities.** It is understood that in connection with and as a result of the consummation of the transactions described, other than as set forth in this Agreement, Purchaser assumes no liability or liabilities or obligations of Seller of whatsoever kind or nature.

8.5   **Refinancing and Assumption of the Practice Debt.** Purchaser understands that the Practice is subject to, and an obligor on, the Practice Debt as well as the real estate lease for the Premises. Seller and her husband are guarantors of such Practice Debt (other than with regard to the Practice's PPP Loan for Covid-19 Relief). Purchaser and the Practice shall use their best efforts to cause the removal of such personal guarantees either by refinancing such Practice Debt or negotiating with the lender and/or landlord to remove Seller and her husband, as applicable, as guarantors (including without limitation by agreeing to personally guarantee such Practice Debt (other than the Practice's PPP Loan for Covid-19 Relief) or lease arrangement). The Practice and Purchaser shall not under any circumstance renew any lease or any other material contractual arrangement if Seller continues, during such renewal term, to be a guarantor of such lease or other arrangement.

8.6   **Liability Insurance.** Following the Closing, Purchaser shall ensure that the Practice maintains comprehensive, public liability, and property damage insurance for the Practice and the Premises with limits and terms similar to those in force immediately prior to the Closing Date.

8.7   **Seller's Treatment of Family Members.** Seller shall have the right for so long as Purchaser holds equity in the Practice to provide dental treatment to his/her family members listed on Schedule 8.8 (the "Family Members") hereto at the Practice's then facility during hours in which the Practice is closed, such facility is otherwise available for use, and upon reasonable prior coordination thereof with the Practice. Seller shall be responsible for payment of all material costs and expenses, including laboratory fees, incurred in providing such dental services, and shall maintain professional liability insurance during such times as treatment is being provided under this section. Further, so long as Purchaser holds equity in the Practice, Purchaser agrees to provide to the Family Members periodic dental examinations, dental cleanings, and perio maintenance, which services will be free of charge other than for material costs and expenses, including laboratory fees, incurred in providing such dental services.

ARTICLE 9
INDEMNIFICATION

9.1   **Survival**. The representations and warranties made by Seller in this Agreement shall survive the Closing Date and shall expire on the twelve (12) month anniversary of the Closing Date; provided, however, that the survival period shall extend until the four (4) year anniversary of the Closing Date with respect to those representations and warranties set forth in Section 3.1 (Organization and Standing), Section 3.2 (Binding Effect), Section 3.3 (Capitalization and Ownership) and Section 3.9 (Taxes) (such foregoing representations, the "Fundamental Representations"). The representations and warranties made by Purchaser in this Agreement shall survive the Closing Date and shall expires on the four (4) year anniversary of the Closing Date. Notwithstanding the foregoing, if a party delivers written notice alleging the existence of an inaccuracy in or a breach of any of the representations and warranties made by another party and asserting a claim for recovery under this Article 9 based on such alleged inaccuracy or breach, then the claim asserted in such notice shall survive until such time as such claim is fully and finally resolved. Other than as set forth above, the representations, warranties and covenants set forth in this Agreement shall survive indefinitely in accordance with their terms unless otherwise specified in this Agreement.

9.2   **Indemnification by Seller.** Subject to the terms contained in this ARTICLE 9, Seller will indemnify Purchaser and her affiliates from and against Losses incurred by any of them, arising out of or as a result of:

(a)   breaches of any of the representations and warranties of Seller set forth in this Agreement;

(b)   breaches of any of the covenants of Seller set forth in this Agreement;

(c)   any amounts payable by the Practice with regard to the PPP Loan for Covid-19 Relief to the extent relating to the period ending on the Closing Date; and/or

(d)   any taxes of the Practice to the extent relating to the period ending on the Closing Date (it being understood that any claim for taxes relating to any period that includes both periods prior to the Closing Date and after the Closing Date shall be appropriately apportioned).

9.3   **Indemnification by Purchaser.** Subject to the terms contained in this ARTICLE 9, Purchaser will indemnify Seller and her affiliates from and against Losses incurred by any of them, arising out of or as a result of:

(a)   breaches of any of the representations and warranties of Purchaser set forth in this Agreement;

(b)   breaches of any of the covenants of Purchaser set forth in this Agreement;

(c)   use by the Practice or Purchaser of Seller's name;

(d)   any of the Practice Debt other than the Practice's PPP Loan for Covid-19 Relief (whether such claims by the lenders in respect of such Indebtedness are made against Seller and/or her family members in connection with a personal guaranty of such Practice Debt or otherwise); and/or

(e)   any other personal guaranty of obligations of the Practice (including in respect of the real estate lease for the Premises) that has been disclosed to Purchaser on or prior to the Closing Date.

9.4   **Indemnification Procedures.** A party hereto that may be entitled to indemnification under this Agreement (an "Indemnified Party") shall give written notice to the party hereto obligated to indemnify her (an "Indemnifying Party") with reasonable promptness upon becoming aware of the claim or other facts upon which a claim for indemnification will be based. The notice shall set forth such information with respect to the claim as is then reasonably available to the Indemnified Party. The Indemnifying Party shall have the right, but not obligation, to assume the investigation and to undertake the defense of such claim asserted by a third party, including the employment of counsel with payment of all expenses, and the Indemnified Party shall fully cooperate in the investigation and defense without cost to her of such claim and make available all records and material requested by the Indemnifying Party. The Indemnified Party shall be entitled but shall not be required to participate in such investigation and defense of such claim and employ separate counsel. The Indemnified Party shall not be liable for any claim compromised or settled without her written consent, which shall not be unreasonably withheld, conditioned, or delayed. The Indemnifying Party may settle any claim without such written consent of the Indemnifying Party, but only if the relief awarded is not enforceable against the Indemnified Party or is monetary damages that are paid in full by the Indemnifying Party. The Indemnifying Party shall satisfy her indemnification obligation promptly upon the determination that such obligation is due. Failure or delay in giving notice of a claim for indemnification and failure to include any specific information with respect to the claim, shall not affect the obligation of the Indemnifying Party, except to the extent that such failure or delay shall have adversely affected the ability of the Indemnifying Party to defend, settle, or satisfy the claim or demand.

9.5   **Certain Limitations**.

(a)   **Basket.** Seller shall not be required to indemnify Purchaser pursuant to Section 9.2(a) against any indemnifiable Losses set forth therein unless and until the aggregate dollar amount of all such Losses incurred by Purchaser exceeds $150,000 (the "Purchaser Basket"), and then only to the extent that Losses exceed such Purchaser Basket; provided, that, notwithstanding anything contained in this Agreement to the contrary, (x) the limitations set forth in this Section 9.5(a) shall not apply to claims based on inaccuracies in or breaches of any of the Fundamental Representations and (y) the amount of the Purchaser Basket that applies to the representations and warranties set forth in Section 3.15 (employment matters) shall be $25,000.

(b)   **Cap.** In no event shall Seller's liability for Losses pursuant to Section 9.2(a) exceed, in the aggregate, $200,000; provided, that, notwithstanding anything contained in this Agreement to the contrary, the limitations set forth in this Section 9.5(b) shall not apply to claims based on inaccuracies in or breaches of any of the Fundamental Representations.

(c)   **Mitigation of Damages**. Each Indemnified Party shall take, and cause its affiliates to take, all reasonable steps to mitigate any Loss upon becoming aware of any event or circumstance that would be reasonably expected to, or does, give rise thereto, including incurring costs only to the minimum extent necessary to remedy the breach that gives rise to such Loss.

(d)   **Insurance Proceeds**. Payments by an Indemnifying Party pursuant to Article 9 in respect of any Loss shall be limited to the amount of any liability or damage that remains after deducting therefrom any insurance proceeds and any indemnity, contribution or other similar payment received or reasonably expected to be received by the Indemnified Party (or the Practice) in respect of any such claim. The Indemnified Party shall use its commercially reasonable efforts to recover under insurance policies or indemnity, contribution or other similar agreements for any Losses prior to seeking indemnification under this Agreement.

(e)   **No-Sandbagging**. Seller shall not be liable under this Article 9 for any Losses based upon or arising out of any inaccuracy in or breach of any of the representations or warranties of Seller contained in this Agreement if Purchaser had knowledge of such inaccuracy or breach on or prior to the Closing Date.

(f)   **Punitive and Exemplary Damages**. In no event shall any Indemnifying Party be liable to any Indemnified Party for any punitive or exemplary Losses, except and to the extent awarded to a third party in connection with a third-party claim.

9.6   **Losses.** For purposes of the foregoing, "Loss" or "Losses" shall mean any loss, damage, injury, Liability, claim, demand, settlement, judgment, award, fine, proceedings, assessments, deficiencies, penalty, tax, fee (including reasonable attorneys' fees), charge, cost (including costs of investigation, third-party expert and consultant fees and expenses) or expenses of any other nature.

9.7 **Exclusive Remedy**. From and after the Closing Date, the exclusive remedy of any party to this Agreement for any Losses or other damages based upon, arising out of, or otherwise in respect of this Agreement are the indemnification obligations of the Parties set forth in this Agreement and the parties shall not have any other liability for any such Losses or damages; provided, however, that the foregoing shall not apply to fraud.

ARTICLE 10
MISCELLANEOUS

10.1 **Applicable Law.** This Agreement and all documents executed and delivered shall be deemed to be contracts under the laws of the State of STATE**** and shall be construed for all purposes in accordance with such laws.

10.2 **Severability.** If any provisions of this Agreement shall be held to be invalid, illegal, or unenforceable, the validity, legality, and enforceability of the remaining provisions shall not, in any way, be affected or impaired.

10.3 **Entire Agreement.** This instrument and the Exhibits attached set forth the entire Agreement between the parties hereto. All negotiations relative to the matters contemplated by this Agreement are merged and there are no other understandings or agreements relating to the matters and things set forth, other than those incorporated in this Agreement. No provision of this Agreement shall be altered, amended, revoked, or waived except by an instrument in writing signed by the parties sought to be charged with such amendment, revocation, or waiver. This Agreement shall be binding upon and shall inure to the benefit of the parties and their respective heirs, personal representatives, successors, and assigns.

10.4 **Mediation Prior to Litigation.** Seller and Purchaser agree that any and all differences, controversy, or claims arising out of or relating to this Agreement, or the breach of this Agreement and any related documents that cannot be resolved by the parties acting and negotiating in good faith, except as to a default in payment under the Purchase Price, prior to the commencement of litigation, shall be submitted to mediation. In the event the parties are unable to agree upon the selection of a mediator, a mediator selected in accordance with the rules of the American Arbitration Association, or its successor shall serve as mediator. In the event litigation ensues notwithstanding such mediation, the costs and expenses of said mediation including without limitation to attorney fees, shall be awarded to the prevailing party in the litigation.

10.5 **Additional Acts and Documents.** Each party hereto agrees to do all things and take all such actions, and to make, execute, and deliver such other documents and instruments as shall be reasonably required to carry out the provisions of this intent of this Agreement.

10.6 **Cost and Fees.** The parties agree that each party shall be responsible for its costs relating to this transaction, including attorneys' fees, broker fees, accountant fees, and Closing costs incurred by that party.

10.7   **Notices.** All notices required or permitted by this Agreement shall be in writing and shall be given by personal delivery or sent to the address of the party set forth below by registered or certified mail, postage prepaid, return receipt requested, or by reputable overnight courier, prepaid receipt acknowledged. Notices shall be deemed received on the earlier date of actual receipt or, in the case of notice by mail or overnight courier, the date of receipt marked on the acknowledgment or receipt. Rejection or refusal to accept or the inability to deliver because of change of address of which no notice was given shall be deemed to be received as of the date such notice was deposited in the mail or delivered by the courier.

If to Seller:

If to Purchaser:

10.8   **Authority.** Each of the parties hereto represents to the other that such party has full power and authority to execute, deliver, and perform this Agreement.

10.9   **Headings for Convenience Only.** The parties acknowledge that the section headings contained in this Agreement are only for the convenience of the parties. The substance and provisions control without regard to said headings.

10.10   **Preparation of Agreement.** The parties acknowledge that this Agreement has been negotiated and prepared in an arms-length transaction and that both Purchaser and Seller have negotiated all the terms contained herein. Accordingly, the parties agree that neither party shall be deemed to have drafted the Agreement and the Agreement shall not be interpreted against either party as the draftsman.

10.11   **Counterparts.** This Agreement may be executed in one or more counterparts, each of which, including those received via facsimile transmission or e-mail (including in PDF format), shall be deemed an original, and all of which shall constitute one and the same Agreement.

[Signatures follow on separate page(s).]

IN WITNESS WHEREOF, the parties hereto have caused this Agreement to be duly executed.

SELLER:

_____

PURCHASER:

_____

PRACTICE:

_____, a Professional Dental Corporation

By: _____
Name:
Title: Authorized Signatory

EXHIBIT 7.5

RESTRICTIVE COVENANT AGREEMENT

This RESTRICTIVE COVENANT AGREEMENT (this "Agreement") is entered into effective as of 11:59 p.m. (Central) on February 28, 2021, and is given by _____ ("Seller") for the benefit of _____ ("Purchaser").

WHEREAS, Seller is licensed to practice dentistry in the State of STATE**** and is engaged in the practice of general dentistry as an employee of _____, and provides such services at _____ (the "Premises");

WHEREAS, Purchaser is licensed to practice dentistry in the State of STATE****;

WHEREAS, this Agreement is a material and separately bargained for part of that certain Stock Purchase Agreement dated effective as of February 28, 2021 (the "Purchase Agreement"), between Seller and Purchaser, whereby Seller sold all of Seller's right, title, and interest in and to all of the outstanding and issued shares of the Practice (collectively, the "Shares"); and

WHEREAS, Seller acknowledges that Purchaser would not purchase the Shares unless Seller agrees to this Agreement.

THEREFORE, in consideration of good and valuable consideration, the receipt and sufficiency of which is acknowledged, Seller warrants and covenants as follows:

1.   Seller agrees she shall not, for a period of three (3) years from the Closing Date, within a ten (10) mile radius of the Premises, directly or indirectly: (a) own any interest in, (b) participate in the management, operation, or control of, or (c) perform any services as or act in the capacity of an employee or agent of any enterprise engaged in the practice of dentistry. In addition, during such three (3) year period, Seller shall not directly or indirectly solicit for dental treatment any patients of the Practice and further shall not solicit any of the Practice's employees to work for anyone other than the Practice.

2.   Seller recognizes that Purchaser would suffer irreparable damage if Seller violates this Agreement. In the event of Seller's alleged breach of this Agreement, Purchaser shall provide written notice of default to Seller by certified mail, return receipt requested. Seller shall have ten (10) days from receipt of written notice to cure the default and comply with the terms of this Agreement. In the event Seller fails to cure the default and comply with this Agreement within the ten (10) day period, Purchaser shall have the right to injunctive relief in order to prevent Seller's continued breach of this Agreement. Seller waives any requirements for Purchaser to post bond in the event Purchaser seeks an injunction against Seller pursuant to this Agreement.

3.   This terms of this Agreement are independent of any other provisions of the Purchase Agreement and have been separately bargained for by the parties hereto. The existence of any claim or other cause of action of Seller against Purchaser shall not constitute a defense to the enforcement of this Agreement by Purchaser.

4.   Seller agrees that the restrictions as to scope, territory, and period of time are reasonable. If any court of competent jurisdiction determines that the restrictions of the above restrictive covenants are too broad to be enforced, it is the parties' intent that such court modify the provisions by narrowing their scope to the minimum extent necessary to permit their enforcement.

Details in Purchase Agreements

As you read the previous first two purchase agreements, you will notice a few similarities and differences in each document. While the first one is short and to the point, the second one is much longer and addresses pretty much every contingency possible.

The third acquisition document is based around a 'stock sale'. This was drafted by our attorney for a specific sale of a practice whereby the seller wanted to pass along the loans, bank accounts, and corporation directly to the buyer. This is non-traditional for most transitions, but might work well for certain situations, including when the doctor wants to exit fast. This could be very typical for situations where a doctor is sick or has an immediate change in family situation. Asset purchases are typically used because they limit any potential liabilities to the new owner, since the new owner is only buying assets and patient charts. Typically the risk in a stock sale is that the purchaser might 'buy' a liability. However, the stock purchase can be written with specific covenants that would protect the buyer from previous liabilities. We also introduce the concept of a bucket system, where the buyer is only liable for a certain dollar amount of damages before the seller picks up the rest - or vice versa. This is a compromise when the seller wants to relieve themselves of future liabilities as well. The advantage is that this is a very fast transaction and the buyer simply takes over the corporation, licenses, bank accounts, and paperwork. The downside is the possible risks. In each of these scenarios, you should discuss the specific details and pros and cons with your attorney before making any decisions.

Legalities of Employee Transition

Next we will address some employee documents. The first agreement includes a table at the end which includes all of the employees, their pay, benefits, and whether they would like to remain working for the next employer. While some sellers are quite open with the fact they are leaving, that is not always the case. If the seller is keeping the transition confidential, it is important to ascertain which employees will stay and which will resign. In most cases, you will want to retain most team members. However, you will need to decide whether to keep the existing team on board with your organization, or whether to pick and choose who stays and who goes. Regardless, we encourage you to use the document found later in the book called 'Termination and Rehire letter'. This document helps to be extremely clear with each team member that they are no longer employed with their former company, and that they are a new employee with your company. We have used this document for years, and even though we are extremely clear with the expectations that they are new employees, there is still often some confusion. We have had employees approach us a year after the transition and ask why they do not have more vacation time. It is during this time that we have to show them the document they signed at the time of the transition that shows them that they are a new employee with your company, and no longer employed by the previous owner.

The next documents we have are the Real Estate Purchase Agreement, then Termination and Rehire Letter, then a Closing Statement, Employment agreement, and Closing Checklist.

REAL ESTATE PURCHASE AGREEMENT

This Agreement is entered into this _____ day of _____, 2021, between **Crown Professional Building Associates, a STATE**** General Partnership ("SELLER")** and **Grain Acres Real Estate Properties, LLC, a STATE**** Limited Liability Company ("BUYER").**

WITNESSETH:

WHEREAS, Seller is the owner of the real estate property at Address****, Lincoln, STATE****, legally described as follows:

LEGAL Description of property STATE****

(the "PROPERTY").

WHEREAS, Buyer desires to purchase from Seller, and Seller desires to sell to Buyer, the Property in accordance with the terms and provisions of this Agreement.

NOW, THEREFORE, in consideration of the mutual covenants and agreements of the parties hereto, the parties hereby agree as follows:

1.   **Property.** Seller shall sell to Buyer and Buyer shall purchase from Seller the real estate described above, together with all buildings and improvements thereon and with any easements and servient estates appurtenant thereto (**the "PROPERTY"**), free and clear of all liens, encumbrances, encroachments and violations of zoning ordinances, but with reservations and exceptions as follows:

   1.1   **Covenants.** Title shall be taken subject to any restrictive covenants, easements, mineral rights, and reservations or conditions of record, which do not interfere or prevent Buyer from Buyer's intended use of the Property.

   1.2   **Exceptions.** Title shall be taken subject to the Permitted Exceptions as defined in Section 5.3.

2.   **Purchase Price.** Subject to the terms and provisions of this Agreement, Buyer shall pay to Seller, and Seller shall accept from Buyer, the sum of $1,087,500.00 as the Purchase Price for the Property (**the "PURCHASE PRICE"**). The Purchase Price shall be paid as follows:

   2.1   **Cash Payment.** Buyer shall pay to Seller the sum of $200,000.00 in collected funds at Closing.

   2.2   **Promissory Note.** At the Closing, Buyer shall execute and deliver to Seller Buyer's Promissory Note in the amount of $887,500.00, bearing interest at 4% per annum, payable in 180 equal monthly installments in the amount of $6,564.00 each, all in the form of the Promissory Note attached hereto as **Schedule 2.2**.

2.3   **Security**. The Promissory Note shall be secured by a Deed of Trust covering the Property being sold and purchased hereunder, in the form of the Deed of Trust attached hereto as **Schedule 2.3**.

2.4   **Personal Guaranties**. As further security for the payment of the Promissory Note, each of the Members of Buyer shall execute and deliver to Seller his Personal Guaranty in the form of the Personal Guaranty attached hereto as **Schedule 2.4** and made a part hereof by this reference.

3.   **Closing and Conveyance.** The closing of this Agreement shall be scheduled for September 1, 2021, at the office of ACCOUNTANT, CITY, STATE****, which Closing shall be conducted by STATE**** Title Company **("CLOSING AGENT")**, or at such other time, place and date as may be mutually agreed upon by the parties hereto in writing **(the "CLOSING DATE")**. The Purchase Price shall be disbursed by and through Closing Agent. Buyer and Seller agrees to retain Closing Agent to close this transaction and shall each pay one-half of the closing charges of the Closing Agent.

3.1   **Filing Expenses.** Seller shall pay STATE**** documentary stamp taxes relating to this transfer and the cost of filing the Deed of Trust. Buyer shall pay the cost of filing the Deed.

3.2   **Warranty Deed.** On the Closing Date, Seller shall convey the Property to Buyer, or Buyer's designee, by warranty deed, free and clear of all liens and encumbrances, special assessments levied or assessed or special assessment districts created as of the date of Closing, and free and clear of any easements, covenants or restrictions filed against the Property on or after the date of the title insurance commitment, subject to all easements, covenants and restrictions of record as of the date of the title insurance commitment which have not been objected to in writing by Buyer pursuant to this Agreement.

3.3   **Prorate Rents**. All rent will be prorated to date of Closing. Any security deposits will be paid to Buyer at Closing.

4.   **Taxes and Special Assessments**. Real estate taxes on the Property for 2020 and all prior years shall be paid in full by Seller on or prior to the Closing Date. Taxes for the calendar year 2021 shall be prorated to the Closing Date based upon the most current mil levy and current assessed value. Seller shall deliver to Buyer on the Closing
Date a title insurance commitment or written statement by the County Treasurer's Office

showing that there are no special assessments of record as of the Closing Date. All real estate taxes to become due after Closing shall be paid timely by Buyer.

5. **Title Insurance.** Seller shall furnish to Buyer a title insurance commitment on the Property issued through STATE**** Title Insurance Company within ten (10) days after the execution of this Agreement by Buyer and Seller. Said title insurance commitment shall show the Buyer as the proposed insured owner and the coverage will be the Purchase Price. The title insurance commitment will show marketable title to the Property in Seller free and clear of all liens and encumbrances. At closing, Buyer shall be furnished a title insurance policy in the face amount of the Purchase Price, subject only to those items shown on the title insurance commitment which have not been objected to by Buyer. The cost of the title insurance shall be divided equally between Seller and Buyer.

5.1 **Objections to Title.** Buyer shall approve or disapprove title to the Property within fourteen (14) business days after receipt of the title insurance commitment. If any defect in title is discovered during the examination of the title commitment by Buyer, Buyer shall furnish Seller with a copy of the attorney's opinion which reflects such defect. Seller shall have a reasonable time to cure such defects, not to exceed 30 days, and Seller shall bear the expense of curing the same. If efforts to cure any such defect fail, both Seller and Buyer shall have the option to rescind this Agreement. In addition to the terms and conditions of this Agreement, the land title law of STATE****, and the title standards approved by the STATE**** Bar Association to the date of examination of title shall serve as a guide to marketability of title.

5.2 **Review of Covenants, etc.** Buyer shall have ten (10) business days after receipt of the title insurance commitment to review all covenants, restrictions, easements and other matters of record affecting the Property. Unless Buyer forwards to Seller a written objection to any such restriction, covenant, easement or other matter of record within ten (10) business days after the receipt of the title insurance commitment and copies of said covenants, restrictions, easements, etc. for the Property, Buyer shall be deemed to have accepted the Property subject to all such restrictions, covenants, easements and other matters of record shown on the title insurance commitment. Seller shall have a reasonable time to cure such objected to restriction, covenant, easement or other matter of record. If Seller is unable to correct or remedy Buyer's written objections within thirty (30) days, this Agreement shall be null and void and of no force and effect, and the earnest money paid herewith shall be refunded to Buyer.

5.3 **Permitted Exceptions.** Any matters reflected in the title commitment to which Buyer does not object shall be deemed to be **"Permitted**

Exceptions."

6. **Environmental Inspections.** Buyer, at Buyer's sole cost and expense, may, if Buyer so elects, conduct environmental inspections of the Property which the Buyer deems necessary on or before the Closing Date. Any Phase I environmental study of the Property shall be prepared by a qualified, independent third party. In the event Buyer, after reviewing the Phase I environmental study, desires a Phase II environmental study be performed, then Buyer may, at Buyer's sole costs and expense, in Buyer's sole discretion, proceed with such Phase II environmental study. If Buyer does not elect to proceed with the Phase II study, or if the Phase II environmental study reveals or discloses any environmental problems with the Property regarding the presence of hazardous substances (as hereinafter defined), Buyer may rescind this Agreement by written notice to Seller, and receive a full and immediate refund of Buyer's earnest money deposit.

7. **Other Inspections**. Buyer retains the right to conduct such other inspections of the Property, including the heating and air-conditioning units, the roof, foundation and structure of any buildings, plumbing, electrical, etc. Buyer may, at its discretion, declare this agreement null and void if any of such inspections reveal deficiencies which, in Buyer's discretion, are unsatisfactory for Buyer's intended use of the Property.

8. **Possession**. Seller shall deliver possession of the Property to Buyer at the Closing Date.

9. **Risk of Loss.** Risk of loss to the Property shall remain with the Seller until the Closing Date, at which time the risk of loss shall pass to Buyer. In the event that the Property is materially damaged, Buyer shall have the option to void this Agreement, unless such damage is repaired by Seller prior to the Closing Date to the sole satisfaction of Buyer.

10. **Representations and Warranties of the Seller.** Seller represents to Buyer that the statements contained in this Section 12 are correct and complete as of the date of this Agreement and will be correct and complete as of the Closing Date (as though made then and as though the Closing Date were substituted for the date of this Agreement throughout this Section 12).

10.1 **Authorization of Transaction.** This Agreement constitutes the valid and legally binding obligation of the Seller, enforceable in accordance with its terms and conditions.

10.2 **Broker's Fees.** Seller has no liability or obligation to pay any fees or commissions to any broker, finder, or agent with respect to the transactions contemplated by this Agreement for which the Buyer could become liable or obligated.

10.3   **Title and Condition of Property**. With respect to the Property:

10.3.1   **Marketable Title**. Seller has good and marketable title to the Property and as of the Closing Date will be free and clear of any security interest, easement, covenants, or other restrictions which impair the current use, occupancy or value, or the marketability of title, of the Property other than Permitted Exceptions and the Leases.

10.3.2   **Proceedings**. There are no pending, threatened, condemnation proceedings, lawsuits or administrative actions relating to the Property or other matters affecting adversely the current use, occupancy, or value of the Property.

10.3.3   **Legal Description**. The legal description of each parcel contained in the deeds transferring the Property describes the Property fully and adequately, the buildings and improvements are located within the boundary lines of the legal description, are not in violation of applicable set-back requirements, zoning laws, resolutions and ordinances (and neither the Property nor the buildings or improvements thereon are subject to "permitted nonconforming use" or "permitted nonconforming structure" classifications), and do not encroach on any easement which may burden the land, the land does not serve any adjoining property for any purpose inconsistent with the use of the land, and the Property is not located within any flood plain or subject to any similar type restriction for which any permits or licenses necessary to the use thereof have not been obtained.

10.3.4   **Governmental Approvals**. All facilities have received all approvals of governmental authorities (including licenses and permits required in connection with the ownership or operation thereof) and have been operated and maintained in accordance with all applicable laws, rules and regulations.

10.3.5   **Leases**. There are no leases of the property to third parties except the existing Lease to _____.

10.3.6   **Options**. There are no outstanding options or rights of first refusal to purchase the Property or any portion thereof or interest therein.

10.3.7   **Possession**. There are no parties in possession of the Property other than Seller and/or the tenants listed in **Section**

10.3.5 attached hereto.

      10.3.8   **Hazardous Substances.** No hazardous substance has been generated upon, manufactured on, produced on, stored on, released on or from, discharged on or from, or disposed of on the Property; and Seller has not received any notice of any proceeding or inquiry by any governmental authority, including without limitation, the STATE**** Department of Environmental Quality, STATE**** Department of Health and Rehabilitation Services, or the United States Environmental Protection Agency with respect to the presence of any hazardous substance on the Property, or the mitigation thereof from or to the Property. The Seller is unaware, and has no knowledge of, any hazardous substances that may have ever been utilized on the Property. The term **"hazardous substance"** shall include without limitation: (i) those substances included within the definition of "hazardous substances," "hazardous materials," "toxic substances," or "solid waste" in Circla, RCRA, and the Hazardous Materials Transportation Act, 49 USC § 1801, *et seq.*, and in the regulations promulgated pursuant to said laws.

      11.   **Representations and Warranties of Buyer.** Buyer represents and warrants to Seller, for the purposes of the Agreement with Seller, that the statements contained in this Section 12 are correct and complete as of the date of this Agreement and will be correct and complete as of the Closing Date (as though made then and as though the Closing Date were substituted for the date of this Agreement).

      11.1   **Authorization of Transaction.** Buyer has full power and authority to execute and deliver this Agreement and to perform its obligations hereunder. This Agreement constitutes the valid and legally binding obligation of the Buyer, enforceable in accordance with its terms and conditions.

      11.2   **Broker's Fees.** Buyer has no liability or obligation to pay any fees or commissions to any broker, finder, or agent with respect to the transactions contemplated by this Agreement for which Seller could become liable or obligated.

      12.   **Conditions to Buyer's Obligation to Close.** The obligation of the Buyer to consummate the transaction contemplated hereby and close on the purchase of the Property is subject to satisfaction of the following conditions:

      12.1   **Representations of Seller.** The representations and warranties of Seller set forth in Section 10 above shall be true and correct in all respects at and as of the Closing Date.

12.2   Legal Proceedings. No action, suit or proceeding shall be pending or threatened before any court of quasi-judicial or administrative agency for any federal, state, local or foreign jurisdiction or before any arbitrator wherein an unfavorable injunction, judgment, order, decree, ruling or charge would (a) prevent consummation of any of the transactions contemplated by this Agreement; (b) cause any of the transactions contemplated by this Agreement to be rescinded following consummation; (c) affect adversely the right of Buyer to own the Property; or (d) affect adversely the right of Buyer to use and sublet all or any part of the Property for any uses intended by Buyer.

12.3   **Seller's Documents.** All actions to be taken by Seller in connection with the consummation of the transaction contemplated hereby and all certificates, opinions, instruments, and other documents relating to effecting the transactions contemplated hereby will be satisfactory in form and substance to Buyer.

12.4   **Reports**. Buyer shall have received reports of all matters, including surveys and environmental reports, which are satisfactory to Buyer in its sole discretion.

12.5   **Title Commitment**. Buyer shall have received a satisfactory title insurance commitment evidencing marketable title to the Property vested in Seller, free and clear of all liens and encumbrances, except easements and restrictions of record.

12.6   **Zoning**. Buyer shall have satisfied itself that the regulations in the Zoning Ordinance of the City of Lincoln applicable to the Property shall not interfere with Buyer's intended use of the Property.

12.7   **Final Inspection**. No more than twenty-four (24) hours prior to the Closing Date, Seller and representatives of Buyer may conduct an inspection of the Property and Buyer shall determine in its sole discretion whether or not the Property meets with its approval. Buyer will be deemed to have accepted the Property if Buyer closes on the transaction on the Closing Date.

12.8   **Waiver**. The Buyer may waive any condition specified in this section if it executes a writing so stating at or prior to the closing.

13.   **Conditions To Seller's Obligation To Close.** The obligation of the Seller to consummate the transactions to be performed by it in connection with the closing is subject to the satisfaction of the following conditions:

13.1   **Buyer's Representations**. The representations and warranties set forth in Section 11 above shall be true and correct in all material respects at and as of the Closing Date.

13.2 **Buyer's Covenants.** Buyer shall have performed and complied with all of its covenants hereunder in all material respects through the closing.

13.3 **Buyer's Documents.** All actions to be taken by Buyer in connection with the consummation of the purchase of the Property contemplated hereby and all certificates, opinions, instruments and other documents required to effect the transfer of the Property contemplated hereby will be satisfactory in form and substance to the Seller.

13.4 **Waiver.** Seller may waive any conditions specified in this section if it executes a writing so stating at or prior to the closing.

14. **Termination.** Certain of the parties may terminate this Agreement as provided below:_____.

14.1 **Mutual Agreement.** The Buyer and the Seller may terminate this Agreement by mutual written consent at any time prior to the closing.

14.2 **Buyer.** Buyer may terminate this Agreement by giving written notice to Seller at any time prior to closing if any of the conditions set forth herein have not been satisfied.

14.3 **Seller.** Seller may terminate this Agreement by giving written notice to Buyer at any time prior to closing in the event the Buyer's conditions set forth herein have not been satisfied.

14.4 **Default.** In the event of a default under the terms and provisions of this Agreement by either party, the non-defaulting party may institute legal proceedings for damages sustained or for specific performance of the terms and provisions of this Agreement.

15. **Miscellaneous.**

15.1 **Survival of Representations.** All of the representations and warranties of the parties contained in this Agreement shall survive the closing hereunder.

15.2 **Rights of Parties.** This Agreement shall not confer any rights or remedies upon any person other than the parties and their respective successors and permitted assigns.

15.3 **Entire Agreement.** This Agreement, including the documents referred to herein, constitutes the entire Agreement between the parties and supercedes any prior understandings, agreements, or representations by or between the parties, written or oral, to the extent they relate in any way to the subject matter hereof.

15.4 **Benefit.** This Agreement shall be binding upon and inure to the benefit of the parties named herein and their respective successors in interest and permitted assigns.

15.5 **Counterparts.** This Agreement may be executed in one or more counterparts, each of which shall be deemed an original, but all of which together will constitute one and the same instrument.

15.6 **Titles.** The leading sections contained in this Agreement are inserted for convenience only and shall not affect in any way the meaning or interpretation of this Agreement.

15.7 **Notices.** All notices, requests, demands, claims and other communications hereunder will be in writing. Any notice, request, demand, claim or other communication hereunder shall be deemed duly given if it is sent by registered or certified mail, return receipt requested, postage prepaid, and addressed to the intended recipient as set forth below.

> If to Seller: Thomas Co-Owner Dentist, DDS
>   ADDRESS
>
> If to Buyer: Grain Acres Real Estate Properties, LLC
>   ADDRESS

Any party may send any notice, request, demand, claim or other communication hereunder to the intended recipient at the address set forth above using any other means (including personal delivery, expedited courier, messenger service, telecopy, telex, ordinary mail, or electronic mail), but no such notice, request, demand, claim or other communication shall be deemed to have been duly given unless and until it actually is received by the intended recipient. Any party may change the address to which notices, requests, demands, claims and other communications hereunder are to be delivered by giving the other party notice in the manner herein set forth.

15.8 **Governing Law.** This Agreement shall be governed by and construed in accordance with the domestic laws of the state of STATE**** without giving effect to any choice or conflict of law provisions or rule whether of the state of STATE**** or any other jurisdiction that would cause the application of the laws of any jurisdiction other than the state of

STATE****.

15.9 **Amendments.** No amendment of any provision of this Agreement shall be valid unless the same shall be in writing and signed by Buyer and Seller.

15.10 **Severability.** Any term or provision of this Agreement that is invalid or unenforceable in any situation in any jurisdiction shall not affect the validity or enforceability of the remaining terms and provisions hereof or the validity or enforceability of the offending term or provision in any other situation or in any other jurisdiction.

15.11 **Expenses.** Both Buyer and Seller will bear their own costs and expenses (including legal fees and expenses) incurred in connection with this Agreement and the transaction contemplated hereby.

15.12 **Best Efforts of Parties.** Seller and Buyer shall use their best efforts to satisfy all conditions contained in this Agreement to assure that every effort will be made to close this transaction.

15.13 **Execution of Documents.** Each of the parties agrees to execute and deliver such other documents and take such other action, whether prior to or subsequent to Closing, as may be necessary to more effectively consummate the intent and purpose of this Agreement.

15.14 **Time.** Time is of the essence in all terms and provisions of this Agreement.

IN WITNESS WHEREOF, the parties have executed this Agreement as of the date first set forth above.

> **SELLER:**
> CROWN PROFESSIONAL BUILDING ASSOCIATES
> By
>   Thomas Co-Owner Dentist, Partner
> By
>   James Co-Owner, Partner
>
> **BUYER:**
> Grain Acres Real Estate PROPERTIES, LLC
> By
>   John Q. Buyer, Managing Member

Schedule 10.3.5
Estoppel Certificate

TO: Crown Plaza Professional Building
        ADDRESS***, Suite A and B
        CITY, STATE ZIP
        ATTN: _____

RE: Lease Agreement and lease of premises at ADDRESS***, Suite ___, CITY, STATE ZIP

To whom it may concern:

This is to certify that as of the date hereof, as follows:

1.   The undersigned is the present owner and holder of the tenant's interest under that certain Office Lease dated January 1, 2015, and that certain First Addendum to Office Lease dated January 1, 2015 (collectively, the "LEASE"), by and between Crown Plaza Professional Building ("LANDLORD") and Tenant Company Name ("TENANT"), covering a leasehold estate in favor of Tenant for space located on lower level of that certain real property owned by Landlord located at ADDRESS***, CITY, STATE ZIP ("PREMISES").

2.   The Lease (i) constitutes the entire agreement between Landlord and Tenant with respect to the Premises, (ii) is in full force and effect, and (iii) has not been modified, amended, supplemented, extended and/or assigned.

3.   The term of the Lease commenced on January 1, 2015, and will expire on December 31, 2025, as set forth in the Lease.

4.   Except as set forth in the Lease, Tenant does not have any right or option to lease additional space in the Premises or to purchase any part of the Premises.

5.   The Tenant has not been assigned, transferred, sublet, hypothecated or encumbered the Property.

6.   Neither Tenant nor, to the knowledge of Tenant, Landlord is in default under any of the material terms, covenants or provisions of the Lease, and Tenant knows of no event which, but for the passage of time or the giving of notice, or both, would constitute a default or event of default under the Lease by Tenant or Landlord. No rental payments have been made more than one month in advance.

7.   Neither Tenant nor, to the knowledge of Tenant, Landlord has commenced any action or given or received any notice for the purpose of terminating the Lease.

8.   Except as set forth in the Lease, (i) Tenant is not entitled to any credit against the payment of rent or other charges under the Lease or to any rent concession, and (ii) there are no offsets or defenses to the payment of rent or other charges payable under the Lease.

9.   Tenant has paid to Landlord (i) a security deposit of $2204, and (ii) all month rent in the amount described in the Lease through DATE_____. Tenant's next monthly rent payment is due on DATE_____, for the month of September.

10.   There are no actions, voluntary or otherwise, pending against Tenant or any guarantor of Tenant's obligations under the Lease pursuant to the bankruptcy or insolvency laws of the United States or any state thereof;

11.   The undersigned acknowledges that Landlord intends to sell the Premises to a third party buyer ("Buyer"). Upon notice of sale and transfer of the Premises to Buyer, Tenant agrees to send to Buyer copies of any written communications to the Landlord concerning the Lease in the manner provided for giving notice in the Lease, at Buyer's address, and if Tenant receives a notice of the Landlord, agrees to begin forwarding rent and notices to Buyer.

        This estoppel certificate is binding upon Tenant and its successors and assigns and may be relied upon by the parties referenced in Paragraph 11 hereof.

        Executed as of _____, 2021.

                                Tenant Company Name, Tenant

                                By: _____
                                Name: _____
                                Title: _____

Grain Acres Dental, LLC
Address
City, State, Zip

To: Employee Name

Our company has purchased the dental practice located at ADDRESS*** from Dr. John Seller. Dr. Seller has terminated your employment with his Company and you are being rehired as a new "at-will" employee with the undersigned company effective as of January 1, 2021 in accordance with our company's policies as will be explained.

The terms of your new employment are as follows: Hourly wage of $_____

Sincerely,
Grain Acres Dental, LLC

_____

Dr. Owner

ACKNOWLEDGEMENT, RECEIPT AND AGREEMENT

I acknowledge receipt of the separate letter from Dr. Seller terminating my employment from his Company and agree to and accept rehire as a new "at-will" employee with Grain Acres Dental, LLC per above the terms and conditions.

Dated this _____ day of November, 2021

_____

Employee Name

Date: January 30, 2021

Seller: Dr. John Seller D.D.S., individually. And Dr. John Seller, DDS doing business as (DBA) "Seller Dental," a sole proprietorship dental practice

Purchaser: Grain Acres Dental, LLC

Office Address: ADDRESS

TERMS OF ACQUISITION

Furniture, Fixtures and Equipment	$25,000
Office Inventory and Clinical and Other Supplies	$25,000
Goodwill	$150,000
Restrictive Covenant 0	

Accounts Receivable $_____

Total Payment to Seller from Purchaser $_____

The parties acknowledge signing and receipt of a copy of IRS form 8594.

By the signature below, Seller confirms the receipt of the purchase payment and the accuracy of this closing statement. _____ John Seller, D.D.S., individually and John Seller, D.D.S., doing business as (DBA) "Seller Dental," a sole proprietorship dental practice

Dated _____, 2021 _____ John Seller

By the signature below, Purchaser confirms it has made the purchase payment to Seller and the accuracy of this closing statement.

_____ Authorized Official of Grain Acres Dental, LLC

Dated _____, 2021

ASSOCIATE DENTIST EMPLOYMENT AGREEMENT

DATED: April 15th, 2021

PARTIES: Dr. John Seller, DDS ("Dentist" or "Employee") and Grain Acres Dental LLC, a STATE**** professional limited liability company ("Employer"), currently located at ADDRESS******. (the " Practice Site").

It is agreed that:

1   At-Will Employment. Employer employs Dentist to provide professional dental services to patients of Employer. The term of Dentist's employment under this agreement shall commence on or about April 15th, 2021 and shall continue until this document is terminated by either party (the "Agreement"). The Employee is employed on an "at-will" basis and the Employer or the Employee may terminate this Agreement without cause on 30-days written notice to the other party. In the event of such termination there will be no further obligations to the other party, other than for payment to the Employee of wages and benefits accrued to the date of such termination.

2   Compensation and Benefits.
2.1   Compensation: The employees base salary for the duration of the agreement is $188,000 per year, or 30% of collections after all adjustments, writeoffs, and payment plan fees. Except as otherwise provided by law, all amounts payable to Dentist pursuant to this Agreement shall be subject to all required and/or authorized payroll withholdings, including, but not limited to, state, federal and local income and employment taxes.

2.2   For purposes of these sections 2.1, the income or expenses to be included in and the mathematical formula for calculating the relevant month's salary period Net services production attributable to the Employee shall be determined in the sole discretion of the Employer from time to time and shall not carry-over from one month to another. Employer reserves the right to at any time during the Dentist's employment to change or increase Dentist's salary or Benefits.

2.3   Benefits: Commencing on or around the start date, Employer shall also pay: premium for professional liability insurance, lab fees (as long as fees are same or lower for the lab Employer uses; e.g., Employer pays $139 for a Full Zirconia including model work), $5,000 annual CE allowance per FTE (Pro-rated if not a Full Time Employee), license renewal, monthly cell phone stipend. Additional benefits may be available and/or agreed upon from time to time through the Employer to be paid for by Employer or Dentist such as disability insurance, accident insurance, life insurance, etc. Employer will not pay for membership in any dental associations or organizations (Example= ADA).

3   Miscellaneous Terms
3.1   Employment. Dentist is employed by Employer to provide dental services to patients of Employer. Dentist agrees to devote Dentist's best efforts to performance of Dentist's duties under this Agreement.

3.2   Schedule. Employer and Dentist shall mutually determine Dentist's work schedule. Some after hours will be expected (Mornings, evenings, Saturdays), including on-call hours. In the event mutual agreement on scheduling is not reached, Employer shall determine Dentist's work location and schedule.

3.3 Standards of Practice. At all times, Dentist shall act in accordance with applicable standards of practice and ethical standards of the dental profession, and shall abide by all protocols of treatment and quality of care policies established from time to time by Employer. Dentist acknowledges and agrees to comply with the requirements of all applicable federal, state and local statutes, laws and ordinances including, but not limited to, laws prohibiting discrimination or harassment of any kind or nature.

3.4 Emergency Services. Dentist shall be reasonably available from time to time to provide professional dental services to patients of Employer or any of Employer's subsidiaries or affiliates and related companies in the Lincoln Nebraska area who have an urgent need for dental services at times when Employer offices are closed.

3.5 Exclusivity. Dentist shall not render professional dental services to any other private offices during the term of this Agreement other than to patients of Employer or any of Employer's subsidiaries or affiliates and related companies in the Lincoln Nebraska area, except to Dentist's family.

3.6 Appearance. Dentist shall maintain a professional appearance during office hours at Employer offices in accordance with the policies established by Employer from time to time.

3.7 Licensure and Qualifications. Dentist shall, at all times during the term of this Agreement, pay for and maintain licensure in good standing as a dentist in the State, including compliance with all applicable continuing education requirements,

3.8 Non-Compete and Non-Solicitation.
3.8.1 Employee acknowledges and agrees that an agreement not to compete with Employer is reasonable and necessary because Employee will have substantial personal contact with patients of Employer. Employee may also have substantial personal contact with patients of Employer's subsidiaries or affiliates and related companies.

3.8.2 During the term of this Agreement, Employee shall not provide care to any patients of Employer or direct such patients to other family health care providers except in furtherance of the best interests of Employer. Employee further covenants and agrees that Employee will not, for a period of one (1) year after leaving Employer (for whatever reason and whether by action of Employee or Employer), initiate any professional contact with, solicit professional business from, or provide professional services to patients whom Employee actually treated and had personal contact while employed by Employer or while assigned to provide dental services to any of Employer's subsidiaries or affiliates and related companies.

3.8.3 During the term of this Agreement, and for a period of one (1) year after leaving Employer (for whatever reason and whether by action of Employee or Employer), Employee shall not cause or encourage any employee of Employer or any of Employer's subsidiaries or affiliates and related companies where Employee provided dental services during the term of this Agreement except in furtherance of the best interests of Employer and with the written consent of Employer.

3.8.4   Employee understands and agrees that the provisions herein are reasonable and may be enforced by Employer seeking injunctive relief, and that the terms of this paragraph shall survive the termination of this agreement.

3.9 Amendment. This Agreement may not be amended other than in a writing signed by both parties.

3.10 Severability.   If any provision of this Agreement is found to be invalid or unenforceable, the remaining provisions of this Agreement shall remain valid and enforceable.

3.12 Assignability. This Agreement shall be personal to Dentist and may not be assigned by Dentist. Subject to this limitation, this Agreement shall be binding on the parties and their respective successors and assigns.

3.13 Governing Law. This Agreement shall be governed by and construed in accordance with the laws of the State of STATE***.

3.14 Notice. Any notice under this Agreement shall be given in writing. Notice to Dentist shall be deemed given when personally delivered or three days after deposit in the United States mail, postage prepaid, as certified or registered mail, return receipt requested, to the address shown on the signature page of this Agreement, or to Dentist's current address as shown in the records of Employer. Notice to Employer shall be deemed given when actually received at its then-current office of the President of Employer.

IN WITNESS WHEREOF, the parties have executed this Agreement as of the date first written above.

EMPLOYER   DENTIST
Grain Acres Dental, LLC, a STATE professional limited
liability company

By: _____   Dr. John Seller, DDS
Authorized Officer

Closing Checklist and Issues

SELLER DENTAL CLOSING DATE: MONDAY, January 30, 2021 9:00 a.m.

	Practice Closing Tasks On Asset Purchase Agreement	**IF AGREED** Insert Initials	
		Purchaser	**Seller**
1.	Purchaser conducted Inventory verification and inspection of assets being purchased prior to closing? (See APA Page XXXX)	_____	_____
2.	Other than as set forth in the APA, there are no additional Excluded Assets or Items from the purchase of the Practice? (See APA Page XXXX)	_____	_____
3.	A list of all computer software, software licenses, and the transfer restrictions, requirements or terms for continuation for the Practice, if any? (See APA Page XXXX)	_____	_____
4.	Copies of all Practice policies, regulations and bylaws? (See APA Page XXXX)	_____	_____
5.	Copies of all Practice contracts, leases, and other outstanding obligations? (See APA Page XXXX)	_____	_____
6.	All professional or other employee contracts, policies, handbooks and/or the specific terms and conditions of all Practice employee salaries and benefits? (See APA Page XXXX)	_____	_____
7.	Copies of all managed care contracts of the Practice in effect between Seller and any third party, if any? (See APA Page XXXX)	_____	_____
8.	The specific space, terms and conditions and/or copies of any leases of any third party on the Property and 2 years' worth of utility expenses on the Property and Premises? (See APA Page XXXX)	_____	_____
9.	Verified copies of all financial records and documents of the Practice along with a certification that such records and documents are true and accurate? (See APA Page XXXX)	_____	_____
10.	Purchaser is entitled to, is hereby transferred, and has received delivery of all "Patient Records," computers, software (licenses, passwords & keys), telephones, telephone numbers, yellow page adds, generic practice names, website access, email addresses, all other miscellaneous tangible and intangible non-cash assets, and is familiar with work in progress? (See APA Page XXXX)	_____	_____
11.	Seller has provided Purchaser a review schedule and list of all employees and copies of contracts or certification of contract terms a of the Practice Closing Date? (See APA Page XXXX)	_____	_____

	Practice Closing Tasks On Asset Purchase Agreement Dated	IF AGREED Insert Initials	
13.	Seller hereby certifies, represents and warrants that Seller has paid all outstanding contractual obligations and paid all employee salaries and benefits as required through the Practice Closing Date? (See APA Page XXXX)	_____	_____
14.	Seller hereby certifies, represents and warrants that Seller has lawfully terminated each of its employees and contractors as of the Practice Closing Date and has or will pay all related employment and social security taxes, benefits, and insurance premiums accrued as of the Practice Closing Date? (See APA Page XXXX)	_____	_____
15.	Seller hereby certifies, represents and warrants that there are no full or partial patient pre-paid fees as of the Practice Closing Date? (See APA Page XXXX)	_____	_____
16.	Seller hereby certifies, represents and warrants to Purchaser to use commercially reasonable efforts to transfer Seller's personal goodwill to Purchaser? (See APA Page XXXX)	_____	_____
17.	Purchaser has been provided an agreed upon list and the amount of accounts receivable either sold or unsold by Seller? (See APA Page XXXX)	_____	_____
18.	Seller hereby certifies, represents and warrants that there are no leases and other contractual arrangements that are not assignable or transferable without the consent of the counterparty? (See APA Page XXXX)	_____	_____

IF EITHER PURCHASER OR SELLER HAVE NOT AGREED AND INITIALED ANY OF THE NUMBERED ITEMS LISTED ABOVE CLOSING SHALL NOT OCCUR UNLESS A NEW AGREEMENT AND COMPLETION DATE ARE AGREED UPON BELOW.

	Practice Closing Tasks On Asset Purchase Agreement Dated XXXXX	IF AGREED Insert Initials	
		Purchaser	Seller
1.	The new agreed upon completion date for item No. ___ above is _____, 202__..	_____	_____
2.	The new agreed upon completion date for item No. ___ above is _____, 202__..	_____	_____
3.	The new agreed upon completion date for item No. ___ above is _____, 202__..	_____	_____
4.	The new agreed upon completion date for item No. ___ above is _____, 202__..	_____	_____
5.	The new agreed upon completion date for item No. ___ above is _____, 202__..	_____	_____

The last few documents hold a lot of value, so we will dig through them and explain why they're needed and important.

Closing Statement

This document is great because at the end of the joint meeting when all of the contracts are finalized and signed, you will need to ensure that the money changes hands in a very simple and clear manner. The closing statement is the simplest version of that. Typically if the bank or buyer comes with a check, then the check is taped to the closing statement and then 2 extra photocopies are made. One photocopy is then given to each of the parties, and the check then goes home with the seller.

Associate Dentist Employment Agreement

On certain occasions, the selling dentist is staying on with the new owner for a period of time to aid in the transition, or to wind down their last few working years with you as the owner/manager. In these scenarios, the dentist employment agreement is useful as a template to rehire the selling doctor. This sample agreement has both a clause about minimum base salary as well as percentage of production. Have your attorney work up whatever option is best for your scenario.

Closing Checklist

One of the most helpful documents included in our acquisition legal paperwork is the closing checklist. On this checklist is every major point that needs to be discussed or signed on closing day. It also gives a place if something is not as expected on closing day, you can add it to the last section and get to it at a date of your choosing in the very near future. In our experience, this has been very helpful and useful as a way to keep the signing ceremony on track.

Final Notes

It cannot be stated clearly enough that these documents are a guidepost for you as you proceed towards an acquisition. A good attorney can take these and edit as necessary to make them work in your situation, but it is never a good idea to do this without legal help. We hope that these have given you a good start to the process and will allow you less stress as you work towards the day you transition in as the new owner.

Notes:

Chapter 6

Transition Day

Congratulations! You have found the right office to purchase in a location that you enjoy and where the economics work out well. You have negotiated an acceptable price, and now it's signing day. Prior to this you will think you have done a bunch of hard work, but trust us when we say the journey has only just begun. The truth is that the rubber meets the road the moment you sign the contract and the keys figuratively, and literally, get handed over to you.

Now we will go through all the major items that will happen during the transition day and week, in a relatively time-appropriate order.

1. Signing Process
2. Meeting with the Team
3. Transitioning the Team
4. Communication with Patients

Signing Process

Usually this happens at a bank, accountants office, or title company when all available parties are present to sign documents, pass over keys, and accept or give payment for assets. This process is usually jubilant, and most of the time everyone is very excited to have consummated the deal. Usually by this point, the documents are all in order, but it's never a bad idea to be over-prepared. The documents in the previous chapter called 'Closing Checklist and Issues' is a great way to make sure everyone stays on the same page with everything that needs to be signed and completed prior to executing all documents.

Meeting with the Team

Sometimes a selling doctor is very open with the team prior to the sale, and in these instances you will get to meet the team before closing. However, when this is not the case, you will only meet them *after* you own the business. At this time, the emotional stress of having the business sold can be a lot for the team, and so don't be surprised with a varying range of emotions. It is usually best if the selling doctor can actually set up a meeting with the team and introduce you to them.

Whenever the first meeting occurs, either before or after the sale,, it is always best to remember to be sensitive to the stress and uncertainty that the team is likely encountering. Rule #1: Bring a gift. The gift cannot totally change the situation, but is common courtesy and will help get you started on the right foot. The gift can either be food or something meaningful to give to each team member. Remember: You are now stepping into the shoes of the beloved former doctor, and that almost nothing will satisfy the normal human aversion to change.

During this first meeting you will want to balance the legal side of the meeting with the emotional side. Of course the former doctor will have to let all of the team know that they are now no longer employed by their former company. There will need to be paperwork distributed to them to inform them that they are now terminated, and potentially rehired by you. (The former employer/dentist should have paid them for their last time period as well as paid out all remaining benefits.)

On the personal side, they will want to know more about you. They will be interested in how you practice, what procedures you do, and the type of person you are. They will likely have many, many questions. This is understandable and expected. However, if they ask questions that you simply do not know the answer to yet. Write them down, and make sure to get back to them at a later date with an answer. They may also ask questions that you might not feel comfortable answering just yet. In these cases set up a time to speak to the person asking the questions to address it privately. Usually a large team meeting is the best way to start the process, but usually it will also take individual meetings that first day to address all other concerns.

Transitioning the Team

After the legal asset transition is complete, it is up to you to handle the next steps from the legal perspective. In many cases, it is appropriate to rehire the entire group, therefore having some of the paperwork ready for that is necessary. You should have their 'Termination and Rehire Letter' covered in the previous chapter already filled out and ready to go. Hopefully each team member will sign it and are grateful to keep their jobs with your new entity, but of course this is not always the case. For a variety of different reasons, some employees may not accept your employment offer. These scenarios happen, it's part of doing business, so try not to take it personally.

There are also scenarios when it is best not to rehire anyone and to start fresh with a new team. When you are unsure who is worth retraining, it is best to meet with the team as a group first, and then quickly move to meet with each team member individually to assess whether they will fit your practice's vision. This process must be handled carefully as tensions are usually high once the 1-on-1 meetings begin. If you take this route, then after all terminated team members are gone, you can then have a more long-form meeting with the remaining team members.

There are also times when you might want to consider trial employment. In these cases you can announce that you are going to keep everyone on for 30 days to ascertain whether they will be a good match for the new culture. The narrative can sound something like,

> *"We truly want you all to stay and work out, but we know that not all team members will enjoy working in a new environment with new stressors and demands. And that's ok.*

Over the next 30 days, we will perform a working interview. At the end of the 30 days, we will then re-offer you a permanent position within the company if warranted. If the relationship between me as the employer and you as an employee isn't going to work out, we should know pretty quickly. Honestly, if it's not a good fit, we should end it as soon as possible so that we can help you find a place that is a better fit for you."

Truth is, there is usually a lot of turnover during an acquisition. Addressing the future turnover up front sets the stage for open communication and clear expectations. However you decide to handle your workforce during the transition, it is always wise to consult an HR company or labor attorney prior to letting anyone go.

Clarity is key during this transition. The big items to explain to the team are that they are no longer working for the former company, they have been terminated, and they are being offered new employment with your company. While it looks like the same office, with the same co-workers, and the practice might even have the same name, it is important to remind them many times that they are now part of a new company. You will have different benefits, different rules, and different expectations.

As they start new employment with you, you will want to give them the customary documents that you'd give any employee on their first day:

- Employee Handbook
- Job descriptions
- Onboarding Packets

Check out Dental Success Network's website, or the Dental Operations Manual by DSN, for full examples of the above documents. These documents, of course, will not be an exact match to what these employees do on a daily and weekly basis. This is understandable, and can be approached as follows:

"I know that this job description does not match your daily tasks identically, but please look it over and use it as a guide as to the format that we'd like to model your job description after. We can work together to create one specific to your position."

Encouraging each team member to write their own job description and procedural frameworks is a powerful way to help them to take a little initiative, and see that their future job will be centered around accountability and checklists rather than pure top-down leadership.

Setting a tone of 'systemization' and accountability from day one might be a big departure from how they were led in the past, but it should be understood that this is how things will be structured going forward. To increase the likelihood of success as the new owner make sure to be empathetic to the change they are going through, and to connect with them on a personal level to better understand their concerns and motivations.

Below is an example of a Hygiene Onboarding packet. These types of documents will help your new employees understand the level of systemization that you wish to see, as well as your expectations for their position.

Dental Hygienist
Handbook

Grain Acres Dental

(Adapted from Dr. Summer Kassmel of Castle Peak Dental, Vail Colorado. Dr. Kassmel is a Blackbelt Coach in Dental Success Institute and also sells a Dental Assisting curriculum through Rocky Mountain Dental Assisting Schools)

Grain Acres Dental

Hygiene Handbook

Table of Contents

Other Documents to be given:
- Employee Handbook
- Clinical Calibration Book
- Tech Systems

Job Description

Grain Acres Dental Core Values:

- Fantastic guest experience
- Always be improving
- Hungry & Humbly confident
- Have each other's backs

The ideal hygienist is:

- Friendly and outgoing
- Dedicated to outstanding customer service
- Gentle with clinical applications
- Organized
- Team Player
- Excellent communicator with staff and patients
- Honest
- Compassionate
- Great with patient education that gives ideal options
- Thorough (Both with explanations and with oral hygiene)
- Respectful of the patient and doctor's time
- Helps patients feel comfortable and confident in their dental care
- Passionate about their job
- Reviews schedule and helps to recognize any inefficiencies
- Energized to hit daily, weekly, and annual goals chosen by the team

Summary: The Dental Hygienist is responsible for patient data collection and documentation, patient education, and the delivery of preventive and periodontal dental treatment as part of the dentist-directed oral hygiene team.

Essential Duties and Responsibilities:

- Ability to take digital X-rays, use intra-oral camera
- Provide quality patient service by delivering thorough patient care, effective communication and personal attention in a gentle and caring manner.
- Assess and plan appropriate dental hygiene care including prophylaxis, scaling and root planing, debridement, periodontal maintenance and adjunct services.
- Complete dental hygiene procedures utilizing hand and mechanical scalers with a high degree of technical skill, and with little patient discomfort
- Conduct a general oral health screening including relevant medical history for each patient and communicate findings to the Dentist.
- Provide accurate and concise patient record charting and complete database information to allow the Dentist to determine the appropriate treatment plan for the patient.
- Provide topical anesthetic and administer nitrous oxide to patients under general supervision by the Dentist.

- Educate patients on proper oral hygiene.
- Responsible for individual professional growth through internal and external training opportunities and continuing education requirements to maintain licensure.
- Set-up and prepare dental hygiene equipment and instrumentation in accordance with established regulations and office guidelines.
- Accurate and timely reporting of all procedures complete with proper documentation in the patient management system program.
- Maintain a clean work environment and dental equipment to meet OSHA and Center for Disease Control sterilization and infection control regulatory standards.
- Adhere to confidentiality, State, Federal, and HIPAA laws and guidelines with regard to patients' records.
- Communicate effectively and develop a strong working relationship with the Dentist and promote teamwork through cooperative and professional behaviors.
- Support business goals by utilizing schedules effectively and supporting the practice revenue objectives.
- Follow and demonstrate commitment to Capital Dental policies, professional expectations, clinical service excellence, and outstanding patient service.
- Other duties as assigned.

Qualifications: To perform this job successfully, an individual must be able to perform each essential duty satisfactorily. The requirements listed below are representative of the knowledge, skill and/or ability required. Reasonable accommodations may be made to enable individuals with disabilities to perform the essential functions.

Education and/or Experience:

- Associate's Degree or Bachelor's Degree in Dental Hygiene required.
- Registered Dental Hygiene licensure in Nebraska is required.
- Current CPR certification required. (If elapsed Capital Dental will set up a time to renew)

Knowledge, Skills and Abilities Required:

- Knowledge of Federal, State and clinic regulations and guidelines for the provision of dental services.
- Ability to operate standard dental equipment including Cavitron, X-ray, Dental Chair and Unit, Sterilizers, Hand Scalers, Curettes and handpieces.
- Strong patient care skills.
- Able to multitask and handle multiple business and workplace changes that may arise.
- Able to communicate clearly and effectively orally and in writing.
- Able to work well on a team and independently.
- Able to perform work with attention to detail.
- Demonstrated ability to maintain a safe and healthy environment for patients and co-workers.
- Ability to respond professionally in stressful situations.
- Possess critical thinking, logic and reasoning skills to identify the strengths and weaknesses of alternative solutions, conclusions or approaches to problems.

<u>Physical Demands:</u>

While performing the duties of this job, the employee is frequently exposed to moving mechanical parts, fumes or airborne particles, risk of electrical shock and risk of radiation. Manual dexterity to operate equipment for proper cleaning and examination. Requires visual and hearing acuity corrected to normal range. Specific vision abilities required by this job include close vision, distance vision, peripheral vision, depth perception, and ability to adjust focus. With or without the aid of assistive devices: mobility, reaching, bending, ability to independently support the weight of an average person, grasping, fine hand coordination, pushing and pulling, and finger/hand dexterity to handle computer, dental and other equipment. Must be able to tolerate prolonged sitting. The physical demands described here are representative of those that must be met by an employee to successfully perform the essential functions of this job. Reasonable accommodations may be made to enable individuals with disabilities to perform the essential functions

Checklists to be Proficient In:

- Daily Checklists for Hygiene
- Phone Skills and Scripts
- Greeting and Start Appointment Flow
- End of Appointment Flow
- Clinical Charting and Treatment Planning Organization
- Presenting Issues/Treatment the Doctor Might Diagnose
- Scheduling next appointment (6-month recall or tx in doctor's schedule)
- Sterilization
- Downtime Schedule maintenance
- Office Cleaning
- Take IO Pictures with IO Camera
- Take Pictures with Extra-Oral Camera
- Take IO Radiographs
- Take Pano/CBCT

- Daily Checklist for Hygiene

Hygienist Daily Checklist

Name_____ Date_____

MORNING CHECKLIST	☐ Turn on all lights, x-ray machines (including pano) in tx rooms/sterilization center/lab ☐ Turn on TV/music in tx rooms ☐ Set up for first appointment ☐ Check room for full day of supplies ☐ Restock rooms if necessary ☐ Make up trays on clean side of sterilization ☐ Check appointments for that day to see if Xrays needed ☐ Check appointments to see for needed treatment ☐ Check schedule for any conflicts/questions – prep for A.M. Huddle

DOWN-TIME CHECKLIST	☐ Call any patients to make sure schedule is full - MOST IMPORTANT ☐ Check other Doctors/Hygiene schedules for efficiency/rooms ☐ Sharpen instruments ☐ Check to make sure sterilization is all up to speed ☐ Check 1 day/1 week schedule, address any issues ☐ Restock rooms as needed ☐ Go through office cleaning checklist ☐ Ask front desk to help with Recall List and other duties

END OF DAY CHECKLIST	☐ Check schedule 1 day ahead - check for interferences/problems ☐ Make sure all rooms are wiped down and ready to set up the next morning ☐ Turn off TV & comp. screen, mouse and keyboard ☐ Suction all lines with Purevac ☐ Restock rooms ☐ Run instruments through the Ultrasonic/package ☐ Load Autoclave with dirty instruments ☐ Package any dirty instruments that have gone through the Ultrasonic and will not fit in the Autoclave, to be loaded in the morning ☐ Prep for Morning Huddle with Route Slips ☐ Make sure all notes are done- run incomplete procedure notes report ☐ Production $_____/ Goal $_____ (Run production report and sign off) ☐ Fluoride at 90% of patients ☐ Sweep Rooms and remove trash ☐ Shut off pumps (last person to leave)

Signature of Manager: _____

Hygiene Morning Huddle Prep									
Appt Time	Pt. Name	Exam Needed	Plus Tx Opportunity	Recare Sched/Fam Needed	X-rays Needed	Notes	Fl-	$$	Re-Appoint
		Y / N							
		Y / N							
		Y / N							
		Y / N							
		Y / N							
		Y / N							
		Y / N							
		Y / N							
		Y / N							
		Y / N							

    a. Daily Checklist is to be fully completed in AM and PM Sections

    b. Downtime duties are to be completed between patients and throughout the middle of the day

    c. Morning Huddle Sheet is to be done either the morning before patients, or previous day

- Phone Skills and Scripts
  - a. Phones should always be answered within the first 3 rings
  - b. Physically Smile before answering so that your voice intonates warmth
  - c. 'Thank you for Calling Example Dental, this is _____, how may I help you?"
  - d. Follow the 3 E's: Empathy, Energy, and Edification
  - e. Scripts for the 7 major categories of phone calls can be found in the Operations Manual
- Greeting and Start Appointment Flow
  - a. Have Route Slip with you to remember name/appointment/details
  - b. Greet patient at the door to the waiting room, close door behind you/them
  - c. Show them where bathroom is, checkout, CBCT Technology, and then proceed to room
  - d. Once in room, point out relaxation/technology (Nitrous for $5, TVs on Ceiling, music)
  - e. Remind them of time allotted for the procedure, ask if they have next appointments
- End of Appointment Flow
  - a. Make sure all treatment is completed in OpenDental (Check w/ Doctor for accuracy)
  - b. Remove patient bib and offer facial wipe if necessary
  - c. Taking Payment in the Treatment Room- follow CC protocol

- d. Otherwise walk up to front desk to take payment if complicated
- Clinical Charting and Treatment Planning Organization
  - a. Understand OpenDental entering existing conditions
  - b. Enter in Treatment plan
  - c. Understand ordering the treatment plan
  - d. Make sure fees are generally correct with insurance or membership plan
- Presenting Issues/Treatment the Doctor Might Diagnose
  - a. Highlight issues you see on x rays or intraorally
  - b. Get to know the doctor's tx planning style so you know what they will diagnose in certain scenarios
  - c. Educate the patient and discuss resolutions (tx needed) so they are prepared when the doctor comes in to diagnose
  - d. Refer to **Example Dental Clinical Calibration Manual** for more details on treatment style
- Schedule Next Appointment
  - a. Schedule Recare for 3,4,6 months
  - b. Make sure recare schedule is appropriate in the 'Family' Module
  - c. If tx is needed, prioritize and know general times for specific appointments
  - d. Schedule needed tx if time allows
- Sterilization
  - a. Ensure that sterilization and lab are clean and that there is no backlog of instruments
  - b. Ultrasonic is emptied of all instruments
  - c. Instruments are bagged and put into sterilizer
  - d. Sterilizer is started if close to full
  - e. Completed sterilizer is emptied of all clean instruments
  - f. Use the Operations Manual picture as a guide
- Downtime Schedule maintenance
  - a. Make sure to call patients on the unscheduled list to fill open holes
  - b. Move patients around to maximize schedule for daily goals
  - c. Make sure schedule moving forward is correct for time and availability
- Room Cleaning Checklist
  - a. Clean floors and countertops, chairs, (chair wheels as needed)
  - b. Take out all trash in treatment rooms and offices
  - c. Take out recycling as needed
  - d. Clean employee Break room
  - e. Vacuum all carpeted areas
- Take IO Pictures with IO Camera
  - a. Use blue DY-80 Camera
  - b. Make sure it's plugged into the USB and has sleeve on it
  - c. Sometimes button on camera doesn't work, so click to take with mouse
  - d. Take pictures as needed and then number them with correct tooth number
- Take Pictures with Extra-Oral Camera
  - a. Open up iphone, go to IOCSnapshot App
  - b. Go to OpenDental Images Folder
  - c. Click the button for iPhone & Aircard
  - d. On the phone the computer ID should pop up on the menu, click it
  - e. Take photos as necessary
  - f. Once back on the computer, label all photos with teeth numbers
- Take IO Radiographs

a. See Operations Manual for specific exposure settings on the handheld x ray machine and Apteryx (digital x ray software) how to document
b. Make sure you have the correct arms, tabs, and rings for the particular type of x ray you wish to take
    i. Posterior PA's- Yellow tab with curved arm and yellow ring
    ii. Anterior PA's- Blue tab with curved arm and yellow or blue ring
    iii. Bitewings- Vertical or Horizontal tab with straight arm and red ring
    iv. FMX- Gray universal ring can be used for PA's and bitewings.
c. Materials Needed
    i. Handheld x ray machine
    ii. Sensor with barrier
    iii. Tabs/rings/arms for type of x ray desired
    iv. Lead apron
d. Know ahead of time which x rays your patient is due for, take accordingly
    i. FMX- All new patients
    ii. Pano- Every 5 years (check ins. frequency, could be less)
    iii. BW- Every 12 months
        1. Check for bone levels, interproximal decay
        2. Possibly less if they have a low caries rate
        3. Higher or lower depending caries risk assessment
    iv. PA-
        1. Anterior teeth at one of the first few visits
        2. Posterior teeth if problems
        3. Implants/Endo - ever year

Key Production Indicators (KPIs)

At Example Dental, we want to hold ourselves to an internal scorecard of being the BEST we can be. Aligning with our core values, we have a few KPIs that are important indicators of 'playing the game at a high level'.

Cheat Sheet for Hygiene (3.3X) @ $37/Hr	
Hrs	**GOAL**
5	$872.14
6	$1,046.57
7	$1,221.00
8	$1,395.43
8.5	$1,482.64
9	$1,569.86

This takes hourly pay X 3.3 X Hours of the day. It also takes into account a 30% Insurance discount. This is very close to true goal.

WIGs for 2021
- Achieve 500 Google Reviews by End-of-Year 2021
- 1,200 New Patients for the year 2021
- $1.5 Million in Revenue for 2021

KPIs for Hygiene to help achieve these goals:
- Net production is 3.3X Hourly Wage
  - If your hourly wage is $35/hour...your goal is to produce $115.50 per hour after all deductions
  - On average this is highly achievable with a typical prophy, exam, and 50% of patients taking BW or 2 PA, Fluoride helps as well
- 90% of Patients getting Fluoride
  - Typically almost all patients can be helped by getting topical fluoride treatment
  - If they fall into a moderate or high risk caries, or other applicable condition, Fluoride should be a recommended treatment
- 90% of patients scheduled for their recare appointments
  - If patients aren't scheduled, they are likely to fall out of our practice and they may go for years.
  - Getting an appointment on the books is of great importance
- 85% Treatment Acceptance Rate
  - We are on the conservative side of the spectrum at Capital Dental
  - Treatment recommended by Doctors in the Urgent or Important Category need to be scheduled
  - Hygiene can help achieve this by educating patients about their condition to be an adjunct voice of the doctor
- 5-Star Google Reviews & New Patients
  - Of course the highest recommendation from any patient is to send friends or give a nice Google Review
  - Hygienists can help by mentioning the giveaways that we have at each office for reviews
  - Also giving out wine, t-shirts, or other gifts can bring forth increased reviews or referrals

30/60/90 Day Goals for Hygiene

1=Rarely; 2= Sometimes;3=Sometimes;4=Mostly; 5=Always

30 Day Goals

_____ Clock in/Clock out

_____ Arrive 15 minutes before morning huddle

_____ Complete Morning Huddle Prep on All Patients for that day

_____ Answer phones in accordance with core values and guidelines

_____ Greet patients and give office tour correctly

_____ Complete Daily Checklists with no error

_____ Able to take Pano / CBCT individually

_____ Able to take IO Pics and IO Radiographs

_____ Able to answer the phone and answer simple questions

_____ Stay on time with appointments

_____ Complete Daily Notes accurately

_____ Follow Hygiene Protocol

_____ Read through the Clinical Calibration Manual for Capital Dental

Areas I feel I excel:

_____
_____
_____

Areas I feel I need help or additional training:

_____
_____
_____

Date Scheduled to Review: _____

Additional training to be completed by: _____

60 Day Goals

_____ Be able to do all 30 day tasks with no supervision

_____ Prioritize daily tasks

_____ Record/Track Daily Production (3.3X Hourly Wage is Goal)

_____ Record and Track Fluoride Production

_____ Keeping sterilization clean and on schedule

_____ Know the schedule and prioritize accordingly
_____ Taking payments in the treatment room

Areas I feel I excel:

_____
_____
_____

Areas I feel I need help or additional training:

_____
_____
_____

Date Scheduled to Review: _____

Additional training to be completed by: _____

90 Day Goals
_____ Do all above 60 day tasks with no supervision
_____ Review Treatment Plans and Schedule
_____ Maintain a Reappointment rate of 85% or higher
_____ Add in Same Day TX (sealants/fluoride) whenever possible
_____ Stay up to date on perio protocol to ensure billing out properly
Areas I feel I excel:

_____
_____
_____

Areas I feel I need help or additional training:

_____
_____
_____

Date Scheduled to Review: _____

Additional training to be completed by: _____

Departmental Assessment Form- Hygienist

Name_____   Date_____

1= Never, 2= Rarely, 3= Sometimes, 4=Mostly, 5= Always

I get my patients back for their treatment within ten minutes of their scheduled appointment time.

1	2	3	4	5

I ask three non-dentally related questions to each patient prior to discussing dental treatment and note it in the designated area.

1	2	3	4	5

I do my best to build rapport and show empathy, courtesy, and compassion to each patient.

1	2	3	4	5

I give a tour of the office and point out high-tech and relaxing features.

1	2	3	4	5

I take a FMP with each patient that I treat at least once a year (every 6months for Perio)

1	2	3	4	5

I take intraoral photos and all appropriate radiographs prior to the doctor's arrival.

1	2	3	4	5

I review the photos and discuss potential restorative treatment with the patient prior to the doctor's arrival.

1	2	3	4	5

The explorer and mouth mirror are clean and conveniently placed on the tray prior to doctor's arrival.

1	2	3	4	5

I educate patients in the proper use of appropriate dental products that would serve to improve their oral health.

1	2	3	4	5

I give oral hygiene instructions to each patient.

1	2	3	4	5

I do the CRAP Handoffs….and use the orange card to speed up Doctor response time.

1	2	3	4	5

I alert the doctor to potential treatment that was discussed with patient.

1	2	3	4	5

I alert the patient to potential treatment that the doctor will most likely treatment plan..

1	2	3	4	5

I take bitewings and full mouth radiographs according to the appropriate interval.

1	2	3	4	5

The patient's most current radiographs, treatment notes and any pending treatment are ready for doctor's review when the exam begins.

1	2	3	4	5

I use the new routing slips to their full potential

1	2	3	4	5

I polish every patient following cleaning, debridement, SRP.

1	2	3	4	5

I floss every patient following polish.

1	2	3	4	5

I keep my treatment room(s) clean and organized.

1	2	3	4	5

I communicate with clarity and respect with all other members of the team.

1	2	3	4	5

I edify doctor and staff to patients whenever possible.

1	2	3	4	5

I review my production reports nightly to ensure all of my procedures are billed out under me.

1	2	3	4	5

I hit my daily production goal with 96% success.

1	2	3	4	5

I help with sterilization, numbing doctor patients, and helping the back office as often as possible.

1	2	3	4	5

I understand the goal of 3.3 X Hourly pay.

1	2	3	4	5

Accountability Agreement: Hygienist

I_____, understand that my responsibilities as a
Hygiene Department include, but are not limited to the duties listed on the
following documents:

1. Hygiene Job Description
2. Hygiene Daily Task Sheet
3. Hygiene Appointment Protocol

Additionally I am aware of Grain Acres Dental's core values as listed below and
will strive to conduct myself in a manner consistent with these values:

Grain Acres Dental Core Values:

- Fantastic guest experience
- Always be improving
- Hungry & Humbly confident
- Have each other's backs

Team Member Signature:_____Date:_____

Practice Owner (CEO)

Signature:_____ Date:_____

Personal Connections

Connecting with your team and letting them know that you care about their personal and professional development is an important aspect of building a strong culture. This can take a long time in normal daily experiences, but we accelerate the process by utilizing an activity that should take about an hour for a team of 6-12 people. We call it the "Focus on You" exercise.

Here is the exercise:

1. Print a page for each team member, and give them a writing surface and allow them to complete the exercise.
2. You lead the activity with this direction:
   a. "This exercise will help all of us get to know each other better, even for those who have known each other for years. For the next few minutes, please fill out the top line yourself quietly. Lets begin."
   b. "In the top Line, fill out what you like to be called. Sometimes your name is Thomas, but you liked to be called Tom. And you might hate it if someone calls you Thomas or Tommy....so write down exactly what you would like to be called." (Wait about 25 seconds)
   c. "In the next line put what you get paid to do. This can be your job description, or really the true essence of what you do." (Wait about 45 seconds, or until everyone is done)
   d. "In the next box, write down "Hot button" topics that you enjoy reading about, talking about or studying. This can be sports, hobbies, health, kids, etc. What is it that 'lights you up' and energizes you?" (Wait about a minute, or until everyone is done)
   e. "In the next box, write down one professional success and one personal success that you have achieved in your life." (Wait about a minute, or until everyone is done)
   f. "In the next box, write down one or two things that you do best. This could be associated with work, or something outside the office." (Wait about a minute, or until everyone is done)
   g. "In the next box, put two goals, one personal and one professional. This could be a long or short term goal.: (Wait about a minute, or until everyone is done)
3. After everyone has their top line filled out, you then pick someone to start with, maybe yourself. Read your answers aloud, and the others around the group will write down these answers onto their sheets. During the time when you're giving out your answers, no one else should talk or interrupt, and when you are completed, they may ask any questions that they have about any of your answers.
4. As you go around the group, you will see that this activity gets you to know a lot about people's hobbies, their wins, their goals, and will hopefully allow you to connect with them at a deeper more personal level.

Focus on You!

Name	What do I get paid to do?	Hot Buttons (Topics I like)	Successes: 1 Professional 1 Personal	What I do Best	Goals: 1 Professional 1 Personal
(You)					

Turnover

Realistically, you are likely to have a fair amount of staff turnover in the first 6 months of practice ownership. While the employees still come to the same building, they now have totally different expectations and a different boss. This stress and change usually leads to disaffection and people will look for a new start somewhere else. This is understandable and to be expected. Do your best to be prepared to onboard and train these employees to your systems, however know that even your best effort to keep them may still end in attrition.

After you have gotten your team up to speed with the new operational flow, the next step is to share the upgrades you have made with the patients. This will include a few things including

1. Letter to patients
2. Email to patients
3. Letter printed out and available at front desk
4. Scripting with Patients to address changes

Below are a few of the sample letters you can use as a template when addressing the improvements. Remember that this letter is discussed in the legal contracts, and is often a shared cost between the buyer and seller. It is also intended to be _for the sole advantage_ of the buyer. The biggest point to remember is that it needs to build credibility and trust in you as the new owner.

Typically it is printed on practice letterhead, but keep in mind that printing, folding and mailing thousands of letters can be cost and time intensive. In the past, we have done this manually with our own team, our own printers in the office, and have paid the 50-cent stamp rate. In the end, we burned through printer cartridges very fast, broke another printer, and took 3 evenings of work to accomplish. It was a nightmare. What's a better system? We encourage you to draft this letter on practice letterhead, and then hire a mail processor to actually print, fold, and mail this for you. Amazingly enough, it will likely cost about 55 cents per letter, due to bulk-mail savings rates on postage.

See below for example letters:

_____

Dear Patient,

Thank you for entrusting your dental care to me for more than 30 years. I am writing to tell you that I have decided to retire from my practice. After practicing for many years, I'm ready to step away. It has been a privilege for me to care for you and your families, which for some includes several generations.

It was my top priority to find the right person to take over the practice, and I am excited to say I have found the perfect match in Dr. _____. Due to his clinical skills and personality, I am sure you will be pleased to have him as your new dentist. He will assume responsibility for the practice on July 1st.

Dr. _____ was born and raised in CITY, and is a graduate of the University of STATE College of Dentistry. Over the past 5 years, he has performed dental mission work in Jamaica and routinely volunteers at the local homeless shelter clinic. He and his wife, _____ are enjoying their first year of marriage and are excited about this opportunity. I feel very confident having Dr. _____ take over my practice, and I am eager for you to meet him at your next dental appointment.

I expect a seamless transition with Dr. _____. He has the support of myself and my staff; all of whom are staying with the practice and are looking forward to seeing you and providing you with the level of care you have come to expect from the office.

I feel blessed to have had you as my patients and friends. Thank you for your loyalty and support. Although I will miss seeing you, I know you are in good hands with Dr. _____.

Sincerely,
Dr. John Q. Seller, DDS

To the best patients in the world,

After 4 years of dental school and 33 years of practicing dentistry, I have determined it is now time for the next chapter in my life, retirement. Although there are things I will miss, such as working with great coworkers and the interactions with many delightful patients, I anticipate the joys of more time spent with my wonderful wife, my children, my parents and now my two grandchildren. I look forward to more time for travel and time at the lake sailing, and the simple joys of gardening, yard work and cooking.

I feel very fortunate and in fact honored to have so many patients express their trust and confidence in me over the years. I have never taken that responsibility lightly. I realize the magnitude of that trust and faith and understand its significance. I do indeed feel honored. As many of you have seen, there have been changes at the office during the past year. Part of transitioning to retirement is to be sure those patients that have had faith and confidence in me are going to continue to be cared for and treated in a manner that best serves them. I am grateful that Dr. _____ has joined the practice to fill the void I leave. I believe she has not only the technical dental skills, but equally or perhaps even more importantly the perspective and caring attitude that serving the needs of the patient is paramount, and that it is their best interest that must be served. I have always believed that if you do what is right for the patient in a fair and honest manner most everything else falls into place. I know that Dr. _____ feels the same sense of devotion and responsibility and it is a great comfort to me to know that all my patients have the opportunity to continue with a very competent compassionate dentist whose values are in the right place.

Over the years I have seen many patients that started with my dad as far back as the sixties when he was on O Street. I have cared for their dental needs, seen them have children, cared for those children, watched them grow up, have children of their own, and yet again provided care for those children. It has truly been a joy, and I feel a closeness and a loyalty to them and again feel very honored to have been allowed that opportunity. Many of you I will miss and forever appreciate your confidence in me. I wish you all the best.

Sincerely,
John Q. Seller

While letters to each mailing address should include every household and will hopefully be received by most patients, there will still be patients that, for one reason or another, will not get the letter. Their address could have changed, or they might have just thrown away the letter. Since our goal is to inform every patient before they come in for their next appointment, we need to find a way to inform them.

We suggest that you will want to follow up the letter with an email. The timing of the email is important, because you will want the letter to hit their mailboxes prior to the email. In order to ensure this occurs, it's best to wait 4 to 5 days after sending the letter before sending out any email announcements.

The email announcement should be the exact same letter above, with links to the updated practice website where there might be more pictures and personal information about the new doctor and team.

Hopefully the letter and email will catch nearly 100% of all patients, but you will still likely see patients walk in the door and be shocked to learn that their beloved doctor has left! For these scenarios, you and your team will need to be prepared to both address it with a physical letter as well as a well rehearsed narrative.

To be prepared for this, have a stack of letters printed out at the front desk for the first 4-6 months of the transition.

The primary goal with a transition script, and printed letters at the front desk, is to build confidence and trust between the new doctor and the patient base. When a senior doctor leaves, the objective is to seamlessly pass on authority and goodwill to the new doctor, so that patients give the new doctor a try before leaving to go to another practice.

Below is a script your team can use as a framework for confirmation calls:
"Hello, this is Susie with Grain Acres Dental just calling to confirm Brian's appointment for 9 am tomorrow for a cleaning. We look forward to seeing you and just wanted to make sure that you received the news about the transition between Dr. Seller and Dr. Buyer. Dr. Seller hand picked Dr. Buyer to take over his practice and as of XXX date, things have been going

smoothly. Dr. Buyer is just the nicest person and very similar to Dr. Seller, we know that you will love him. Can't wait to see you tomorrow!"

In this message script, you hit the major points:

1. Confirmation of the appointment
2. Reminder of the transition that they have hopefully already received
3. Transfer of Trust between Dr. Seller and Dr. Buyer
4. "Assume the YES" that they will stay with the practice and continue care with you

You will likely encounter situations that will dictate modifying this script. These could include transitions that occurred due to doctor sickness or other emergent factors that may change the tone of the narrative. While it doesn't happen often, these situations do occur and team members may need guidance and preparation for these difficult conversations.

Here is a script for a patient who has arrived at the practice in person and is not aware of the transition:

Team:

Good morning Brian, we have you here for your 9 am cleaning. Has anything changed with your address or insurance?

Brian:

Nope, all the same.

Team:

Great, and did you hear the news about the doctor transition?

Brian:

No, is Dr. Seller gone?

Team:

Oh I'm sorry, we sent out letters and emails last month about the transition. In the past year, Dr. Seller started looking to retire and hand picked Dr. Buyer to take over care of his patients. Dr. Buyer's a very skilled doctor and all of our patients who have met him, love him. Everyone else is still here and you'll get to meet Dr. Buyer in just a few minutes!

Mitigating Post Transition Patient Attrition

One of the primary benefits of mastering patient communication is to mitigate attrition. Even though it may feel like overkill to send out letters, emails, and scripts for crucial conversations, it is important to control the narrative to as many patients as possible.

At this point, you might be wondering, what is an appropriate turnover rate during a transition? The truth is that each situation is variable and the percentage of patients who leave a practice in the first year can vary significantly amongst transitions. On average throughout all situations, however, the average typically falls between 70%-90% retention of patients throughout the first year.

To achieve the highest percentage possible, it pays to be extremely prepared. This preparation includes but is not limited to: excellent communication, a solid operational plan from you as the owner, and the ability to build trust and rapport quickly. If you can execute on all of these things well, you are likely to experience a smooth and successful transition.

A challenge that we often encounter when a new doctor takes over a practice from a late career dentist is a general trend of under diagnosed/undiagnosed dentistry. This manifests itself with very low periodontal treatment percentages in the hygiene department (AKA-"Bloody Prophies"); multiple "watches" on teeth that have active decay, and teeth that have been patched numerous times and need to be crowned.

There are many factors that lead to this phenomenon including but not limited to: diminished eyesight of a selling doctor, the departing doctor's unwillingness to have difficult conversations with long-time patients, and years or decades of performing clinical dentistry which may have led to apathy and burnout. When this pattern arises, it is important to take the appropriate steps to minimize patient attrition and following the transition and provide ethical and acceptable clinical care.

Treatment planning can be especially challenging when a patient base has been subjected to years of underdiagnosing and "supervised neglect". You might feel like every patient has large treatment plans that they are not expecting. Patients might push back against these treatment plans very hard because, "Dr. Seller never told me about these things." This happens in a large majority of transitions, and so it's good to plan on mitigating these interactions.

Effective communication and handling these situations delicately with the utmost professionalism could make the difference between 10% attrition and mass patient exodus following the transition. A great rule to live by throughout your dental career is to never speak negatively about another colleague to a patient. This is especially important when you take over a practice and begin interacting with the existing patient base.

Although there will certainly be times when you disagree with the previous doctor's diagnosis and treatment plans - and may even have to deal with subpar clinical outcomes, it is important to keep your comments to patients as positive as possible.

Keep in mind that there is a high likelihood that the patient base has genuine trust and affection for the previous doctor and being overly critical could very quickly erode the trust that you are trying to establish.

We recommend a conversation that sounds something like this:

"It looks like Dr. Jones did a great job caring for your smile over the years by patching several of your teeth and keeping them functional. It is really impressive that these fillings have lasted for x years. That really says a lot about Dr. Jones's quality work. As you can see though, *(at this point you can show intraoral pictures of the patient's teeth that need treatment)*, a few of these teeth are finally starting to break down. Another patch would weaken these teeth to the point that they'd likely break soon after. You have some other teeth that will eventually need some attention but here are the two that will need crowns immediately before we end up in a situation when they can no longer be fixed."

(OR)

"It looks like Dr. Jones and Sarah have done a good job keeping your teeth clean over the years and I see from your records that you have been doing your part by coming in consistently every 6 months for the last 5 years. Great job! After taking your gum measurements today, we saw quite a bit of bleeding and even a little bit of puss coming out of your gum tissues in these areas. (Good time to show intraoral pictures of bleeding and purulence.) These are actually areas where you have an active infection in your gum tissue. New studies have shown that this type of infection can lead to a host of overall health complications and tooth loss. The good news is, we now know that certain procedures that we perform at this office can eliminate this infection and decrease the risk of tooth loss and system health issues..."

Notice that there is always an effort to compliment the previous doctor and team members for the previous work that they have done, even if it needs to be replaced. It is also important to be careful not to overwhelm the patients with huge treatment plans right from the beginning of your tenure. Nothing causes a patient to leave a practice faster than a $25,000 treatment plan from a new dentist after the previous dentist just gave them a clean bill of dental health just six months earlier.

The other key is using the words, "What we now know". This implies that since Dr. Seller has left, something has changed in the way we treat dental disease. It doesn't negatively speak to Dr. Seller's treatment plans, but it says that now there is a new modality for treatment. It also implies the collective 'we', which means 'All of Dentistry'. When using this statement, it carries a lot of proverbial weight, as well as keeping the statements about the previous dentist positive. In summary, get good at saying, "What we now know..."

It's best to make modest recommendations and start the rebuilding process slowly. Overall, you should definitely let people know about every problem, but at first you might lean towards the most conservative treatments if possible. This might be, "I see a few dark cracks here that will probably need some treatment in the near future, but today I only see one that has active decay. The one with active decay will need a crown, however these others can be monitored for a little while if you are ok waiting on treatment for those teeth." If you go into these conversations with the right mindset, tact and professionalism, you'll be able to retain most of the patient base and build a solid foundation of trust that will eventually grow into a wildly successful practice.

Overall the transition process can be both invigoration and exhausting at the same time. Keep in mind that you are trying to establish yourself as a competent, compassionate and acceptable replacement for a doctor that has built trusting relationships for years. This is no small feat and many patients will initially view you with caution and skepticism. You are literally auditioning for a part.

Be kind, be patient and be professional, and you will build trust and credibility quickly.

In order to continue to move towards the vision of your ideal practice, we'll now cover some of the next key areas in a smooth transition.

Chapter 7

Technology after the Transition

In the weeks and months before a transition, you'll have a chance to thoroughly assess the technology and infrastructure of the practice. Hopefully with a good amount of presale analysis, you will get a good handle on the quality of the setup. Through the presale analysis, you'll also be able to identify which items are good for a few more years, versus what might need to be updated immediately. This analysis needs to happen for both hardware and software.

Where to Start

When you acquire a practice that already has a level of technology integration, the previous owner will most likely have a technology firm or person they are working with that has helped them to implement these systems. In this case, you will want to assess whether they are a good fit with you, and whether you will continue to use them. The questions below will help you analyze whether to continue working with this firm:

How to Hire or Evaluate a Technology Firm:

Insider Tips:
- Most tech salesmen have incentives that do not always align with your best interest
    - They make more money when you spend more money
- Do not sign up for a a high monthly recurring service
    - Try to find a service that charges per hour, typically $80-150/hour
- Get recommendations from other dental offices

Questions to ask the tech service:
- What are your preferred backup methods?
    - Methods should include cloud and local hard drives
- Ask for the number of clients they currently service and for referrals from existing clients- similar in size to your dental office
- Do you know how to set up an active directory from scratch?
- Do you have a list of clients?
- How do you structure recurring maintenance fees? What do you charge for (make sure they aren't nickel and dime-ing you on everything)?
- Do you have warranties on services provided?
- What are your holiday/after hours policies?
- What is your response/turnaround time on emergencies issues?
- How many employees do you have vs how many clients?

- What is your familiarity with dental tech?
- Is your software/service HIPAA compliant?
- If my server went down, how fast could you physically be on site?

After you find a firm that is a good fit for you and at the price point that you can afford, it is now necessary to work together with them on a plan to ensure that all technology is up-to-date or on a schedule to be updated.

Hardware Analysis and Upgrades

Server

If you are looking for a server, you will have to rely on your technology firm for guidance. These people should know exactly what to look for that appropriately matches your practice situation and plan for growth. If the server is relatively new and still reliable for a few years, you can move on to other items and update this technology at a later date. If the server is older or does not contain some of the backup capabilities needed however, then you might need to replace it immediately.

Here are a few good server options. On the lower-cost end, you could build something similar to this Intel Xeon 8 Server.

1	Intel Xeon 8 Core Business-Class Server	$ 2,865.00	$ 2,865.00
	Includes the following: Intel Xeon processor (8M Cache, 3.40 GHz), 16GB RAM, mirrored (RAID 1) 2TB Enterprise Ultra Fast hard drives, Intel RAID controller, internal DVDRW, integrated video, 2-port SuperSpeed USB 3.0 card, 1GB server network card & 1GB failover network card		

If you're looking to build a larger practice or possibly run multiple locations off of one server, however, you'll need to go with more capacity. In those cases, here's an option from another manufacturer, HP. On this server bid, you will see a few things that stand out that are important for organizations that want 99.999% up-time during the course of a year. (That means only approximately 4 hours of down-time per year.)

One of the first things to notice here is the dual power supply. In this scenario, there are two power sources to the entire server. If one were to break down, the server can still run on the other power supply, and a service technician could actually replace the second power supply at the appropriate time. The other option is the RAID controller and hard drives. A RAID setup is basically a constant backup between two hard drives, so that no matter what happens, your data is secure and

HP Proliant ML350 Gen 10 Brand Server

- Single Xeon Server Motherboard
- Tower Server Case
- 1 Intel Xeon Processor
- 32 GB Ram
- Dual Power Supply
- Raid Controller
- 2 – 960 GB SSD Hard Drives
  - Raid 1 Operating System
- Windows Server 2019
- 3 Year Warranty

Total System Price $4,700.00

lives on one or both of the hard drives. If a hard drive breaks and you need to replace it, you could actually pull the hard drive out while the server is still active and powered. Replacing a broken hard drive while the server is still on, the new hard drive will program and be able to upload all of the data from the functioning hard drive. Of course this does not mean that you should eliminate either local backups or cloud-based backups, but this is a great way to ensure that your server will be up and running for each day you need it to.

Workstations

In many acquisitions, the workstations are not ideal for the way the new doctor will be working. When this occurs, the new doctor may need to purchase all new workstations. Although this can be costly, it is worth it to ensure that the practice runs smoothly and that the technology aids rather than hinders the practice's process.

OptiPlex 3080 Micro

$639.00 $1,098.57
You Save $459.57 (42%)
Free Shipping

- 10th Generation Intel® Core™ i5-10500T
- Windows 10 Pro 64bit English
- 8GB, 1X8GB, DDR4 non-ECC Memory
- M.2 256GB PCIe NVMe Class 35 Solid State Drive

If you have to purchase new equipment, you will need to select the appropriate workstation computers for each operatory and desk in the office. While these can get quite expensive, we have found it is possible to control costs if you have the right practice management software. If you use OpenDental, for instance, you will find that you do not need a fancy PC to run the software. Even most imaging software can run using most workstations.

The computer shown to the left is the ideal practice computer for 90% of all uses (We will discuss CBCT uses below.) You should ideally have an i5 Intel Processor, 8 GB of Memory, and at least 256 GB hard drive. You could even go with a 500 GB hard drive, but that is not always needed. In general, $600-$850 per computer is sufficient. Also, remember that this does not include screens, mouse, keyboard, or any other accessories. Those will all be an additional expense and will need to be added to the budget.

If you plan to be doing a lot of CBCT and 3-D planning, you'll want to supercharge the workstations that you'll be using for those needs. In these instances, you will not want a 'small form factor' computer, because you may need to add a graphics card into the workstation in order to process the CBCT images. In general, you might need to spend about $2,000 per computer that can manage all of those computing needs.

Cone Beam CT Machine or Pano

Many selling doctors these days have not yet invested in a CBCT, due to the fact that this type of large investment late in a career usually yields a poor return-on-investment. If this is the case for the practice that you are purchasing, you might be considering a CBCT purchase to add to the office's technological offerings to enhance diagnosis and advanced clinical procedures.

One of the most economical ways to go about buying a CBCT for a new practice is to go with the company called Renew Digital. They are a national company that sells new and lightly used Panos and CBCT machines. They are extremely economical and they even send the computer and a technician to come install the equipment for you. In our experience, their customer service is excellent and the quality of their equipment is good.

Another option to consider is buying through group deals, like the ones we offer inside of the Dental Success Network. Our network has negotiated deals that are not published to the general public due to confidentiality agreements. You can also find new units with perks and warranties for the same price you will pay for a used unit - with a few options that may include a CBCT, computer, delivery and warranty for under $47,000. Check out the Dental Success Network Vendor Page for more details on these deals.

Practice Management Software

Once you start evaluating a few potential acquisitions, you are likely to come across the names of softwares that you may have never heard of before. This can raise the question of whether this is legitimate software or who the selling doctor purchased it from. Unfortunately, this is not an uncommon occurrence. We've even come across a selling doctor who created his own software that ran on a mid 90's PC with a 3.5" hard-disk.

Early on in your ownership journey, we encourage you to switch to a software that is well-known and respected in the industry and that you are comfortable and familiar with. While we know there is a lot of stress at the beginning of a transition, this is crucial for a few reasons. The main reason is that it will make your life easier and will allow you to practice with speed and efficiency. Switching can also mitigate the risk of embezzlement. According to some statistics, over 70% of dentists will be embezzled from at some point in their career. If you take over a practice and do not have a clue of how to navigate the software, your risk of embezzlement goes up astronomically.

While there are seemingly endless solutions for dental software, there are a few key players that have risen to the top of the market when you're looking for the main practice management platform. Eaglesoft, Dentrix, and OpenDental are all the main names in software, but one stands out for a few reasons.

We encourage, and are very open about our favorite practice management software, OpenDental. The primary reason is that it is the only software that is truly 'open'. While it is not free, it is very reasonably priced, bordering on absurdly cheap. The customer basically only pays for ongoing support fees. As of this writing, the support fees are around $180/month for the first 6 months, and drop lower after that. The company encourages you to vote on new features and updates the software often to fix bugs and add improvements. This crowd-sourced approach to development has made them a fan favorite for more than a decade. Here's something Dr. Addison has written about them and why they are steadily growing in market share:

We are at a tipping point. In the next few years, Open Dental is going to be the most widely used software in dental- and every other platform will be a minor player. Place your bets now. Why should we be so confident about this?

Nathan Sparks, the CEO of Open Dental (OD), knows that OD was a startup software created by a user who just wanted it to work for what they needed- particularly for his brother, and getting better reports. So why is this startup going to rule the marketplace? Here's my bet- Disruptive Innovation.

For those who haven't heard of the term, I suggest you Google it and watch Clayton Christensen- a Harvard Business professor and author of the book 'The Innovators Dilemma'. In the book, he explains how late entrants join a market and may offer a seemingly less quality product. They are often short on cash, resources, and potentially short on technology (Think Apple 1985). There are established players in the industry, that should be able to evolve, and they have all the cash and resources in the world (Think Microsoft).

The smaller players are able to maneuver the marketplace and technological curve much faster, and develop technology that tackles the needs of the customer more closely than large corporations- where the timeline for development may take many years.

From Dr. Christensen:

Characteristics of disruptive businesses, at least in their initial stages, can include: lower gross margins, smaller target markets, and simpler products and services that may not appear as attractive as existing solutions when compared against traditional performance metrics. Because these lower tiers of the market offer lower gross margins, they are unattractive to other firms moving upward in the market, creating space at the bottom of the market for new disruptive competitors to emerge.

In the case of OD, they started small- solving the problems of just Dr. Jordan Sparks' office. As a dentist, he knew what the dental industry actually needed. Rather than being driven by a large player like Henry Schein, Dr. Sparks could actually design software that solved the solutions on the ground level for all in the dental field. Oddly enough, he built it on a platform- SQL Server- that is easily attainable, and open-source. OD was also cheaper than all other options- both to start and in monthly costs. It started as a no-frills product, attacking the bottom of the market. This would make it seem like a low-quality product. That couldn't be further from the truth.

That's where Disruptive Innovation happens- at the 'seemingly' bottom of the market. For years, OD has functioned as a product that has no marketing team, and where users vote on the next feature to be added by the development team.

At first, Henry Schein and others didn't even pay attention to the fly on the wall. OD was just an upstart like all the rest. HS had the money, and they were building products like Dentrix Ascend. Dentrix Ascend was meant to be the next 'Sustaining Innovation' where all the data could be in the cloud. This has turned into a colossal failure, and they are seeing users flee as fast as they can 're-brand' and re-unveil the software.

OD has now morphed into a major, strong dental platform. Used by corporate groups that have over 120 offices, down to the boutique dental office on the street corner. The different services that can sync into the software make it usable by many varieties of users. The reporting features make it very clear, and you can easily add more 3rd party reporting software to get higher level reports.

Since 'Disruptive Innovation' is a theory only coined in the last 20 years, it's entertaining to see it happening in the dental field. One of the most special things- and why this theory applies accurately – is that OD asks it's users every day to Vote on features they want. They are crowd-sourcing the next developments that users want to see. Even the CEO is on a Facebook group asking and responding to the day-to-day issues that come up.

It is because of Disruptive Innovation that Open Dental is going to be the biggest dental software in the next few years.

- *Dr. Addison Killeen, Posted on Dental Success Network*

The above information points to a bit of the advantages of OpenDental over its competitors. But if we were to actually list it out, here are the big advantages, in order of priority:
1. You own your entire database and all the data within it, 100% control
2. Customization of the software to meet your needs
3. Modularity- meaning you have the ability to utilize many 3rd party softwares that work well with OpenDental's platform
4. The ability to use from the cloud if that is your preference
5. The ability to use many different imaging softwares
6. Lowest price

Remember to check out the end of the book to see the OpenDental Startup Guide Manual and links to videos on Dental Success Network.

Imaging

Occasionally, the practice already has an imaging software that works well with the sensors that they use. In these cases, we usually recommend that you keep this software and use those sensors as long as they deliver a high quality image. If they are not up to your standards, you may need to consider purchasing new sensors, or buying new sensors and software.

If you are looking for new imaging software, we encourage you to try out Apteryx XRayVision and XDR. We endorse these two softwares because they also work with many different brands of sensors. It cannot be stated enough, we will only recommend softwares that will work with many different types of hardware. Any software that locks you into one specific type of sensor is most likely a bad idea.

Insurance Verification

With the amount of activity that occurs at the typical dental office front desk, most team members report varying levels of stress on any given day. This feeling is heightened significantly during a transition. In order to lessen this stress, you may want to consider outsourcing certain administrative tasks like insurance verification. Two companies that we've found useful for insurance verification are Verrific and Verifixed. Verrific integrates well with OpenDental. To get an insurance breakdown on a patient, the staff member presses a button, sends it out, and within a day or two the information comes back in a fully uploadable file containing patient eligibility and insurance benefits.

Phones

If you are considering upgrading your phones, we've had good luck with Mango Voice. Mango Voice is the overwhelming favorite with the members of the Dental Success Network. You can switch over your old phone number, including phone hardware, for an all inclusive price of $25/phone/month. Usually when you pay for a full year upfront, you will get the phones for free. The system also allows for a digital fax line.

Mango also has a few features that work well with all the other softwares. The system integrates an app with your personal cell phone that allows you to call or receive calls from your office as if you were physically there. They also record all calls for quality assurance purposes.

Analytics

Analytics platforms can take pertinent data from the practice's management software and display it in a convenient user friendly interface. The largest in the industry is Dental Intelligence. This platform, usually called by their shortened name of Dental Intel, has an active web-based dashboard. The cost for Dental Intel is usually much higher, and we are not usually fans of expensive options.

Divergent Dental differs in that it does not have a web platform. This company sends out executive-style reports each morning, night, week-end and month-end. These reports can be emailed to anyone on the team, and are a succinct way to look at the practice from an analytical perspective. For less than $200 a month, this software is a DSN favorite.

HR and Payroll

Another software that is quite popular by the DSN members is Gusto- for payroll and HR needs. They are an extremely simple platform that can help you manage payroll, onboarding, and the

HR needs of the typical small business. They continually add functions and services on an almost monthly basis, including QSEHRA monthly healthcare stipends and 401(k) offerings.

For other Human Resources needs bordering on legal help, we also can recommend CEDR. Paul Edwards, the CEO of CEDR, has been helping dentists for many years, and we can personally attest to the success with their help navigating difficult employee situations. Dealing with the specific HR laws of your state may be a nightmare, but their team of attorneys that specialize in the dental field can help you as you deal with problems that arise.

Summary of all Softwares

In all, this 'stack' of softwares have become member favorites amongst DSN members for their cost, customer service and quality.
1. OpenDental
2. Apteryx or XDR
3. Mango Phones
4. Divergent Dental Analytics
5. Gusto
6. CEDR

As a new business owner you have the opportunity to choose the software that will enhance your practice management experience. Remember that in order to be successful in this transition, you do not have to reinvent the wheel. Following what many other experts have done and utilizing tools that they implement is going to be the fastest route to realizing your ideal practice. We hope that the notes in this chapter have helped introduce you to some efficiencies that will help you save time and money moving forward.

Chapter 8

Cash Flow and Insurances

In comparison to a Start Up, the financials of an Acquisition are favorable in the beginning because you have purchased an existing business that has a history and cash flow to sustain you. Regardless of this benefit, there is still stress during the transition. Credentialing with insurance companies, dealing with patients who are not trained to pay on the day-of-service, team and HR challenges, and countless other factors- all lead to a delayed cash flow in the beginning compared to what you can expect at the 3-6 month mark.

In order to understand the nuances of what is occurring in your practice from a financial perspective, it is important to know how to read and analyze different types of financial reports.

Reading Financial Reports

Your accountant will likely give you three reports each month. The first is called the Balance Sheet. Like it's name implies, it balances debt and assets. Here are some notes on the balance sheet for simple reference:
- Balance Sheet (Statement of Financial Position)
    - Point in time "snapshot" of financials
    - Shows-
        - What you own (Including Bank account balances)
        - What you owe (Loans and such)
        - Balance or financial position
    - You can have a negative "Net Worth"
    - Should grow (positive) over time
        - Successive statements identify trends

A sample balance sheet is displayed on the following page. In this example, all of the assets are listed at the top. In an acquisition, there will be a few key items including the assets that you purchased from the seller, as well as the 'goodwill' of the seller. Underneath that is the liabilities that you have with any bank. All loans are included in this second portion.

The final number is your net worth. This is the 'intangible' value of the practice at any point in time. This is purely a financial metric, and should really not be used for anything more than purely internal documents. This is not the 'value' of the practice in reality- which would be calculated by a totally different method.

ASSETS

    Cash/Cash Equivalents
        Checking Account 3,050
        Credit Union Savings   4,000
        Money Market Account   7,500
        Life Insurance Cash Value 8,000 22,550

    Personal Use Assets
        House 135,000
        Automobiles 28,000
        Personal Property   52,000   215,000

    Business Use Assets
        Dental Practice   200,000   200,000

    Investments
        Stock Portfolio   7,800
        Mutual Funds   6,500
        SEP / IRA's 18,980   33,280   470,830

LIABILITIES

    Short Term Liabilities
        Credit Card Balance   950   950

    Long Term Liabilities
        Auto Notes Balance 4,920
        Home Mortgage Balance 87,900
        Dental Practice   150,300
        Student Loans   100,000   343,120   344,070

NET WORTH   126,760

The next two statements are very similar. One is the Profit and Loss statement (income Statement or "P&L"), and the other is the cash flow statement. Here is a quick run-down on P&L.

- Income Statement (Profit and Loss Statement)
  - Shows money flow over time
    - Month, quarter, year or other
  - Indicates taxable income and expense items
  - Indicates a profit or loss
  - Two types-
    - Cash- what goes in versus what comes out

- Accrual- what goes in versus expenses that come out later (ex: lab fee)
  - **We think this is a more accurate method for managerial purposes**
- Real world
  - Shows what 'profit' was made, before the next three items:
    - Does not show actual cash in hand
      - This is on the balance sheet
    - Does not show debt payments
      - Remember that debt payments do not impact taxable profits

The income statement is the most useful statement that you will want to look at after the end of each month. Typically your accountant or bookkeeper will take about 10-12 days to go through all income and expenses to clean everything up. They should then send you a preliminary statement that you can review. In this process, you will want to double check all expenses to make sure that they are categorized correctly. Incorrect categorization of expenses will make your reports inaccurate and unhelpful.

The most detailed statement, which looks very similar to the Income statement, is the Cash Flow statement. Here are the quick notes on this type of document:

- Cash receipts and disbursements over a time
- SImilar to Income Statement and P&L
- All inflows equal all outflows

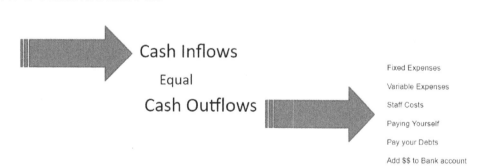

- Cash in:
  - Patient Payments
  - Insurance Payments
  - Borrowing
  - Savings
- Cash out:
  - Pay bills
  - Pay loans
  - Pay taxes
  - Personal living expenses

- Cash in must meet or exceed cash out
  - Non-payment
  - Bounced checks
- Shows spending patterns, savings, and investments

Below is a report by Custom Practice Analytics, a company founded by Dental Success Network Faculty member Jake Conway. This is the best visual representation of a cash flow sheet we have seen. It encompasses all expenses, where the money is going, and your take-home pay after all expenses have been paid. (https://custompracticeanalytics.com/)

Overall, having a good grasp on the financials of the practice from the beginning will be key to long-term success. Even if the numbers do not interest you, there is a huge value to being familiar with how money flows through the practice in order to be able to make managerial decisions as you grow.

Cash Flow in an Acquisition

As you transition the practice, collections may turn out to be lower than you expect during the first few months, and costs might be much higher than normal. This often occurs because of the need to purchase equipment and supplies. For this reason, plan for collections to be slightly lower and be prepared to use a bank line of credit or working capital loan to float your expenses if necessary. Collections will lag mainly due to insurance payments, credit card payments, and possibly slower patient payments. Any sort of payment plan may add to this trend.

If you have purchased the accounts receivable, you will have the benefit of immediate cash flow coming in from the collections of the selling doctor. This cash comes in handy when paying for supplies, payroll, and miscellaneous costs during the first few months of business ownership.

If you do not purchase the accounts receivable, you will most likely need to have that line of credit ready to use for a month or two until your collections catch up. To plan out potential costs during this time, you will need to forecast enough cash to cover for payrolls, rent, supplies, etc for those first two months.

Oftentimes, the selling doctor may have a drop in production and collections during the last few months of ownership. There are many potential reasons for this occurrence- the doctor may not wait to start cases he or she cannot finish or may just want to coast to the finish line. Regardless of the reason for the dip, it will most definitely affect cash flow in the first few months for the new owner. Whether this common scenario will play out will not typically be discovered until the transition is complete, as the seller is not always obligated to share financials with the buyer after an accepted offer has been made.

Always try to remember to anticipate the worst case scenario and be prepared for as many potential cash flow challenges as possible.

Upgrading the Practice

In most practice acquisitions, the buyer will need to make some degree of upgrades to the practice. This may include cosmetic upgrades or technical upgrades such as computers, servers, equipment, digital sensors, or a CBCT. These large expenses should have been planned already, and your bank should help finance these expenses from the beginning. The goal should be to finance as many upgrades over a few years to protect the cash flow in the first few months. If you are clear and organized about what capital is needed, most banks will be open to financing these improvements.

Overhead

Much like cash flow, overhead will almost always be elevated during the first few months following transition. In most cases this occurs because you will likely have a legacy staff cost and other costs that were held over from the selling dentist. But, as you start to get a handle on all of the vendors and costs within the practice, you will begin to pick and choose your preference for vendors and service providers. Over time your overhead should decrease as you manage expenses better.

Accounting/Bookkeeping Principles

During this transition, you may choose to start a new relationship with an accountant or bookkeeper to be an extension of your team. Here are a few things to consider during the selection process.

The first consideration is accrual versus cash accounting basis. We recommend the accrual method because it takes into account when the expense was incurred, not necessarily when it was paid. Sometimes bills are incurred on a credit card in January, but will not be paid until February or March. For reporting and management purposes,we find it useful to utilize accrual accounting to make accurate financial decisions regarding expense allocation throughout a particular month.

Another scenario that we often see with many accountants is delayed reporting. It is not unreasonable to expect your income statements, or P&L reports, by the 12th of the month. Some accountants will even try to convince you to accept quarterly statements, and this is even worse. We firmly believe it is virtually impossible to manage a practice effectively unless reports are provided monthly in a timely manner.

Monthly Break Even (MBE)

One of the first things that you will want to calculate as expenses start to stabilize at month 2 or 3 is the monthly break even point. This is the addition of all of the fixed and average variable expenses, plus any debt service. Debt service would include interest and principal payments made on practice notes, equipment loans, and lines of credit.

Ideal Numbers

As your revenues and expenses start to level out, you can start to gamify the numbers. We use the term gamify because getting more profitable can be viewed as a game, similar to golf, where we are challenged to improve over time and try to get better. Just like golf, there is a 'par' or break even score. The goal is to spend equal to or less than the target score per category. These are the average numbers per category that we have seen across the industry for high-performing practices. Here's a list of some of the major areas and targeted overhead numbers:

Variable (low hanging fruit)
- Supplies 5%, Ideal 4.5% or lower
- Lab 9%, Ideal 7% or lower
- Combined Supplies/Lab 14%, Ideal 11.5% or lower
- Marketing 4.5% (depending on the situation)
- Offices expenses 1.2%
- Other expenses 5.5%, Ideal 4.5
  - Merchant fees
  - Patient refunds
  - Continuing education

Fixed
- Payroll 30%, Ideal 25% or lower
  - Front/back office 16%, Ideal 13% or lower
  - Hygiene 9%, Ideal 8% or lower
  - Fringe benefits 2.5%, Ideal 2% or lower
- Facility/Equipment 9%, Ideal 7% or lower
  - Rents
  - Utilities
  - Equipment repair
- Knowing and correcting your variable costs will lower your overhead

- Increasing collection and lowering fixed costs leads to lowering your overhead

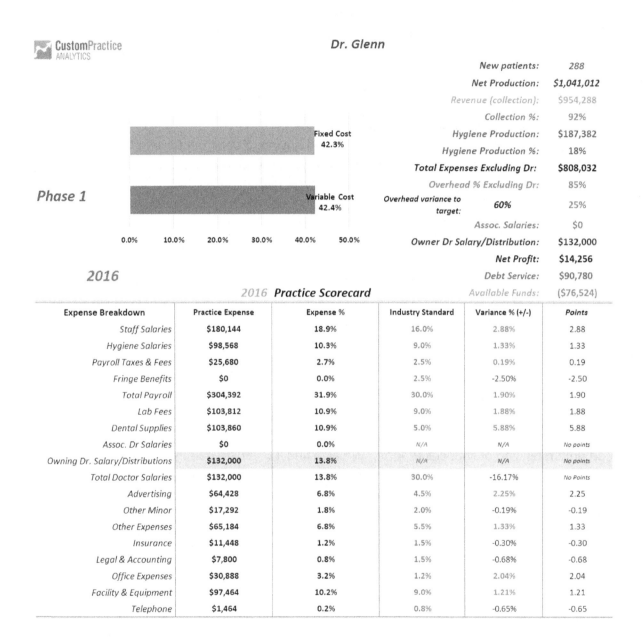

CustomPractice ANALYTICS

Dr. Glenn

New patients:	288
Net Production:	$1,041,012
Revenue (collection):	$954,288
Collection %:	92%
Hygiene Production:	$187,382
Hygiene Production %:	18%
Total Expenses Excluding Dr:	$808,032
Overhead % Excluding Dr:	85%
Overhead variance to target: 60%	25%
Assoc. Salaries:	$0
Owner Dr Salary/Distribution:	$132,000
Net Profit:	$14,256
Debt Service:	$90,780
Available Funds:	($76,524)

Phase 1

Fixed Cost 42.3%

Variable Cost 42.4%

0.0% 10.0% 20.0% 30.0% 40.0% 50.0%

2016

2016 **Practice Scorecard**

Expense Breakdown	Practice Expense	Expense %	Industry Standard	Variance % (+/-)	Points
Staff Salaries	$180,144	18.9%	16.0%	2.88%	2.88
Hygiene Salaries	$98,568	10.3%	9.0%	1.33%	1.33
Payroll Taxes & Fees	$25,680	2.7%	2.5%	0.19%	0.19
Fringe Benefits	$0	0.0%	2.5%	-2.50%	-2.50
Total Payroll	$304,392	31.9%	30.0%	1.90%	1.90
Lab Fees	$103,812	10.9%	9.0%	1.88%	1.88
Dental Supplies	$103,860	10.9%	5.0%	5.88%	5.88
Assoc. Dr Salaries	$0	0.0%	N/A	N/A	No points
Owning Dr. Salary/Distributions	$132,000	13.8%	N/A	N/A	No points
Total Doctor Salaries	$132,000	13.8%	30.0%	-16.17%	No Points
Advertising	$64,428	6.8%	4.5%	2.25%	2.25
Other Minor	$17,292	1.8%	2.0%	-0.19%	-0.19
Other Expenses	$65,184	6.8%	5.5%	1.33%	1.33
Insurance	$11,448	1.2%	1.5%	-0.30%	-0.30
Legal & Accounting	$7,800	0.8%	1.5%	-0.68%	-0.68
Office Expenses	$30,888	3.2%	1.2%	2.04%	2.04
Facility & Equipment	$97,464	10.2%	9.0%	1.21%	1.21
Telephone	$1,464	0.2%	0.8%	-0.65%	-0.65

Above is the example scorecard by Custom Practice Analytics that we use inside of the Dental Success Institute to track our members' financial progress. As you can see, this shows the target range expenses for a practice that is trying to get to 60% overhead. Remember what Karl Pearson, the father of statistics once said, "That which is measured, improves. That which is measured and reported, improves exponentially." This is commonly noted as Pearson's Law. To achieve success in your business, you will want to be fanatical about measuring and improving. Scorecards like this, paired with a monthly cadence of analytics, will lead to exponential growth and profitability for you, the business owner.

As you start to get a handle on your new acquisition, you will likely have questions about when to add more hygiene hours, when to add another assistant, or open up another operatory. Here are some of the most common symptoms we see that indicate it may be time to expand.

- When to add more Hygiene Hours
    - Hygiene booked out (85%+) for 3+ weeks
    - Booking out new patients more than 14 days
    - New patient flow is maintaining/increasing
    - Recall/Reactivation is happening and having to book out far into the future
- When to add another dental assistant (If the practice can handle it)
    - Patient volume in general is increasing
    - No overflow time
    - Same day treatment trending down
    - New patient flow is throttled
- When to look at adding an associate doctor
    - Periodic plus new patient exams exceed 125-130+ per doctor on a consistent basis
    - Doctor booking out operative more than 4 weeks

Trying to discuss the entire overhead and financial process for a practice could alone fill a 300+ page book, but we hope that some of the basics covered in this chapter have been a helpful resource. Remember that in order to be a sophisticated business owner, you will need to have a deep understanding of financial reports. We also find it useful to gamify those reports and to constantly work towards improving the profitability of the practice. While the numbers at the beginning will not look good, using the documents and resources in this book will make sure you are prepared for the first few months when you actually do not make any profit. Finally, remember as you grow and the profitability increases there will be certain benchmarks that let you know when it is time to grow and expand to further utilize the resources of the practice that you have built.

How to Manage Insurances

One of the most misunderstood, and likely ignored, topics during an acquisition is fee negotiations and credentialing. However, this decision makes a monumental difference in the financial success, and stressors, of a practice once the buyer takes over. One of the best outcomes is when the buyer can achieve a significantly higher fee schedule than the selling doctor, but this is not always easy or advised.

The major determining factor in this decision is cash flow. When it comes to credentialing, the buyer is faced with a bit of a 'rock and hard place' dilemma of two tough choices. The choice centers around whether to negotiate first on a new tax ID and then credential, or go through the path of quickest credentialing by inheriting the seller's contracts. We have done both, and there are advantages to each strategy.

New Tax ID and Credentialing from Scratch

A new tax ID is one of the best weapons a dentist has that, if used right, can provide one of the highest fee schedules in the area. A new tax ID often gets the highest reimbursements because of the flexibility it provides the dental office. While this is extremely counterintuitive, the field of fee negotiations and credentialing is far more convoluted than what most people believe due to a lot of 'shared networks' and 'umbrella networks'. A skilled negotiating and credentialing company can utilize the new tax ID in the most optimized way to get the best possible insurance reimbursements. We do not suggest negotiating on your own.

We discussed this with Vivek Kinra of PPO Profits. PPO Profits has done work on hundreds of acquisitions, and the fee differences between what the seller had and what the buyer got on a new tax ID is often very significant. Very often we see that sellers have not increased fees in many years, they have very low fees negotiated, and a very convoluted poor credentialing structure. In cases such as these, Mr. Kinra saw that proper negotiations and credentialing led to a 60-80% improvement on negotiated 'in-network' fees. One downside is that negotiating and credentialing on a new tax ID greatly **increases the timeline** before the buyer becomes fully credentialed and contracted with the insurance companies.

This absolutely slows cash flow, so be aware of that downside. The timeline varies between insurances, but in the best case, it's often 4 months but some insurances like Aetna and Metlife can take a year depending on some other circumstances.

Beware, this option almost always creates some friction between the new doctor (who wants the highest fees) and the front office team (who wants simplicity). No matter what anyone does, choosing this option should be done with a clear understanding that the first year for the dentist, patients, and front office team will be very frustrating. However, the key here is to understand and manage the frustrations, and embrace the reality that this option will be very rocky. This is the option for doctors who are willing to go through a year of administrative pain to get the best possible fees from there on out.

Mr. Kinra also gave some interesting perceptions on dentists who went through with the new tax ID and negotiation process. He said that 100% of dentists who go through renegotiation somewhat regret it *while* undergoing the process, and at the same time 100% of dentists polled say they are glad they went through option two and would do it again. When choosing a firm to help you navigate these tricky waters, we would expect that a good negotiating/credentialing firm be super clear with the expectations and super tight with communication with the office. Additionally, it is imperative that the entire front office team is part of the process from the get go and are empowered to be able to get through the impending challenges that await them for the first year.

The largest downside to negotiating a new fee schedule with a new Tax ID is that cash flow is slow. If you can manage it, then we do suggest trying this option. However, if cash flow is a concern and you do not have a large line of credit with the bank, then we do not suggest trying this option, even though it is desirable.

Inherit the Fee Schedules from the Seller

This option leads to the fastest credentialing and contracting (note credentialing and contracting are two different terms), but you have now just inherited fees from the seller and you will begin building claim data that insurance companies can access. This option is good for the short term for buyers - as the patients may see very little (if any) difference as they see the new doctor. However, it is less desirable for the long term because the web of poor credentialing often becomes so entangled that most offices deal with this problem by simply not exiting these poor plans. Depending on the seller's contracts, the buyer may have also inadvertently inherited a credentialing spider web that most offices never bother untangling. Additionally, if you now decide to engage an outside negotiating company, it becomes far more challenging to get the same top fees and structure the credentialing properly.

We suspect that most often prospective buyers have no idea about the two options and the benefits of each. Ideally, any buyer should be totally aware of the options, and make a focused decision on how they want to credential. We think that accepting the fee schedules of the seller is what most dentists go through because the office manager or the insurance coordinator of the seller simply takes over the credentialing process. They can simply call the insurance companies and complete the 'port of authority' or 'change of ownership' form to transfer the contracts to the new buyer.

While both options are less than ideal, the buying doctor should carefully evaluate the business conditions and cash flow of the office to make the decision. If he/she selects a new tax ID and negotiations, and would like to use a credentialing company, then it is ideal to get the front office team's buy-in and getting them involved as early as possible including while interviewing credential firms.

In summary, you can go with a quick option which preserves cash flow where the buyer takes over the sellers contracts and networks. This provides a quick and easy option, but stunts the ability to renegotiate later. The more difficult short term option is to negotiate a new tax ID, and while this creates more headaches in the short term, it can provide for much higher reimbursements in the future.

Difficulties in Change

No matter which option you choose, there will be a certain amount of time that you are considered 'out of network'. During this time, make sure to ask each insurance company for their particular set of rules. Some of them will want you to hold claims for a few weeks until you are in-network, while some will not back-date any claims in which case you will need to submit claims out of network. For these claims, you will need to make a decision as to whether you will charge for their out-of-network fees, or give some sort of a discount.

Another challenge that may occur in these scenarios is that the payment often gets sent to the patient.

Here are some ways these situations can be handled:

1. Require that the patient pay up front for their entire bill and let them know that their insurance company will send them a check (not encouraged unless selling doctor did this previously)
2. Wait until insurance pays and then bill the patient (more palatable option)
3. Wait until insurance pays, and have patient bring in a check to you (endorse the check to your practice on the back), make write-offs for any amount over what insurance pays (possible best option)

In any of the options above, your solution might change if the charges are for preventative services versus restorative. With restorative, we will often require the patient to make their co-pay on the day of service, and allow any other balances to wait until the insurance has come back.

The most important measure here is that the practice needs to be flexible. Remember that in an acquisition there is a lot of uncertainty with patients and you must do everything you can to build trust as quickly as possible.

In case you go with option one and do it in house, use the sample spreadsheet to the right- the Insurance Verification Checklist. Download from the link to the right.

Insurance Company

	Terminated Old Doctor	Recieved all paperwork to complete	Paperwork Submitted to Company	Recieved Confirmation that they have paperwork	In-Network	Contact Name and Information	Notes
Aetna	☑	☑	☑	☐	☐		Most recent mailed paperwork
Ameritas	☐	☐	☐	☐	☐		
Assurant	☐	☐	☐	☐	☐		
Blue Cross	☐	☐	☐	☐	☐		
Cigna	☐	☐	☐	☐	☐		
Connection	☐	☐	☐	☐	☐		
Delta Dental	☐	☐	☐	☐	☐		
Guardian	☐	☐	☐	☐	☐		
Humana	☐	☐	☐	☐	☐		
Maverest	☐	☐	☐	☐	☐		
MetLife	☐	☐	☐	☐	☐		
Principal	☐	☐	☐	☐	☐		
United Concordia	☐	☐	☐	☐	☐		
United Healthcare	☐	☐	☐	☐	☐		

Here is a resource to help you to manage the different timelines for each insurance network or umbrella network. Make sure that either you, or a very detail-oriented front desk employee, is doing all of the paperwork and completing this process for you.

Taxes in Your Transition

The Purchase Process

As your first year of practice ownership comes to a close, you must begin to think about taxes. If any profit was generated, you may be looking at having to write a check to the IRS. The good news is you will have the depreciation from the purchased assets to deduct against the taxes owed for the year.

In this scenario, look to the IRS Form 8594 discussed in Chapter 4 to see exactly how much depreciation you will be able to take in the first year. Most of the time it is the entire amount listed on that form.

Optimization

A smart business owner will try to take legal advantage of anything they can to ensure that they pay the least amount in taxes, while investing any available capital into the business. Most accountants will be able to help with many of these strategies , but it is very important to find an accountant who has a sound knowledge of the dental industry in order to help in all facets of the business and tax planning. Here are a few of the items to review with your tax professional:

- Vehicle allowance: Your business can legally pay for a portion of your vehicle for business purposes. Discuss with your accountant the best way to pay for a portion of the vehicle through the company or for any deductible automobile expenses.

- Meals and Entertainment: There are legal ways to deduct meals and entertainment if the expenses were business related. Discuss the specifics with your tax professional.

- Cell Phone and Internet: In this day and age, having a cell phone is a necessity for a business owner. We are on call for our patients much of the time. It is acceptable to run cell phone expenses through the practice. If we have a 'Home Office', it is also legal to pay for a portion of our home internet, to work on payroll, accounting, statistics, and completing patients' charts at night.

- Home Office: Most business owners use their home as a 'home office' for varying periods of time. For periods of 10-12 hours per week, the IRS will allow the expense of an office at your residence. One way to calculate this deduction, add up all the square feet of the home office, and research a market rate per sq. ft. per year in your area. The other method is called the 'Safe Harbor'. The IRS has defined a normalized method to rent your residence, and this is $5 for up to 300 Sq. Ft. of your home. The total in this scenario is $1,500 rent payment to yourself each year for rent.

- Renting Your Home: It is legal for you to rent your own house for work related events for up to 14 days per year at a normal market rate. In order to do this, ask for 3 competing bids from local establishments on a room rental. When you have collected competing bids, shoot for times of the year that may be at the higher end of the spectrum. Be sure to check with your CPA before counting this as a business expense, as it is becoming increasingly scrutinized.

- Travel: Many times there are CE courses offered in distant and exotic locations. These trips can be written off if they are considered "ordinary and necessary" to run your dental business. If you choose to take your spouse, their flight may not be a necessary business expense, but the hotel room for you is surely ordinary and necessary.

- Other business expenses: Remember that any item or asset that is used for business, can legally be purchased by the business.

In general, taxes are a part of life. You have to pay them, and you will most likely pay quite a substantial amount. The key to being successful is using the tax code to your advantage and to pay the correct amount, not overpay. This is why it is incredibly important to shop around for advisors and an accountant who can help you to legally minimize your tax liabilities.

Notes:

_____

_____

_____

_____

_____

_____

_____

_____

_____

_____

_____

_____

_____

_____

_____

_____

_____

_____

_____

_____

_____

_____

_____

Chapter 9

Marketing and Rebranding

On rare occasions, a practice acquisition will come with a great brand, long history, and good reputation in town. In these cases, it often means that there is strong new patient flow, solid production, and no need to change much in order to gain traction in the community. If you have found a practice like this, consider yourself extremely fortunate. Typically these practices are few and far between. If you buy a practice like this, then you might only need to only maintain or improve your marketing, without the need to completely rebrand.

More often, practices come with virtually no brand awareness, or even an undesirable brand. These cases warrant the need for a complete rebranding of the office more centered around you and the services that you offer.

We often see a practice that has named the office after themselves, and with virtually no brand. They are often called, "John Seller D.D.S., P.C." with no icon, no color palette, and no brand. While this was very standard about 25 years ago, it is a recipe for disaster in today's connected world.

Remember that Dental Success Network has a 4 Hour Marketing Course taught by Dr. Addison Killeen and DSN Faculty Member Ryan Gross, the CEO of myCMOshare. This course is a good synopsis of all the marketing techniques and expands on a lot of the information found in this chapter. Use the QR Code Here to watch the course on DentalSuccessNetwork.com during your Free Trial:

SCAN ME

From the time you begin considering acquiring an office, you will want to be thinking about how to handle the brand and marketing after the transition. But before we dig too deep into any of the strategies, let's identify the difference between 'brand' and 'marketing'.

Difference between Brand and Marketing

While many people think that marketing is all about 'advertising', it actually is not. Examples of advertising include buying ad space in different mediums like radio, billboards, and mailers. While this is part of the overall plan, it is not all-encompassing. Marketing includes all of your activities from the physical space you have, to your communication methods with your patients, to your advertising, to your patient experience, all the way through your patient follow-up.

All of your marketing activities however, are based around your *brand*. Creating a brand is often well executed by corporate dentistry and they often spend large amounts of money to develop and push it out to the masses. They often spend hundreds of millions of dollars across the industry on web-advertising, Nascar sponsorships, and TV ads in order to become recognizable to their target audience. Recently, we were even talking to an entrepreneur who sold his business for $1.2 Billion about 6 years ago to IBM. He shared that during his merger and acquisition, they actually assessed that his brand added another $100 Million to the purchase price! Quite simply, brand matters. It matters to big corporations, and it matters in our communities as we do our best to position our practices as the best option for new and existing patients.

ReBrand

Your new brand is something that will be with you for a long time, so as you start to make decisions on names and branding, it is important to consider the entire package. Assess whether the previous brand is something you want to model or sharply diverge from. On some occasions it is possible to incorporate the previous name and logo into your new brand. In these cases, you will want to get some help on how to create the new brand in a way that incorporates colors, themes, or references back to the old brand.

If you choose to go with an entirely new brand, you will have much more freedom. If you elect to start with a clean slate, reflect on what makes you different from all other offices in town. If you need more clarity in this area, go back to the first chapter on Vision. You will want to market an experience, so keep that in mind as you develop your brand. No matter what the previous practice looked like, you can decide from this day forward what your practice will be and how it will be unique.

How do you want your patients to feel when they walk in the office? Creating your desired experience includes the logo colors that you select all the way through the colors you paint the walls. Be deliberate to make sure your practice interior matches the brand and experience you're going to be putting out into the world. As you start to create this, you'll constantly be asking yourself, "What is my story?"

Changing a Name

We have both gone through multiple practice name changes and we admit that the process can be challenging. The most difficult part is finding a unique name that encompasses the style of dentistry you practice, the city you are in, and the level of quality that you want to convey. It's a difficult balance! In many cases, we started by flipping through a phone book and searching for words, neighborhoods, and geographies that matched the feeling we were trying to capture. Once you get a list going, ask any trusted advisors around you for their thoughts.

Here are some parameters to keep in mind when renaming and rebranding a practice:

- Easy to say
    - Needs to be something short, simple, and have good/positive vibes. Your staff will be saying it a lot, find something catchy.
- Easy to spell
    - Something that has a 'tch' in it, or a 'ae' or 'ou'...probably not good. Those can often be difficult to spell, which can impact branding. You want your name to be more similar to a name brand drug like Lipitor......less like something hard to spell like 'Atorvastatin'.
- Good connotations
    - You want your name to elicit positive emotions. Think of locations that are nice, gentle, airy, beautiful...they have prefixes like 'beau' or endings like 'lux'. Beau means beauty, lux means luxurious....having a slight change in the letters, but still sounding or looking like the word of origin will have a greater chance of having a positive effect on the brain.
    - Positive sounding words to copy parts of: absolutely. accepted. acclaimed. accomplish. accomplishment. beaming. beautiful. believe. beneficial. bliss. calm. celebrated. certain. champ. champion. dazzling. delight. delightful. distinguished. earnest. easy. ecstatic. effective. fabulous. fair. familiar. famous. generous. genius. genuine. giving. handsome. happy. harmonious. Healing.
    - Think of two nonsense words: Mar or Zeg. Which is positive, which is more negative. You likely picked Mar as the positive word. Why? Your brain may have connected the letter Z in Zeg which is more commonly associated with movie/TV villains...and the word Mar is similar to 'mer' which is latin for sea...which could be seen as calming.
- Somehow connected to your area, mission, or specialty
    - Pick something like a tree, a river, something that connects with your base. If you're in the mountains, perhaps a name that connects with that. If you're in the plains, a name like 'Prairie Skies' is a good starting point.
- Decent Web address URL
    - Even if your selected practice name isn't available in the simple NAME.COM format, you can still select something similar that's easy to remember. Research the availability of MYNAME.com...or include the location NAMECITY.COM. Disney has many URC's that use 'MY' as the prefix.
- Iconography that can make it work
    - The last step after you have selected a name is to create iconography- or the little logo image. Go to Logocontest.com to pay $200 down, you'll get dozens of ideas for a logo. You can then select a winner, who then gets the $200. From there, you can work directly with that designer to improve and finalize the logo. These websites are also great for brainstorming and generating ideas. You can then use a different designer for the final icon/logo.

Searching for available existing Trademarks and Website URLs is a first step before settling on a name and design. In many cases, the name or URL you want may already be taken. While this can be discouraging to have to keep researching new names, remember that there may be other combinations that may make your website URL more memorable. This could include using the word 'my' in front of the name, or even going with a '.co' or '.net' domain name extension.

If the corporation name and your brand name are the same, it lessens any confusion, but they do not necessarily have to be the same. In our examples, we used 'Grain Acres Dental LLC' as the entity, but the practice name does not have to be 'Grain Acres Dental'. It could be called something like 'Smile Dental', and then when deposits are put into the bank all checks are endorsed with a stamp that says 'Grain Acres Dental LLC dba Smile Dental'. The "dba" stands for "doing business as" and allows you to have a different LLC or PC name than your marketing or branding name.

Logo Icon Design

A brand is much more than a logo, but the logo is where it all starts and can make a huge difference in the ease of spreading the message. As you design your logo, consider how it will appear in different settings:
- Billboard appearance
- Printing appearance (shirts)- keep it simple
- Stitching appearance on shirts - embroidery can be difficult if logo is too complicated
- Make sure the colors you pick match the feel/brand
- Choose clean colors with no gradient
- Pick a logo that is easily definable
- Draw familiarity from local landmarks

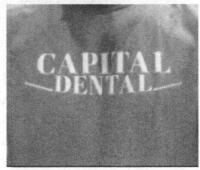

Be sure to lean on expert help throughout the process. In the past, we have used 99designs or logocontest.com to help us generate our initial concepts and rough design, but in the end we then take the initial ideas to a trusted graphic designer to complete the project. A good graphic designer will understand what different colors convey, how they interact with each other, and guide you towards the ideal color palate for your project.

One thing that you will want to provide initially is your color preferences. Here's a summary of colors and the main words that they are usually associated with.

RED

MEANS:
passionate
active
EXCITING
bold energy
youthful
physical
PIONEERING
leader willpower
confidence
ambition
POWER

BRANDS:
Kellogg's
Virgin / LEGO
Coca-Cola
Nintendo
Red Bull

PINK

MEANS:
love **calm**
respect
WARMTH
longterm
feminine
intuitive **care**
assertive
sensitive
NURTURE
possibilities
UNCONDITIONAL

BRANDS:
BBC
three
Barbie
COSMOPOLITAN
VICTORIA'S SECRET

PURPLE

MEANS:
DEEP
creativity
unconventional
original
stimulation
individual
WEALTH modesty
compassion
DISTINGUISHED
respectable
fantasy

BRANDS:
Cadbury
YAHOO!
Hallmark
Milka
Zoopla.co.uk

NAVY

MEANS:
trust order
LOYALTY
sincere
authority
communication
confidence
PEACE integrity
control
responsible
success
CALM masculine

BRANDS:
f
Reebok
British Gas
t / GAP

GREEN

MEANS:
BALANCE
growth
restore
sanctuary
EQUILIBRIUM
positivity NATURE
generous
clarity
prosperity
good judgement
safety stable

BRANDS:
bp
Holiday Inn
tic tac
LACOSTE

BLUE

MEANS:
spirit
perspective
CONTENT
control
rescue
determination
self-sufficient
modern **goals**
aware PURPOSE
OPEN
ambition

BRANDS:
intel
Blu-ray Disc
skype
W

ORANGE

MEANS:
INSTINCT
WARMTH
gut reaction
optimistic
spontaneity
extrovert
social NEW IDEAS
FREEDOM
impulse
motivation

BRANDS:
Fanta
orange
Penguin
MasterCard
bitly

As you are picking some of the primary colors and design features, you will also want to double check that your design and colors aren't too similar to the competition around you. There's lots of tooth-shaped logos. There's also a good chance that even your creative graphic designer will design something that resembles what someone else already has. For this reason, it is important early on in the logo design process to familiarize yourself with the logos and names of the competition in the area and plot those out so that you can create a logo that is memorable and unique.

The signage on the outside of the building is very important because it is going to be one of the first things that the public will see when they pull up to your new practice. This is one area where we believe you should go the extra mile in making sure that it is reflective of the quality and type of dentistry that you will be doing. This could be a lighted box, or even higher end like custom cut-out letters that are each individually backlit. Typically a nice building-mounted sign will cost anywhere from $5,000-9,000, so make sure this is accounted for in your startup loan package.

Roll Out Phase

Once you have your logo and branding established, you will want to begin strategizing the best ways to share your new brand with the existing patients and community at large. Obviously the first communication with your patients after the transition will be a letter sent out to all patient families. We do not believe it is wise to try to rebrand in this letter. The goal of this correspondence should be to focus 100% on introducing the doctor and building up the authority and trust.

After a month or two, it might be a more appropriate time to roll out the new brand and name (if there is going to be a name change). As discussed in earlier chapters, we understand that cash flow is sometimes irregular in the beginning. For this reason, if you are planning a large rebranding effort, it might be more economical to change the website and print materials internally in the beginning. After those changes are made, you could change exterior signage shortly after. Plastic tarp-signs that cover older signage are a good transitory step prior to investing in a new exterior signage.

If you plan to hire an internal professional or outsourced company to help with your marketing needs, here are some things to consider:

Hiring a Marketing Company/Person
Questions to ask-
- Have you ever managed social media for a business?
- Walk me through the steps of how you would create an engaging facebook post?
- Have you ever set up a facebook ad? Or do you just 'boost' posts?
- When creating a facebook ad, billboard and/or print ad, what kind of audience do you think you would want those ads to appeal to and how would you achieve that?
- What are the most important skills you have learned that you think would be important for this position?
- Are you more of a detail-oriented or big picture person and why?
- Tell me about a time when you created content for an email and the process you went through to create it?
- How have you measured success in your current/past marketing role?
- Give an example of a goal you had to achieve in a marketing role and what steps you took to achieve it?
- What kind of management style do you prefer?
- What motivates you to work hard and do well?
- Tell me about a project you have worked on that you are most proud of?
- Tell me about a position you've held where you have managed multiple projects, vendors and timelines.
- What do you do to stay organized?
- Do you prefer to do your own graphic design or work with graphic designers to execute projects?
- Tell me about a position where you worked with someone in a creative position and how you directed them to get the results you were looking for.
- Our priority is to give patients the best experience they can have when visiting us. What could you do in this position that could help give patients a positive experience?

While we have had amazing success and tragic failure with marketing people, if they are the right fit, we see great value in their expertise. We have found the best outcomes come from those that are intimately involved in your decision-making, and know you well. Larger companies often offer less individual attention and we've enjoyed working with smaller, high quality boutique firms. But, whether you hire someone to help or not, you'll need to keep the process moving along. While you can save a considerable amount of money by doing this yourself, be sure that you have the personal bandwidth to take on a project of this scope. The next step is budgeting and timing. Calculate how much you'd like to invest in marketing each month, and create a calendar of what you'd like to focus on during specific periods of time:

- Where do you want the money to be spent? (internal or external marketing)
- How are you going to track which methods are effective and which are not?
  - Bigger investment = faster results and longevity of patients (reach more ideal patients)

One element of the marketing system that we encourage you to focus on is keeping all of your ideas and marketing efforts in a large spreadsheet and using it to keep track of your results. This data will allow you to pivot and eliminate underperforming efforts and increase resources to the most successful efforts. The table pictured here will help you to track your ideas and determine where you will want to spend money over the first few months. The next table shows all internal marketing and signage spend. Oftentimes, internal marketing is more effective than external campaigns. Hopefully patients love meeting you as their new doctor, but to give away a YETI mug or bottle of wine sets you apart on an entirely different level. Remember that spending money on patients that are already in the chair can be a very good investment. (However, if you're going to do a bulk purchase of any items like stainless steel mugs, tee-shirts, or other branded materials, you should go through the rebranding process first.

Total Spend	% Spend	Total $	Month 1	Month 2	Month 3
TOTAL					
Branding/Plan					
Signage					
Internal					
YETI Mugs					
YETI Coolers					
Wine/Drinks					
T-Shirts					
Coffee Gift Cards					
Other Referral Gifts					
Paperwork					

The next table pictured here shows some external marketing ideas. While it is not all encompassing, it will give you some idea of what you can do with some of your marketing spend. We do not encourage you to consider these types of campaigns in the first 6 months of an acquisition.

As you are pondering your marketing and possible rebranding efforts, remember that for the first 6-12 months of your transition, your entire goal is to minimize attrition of existing patients. Your primary objective should be to meet and gain the trust of hundreds or thousands of patients. While getting new patients is great, your plate should be full trying to serve the existing patients.

External				
Website				
Google Ads				
Facebook Ads				
Billboards				
Radio				
Television				
Guerrilla Marketing				
PostCards				

At some point between 3 and 6 months into the transition, your 'whirlwind' of activity will begin to calm down, and you will have more time to focus on a rebranding effort. When you come to this point, you will surely want to set a budget. We do not suggest that you allocate a large amount of capital to do this. Rather, we believe that you should try to keep your normal marketing spend at a percentage up to 5%. The money you have budgeted for the 'rebrand phase' is going to be focused on branding, as opposed to building authority or patient acquisition.

The 'rebrand phase' of marketing should take no longer than a few months. Following this phase, attention can be shifted back to SEO, external marketing, internal marketing, and other traditional efforts of practice building.

Continued Efforts

After getting stabilized and possibly rebranded, marketing techniques should begin to diversify with a focus on achieving an acceptable ROI on new patient acquisition.

We typically recommend setting a budget of 4.5% of total revenue dedicated to marketing spend. In the practices that have underutilized spaces, or are in growth mode, this can be elevated for a period of time.

It's important to determine whether the practice can handle a large influx of new patients, and whether an increase in marketing spend is the right strategy. Percentages sometimes get as high as 10%-15% for a few months. When revenue begins to increase significantly, you can begin to dial the spending percentage back. As with everything in practice ownership, the location and market saturation will have a large effect on how aggressively you will need to market.

Here are a few questions that you will want to answer when deciding the amount to budget for marketing spend.

- What is the cost difference between internal versus external marketing?
  - We typically see a 25% spend internally, and a 75% spend externally. This 25% internal spend is described later in this chapter.
- Where is the best return on investment?
  - The answer to this question is almost dependent on the demographic and the population that you will be serving. While there is an absolute formula, the foundation for almost all successful marketing is a good website.

Web Presence

Your website and web presence is often your best return on investment. Although building a quality website can be costly, it often becomes the single largest referral source for most new practices. Usually a practice being purchased comes with a website. If the existing website is already gaining a lot of new patients and has a good history, it may be best to keep the existing provider or host. In these cases, make sure to gain ownership and control of the site on the day that you purchase the practice. If the seller does not grant access, it can be very challenging to gain control of the website if the seller has moved out of the area or becomes difficult to reach.

As you evaluate a company and or marketing coordinator, utilize the questionnaire in this chapter as a vetting tool. If the company you are using is well established in the dental profession, be sure to ask for references and ask about their experience. Most of these will be overwhelmingly positive, especially if the company provided them, but you may be able to get more specifics regarding their service.

Website

Websites vary significantly based upon the primary focus and branding of the practice. The user experience for most websites however will be quite similar. Here are some general notes on websites and traffic patterns.

- Create a funnel for website traffic leading to a higher probability of scheduling
- 50% of your website traffic will be to the doctor's 'about' page followed by financially related details of the practice:
  a. Are you in network with their insurance?
  b. Do you have a savings plan for uninsured patients?
  c. Do you offer payment plans for larger treatment plans?
- Show office fees on the website. Although it is rarely done, we believe that it is acceptable to post this information because it can potentially lead to a greater likelihood that a patient will schedule because they know what their financial obligation will be. This also may serve to build trust by demonstrating transparency.

Once your website is live, you'll need to evaluate its performance. Here are some of the details you'll need to track:
- Where is the traffic coming from?
- What is the bounce rate?
- What are the highest visited pages on the website?
- Is the traffic a result of phone calls leading to website visits or vice versa?
    - Phone calls require a 95% or higher answer rate, remember that missed calls equals missed opportunities to schedule.

One often-missed opportunity with many practices is not having an online scheduling option. In our experience, online scheduling options on dentist's websites results in not only more new patients, but Google and other search engines rank them higher.

Facebook

Similar to the website, make sure you are given instant Admin Access to the company facebook page if there is one on the day you take ownership of the practice. At that point, remove all other parties who are Admin or Managers on the page.

Most target demographics for dental offices focus on the female 25-45 age range. This is also one of the largest demographics on the Facebook platform. For this reason, Facebook advertising should be part of your marketing plan.

It is key to establish an organic presence on facebook, creating connections with the doctor at regular intervals every week. Most of them can be regular posts, with the occasional boosted post added to the mix. (As well as Facebook Ads.)

Keep in mind that Facebook will typically not generate new patients instantly. The upside to utilizing Facebook is that it allows you to build a connection with a potential patient, which could then lead to a website visit and eventually a scheduled appointment.

Facebook 'Reach' is by far the most important statistic to monitor and track when periodically checking Facebook statistics.

Google MyBusiness

Google is the largest platform in the world and can generate patients for you, or make you invisible to the world. In order to use it to your benefit, you'll want to use every tool that they offer to become as prominent as possible. Creating and maintaining a Google MyBusiness page is an important step.

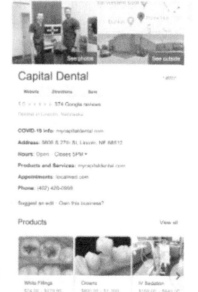

During the transition process, be sure to also gain access to the Google MyBusiness page and remove any other users. After this is complete, you can use the page as a tool to generate new patients.

Getting as many 5-star Google Reviews as possible is of the utmost importance. These reviews can move a new practice into the top ranking on Google without years and years of SEO and website history. Getting as many 4 and 5 star reviews as quickly as possible should be one of the top initiatives for you and your team.

Many dentists under utilize certain aspects of the Google page. This includes the 'Products' page as well as any other links that you can input into the page. While most dentists do not sell 'products' as a major part of their businesses, we do fillings, crowns, dentures, implants and other treatment that people are seeking. Be sure that your page has pictures, links, and prices for various types of procedures to ensure that Google ranks your website higher.

Internal Marketing

Internal marketing can be instrumental in gaining new patient referrals and for creating an amazing patient experience. Creating an exceptional patient experience will also increase the likelihood that patients will leave positive, 5-star Google reviews.

So, what strategies can we deploy in internal marketing to help create an unforgettable patient experience? It starts with systems like the phone scripts, the new patient tour, developing connections with patients in the office, and reducing discomfort (sedation or painless injections). It also includes some things that might not typically be include in marketing:

- Patient Experience
  - Obviously you and your team must create a great patient experience from beginning to end. Engage in real personal interaction, CARE about your patients, and work on connecting with people at a deeper level. If you do that, no matter how it's executed, your patients will become raving fans.
- Scripts for phone
  - There are only a few categories where most callers fall into...work to develop and role play scripts that account for each type of caller. This should be part of your operations manual.
- Transfer of Trust scripts
  - During each transition in the patient flow, you should perform a transfer of trust. This should include edification of the team member that you are handing off to. This should also be in your operations manual.
- Texting/Voicemails after difficult procedures(Implants, Endo, Extractions, Sedation)
  - After any procedure requiring anesthesia, the doctor or staff should text or call the patient to check in. This is one of the most well regarded gestures of kindness and empathy. If you don't want patients to have your direct cell phone number, you can always use a Google phone # for patient-only contact.
- Continuity of Brand In-Office
  - Internal Office Paperwork
    - Brochures and items that are custom branded do your office. These could include informational brochures on extractions, implants, sleep apnea, caries risk, periodontal risk. Examples are shown:

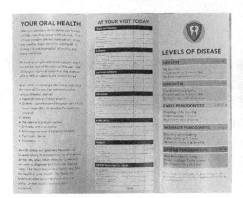

- **Business Cards/Reappointment Cards**
  - Custom business cards are commonplace these days. Remember that the quality of the card is often associated with the quality of perceived care that patients will receive in your office. Do not go cheap on these, invest in a higher quality card, heavier stock, etc. Also make sure that they look professional and do not have pixelated images or poor quality printing.

  -

- **Patient Giveaways:**
  - T-shirts
    - In our offices we give away t-shirts intermittently. We create new t-shirt designs every few months that have attractive images on them associated with the season. Staff love them, and when given out, they are rolled up, tied with a bow, and a business card. (About $6.50 per t-shirt is the cost.) These are more expensive than other giveaways, but they become walking billboards for you and have a very high perceived value.

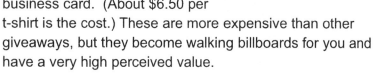

  - Wine
    - We go to Trader Joes or other stores and purchase cases of inexpensive bottles of wine then wrap them in a clear plastic bag from Amazon.com, place a nice sticker on the bottle, and tie them up with a bow. Each employee gives

out 1 bottle of wine per day. It's part of their daily checklist to give one out to anyone they choose.
- ○ Steel-insulated Cups
  - ■ Go to Alibaba.com to purchase, or else use my contact at this company: They are about $4.50 for a 20 oz. mug that is EXACTLY the same as Hydroflask. (They are prohibited from printing Hydroflask on the bottle)

- Google/Facebook Reviews:
  - ○ We have found that Swell is the most effective software for getting more google reviews. Although there are many options, Swell does a great job in getting reviews faster than any other texting-solution.
  - ○ Giveaways
    - ■ Our most popular giveaway is a YETI Cooler, place it somewhere conspicuous in the office with a sign that explains that each month or two you will give it away to a lucky winner. To enter, simply leave a google review.

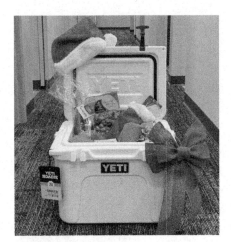

- ○ Email Batching to patients
  - ■ Pull all emails from the past 6 months, send them emails. Use a service like MailChimp or ActiveCampaign to send emails to these patients if you do not have a service like Flex. These emails should thank them for being a patient, and remind them how important google reviews are to your business. In this email, tell them how much reviews mean to your business and ask them if they would kindly write a review for you.

- Cards to Patients:
  - New Patients
    - Custom printed cards with a message of gratitude and additional space to customize. Must be high quality card-stock

      Dear (patient),

      Thank you so much for referring a friend to our clinic recently. It means a lot that you trust us with your care, and in turn tell other people about us. As a gesture of our appreciation, grab a smoothie or coffee on us. Enjoy!

      Thanks,
      Dr. Costes & Team

  - Special Occasions
    - Using the same card as above, a staff member can write a personalized message for a special occasion occurring in the patient's life, a get well soon message, or condolences for a lost family member.

Although these internal strategies seem like overkill to the typical general dental practice, we believe that they create an amazing patient experience that goes far beyond what other practices are willing to do. When this much focus is placed on recognizing patients, the dividends of your kindness, empathy and attention will pay off for decades.

External Marketing

Some external marketing campaigns can generate many new patients, and some can be a complete dud. Finding out which type of marketing generates a favorable ROI and which does not can take time and lots of trial and error. Most strategies are market and demographic specific so testing and tracking are imperative.

Here's a few of the methods that we have tried in the past:
- Google Ads
  - While it is important to make sure to stay within a certain budget, Google Ads typically provide a favorable return on investment.
- Facebook Ads
  - These are a useful, low-cost marketing strategy to generate more awareness about your practice. A budget of around $300 per month is usually sufficient.
- Postcards
  - Postcards can be very successful with some demographics. If results are positive in the first few attempts, repeat 5-6 times. After this initial wave, decrease frequency to every 2-3 months.
  - People who are 20-55 respond surprisingly well to postcards.
- Billboards

- ○ Billboards offer mixed results but can be effective in some markets. Cost can range from $600-4,000 a month depending on the traffic and size of your market.
- Radio
  - ○ We have not seen great return on investment from radio ads.
- Guerrilla
  - ○ Creative and unconventional marketing strategies that cost very little. They sometimes work well, but can be difficult to measure.

Tracking Return on Investment

The most important element to a successful marketing plan is to ensure that each avenue of marketing is measured and the effectiveness compared. In order to do this accurately, you will need to keep track of your spending, and how each patient ended up in your practice.

Part of this analysis includes your website and phone number. For trading purposes, we suggest that you place customized phone numbers on them. Using different phone numbers allows you to track exactly where each new patient is coming from. Note: This tracking strategy can cause confusion in the patient base if too many tracking numbers are being used at one time, so do your best to limit the tracking numbers as much as possible.

The tried and true method of tracking is to simply ask the patient how they heard about your office. Once they share this information with the team, it should be documented in the patient's chart.

Another way to track return on investment is by delineating the value of each patient. For example, if you are marketing for 'All on X' procedures, these patients are worth much more than the typical cleaning patient. Tracking the type of production that each of these patients is completing is also important.

Here are some of the charts that we use in our evaluation of marketing effectiveness. In general, we have noted that the more visitors to a website usually means more new patients, which leads to more production and revenues. When you see a graph like the one above, you'll know that things are going well for a practice, as web visits are begetting production. All lines are moving in a positive direction.

Some marketers only measure "leads" generated by their marketing efforts. These reports shown here are quite different. The first one shows a market research type graph of your website total traffic from search websites versus those of your competition. This is compiled by our website firm, and they do this analytics dump each month and email us the results. Although effectiveness is sometimes measured by whether you are showing up in the top 3 of any given search term, these results can be misleading. Many people use the search terms 'dentist' and the city and state. The cumulative addition of all other dental search terms however dwarfs this number. If you are only focused on being the #1 dentist if someone searches 'dentist san antonio tx', for instance, you may be missing out on many other leads that might be valuable if other search terms were used.

A strategy that attacks many keywords at the same time can actually get more web traffic across multiple search terms, as opposed to having all of your SEO focus on just one type of search.

In all, effective marketing can potentially be one of the factors that skyrockets your business to new heights. To execute this correctly, it will require a focus on branding, external marketing, internal marketing and tracking.

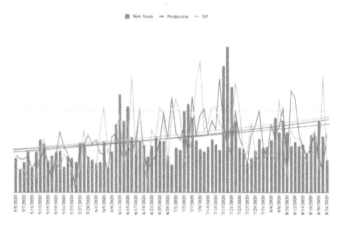

We gained just over half a point of visibility last month and moved up a rank to second in overall search visibility

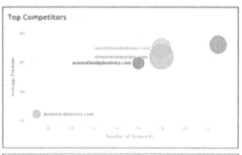

Notes:

Chapter 10

As the Whirlwind Slows

In their book, the 4 Disciplines of Execution, Chris McChesney, Jim huling, and Sean Covey describe a phenomenon that they call the "whirlwind." This term refers to the frenzy that occurs everyday in a busy business environment. In a dental office, this includes simultaneously managing the team, the patients, the vendors, clinical care and overall business operations. The reality of being a dentist in a transition can be overwhelming and exhausting. Having been through many start-ups and acquisitions= both smooth and turbulent, we know first hand that there will always be obstacles, challenges and stressful moments.

We also know that as you work in a practice over time that the whirlwind will eventually calm down. As it does, you will get the opportunity to expand your focus to other aspects within the practice that require attention. The best place to start in order to move from chaos to efficiency and order is the implementation of systems.

Systemization

Contrary to popular belief, operational systemization is not a finite practice. It is rather, an ongoing fluid process that is constantly changing and evolving as your practice, team and skill-set changes and evolves. While we've written an entire manual dedicated to systemization, (The Dental Operations Manual), in the pages that follow, we will give you an overview of our Elite Practice Blueprint, which is the foundational framework for turning your practice into an efficient, profitable, sophisticated business.

Prioritization

Next, you will see the major categories of the Elite Practice Blueprint: Foundation, Operational Systemization, Lifetime Patient Experience, New Patient Acquisition, Human Resources and Overhead and Cash Flow control.

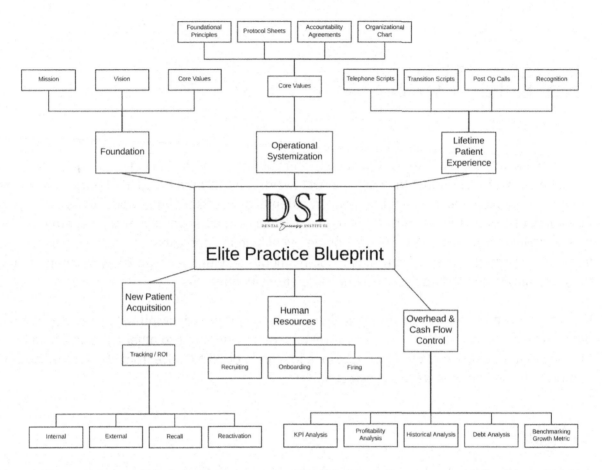

The pages that follow will give printed examples on digital access to several documents that will help you to master all six pillars of the Elite Practice Blueprint. If you haven't already done so, pick up a copy of The Dental Practice Operations Manual for a deep dive into each category and process.

Sample Table of Contents Includes:
- Foundational Principles
- Organizational Chart
- Protocol Sheets
- Accountability Agreements
- Patient Experience and Phone Scripts
- Monthly Performance Reviews
- Ideal Set-Up Pictures
- Common Area Pictures
- End of Day Protocol
- Downtime Protocol
- Universal Onboarding Documents
- Positional Onboarding

Organizational Chart

From day one you will want to have an organizational chart. Here are some main points to consider:

- As CEO you should strive to have the smallest number of people reporting directly to you as possible.
- No more than one person should fill a role, but a person can fill more than one role.
- A person can have more than one direct supervisor from different departments. (clinical/administration)

To create your own organizational chart, follow these steps.

- List out all positions in your organization
- Give each employee a title
- Designate a lead for each department
- Draw out organizational chart according to your practice's internal hierarchy

An example is below:

Example Dental

As you go about the process of doing this yourself, we have found it beneficial to use the software called LucidChart to help create beautiful flowcharts like this.

Systemization Jumpstart

Rather than fill hundreds of more pages in this book on systemization, we suggest that you model what has already been built. Remember that members of the Dental Success Network get access to the Operations Manual Templates. To get immediate access, simply head to the website and sign up for a free trial and feel free to download any documents that you need. There are hundreds of pages of documents to help jumpstart your own operations manual.

One of the best ways to avoid getting lost and overwhelmed during the systemization process, we suggest downloading the systemization jumpstart. This packet includes daily checklists, patient experience touch-points, and follow the dollar exercises. By far the most impactful are the daily checklists. These lists are meant to remind each team member of exactly what they should be focusing on throughout the day. This can include a morning protocol, down-time protocol, and end of day protocol.

Here is a copy of the Daily Task list for a clinical assistant and front office assistant. These were created on Google Sheets, and can be copied from the DSN document vault. Use these as the framework for building your own, and look at other tabs in the document to see what other checklists you could create for your practice.

Assistant Daily Checklist

Name_____ Date_____

Room 2   Room 5   Room 6

MORNING CHECKLIST

- ☐ Turn on pumps
- ☐ Turn on Tanks of Nitrous & Oxygen
- ☐ Make sure water bottles are full and add capsules of water cleaner
- ☐ Turn on TV/music in tx rooms, go to phone and pick relaxing station on 'Soundtrack' app
- ☐ Turn on all lights, x-ray machines (including pano) in tx rooms/sterilization center/lab
- ☐ Fill Ultrasonic with water and cleaner, package instruments when finished shaking
- ☐ Empty clean Autoclave
- ☐ Load sterilizer with dirty instruments that did not fit, packaged the night before, start if full

- ☐ Set up for first appointment
- ☐ Restock rooms if necessary
- ☐ Make up trays on clean side of sterilization
- ☐ Check schedule for any conflicts/questions – prep for A.M. Huddle

DOWN-TIME CHECKLIST

- ☐ Check with Hygiene to see if they need help
- ☐ Check other Doctors/Hygiene schedules for efficiency/rooms
- ☐ Check to make sure all lab cases are scheduled
- ☐ Check to complete any needed labwork
- ☐ Check 1 day/1 week schedule, address any issues
- ☐ Restock rooms as needed
- ☐ Go through office cleaning checklist
- ☐ Ask front desk to help with Recall List and other duties

END OF DAY CHECKLIST

- ☐ Check schedule 1 day/1 week ahead
- ☐ Check to make sure all AM lab cases have arrived
- ☐ Turn off TV & comp. screen, mouse and keyboard
- ☐ Suction all lines with SlugBuster
- ☐ Restock rooms
- ☐ Make sure all notes are done- run incomplete procedure notes report
- ☐ Sweep & Take out Trash
- ☐ Prep for Morning Huddle with Route Slips

Make sure all rooms are wiped down and ready to set up the next morning
- ☐ Load Autoclave with dirty instruments
- ☐ Run instruments through the Ultrasonic/package
- ☐ Drain Ultrasonic
- ☐ Package any dirty instruments that have gone through the Ultrasonic and will not fit in the

- ☐ Shut off Oxygen & Nitrous Tanks
- ☐ Shut off pumps (last person to leave)

Signature of Manager: _____

Check in/ front office Daily Checklist

Name_____ Date_____

MORNING CHECKLIST

- ☐ Check all message services (Phone, Email, Texts in Flex)
- ☐ Review daily doctor schedule for openings/opportunities
- ☐ If any open time, call patients on ASAP list
- ☐ Open the office
- ☐ Turn HVAC/Fan to on
- ☐ Turn CBCT/Pano on
- ☐ put out sign in front of office
- ☐ Review unscheduled list and call to schedule as needed- Divergent document sent by email
- ☐ Check VoiceMail
- ☐ Check Email for same-day changes
- ☐ Prepare for morning Huddle/ see morning huddle sheet
- ☐ print daily schedule
- ☐ Check Texts in Flex for same-day changes
- ☐ Review daily revenue goal for office
- ☐ Review Schedule to see any opportunities / same day treatment
- ☐ Verify monthly benchmark calendar is up-to-date and team is aware of goals
- ☐ Check to see if any appointments need to be re-called
- ☐ Check office for cleanliness throughout- note and pass along task to other staff
- ☐ Pictures of all patients taken and added to charts throughout the day
- ☐ Check patients to see who needs Updates- on Flex send again if needed
- ☐ Enter Insurance Payments/ EFTS/Mail payments

DOWN-TIME CHECKLIST

- ☐ Check mail after 11:30 am
- ☐ Clean waiting room
- ☐ Call 3 patients on unscheduled treatment list
- ☐ Verify that all unnecessary items are put away from counters, desktops, etc. and are in appropriate
- ☐ Look for and recognize potential schedule conflicts for following day so they can be resolved.
- ☐ Check in lab cases as they come in, make sure appointments are set up
- ☐ send pre-auths as needed

END OF DAY CHECKLIST

- ☐ Send claims through clearinghouse
- ☐ Speak with Doctor wrapping up day/budget/staff
- ☐ Look for and recognize potential schedule conflicts for following day so they can be resolved.
- ☐ Check supplies daily and reorder as necessary keeping to the office budget.
- ☐ All notes completed for the day- run incomplete procedures notes
- ☐ Verify that all unnecessary items are put away from counters, desktops, etc. and are in appropriate
- ☐ Clean workstation/area
- ☐ Vacuum as needed
- ☐ Today's production $_____/ Goal $_____
- ☐ Tomorrow's production $_____/ Goal $_____
- ☐ Print Daily payments report and make sure everything matches
- ☐ make Deposit slip
- ☐ Turn off Pano/CBCT/ turn AC to auto
- ☐ Take Checklist to Manager

Signature of Manager: _____

Once you've created your daily task lists, continue on with other aspects of creating a systemized practice. The flow chart below shows some of the biggest items to focus on during your acquisition journey.

Identify Systems to be Created	Patient Touch Point Exercise Follow the Dollar Exercise Time Journal Exercise
Create Systems	Time Journal Exercise Positional Authorship
Organize Systems	Operations Manual
Implement/Trai	Onboarding Process
Management/Accountabilit	EOD Protocol Weekly Growth Meetings Monthly Performance Reviews
Ongoing Refinement	Weekly Growth Meeting Monthly Calibration Meeting Annual Planning Meeting

- Patient Touch Point Exercise
  - In this exercise, follow a patient from their first interaction with your practice, throughout the process, up until they pay and leave with a rescheduled appointment. In general, you will want a rough script for each touchpoint.
  - For example, sometimes a patient will call and request an appointment and is ready to schedule. This is straightforward and the person answering the phone will get them scheduled. However, a caller wants to know prices and insurance information. For these cases, the team must have adequate training to field these types of questions.

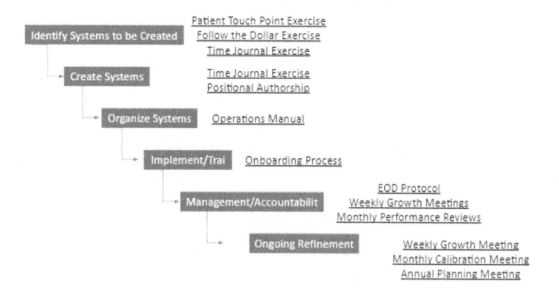

1. Task: Initial Phone Call / Confirmation Call - Front
Team Position(s) involved (i.e. front office/back office, etc.):

Protocols that need to be created (before/during/after task):

2. Task: Patient Check-In - Front

3. Task: Treatment Plan Presentation - Brock/TC

4. Task: Patient Check Out - Front

5. Task: Claim created and Sent - Billing Dept

6. Task: A/R Analysis - CFO/CEO/OM

7. Task: Entering payment in PMS - Front/Billing

8. Task: Bank Deposits - Front

9. Task: Day Sheet Reconciliation - OM

10. Task: Statements Sent to Patients - Billing/Front

- - Here are the main touch points that should be scripted, streamlined and roll played until mastered:
    - First phone call
    - Reminder phone call
    - Greeting when entering practice
    - Calling patient back to the operatory
    - Patient Tour of the practice upon first visit
    - Seating Patient into the Chair, Building rapport
    - Handoff from Assistant to Doctor
    - Handoff from Doctor to Treatment Coordinator
    - Collecting at the end of the appointment
    - Rescheduling at the end of the appointment
    - Walking out and finishing up appointment

- Follow the Dollar Exercise
  - This exercise is similar to the Patient Touch Point exercise but from a financial perspective. You will need to list in order each time money or payment is discussed, billed, or collected as well as the team member associated with the task. Here's an example sheet you can copy and work through:
- Time Journal Exercise
  - CEO/Doctor
    - For a period of five days, journal your activities from the time that you wake up until the time you go to sleep
    - Highlight in yellow, all of the activities that can be eliminated or delegated out for less than $100 (or what you think your hour is worth)
    - Highlight in blue, all of the activities that cannot be eliminated or delegated out for less than $100
    - Definitions: Yellow time- low value activities, Blue time- high value activities, White time- Free time
    - The goal is to replace as much yellow time with white time and blue time
  - Team Protocol Sheet
    - For a period of three days, have each team member journal their activities from the time that they arrive at work until the time that they leave for the

TIME JOURNAL   DSI

Today's Date _____

Time	Tasks
4:30AM	
5:00AM	
6:00AM	
7:00AM	
8:00AM	
9:00AM	
10:00AM	
11:00AM	
12:00AM	
1:00PM	
2:00PM	
3:00PM	
4:00PM	
5:00PM	
6:00PM	
7:00PM	
8:00PM	
9:00PM	
10:00PM	
11:00PM	
12:00AM	

day
- Schedule a meeting with each team member to review their journal
- Identify tasks that are continuously repeated throughout the day, redundancies, inefficiencies and overlaps in operations
- Name each chuck of tasks (verifying insurance, setting up treatment rooms, etc.)
- Allot time and give a deadline for each team member to summarize how they perform each chuck of tasks
- Schedule a follow up meeting with each team member and review their summaries and convert them into checklists and protocols (their feedback and authorship is key in this step)

While this is far from an all-inclusive list of systems that need to be created to run a smooth and profitable operation, it is a good start. As mentioned earlier, you will never be "finished" with this process as you will forever be growing, changing and evolving as a team, owner and practice.

Remember that inside the Dental Success Network, we have the full Operations Manual available for Download. In order to access the file as a member, scan the code here and click the button: Download Ops Manual.

Notes:

Chapter 11

Hiring and Onboarding New Team

It is an understatement to say that the job market has been on a roller coaster for the past few years. We have heard from many dentists around the nation that finding qualified employees is now tougher than ever. Many report that they struggle to even get applicants to show up for interviews.

It is not uncommon to experience 100% turn over of your team members in the first two years of ownership. With this in mind, it is important that you get extremely well versed in systems to hire, onboard, and run the 'people' side of your business.

In order to lead an organization effectively, it is important that you clearly convey your expectations for each role within the practice. Designing onboarding protocols and systems with this in mind will greatly increase the likelihood that your team members will be successful in their positions.

Putting together all of these hiring and onboarding documents can be mind-boggling. This chapter is dedicated to simplifying the important and complex topics. Below is a list of the elements that are important to include in the Hiring and OnBoarding portion of your practice's operations manual:
1. Organizational Chart
2. Job Descriptions
3. Hiring Advertisements
4. Interview Process
5. Onboarding Process
6. Specially for Startups- what are the first positions to hire for?

It is important to remember that each place on the org chart can only be occupied by one person, however a person can reside in more than one place. If we were to turn this example into an image, it would be shown to the side here. In essence, your new office

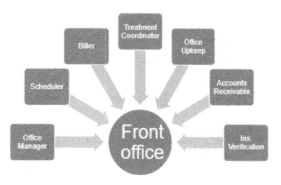

manager can also be your 1. Insurance Verification, 2. Scheduler, 3. Biller, and 4. Treatment Coordinator. So, one person can sit in 5 or more seats, but there should not be two office managers.

Once we have the positions defined by name, we must clearly define the duties associated with each role. This will need to be described in careful detail and reviewed with each team member.

Job Description

A job description is quite simply the list of tasks for a job. If you currently work at a practice prior to acquisition, observe the varying tasks that are being performed by each team member and list those out in careful detail. The more detail that you can include, the greater the likelihood that those duties will be completed thoroughly and correctly.

When creating ideal Job Descriptions we have found it helpful to envision your "perfect" team member. What qualities does he or she possess? How do they work with other team members? During this process, determine which traits are non-negotiable versus which are just a bonus. Having these parameters clean prior to the interviewing process will almost always save time and produce a superior team.

At the end of this chapter we have included examples of job descriptions for Dental Assistants, Hygienists and Front Office Coordinators.

Hiring is Marketing

When you begin recruiting to fill a position on your team, it is important to attract the most qualified applicants possible. To make sure that this occurs, you will need to take off your administrator's hat and start thinking like a marketer. Crafting a story that allows the potential team member to envision themselves on the team typically produces great results. Explicitly describing the culture and values of the office and the fact that you value the community and provide exceptional care to the patients will also separate your post from the more traditional "help wanted" ad.

Here's the major items to include in the job advertisement:
- Job listing headline
- Position and practice overview
- Responsibilities/expectations
- Job skill requirements
- Compensation
    - Use Payscale.com to compare what current salary expectations are for that position
- Include detailed application instructions to separate applicants, who are detail oriented and follow directions
    - Ex: What is your favorite candy? Who is your favorite basketball team?

Here's an example of ours:

Dental Assistant at Example Dental

Salary: ranging from $13-19 per hour depending on experience
Employment type: full-time

An exceptional person is needed to join our team. If you feel bored and unappreciated with your current job and you think you have the talent to be a valuable team player- we'd love to meet you!

Our practice is looking for an exceptional person to join our team. Our dental group offers:
- Positive family-oriented environment
- A team dedicated to making dentistry a better experience
- Paid Vacation and Sick Time
- 401 K
- Opportunities to grow professionally

To Apply- fill out the application, email a resume to (XXXXXXXXX), but make sure to include what your favorite candy is in the subject line, (Dr. Smith is addicted to Rolo's in his smores right now!).

If you're truly driven, you could speed up the hiring process by taking our personality tests here: https://www.ondemandassessment.com/link/xxxxxxxxxxxxxx

Job description
We are looking for an exceptional Dental Assistant that would be responsible for:
- Keeping the guest experience fantastic
- Assisting Doctors with procedures
- Helping answer phones when available
- Keeping the flow of the office sustainable with guest experience

Required Skills :
- X-ray certified
- Coronal polishing
- High school diploma or GED

Company Description:
Our dental practice provides comprehensive care for all ages and all dental needs. We offer a full range of services, including IV sedation and wisdom teeth extractions, implants, and all other types of general dentistry. Dr. Smith is driven to create the best guest experience at a fair price, and our practice has grown exponentially since it started two months ago. Check out our

webpage at **XXXXXXX.com** for more information on what we do and how we can say 'Relax, Dentistry is Different Here."

In this ad, you will notice we hit all the major points. "Selling" the office to the prospective applicant is very important. Sharing the required skills is next. Sprinkled in there are a few special instructions to see if they can follow directions. If they complete these tasks, it shows that they have an attention to detail that is above average. Now that you have the advertisement written, you will need to decide where to place it. Here's what has worked well for us:

- Indeed
- Craigslist
- Facebook
  - Private ads
  - Facebook groups
- Local Job Boards
  - Google for your area- any schools?
- Professional Organizations
  - State Dental Board

Once you start getting applicants, you can begin the interview process. For positions that you need to be filled on opening day, start the process about 2.5 months before your projected start day. Planning this far out will give you sufficient time to interview without having to be rushed into making a hiring decision.

Interview Process

Once you have a stack of applications, you can begin to sort through them in a systematic manner. Here are the steps to the interview process:

1. Phone Interview
2. Skills Testing
3. In-Person Interview
   a. Reference Check
   b. Background Check
4. Working Interview (In some scenarios)

Phone Interview

The phone interview is the step in the process that can actually save you time down the road. It should be a quick (less than 10 minute) phone call with an applicant that quickly covers the highlights of the job

Phone Interview Hot Sheet

Applicant Name:_____ Date:_____

Position Title:_____

Availability: Full Time / Part Time

Desired Salary Range:_____

Experience (Years): <1   1-2   3-4   5-6   6+

On a scale of 1-10 rank: Total:_____
  Personality:_____
  Attitude:_____
  Professionalism :_____
  Eloquence:_____
  Knowledge of position:_____
  Culture Fit:_____

Notes:

and their history and background. During the phone interview you will want to gather this information:

1. What is their pay range?
2. When could they potentially start?
3. Do they have acceptable people skills?
4. Do you have a good feeling about them?

When going through this process, we like to have a quick phone interview sheet to use as a framework during the call. See below.

(Check out the document vault for the phone and in-person interview help sheets.)

Phone Interview

Name: _____   Reason for wanting to change: _____

Energy   1 2 3 4 5   People Skills   1 2 3 4 5

Tell me a bit about yourself?
What attracted you to apply for this position?
How would you describe your work style?
What can you tell me that isn't on your resume that is important for me to know about you?
Why are you leaving your job/why are you looking elsewhere?
What questions can I answer for you?

Once they have completed the phone interview, you will want to let them know as quickly as possible whether they will continue on in the process or not. If they are to continue on, you will want to email them the skills assessment link.

Skills and Personality Testing

As you consider the skills and personality testing format, you will have two different options. One is the free option, which could include websites like 16personalities.com or online DISC assessments. In these assessments, you will get personality testing and a fairly good feel for the applicants. These aren't overly descriptive however, and may leave you wanting more information.

On the skills testing side, we haven't found any free tests out there. However, if you have the time, you could always write your own skills tests, and see if applicants can complete a series of specific tasks. For example, you could deliver a series of instructions about creating a spreadsheet in Excel, and see if the applicant can complete it and email the file back to you. Here's some quick notes on free tests:

- Personality tests
  - DISC
    - Quick, simple and to the point
  - 16personalities.com"
    - In depth
    - Shows how they operate in different environments
- Skills test
  - Build your own

As you look at paid resources, there are a couple of good choices. The best one that we've come across is called HireSelect by the Criteria Corporation. The tests given out by HireSelect are both high in quality and in the range of tests they offer. They can do multiple different types of personality tests that are rated against the job you are hiring for. They can also give skills tests on Word, Excel, Web knowledge, computer literacy, and typing speed. Here's a quick summary of the options you have for paid testing.

- Personality tests
  - Criteria Corp (Hire Select)
  - Kolbe Index
- Skills Test
  - Criteria Corp (Hire Select)
  - Indeed

On the following 8 pages are the examples of the tests that we use including the Personality profile, the Cognitive Aptitude Test, and the Computer Literacy and Internet Knowledge Test.

After reviewing these skills tests and making sure that you think they might be a good fit in your company, the next step is the In-Person Interview.

> PERSONALITY TEST

Employee Personality Profile

s a personality assessment that measures twelve traits. Scores for each trait are
l as a percentile ranking, which reflects how a person scored on that trait relative to
takers. There are no "high" or "low" scores on the EPP; rather, people with certain
to be a better fit for certain jobs. The EPP contains a series of job-specific
ks that assess how good a fit a person's personality is for a given position.

Results Summa

77%

Analyst Match

)etails

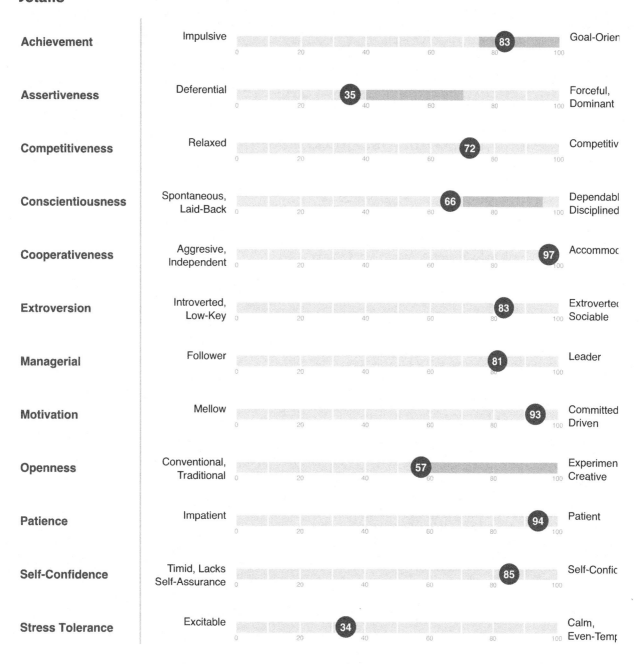

Trait	Left label	Score	Right label
Achievement	Impulsive	83	Goal-Orien
Assertiveness	Deferential	35	Forceful, Dominant
Competitiveness	Relaxed	72	Competitiv
Conscientiousness	Spontaneous, Laid-Back	66	Dependabl Disciplined
Cooperativeness	Aggresive, Independent	97	Accommoc
Extroversion	Introverted, Low-Key	83	Extroverteo Sociable
Managerial	Follower	81	Leader
Motivation	Mellow	93	Committed Driven
Openness	Conventional, Traditional	57	Experimen Creative
Patience	Impatient	94	Patient
Self-Confidence	Timid, Lacks Self-Assurance	85	Self-Confic
Stress Tolerance	Excitable	34	Calm, Even-Temp

core Explanation

Achievement Percentile — 83

e Achievement (ACH) scale score reflects an individual's ability to follow ough and complete tasks and to achieve specific goals. It is also related the amount of interest that a person has in intellectual or conceptual rk. The ACH score in the 83rd percentile for this person indicates he or e consistently achieves and follows through. This person is likely to rform at an above average level at work or in a career, and has an ove average level of attention or energy available for intellectual asoning or conceptual work. This person is likely to be successful in ademic activities. The ability to perform and follow through is likely to be parent at work or in this individual's career history.

Assertiveness Percentile — 35

e Assertiveness (AST) scale score provides a gauge of an individual's ectness in expressing himself or herself and in dealing with others. This rson's AST score in the 35th percentile indicates an individual who is atively unassertive.

Competitiveness Percentile — 72

e Competitiveness (CMP) score reflects the need to win, to perform tter than others, or to surpass standards of achievement or rformance. This individual's CMP score in the 72nd percentile suggests at he or she is likely to value competitiveness, but only in areas that are rticularly important to him or her.

Conscientiousness Percentile — 66

e Conscientiousness (CON) scale is an indicator of a person's ndencies with respect to being deliberate, self-disciplined, organized and pendable. This person's score in the 66th percentile suggests he or she reliable, hard-working, careful, and organized. Individuals with scores in s range tend to be goal-oriented, dependable and persistent in work ttings.

Cooperativeness Percentile — 97

e Cooperativeness (COP) score indicates a person's level of comfort in rking closely with others and in taking the lead from others. A low COP ore does not necessarily indicate uncooperativeness, but may indicate lependence or aggressiveness in dealing with others. This COP score in e 97th percentile suggests that this person is likely to display a high level cooperativeness.

Extroversion Percentile — 83

e Extroversion (EXT) scale score indicates the degree to which a rson sees himself or herself as socially outgoing. For this individual, the T score in the 83rd percentile indicates a person who is likely to see nself or herself as extroverted. He or she is likely to be seen as more tgoing than most in business or social situations.

Managerial Percentile — 81

The Managerial (MGT) score represents the degree to \ person's work strengths combine with his or her achieve motivation, interpersonal strengths, and inner resources pattern similar to that of individuals in managerial and sɪ roles. This individual's MGT score in the 81st percentile that his or her general characteristics are moderately sir those of individuals in management or supervisory roles person is likely to be able to delegate authority and to h ability to inspire and motivate others. This person may b having moderately good overall management potential.

Motivation Percentile — 93

The Motivation (MOT) scale score is intended to repres person's inner drive, commitment to achieve, and the st inner emotions, needs, and values. This MOT score in t percentile indicates a person whose motivation or inner relatively strong.

Openness Percentile — 57

The Openness scale measures the extent to which an iɪ imaginative and creative, as opposed to down to earth a conventional. The Openness score of 57th percentile inɑ someone who scored in the middle range in Openness. individuals are generally practical and down to earth. W averse to experimenting, such individuals often prefer conventional approaches and routines. People who sco middle range are generally able to strike a balance betw detail-oriented and not losing sight of the "big picture."

Patience Percentile — 94

The Patience (PAT) scale indicates a person's ability to cope with frustration encountered in completing tasks oɪ conflict-laden situations. This individual's PAT score in tl percentile suggests that he or she is more patient than ɪ

Self-Confidence Percentile — 85

The Self-Confidence (SCN) score is an indicator of the l confidence and self-assurance an individual brings to hi work. The SCN score in the 85th percentile suggests thɪ is, in general, self-confident and self-assured.

Stress Tolerance Percentile — 34

The Stress Tolerance scale measures the ways in whicɦ respond to stress. The Stress Tolerance score of 34th p indicates this individual will generally be calm and even- though they may sometimes respond emotionally to eve under stressful conditions. People who score in the midɑ for Stress Tolerance generally do not worry too much ak others perceive them, and are able to accept constructiⱱ criticism

Manager — 71%

t important score for managers is the Managerial trait, where
ers tend to be a better fit for such roles. Higher scores in
iveness and Assertiveness are also characteristic of the
benchmark. On the other hand, low to medium scores in
iveness are appropriate for people in managerial roles,
being too accommodating and empathetic can be a
e to effective and objective decision-making. As a group,
s also tend to have above average scores in Extraversion.

Accounting/Finance — 76%

ge, accountants tend to be considerably more introverted
rest of the population, reflecting the fact that their jobs do not
olve a high degree of social stimulation. They also tend to
er than average scores in Openness, reflecting their
ce for the traditional and conventional over the experimental
e. The benchmark for accountants is also characterized by
n average Assertiveness scores and high scores in
itiousness.

Administrative Assistant — 91%

inistrative Assistant benchmark includes high scores in
iveness and Conscientiousness, both of which have been
high performance in these positions. High scorers in
iveness tend to be accommodating and easy to manage, and
ers in Conscientiousness tend to be organized, careful and
Administrative Assistants also tend to have lower than
scores in Assertiveness.

Analyst — 77%

e most prominent traits in the Analyst benchmark profile is
s, in which analysts as a group score almost one standard
higher than the rest of the population. This reflects their
r problem solving and their intellectual curiosity. They also
core highly in Achievement and in Conscientiousness, and on
have slightly higher than average scores in Assertiveness.

Bank Teller — 90%

Teller benchmark is characterized by high scores in
iveness and Patience, which is typical for a customer
riented position. As a group, Bank Tellers also tend to have
er than average scores in Assertiveness and Openness.

Collections — 73%

ctions benchmark is very similar to the Sales benchmark, as
iveness, Assertiveness and Extraversion are all correlated
ess in both sales and collections. High scores in
itiousness and Stability are also assets for collections agents.

Customer Service — 83

ustomer Service benchmark features high scores in
erativeness and Patience, both of which are important for
ng positive customer experiences. High scorers in
cientiousness tend to be reliable and careful, and those in
mer Service positions also tend to have lower than averag
ness scores.

Front Desk/Reception — 85

eceptionist benchmark is similar to the Customer Service
scores in Conscientiousness, Cooperativeness, and Patien
tant in this position, and receptionists also tend to have lov
ange scores in Assertiveness.

Medical Assistant — 81

ledical Assistant benchmark is similar to the Customer Se
. High scores in Conscientiousness and Cooperativeness
in patient-facing positions. High scores in Conscientiousne
set for Medical Assistants, as deliberate, careful, and deta
ed people will be more likely to prosper in these positions.
ge scores in Openness are also typical.

Production/Manufacturing — 72

nufacturing positions, Conscientiousness and Cooperative
been shown to positively correlate with performance. High
s in Conscientiousness tend to be careful and dependable
corers in Cooperativeness can be easier to manage. Proc
nnel typically have lower than average Openness scores a

Programmer/Developer — 83

ammers and software engineers tend to be significantly m
erted than the general population, reflecting the fact that th
-day jobs often do not involve extensive social interaction
, programmers also have much higher than average score
ness, a function of their high degree of intellectual curiosit
villingness to experiment. Programmers also typically are
corers in Assertiveness or Conscientiousness, and have l
verage scores in Stability.

Sales — 68

ales benchmark features high scores in Competitiveness,
vement and Extraversion. Each of these has been shown
ate with success in sales roles. Salespeople tend to be m
ive than average, and commonly have lower than average
erativeness scores, as being too accommodating can be a
y in effective sales closing.

Interview Questions

Achievement

Jessie scored in the range for Achievement. Questions to confirm this include:

- Tell me about your experience in defining long-range goals. Be specific and discuss how you set a particular goal, how you measured progress towards the goal, and how successful you were.
- Describe a time at work when you set a series of small goals to achieve a bigger underlying goal.
- Talk about your strategy at work to ensure that you are able to follow through in completing all of your various tasks, projects, and goa

Assertiveness

Jessie scored below the range for Assertiveness. Questions to explore this include:

- Give an example of how you have had to be firm and direct with someone you managed because of their failure to meet expectations
- Give an example of how you have had to be firm or uncompromising with someone in order to accomplish a work-related goal.
- Describe a time that you spoke out on an issue of importance to you, even though you knew it would not be well received (by co-work

Conscientiousness

Jessie scored below the range for Conscientiousness. Questions to explore this include:

- Tell me about a time when your organizational skills helped you solve a problem or challenge at work.
- Describe a specific thing you've done to try to improve your organizational skills.
- Describe a time when you went out of your way to make sure that a task or project was completed on time.

Openness

Jessie scored in the range for Openness. Questions to confirm this include:

- Tell me about a time when you encountered a change in the way things were done at your job; describe this change and how you responded to it.
- Discuss a time when you needed to be creative at work.
- Discuss your preference for working with clear and conventional tasks versus working with creative and open-ended tasks.

lidity & Response Style

Validity and Response Style scales represent the individual's level of attention to the meaning of EPP statements (Inconsistent sponding) and tendency toward positive (Self-Enhancing) or negative (Self-Critical) self-presentation.

Inconsistent Responding (INC)   0

Inconsistent Responding (INC) score of 0 indicates that person paid appropriate attention to the meaning of EPP tements when giving responses, and is not likely to have ponded carelessly or in a completely random fashion.

Self-Critical Score (CRT)   12

In addition, the **Self-Critical (CRT) score** in the 12th percentile suggests that this individual may be less likely than most to make statements that are highly self-critical or reflect weaknesses. These scores and the Self-Confidence score in the 85th percentile suggest a person who will confidently give the best possible self-presentation and leave others with a favorable impression.

Self-Enhancing Score (ENH)   91

s person obtained a **Self-Enhancing score (ENH)** in the st percentile. This style of self-presentation is somewhat re positive than that of most people. This is often a aracteristic of job applicants or others trying to make a od impression in business, social, or other situations, or it y reflect an individual who is confident about identity, work bits, or capabilities. Others are likely to describe this son's self-regard as highly positive.

Computer Literacy & Internet Knowledge Test

The CLIK is an assessment of basic computer proficiency. It measures a person's ability to use Internet browsers and common desktop applications such as email and word processing programs.

Results Summary

Proficient
Overall Rating

Overview

Not Proficient		Proficient	Highly P

17

Candidate Responses

Correct? Simulation 1 (Total Time Taken: 64 seconds)

- ✓ Open a document
- ✗ Minimize a window
- ✓ Address an email (To, Cc, Subject)
- ✓ Copy and paste
- ✓ Send an email

Correct? Simulation 2 (Total Time Taken: 58 seconds)

- ✓ Maximize a window
- ✓ Use the browser address bar
- ✓ Create a new browser tab
- ✓ Use the Favorites/Bookmarks menu
- ✗ Perform simple Bing search

Correct? Multiple Choice

- ✓ 1. To go to the previous web page in an internet browser, you would click:
- ✗ 2. To move the browser window around the desktop, you would need to begin by clicking:
- ✓ 3. When filling out an online form, the Tab key usually moves the cursor from one field to the next.
- ✓ 4. Putting a file in the Recycle Bin permanently deletes it from your computer.
- ✓ 5. Which password is the most secure?
- ✓ 6. To restore the minimized window, you would click:
- ✓ 7. To bring up a contextual menu like the one below, you would:
- ✓ 8. Which of the following will NOT allow you to print a browser web page?
- ✓ 9. Which of the following is a common document format found on the internet?
- ✓ 10. To find text on a web page, you would press:

APTITUDE TEST

Criteria Cognitive Aptitude Test

he CCAT measures cognitive aptitude, or general intelligence. This test provides
n indication of a subject's ability to solve problems, digest and apply information,
arn new skills, and think critically. Cognitive aptitude is one of the most accurate
b predictors of job success for any position.

Results Summary	
34	**84**
Raw Score	Percenti

---

law Score

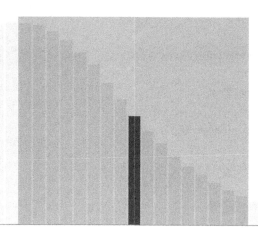

l 2 3 4 5 6 7 8 9 10 11 12 13 14 15 16 17 18 19 20 21 22 23 24 25 26 27 28 29 30 31 32 33 34 35 36 37 38 39 40 41 42 43 44 45 46 47 4

Selected Score Range

Analyst
Suggested Range: 26-42

 ✓ In R:

---

lesults Details

ssie Hain achieved an overall score of 34, which means Jessie answered 34 questions correctly. This corresponds to a perce
nk of 84, meaning Jessie scored better than 84% of the people who have taken this test. Below are details of how Jessie perf
specific sub categories.

Spatial Reasoning Percentile	**85**

bility to visualize, make spatial
dgements, and problem solve;
rrelated to general intelligence.

Verbal Ability Percentile	**85**

Reasoning and comprehension of
words, constructive thinking, and
attention to detail.

Math & Logic Percentile	**ε**

Ability to reason using numbers a
numerical concepts. Also measur
logic and analytical thinking.

Suggested CCAT Score Ranges by Position

*Based on national norms compiled by (

Jessie Hain | Score: 34

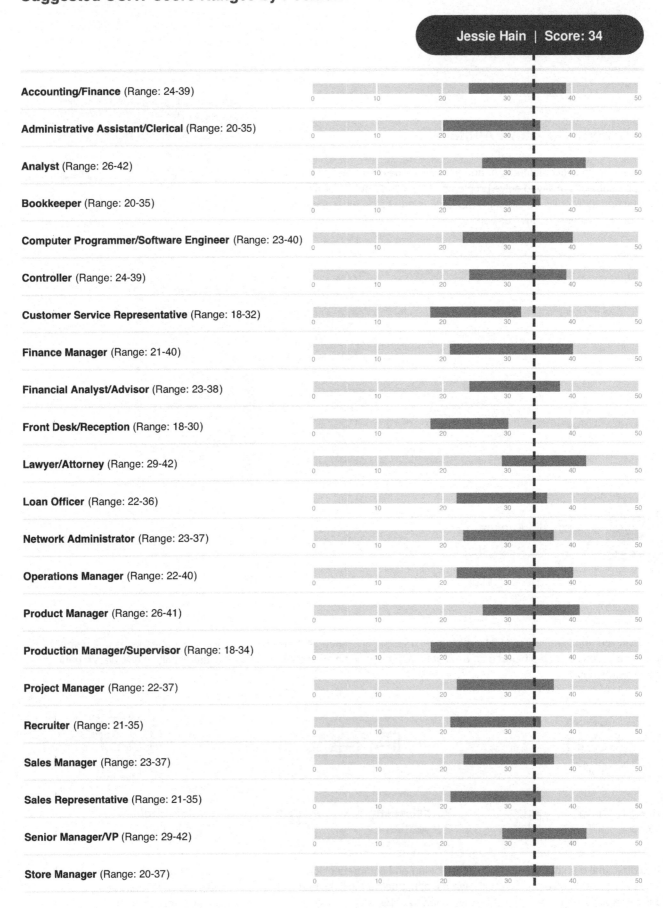

Accounting/Finance (Range: 24-39)

Administrative Assistant/Clerical (Range: 20-35)

Analyst (Range: 26-42)

Bookkeeper (Range: 20-35)

Computer Programmer/Software Engineer (Range: 23-40)

Controller (Range: 24-39)

Customer Service Representative (Range: 18-32)

Finance Manager (Range: 21-40)

Financial Analyst/Advisor (Range: 23-38)

Front Desk/Reception (Range: 18-30)

Lawyer/Attorney (Range: 29-42)

Loan Officer (Range: 22-36)

Network Administrator (Range: 23-37)

Operations Manager (Range: 22-40)

Product Manager (Range: 26-41)

Production Manager/Supervisor (Range: 18-34)

Project Manager (Range: 22-37)

Recruiter (Range: 21-35)

Sales Manager (Range: 23-37)

Sales Representative (Range: 21-35)

Senior Manager/VP (Range: 29-42)

Store Manager (Range: 20-37)

In-Person Interview

The in-person interview can be stressful and haphazard the first few times that you do it, but as with most things- systemization works. Here are the major points regarding an in-person interview that has helped us through the years.

- Ask the applicant to explain what the position is or entails in their own words.
- Questions to ask during the interview-
  - Can you tell us about yourself?
  - Explain what drew you to this position.
  - Can you give me an example of a time that you made a mistake and how you handled it?
  - How comfortable are you in your skills with (position required skill)?
  - (Role playing scenarios based on position)
    - Examples-
    - Back office- Have the applicant present a treatment plan like they would a patient and explain financing and insurance coverage
    - Front office- Have interviewee check a patient out, schedule next appointment, collect payment, and answer an "incoming phone call"
    - Office manager- Have interviewee role play a call with a difficult patient who wants a refund or a situation where they must confront a subordinate about a mistake that was made
  - Compensation-
    - When you left your previous position what was your level of compensation?
    - What is your preferred compensation range for this position?
    - Do you mind if we contact your previous employer? If no, why not?
- **Don't ignore a gut feeling**

Attached in the document vault is the In-Person interview help sheet. Take, customize, and use this sheet as you go through the interview process with applicants. Since in many instances you will not have an office yet, try to do the interviews at a coffee shop or other fast-style restaurant.

After the interview process, you will want to check references. While this is mostly a routine exercise, you will sometimes find out interesting facts about an applicant. These are usually 5 minute phone calls, and is an important part of the process that should not be skipped.

  - Always check references
  - Call previous employers
    - "Tell me about the time you worked with them"
    - MOST IMPORTANT QUESTION
      - "Would you hire this person again?"

Background Check

If the applicant has good references, then the next step is the background check. This step is usually relatively inexpensive, but should always be done. The cost is typically $12-25 based upon the number of states they have lived in.

This is how we approach the background check with potential employees,

> *"At this point in the process we run background checks on all potential applicants, and I will run yours today since you are at the final stages of the interview process. Is there anything I should know about that may come up on the background check?"*

With this statement, you will give them an opportunity to explain anything that may appear on the report, but it's also the way they address a potential issue. If they come right out and share a mark on their record, we give them bonus points for honesty and candor. When nothing is shared and a negative report is delivered, we typically eliminate that applicant from contention. In many instances, you will also want a working interview. This is only applicable after you own an office, but the working interview can often help to demonstrate how a potential applicant will handle real life situations. Here are some notes on working interviews:

- Regarding compensation, find the range and pay them towards the lower end for the day
- If hired, can add working interview compensation to first paycheck
- If not hired, have check ready for end of day
- Test direct skills- back office skills, insurance verification skills, phone skills, etc.

If the applicant feels like a good match, you can offer them a position. This can be done verbally and followed up with a written offer letter.

Offer Letter

Here's an example offer letter that you can edit for your own purposes. Sometimes the legalities of this type of letter differs from state to state so make sure to have a state-specific HR professional take a look vefore you send it off.

Dear Keith Beasley,

Acme Co. (the "Company"), is pleased to offer you employment with the Company on the terms described below. This offer of employment is conditioned on your satisfactory completion of certain requirements, as more fully explained in this letter. Your employment is subject to the terms and conditions set forth in this letter.

• Position. You will start in a full-time position of Business Analyst. In this capacity, you will perform duties and responsibilities that are reasonable and consistent with such position as may be assigned to you from time to time. You will report directly to Ronna Marquis. You agree to devote your full business time, attention, and best efforts to the performance of your duties and to the furtherance of the Company's interests.

• Compensation and Employee Benefits. In consideration of your services, you will be paid $50,000.00 per Year, payable in accordance with the standard payroll practices of the Company and subject to all withholdings and deductions as required by law. As a regular employee of the Company you will be eligible to participate in a number of Company-sponsored benefits.

• Employment Relationship. Employment with the Company is for no specific period of time. Your employment with the Company will be "at will," meaning that either you or the Company may terminate your employment at any time and for any reason, with or without cause. Any contrary representations which may have been made to you are superseded by this offer. Although your job duties, title, compensation and benefits, as well as the Company's personnel policies and procedures, may change from time to time, the "at will" nature of your employment may only be changed in an express written agreement signed by you and the Company.

• Contingent Offer. The Company reserves the right to conduct background and/or reference checks on all prospective employees. Your job offer is contingent upon clearance of such background and/or reference check as applicable. This offer will be withdrawn if any of the above conditions are not satisfied.

• Company Policies and Additional Agreements. As an employee of the Company, you will be expected to abide by and adhere to the Company's rules and standards. As a condition of your employment, you will be subject to all applicable employment and other policies of the Company. You will also agree to execute any additional agreements required by the Company at the start of your employment. You further agree that at all times during your employment (and afterwards as applicable), you will be bound by, and will fully comply with, these additional agreements.

• Continuing Obligations. By signing this letter, you confirm with the Company that you are under no contractual or other legal obligations that would prohibit you from performing your duties with the Company. You further confirm that you will not remove or take any documents or proprietary data or materials of any kind, electronic or otherwise, with you from your current or former employer to the Company without written authorization from your current or former employer, nor will you use or disclose any such confidential information during the course and scope of your employment with the Company.

• Entire Agreement. This letter and other accompanying documents supersede and replace any prior understandings or agreements, whether oral, written or implied, between you and the Company regarding the matters described in this letter.

If you wish to accept this offer, please sign and date below. As required, by law, your employment with the Company is also contingent upon your providing legal proof of your identity

and authorization to work in the United States. This offer, if not accepted, will expire at the close of business on February 22, 2021.
We look forward to having you join us no later than March 1, 2021.

Very truly yours,
By: Steven Smith
  (Signature)
Name: Steven Smith
Title: CEO

ACCEPTED AND AGREED:
Keith Beasley
(PRINT EMPLOYEE NAME)

_____
(Signature)
February 22, 2021
Date
Anticipated Start Date: March 1, 2021

_____

Hopefully you have built up enough authority with your advertisement and interview process that this applicant will jump at the chance to work with you. In that case, they will get moved onto the next steps of the process- the OnBoarding System.

Onboarding

The onboarding process in many dental practices is broken or non-existent. It often consists of a mix of instructions to 'follow-the-trainer' and 'watch me do this once'. After the new employee watches one of your team members a few times, they are often expected to know exactly what to do and how to do it.

A much more effective and efficient way to onboard team members involves proactively creating systems that help train and support an employee with clarity and clear expectations. These expectations should be very detailed, and time bound. In our sample documents, we have laid out these benchmarks in a 30-60-90 day format. These expectations specify what proficiencies are at 30 days, 60 days, and 90 days. The 30 day list is relatively rudimentary. At 60 days, they will be expected to know and be proficient in all items from the 30 days list, plus added responsibilities, skills, and knowledge applicable for a more seasoned employee. At 90 days, the employee should 'graduate' from the official onboarding process and become a full fledged employee. If they cannot complete many of the duties of the 90 day checklist, however, they can be kept on probation for another 30 days. If there are multiple points of failure it may be time to consider termination so that you can free them to seek a position where they can succeed.

Throughout the process, you will need to have an infrastructure in place that will facilitate growth and proficiency. Here's a quick list of considerations to reflect upon throughout this process:
- What does success in this position look like?
- Have all resources been provided to facilitate success?
  - Education- Show, tell, do
  - Online Videos
  - Written Workbooks
- Set benchmarks and deadlines for skills proficiency
  - 30,60,90 Benchmarks
- Pair with a mentor
  - Make sure mentor/mentee are working well together
- Recognize progress
  - Be positive and not always correcting mistakes
- Encourage questions and feedback
  - Make sure the new hire is being heard
- Maintain disciplined adherence to the onboarding cadence
  - Be present and keep up on progress
  - Set Calendar reminders on your calendar to follow up with them

At the beginning of the onboarding process, we recommend having everything in a packet for review and to give to them on their first day. This includes all the administrative HR packets and other checklists, documents, and the 30-60-90 day benchmarks. Below is a list of items that you might consider including in an onboarding packet:

Universal Onboarding Checklist
- History of practice
- Practice owners bio
- Team members and positions
  - Ask staff for their bio for the new hire to get to know them
  - Ask for a bio from the new hire
- Foundational Principles
- Handbook Policies
- Benefit package Information
- Meetings and performance reviews on schedule
- Onboarding scheduled with _____(Mentor)

Positional Onboarding
- The training should include but is not limited to:
  - Patient touch points and verbiage
  - Protocol sheets for each set of duties they will encounter
  - Accountability agreements
  - 30-60-90 day expectations
  - Weekly benchmarks and check-ins

Onboarding Cadence
- 3 days Universal Onboarding-Universal trainer
- Positional training 90 days+
- Weekly check-ins with trainer/supervisor
- Participation in weekly team growth meetings (lead measures)
- Monthly performance reviews with 30/60/90 day assessments
- Ongoing cultural, procedural/clinical mentorship and guidance

This is an exhaustive list, feel free to include, exclude or customize as you see fit. On the next few pages you will see an example packet for the Dental Assistant position, and there are specific packets for other positions in the online document vault.

Here's the list of items that we include in the Onboarding Folder for each position of the practice:
1. Welcome Emails per position
2. Universal Onboarding Document
3. Book per position

Sample Welcome Email:

Hello!

We are glad you've decided to join the Capital Dental team! We have an amazing team dedicated to creating a better dental experience, and we hope that you can get up to speed with our systems so that you feel comfortable from the first day.

You should have received an email from our payroll service 'Gusto'- which will allow you to accept the job offer, as well as put in all your personal information. It's all done digitally now, so make sure to find that email in case it might have gone to your spam folder. (Remember on your first day to also bring 2 forms of ID as well- Drivers License, Social Security Card, or Passport.)

So first things first, we run on a set of core values that are the most important rules that we live by in the practice. We also have a mission and vision for where these rules will take us as we grow. Read this **Mission, Vision, Core Values document,** *there may be a test- so memorizing these is a good idea!*

To get a general sense of how we run as an office and how to do a few things around the office, we created a 'Universal On-Boarding' document. Read that **HERE**. *With any job, there's usually a legalese manual. It's boring and filled with a bunch of policies, however it does cover a lot of what it means to be a good employee with our company. So grab a coffee and read that* **HERE**.

For your position as a Dental Assistant, there's a few documents that outline exactly what you will be doing as well as a few videos that will help you understand Open Dental better. Read and watch those below:
- *Job Description for Dental Assistant*
- *Clinical Setups*
- *OD Video Overview*
- *OD Clinical Videos*
    - *Clinical 1- Entering Tx*
    - *Clinical 2- Clinical Notes*
- *If you have any certifications for your degree or skills, like radiology or coronal polishing, please bring a copy of that on your first day as well.*

All our doctors and hygienists run by a general set of guidelines set up by our Doctors. We tried to codify these diagnoses and treatments as much as possible. It's a huge book, and is really just a primer on what and how to do things. It's not required reading but if you ever want to flip through it, you can read it **HERE**.

Overall we run a different sort of practice. It's based on the first core value of 'Fantastic Guest Experience'. All the systems listed above create a guest experience that is relaxing, well-timed, and smooth. We want every player on the team to be an All-star, and we feel these systems get us there. If you have any questions, please don't hesitate to reach out to us, Dr. Buyer at (402) XXX-XXXX or Dr. Associate at (402) XXX-XXXX.

Thank you again, we look forward to starting this adventure with you!

Grain Acres Dental Team

Here's an example of the Universal OnBoarding Document that we have for employees to get a quick run-down on how we run the practice:

Universal On-Boarding

1. Core Values
   a. Fantastic Guest Experience
   b. Always be Improving
   c. Hungry and Humbly Confident
   d. Have Each Other's Backs
2. Cadence of Accountability-
   a. Morning Huddles
      i. Start promptly at 7:45am each morning before we see patients
      ii. Each column (hygiene 1/2/3, doctor 1, surgical 1/2) will go through each of the following about pts in their column:
         1. Pts with balances
         2. Other treatment in their chart not yet scheduled that could potentially be completed same day, schedule allowing
         3. Scheduling conflicts/issues
         4. Note if a pt is being seen by hygiene or doctor before/after coming to your chair
   b. Weekly Growth Meetings
      i. Every Tuesday over lunch (30mins weekly/1.5hrs monthly)
      ii. Each person chooses a lead measure to focus on pertaining to their position (See hyperlink for examples of lead measures for each position
      iii. During the weekly meeting each person is held accountable for meeting their lead measure they chose the previous week (was the goal met or not), new or different goals are created for each staff member
   c. Quarterly Off-Site Meetings
      i. 4(ish) hour meeting held quarterly to review newly implemented policies or procedures
      ii. Team bonding time
      iii. Discuss/resolve issues noticed since the last meeting

3. Payroll- How it works
   a. Gusto (third party payroll service) - how you get paid
   b. Bi-weekly pay system
4. Employee Manual- Link to document
5. Where to park

6. How to clock in
    a. Log in to Open Dental
    b. Click the "Manage" tab on the left hand side
    c. Find your name under the list of employees and click on it
    d. Under displayed time choose either click Clock In, or choose "Home/Lunch" and click Clock Out For

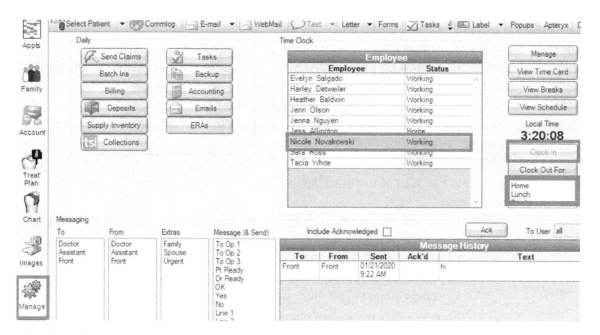

7. Break room etiquette and where to store items
    a. Any food in the cupboards is up for grabs- help yourself
    b. We are all coffee fiends so whoever is available make a fresh pot before huddle/first pt :)
    c. Wash your OWN dishes
    d. There are lockers in front of the fridge with locks if you want to keep your purse/coat/personal dry foods in them
    e. We are all responsible for keeping the break room tidy and somewhere appealing enough to eat in
8. How to use OpenDental (DOCUMENT)
9. How Chairs work-
    a. Each chair is pre-programmed to tip the pt back and set them up per the Dr's preference
        i. Click the A on either side of the back of the chair to tip the pt back
        ii. Click the E on either side of the back of the chair to sit the patient back up
        iii. Adjust the tilt or base of the chair with the respective arrow buttons
    b. Why Surgical Chairs are different
        i. The base of the surgical chairs raise all the way up so the doc/assistant can stand for surgery
10. How Clear Tubs are meant to work
    a. Referred to as "el cheapo's"

  b. Meant to help reduce hallway traffic by keeping stock in each room

  c. One box should have all disposables (2x2 gauze, cotton rolls, cotton tipped applicators, hve/saliva ejector tips and any anesthetics/needles)

  d. The other box (doctor side) will have restorative materials (composite, etch, prime/bond, flowable, composite gun etc) See pictures in Op Manual for reference

11. How Nitrous Works - Link to video and document

12. Sedation protocol- Link to video and document

13. How Suction and Pumps Work

  a. Pumps are turned off each night by the last person out of the office, and turned back on again by the first person to arrive the next morning

    i. On/off buttons located right next to the back door

  b. Traps are changed weekly in each operatory- you are responsible for your own room

14. How Sterilization works/flows

  a. The lab is the start of the sterilization area, the lab is included in the "dirty side" of sterilization

    i. Starts with the grinder→ sink → vibrating machine/lab handpiece/suck down stint machine

    ii. "Dirty side" continues to ultrasonic unit → sink → packaging area

    iii. Two utraclaves separate the dirty side of sterilization from the clean side (NO DIRTY GLOVES SHOULD TOUCH THESE MACHINES) {open/remove trays with clean ungloved hand, load trays with gloved dirty hand}

    iv. Ultraclaves are unloaded to the right of the machines to the clean side of sterilization, items will then be placed on trays or put away in clean cupboard to the right of the counter

15. How Pano/CBCT Work - Link to video and document

16. Organizational Structure- Link to document

17. Who to call when sick

  a. Office Manager - Phone number

  b. Group Chat if looking for coverage

18. Who is manager/supervisor

  a. Dr. Killeen / Dr. Chapek at the moment

19. How Sedation patients are scheduled

  a. 1st is consult for 30-50 minutes in 3rd column

  b. Sedation appointments are 1.5hrs-2hrs and several things are required prior to scheduling

    i. NEED:

      1. Referral from general dentist

      2. Track pt info on oral surgery spreadsheet

      3. X-rays/Pano for 3rds

      4. New Patient paperwork filled out

      5. Sedation Videos watched

20. Flow of a Patient through the office
    a. Pt enters the practice and checks in with front desk
    b. Assistant/Hygienist brings pt back (gives office tour if new patient) and seats them in the operatory
    c. If possible the assistant will check pt out for services completed that day
    d. Hygiene will be trained to check out for fluoride to avoid congestion at check out up front
    e. If not able to check pt out (questions/large balance) bring pt up to the front to one of the two check out stations
    f. If noone is available at the designated checkout take pt to front desk or seat pt in waiting room and let them know that someone will be with them asap
        i. Leave completed routing slip with Tacia face down at her desk so she knows to help your pt next

Here is the example of the Dental Assistant Handbook. In the document vault, you will have access to examples for multiple positions as needed.

Dental Assistant

Handbook

(Adapted from Dr. Summer Kassmel, Castle Peak Dentistry, Vail Colorado)

Capital Dental

Dental Assistant Handbook

Table of Contents

Other Documents to be given:
- Employee Handbook
- Clinical Calibration Book
- Tech Systems

Job Description

Capital Dental Core Values:

- Fantastic guest experience
- Always be improving
- Hungry & Humbly confident
- Have each other's backs

The ideal assistant is:

- Friendly and outgoing
- Dedicated to outstanding customer service
- Gentle with clinical applications
- Organized
- Team Player
- Excellent communicator with staff and patients
- Honest
- Compassionate
- Helpful with every other area of the office

Summary: Assists Dentist during examination and treatment of patients, administers company policies and regulatory compliance and maintains dental supplies are stocked for procedures. It is essential to be flexible, friendly and work in a team environment. In addition, the Dental Assistant must display excellent communication skills and a commitment to patient care.

Essential Duties and Responsibilities:

- Ensure quality patient service by providing thorough patient care, effective communication, and personal attention in a gentle, caring manner.
- Prepare the treatment rooms, patient records, equipment and necessary instruments for dental procedures in accordance with universal safety precautions and other safety standards.
- Provide chairside assistance to the Dentist including but not limited to basic and complex restorative, surgical, endodontic, pediatric, emergency and preventive dental treatment procedures.
- Take dental impressions.
- Record accurate and concise patient/treatment information and clinical notes into dental programs as instructed by Dentist.
- Explain to each patient the purpose and process involved in their dental care and reinforce the treatment plan prescribed by the Dentist.
- Explain consents in detail, answer patient questions and obtain patient signatures.
- Expose quality radiographs; date and label properly.
- Perform various laboratory procedures (pouring study models, fabricating bleaching trays, etc.)
- Maintain sterilization area as clean and organized

- Support business goals by utilizing schedules effectively and supporting the practice revenue objectives.
- Effectively communicate and develop a strong working relationship with the Dentist and promote teamwork through cooperative and professional behaviors.
- Follow OSHA and CDC Guidelines for a clean workplace.
- Maintain dental equipment in proper working order.
- Conserves dental resources by using equipment and supplies as needed to accomplish job results.
- Ensure operation of dental equipment by completing preventive maintenance requirements, following manufacturer's instructions, troubleshooting malfunctions, calling for repairs, maintaining equipment inventories, and evaluating new equipment and techniques.
- Responsible for stocking treatment areas.
- Contribute to team effort by accomplishing related results as needed.
- Conduct work in compliance with Federal, State, and other regulations, (i.e. OSHA, HIPAA, ADA, etc.) and clinic policies and practices.
- Other duties may be assigned.

Qualifications: To perform this job successfully, an individual must be able to perform each essential duty satisfactorily. The requirements listed below are representative of the knowledge, skill, and/or ability required. Reasonable accommodations may be made to enable individuals with disabilities to perform the essential functions.

Education: High School diploma or GED, Radiology and Coronal Polishing Certificates encouraged

Knowledge, Skills and Abilities:

- Ability to effectively manage more than one activity at a time required.
- Ability to work well on a team.
- Ability to provide accurate and precise attention to detail.
- Ability to effectively assist providers.
- Ability to be well-organized and reliable.
- Ability to make anterior and posterior temporary crowns with good margins and contacts.
- Ability to maintain professional and technical knowledge.
- Ability to exhibit a positive attitude required.
- Knowledge of Open Dental software, MS Outlook, Work and internet search engines preferred.
- Specified training courses as mandated by State for certification, licensure or registration requirements.

Physical Demands: While performing the duties of this job, the employee is regularly required to talk and hear. The employee is frequently required to stand, walk, use hands to finger, handle or feel, and reach with hands and arms. The employee is occasionally required to climb or balance, stoop, kneel or crouch. The employee must occasionally lift and/or move up to 25 pounds. Specific vision abilities required by this job include close vision, distance vision, peripheral vision, depth perception, and ability to adjust focus. The physical demands described here are representative of those that must be met by an employee to successfully perform the essential functions of this job. Reasonable accommodations may be made to enable individuals with disabilities to perform the essential functions.

Checklists to be Proficient In:

- Daily Checklists for Dental Assistant
- Phone Skills and Scripts
- Greeting and Start Appointment Flow
- Room Setups according to Plan
- End of Appointment Flow
- Clinical Charting and Treatment Planning Organization
- Sterilization
- Office Cleaning
- Take IO Pictures with IO Camera
- Take Pictures with Extra-Oral Camera
- Take IO Radiographs
- Take Pano/CBCT
- Schedule a Crown Seat
- Making Platelet Rich Fibrin (PRF)
- Sending Cases to the Laboratory
- Making Bleaching Trays or Essix Trays
- Setting up Surgery and IV appointments

- Daily Checklists for Dental Assistant

Assistant Daily Checklist

Name_____ Date_____

Room 2   Room 5   Room 6

MORNING CHECKLIST	☐ Turn on pumps
	☐ Turn on Tanks of Nitrous & Oxygen
	☐ Make sure water bottles are full and add capsules of water cleaner
	☐ Turn on TV/music in tx rooms, go to phone and pick relaxing station on 'Soundtrack' app
	☐ Turn on all lights, x-ray machines (including pano) in tx rooms/sterilization center/lab
	☐ Fill Ultrasonic with water and cleaner, package instruments when finished shaking
	☐ Empty clean Autoclave
	☐ Load sterilizer with dirty instruments that did not fit, packaged the night before, start if full
	☐ Set up for first appointment
	☐ Restock rooms if necessary
	☐ Make up trays on clean side of sterilization
	☐ Check schedule for any conflicts/questions – prep for A.M. Huddle

DOWN-TIME CHECKLIST	☐ Check with Hygiene to see if they need help
	☐ Check other Doctors/Hygiene schedules for efficiency/rooms
	☐ Check to make sure all lab cases are scheduled
	☐ Check to complete any needed labwork
	☐ Check 1 day/1 week schedule, address any issues
	☐ Restock rooms as needed
	☐ Go through office cleaning checklist
	☐ Ask front desk to help with Recall List and other duties

END OF DAY CHECKLIST	☐ Check schedule 1 day/1 week ahead
	☐ Check to make sure all AM lab cases have arrived
	☐ Turn off TV & comp. screen, mouse and keyboard
	☐ Suction all lines with SlugBuster
	☐ Restock rooms
	☐ Make sure all notes are done- run incomplete procedure notes report
	☐ Sweep & Take out Trash
	☐ Prep for Morning Huddle with Route Slips
	Make sure all rooms are wiped down and ready to set up the next morning
	☐ Load Autoclave with dirty instruments
	☐ Run instruments through the Ultrasonic/package
	☐ Drain Ultrasonic
	☐ Package any dirty instruments that have gone through the Ultrasonic and will not fit in the Autoclave, to be loaded in the morning
	☐ Shut off Oxygen & Nitrous Tanks
	☐ Shut off pumps (last person to leave)

Signature of Manager: _____

Assistant Morning Huddle Prep						Emergency Times:		
Appt Time	Pt. Name	Todays TX	Balance Due?	Plus Tx Opportunity	Recare Sched/Fam Needed	X-rays Needed	Notes	

    a. Daily Checklist is to be fully completed in AM and PM Sections

    b. Downtime duties are to be completed between patients and throughout the middle of the day

    c. Morning Huddle Sheet is to be done either the morning before patients, or previous day

- Phone Skills and Scripts
  - a. Phones should always be answered within the first 3 rings
  - b. Physically Smile before answering so that your voice intonates warmth
  - c. 'Thank you for Calling Capital Dental, this is _____, how may I help you?"
  - d. Follow the 3 E's: Empathy, Energy, and Edification
  - e. Scripts for the 7 major categories of phone calls can be found in the Operations Manual
- Greeting and Start Appointment Flow
  - a. Have Route Slip with you to remember name/appointment/details
  - b. Greet patient at the door to the waiting room, close door behind you/them
  - c. Show them where bathroom is, checkout, CBCT Technology, and then proceed to room
  - d. Once in room, point out relaxation/technology (Nitrous for $5, TVs on Ceiling, music)
  - e. Remind them of time allotted for the procedure, ask if they have next appointments
- Room Setups according to Plan
  - a. See Operations Manual to see how each setup is done
- End of Appointment Flow
  - a. Make sure all treatment is completed in OpenDental (Check w/ Doctor for accuracy)

- b. Remove patient bib and offer facial wipe if necessary
- c. Taking Payment in the Treatment Room- follow CC protocol
- d. Otherwise walk up to front desk to take payment if complicated
- Clinical Charting and Treatment Planning Organization
    - a. Understand OpenDental entering existing conditions
    - b. Enter in Treatment plan
    - c. Understand ordering the treatment plan
    - d. Make sure fees are generally correct with insurance or membership plan
- Sterilization
    - a. Ensure that sterilization and lab are clean and that there is no backlog of instruments
    - b. Ultrasonic is emptied of all instruments
    - c. Instruments are bagged and put into sterilizer
    - d. Sterilizer is started if close to full
    - e. Completed sterilizer is emptied of all clean instruments
    - f. Use the Operations Manual picture as a guide
- Office Cleaning
    - a. Make sure office cleaning checklist is completed daily/weekly as needed
    - b. Clean floors in treatment rooms
    - c. Clean countertops in all areas
    - d. Clean front and employee bathrooms according to checklist
    - e. Take out all trash in treatment rooms and offices
    - f. Take out recycling as needed
    - g. Clean employee Break room
    - h. Vacuum all carpeted areas
- Take IO Pictures with IO Camera
    - a. Use blue DY-80 Camera
    - b. Make sure it's plugged into the USB and has sleeve on it
    - c. Sometimes button on camera doesn't work, so click to take with mouse
    - d. Take pictures as needed and then number them with correct tooth number
- Take Pictures with Extra-Oral Camera
    - a. Open up iphone, go to IOCSnapshot App
    - b. Go to OpenDental Images Folder
    - c. Click the button for iPhone & Aircard
    - d. On the phone the computer ID should pop up on the menu, click it
    - e. Take photos as necessary
    - f. Once back on the computer, label all photos with teeth numbers
- Take IO Radiographs
    - a. See Operations Manual for specific exposure settings on the handheld x ray machine and Apteryx (digital x ray software) how to document
    - b. Make sure you have the correct arms, tabs, and rings for the particular type of x ray you wish to take
        - i. Posterior PA's- Yellow tab with curved arm and yellow ring
        - ii. Anterior PA's- Blue tab with curved arm and yellow or blue ring
        - iii. Bitewings- Vertical or Horizontal tab with straight arm and red ring
    - c. Materials Needed
        - i. Handheld x ray machine
        - ii. Sensor with barrier
        - iii. Tabs/rings/arms for type of x ray desired

           iv.   Lead apron
- Schedule a Crown Seat
  a. Allow 2 weeks for Precision Aesthetics (lab) to fabricate crown
  b. 30 mins for appointment (10-10-10) in overflow column if possible
  c. Schedule while patient is in the chair if possible in order to avoid congestion up front
- Making Bleaching Trays or Essix Trays
  a. Maxillary and mandibular alginate impressions, capturing all margins
  b. Pour up models in lab with green or buff stone (personal preference-green sets up faster), let stone set up
  c. Separate models from alginate
  d. Trim the models with the grinder, making sure the palate is either empty or has a hole in it to allow maximum suction so the trays fit correctly
  e. Hand scale models to define margins and get rid of any bubbles or imperfections in stone
  f. Heat up vacuum machine in the lab
  g. Melt the Soft EVA .040 bleach tray material and vacuum to models
  h. Let the material cool down and then separate the material from the models
  i. Cut out the bleach trays and scallop trays along the defined margins
- Take Pano/CBCT
  a. See document
- Making Platelet Rich Fibrin (PRF)
  a. See document
- Sending Cases to the Laboratory
  a. See document
- Setting up Surgery and IV appointments
  a. See Setup document

30/60/90 Day Goals for Dental Assistant

1=Rarely; 2= Sometimes;3=Sometimes;4=Mostly; 5=Always

30 Day Goals

_____ Clock in/Clock out

_____ Arrive 15 minutes before morning huddle

_____ Answer phones in accordance with core values and guidelines

_____ Greet patients and give office tour correctly

_____ Complete Daily Checklists with no error

_____ Able to take Pano / CBCT individually

_____ Able to take IO Pics and IO Radiographs

_____ Able to setup rooms according to plans

_____ Able to answer the phone and answer simple questions

_____ Stay on time with appointments

Areas I feel I excel:

_____

_____

_____

Areas I feel I need help or additional training:

_____

_____

_____

Date Scheduled to Review: _____

Additional training to be completed by: _____

60 Day Goals

_____ Be able to do all 30 day tasks with no supervision

_____ Prioritize daily tasks

_____ Able to assist with Hygiene or Doctor Treatment planning and charting

_____ Keeping sterilization clean and on schedule

_____Know the schedule and prioritize accordingly

_____ Ability to put in lab cases in the computer accurately

_____ Ability to schedule crown seat appointments accurately

_____ Taking payments in the treatment room

_____ Be able to locate office forms in the computer

Areas I feel I excel:

_____
_____
_____

Areas I feel I need help or additional training:

_____
_____
_____

Date Scheduled to Review: _____

Additional training to be completed by: _____

90 Day Goals
_____ Do all above 60 day tasks with no supervision
_____ Check out patients: Collect correct $ and schedule patients accordingly
_____ Review & Present treatment plans
_____ Payment plans for patient's according to office guidelines using Flex
Areas I feel I excel:

_____
_____
_____

Areas I feel I need help or additional training:

_____
_____
_____

Date Scheduled to Review: _____

Additional training to be completed by: _____

Departmental Assessment Form- Dental Assistant (Done Monthly)

Name_____   Date_____

1= Never, 2= Rarely, 3= Sometimes, 4=Mostly, 5= Always

I come prepared to morning huddle, and bring energy to start the day.

      1   2   3   4   5

I greet patients warmly and give the office tour according to the standard script.

      1   2   3   4   5

I seat the patient, adjust the headrest to comfort and then do patient napkin.

      1   2   3   4   5

I ask three non-dental questions and record the date and responses in our office designated area.

      1   2   3   4   5

I verify treatment that will be performed, take blood pressure as needed and record that in the chart notes immediately.

      1   2   3   4   5

I verify all appropriate equipment, materials, and instruments are set-up according to standardized protocol.

      1   2   3   4   5

I brief the doctor on whether the patient is existing or new, the treatment that will be completed during visit, or if there is any significant health history.

      1   2   3   4   5

I make sure that the most current radiographs are ready for doctor to review.

      1   2   3   4   5

If the patient is new to the office, I introduce them to the doctor.

      1   2   3   4   5

After treatment I escort the patient to the front office -side check-out area

      1   2   3   4   5

I follow the NDTR protocol.

      1   2   3   4   5

I sterilize and place barriers according to standardized protocol.

      1   2   3   4   5

I complete chart entries prior to day's end.

      1   2   3   4   5

I show empathy and concern when talking to patients.

      1   2   3   4   5

I edify doctor and staff to patients whenever possible.

      1   2   3   4   5

I communicate respectfully and effectively with the entire team in the practice.

      1   2   3   4   5

I turn in my end of day sheet to OM nightly.

      1   2   3   4   5

I follow the core values of the practice on a daily basis.

      1   2   3   4   5

I stay busy with tasks and check in with my manager frequently if I have unused time.

      1   2   3   4   5

I try to grab the phone ASAP if I hear it ringing.

      1   2   3   4   5

I help hygienists with probing when I have free time.

      1   2   3   4   5

Accountability Agreement: Dental Assistant

I_____, understand that my responsibilities as a Dental Assistant include, but are not limited to the duties listed on the following documents:

1. Dental Assistant Job Description
2. Dental Assistant Daily Task Sheet & Weekly Task Lists
3. Room Setups, Protocols and Procedures

Additionally I am aware of Capital Dental's core values as listed below and will strive to conduct myself in a manner consistent with these values:

Capital Dental Core Values:

- Fantastic guest experience
- Always be improving
- Hungry & Humbly confident
- Have each other's backs

Team Member Signature:_____Date:_____

Practice Owner (CEO)   Signature:_____ Date:_____

Chapter 12

What to do When...

There are countless unanticipated situations that occur during dental practice transitions. We took some of our experiences as well as some compiled from selected members of DSN and shared them in this chapter. Hopefully you will learn some lessons as well as get a good laugh or two from the stories in this chapter.

15 Minutes Late is Okay

A doctor once told us that his patient base had been "trained" by the previous owner and team to be consistently late. This scenario occurs for a number of different reasons ranging from poor team communication to the absence of consequences for undesired behavior. The first step to rectifying this trend is to begin to communicate the new expectations to the patient base and to roll play the appropriate language with the team. A firm but reasonable response to a patient may sound something like this:

Thank you for letting us know that you'll be 15 minutes late, Mrs. Jones. Since we only had 60 minutes scheduled with Dr. Buyer for this appointment, unfortunately we will not be able to complete the entire treatment we had planned for today. We are booked solid so in respect to our other patients, we have to stay on schedule.

Handling a situation in this manner demonstrates to the patient that your time is valuable and that other people are affected by their tardiness. Secondarily, this also shows that you are a busy practitioner that cares for many people. This further adds to your authority and the value patients place on your time. After all, no one wants to be treated by a dentist that isn't regarded highly enough to have an extremely busy practice.

It is also important to establish set policies for scenarios that are bound to arise regarding late patients and rescheduling. Let's say for instance that a patient walks in at 9:15 for their 9:00 appointment. What's your policy? How late can a patient be and still be treated?

Here are some suggestions:
1. A patient will be reappointed if they show up more than 15 minutes past their appointment time.
2. A patient should be scheduled a minimum of 4 weeks out when they are rescheduled for being late or missing an appointment. This will cause an inconvenience for the patient and reinforce the value of your time and the importance of arriving on time.

3. If a patient is a repeat offender for showing up late or missing appointments, allow them to schedule only on a "same day" basis.

Overall, communication and consistency will be the key ingredients to controlling patient behavior. Some patients will conform very quickly to the new policies while others will not. In the latter cases it is better in the long run to allow patients who do not respect you or your team's time to leave the practice.

Payment Due

One of the fastest ways to find yourself in a cash-flow or accounts receivables crisis is the "We will send you a bill" policy. The supermarket wont send you a bill for your groceries. They expect payment at the time you receive your goods. In much the same way, it's imperative to collect the patient's payments, whether it's fee-for-service or the PPO deductible and co-pay at the time of service. Once again, communication, scripting and roll playing with the team is your best ally in enforcing this office policy.

The conversation can be as simple as this: "Mrs. Jones, it's so nice to see you today! Our policy is to collect the patient portion at the time of service. It looks like we have you here for this procedure today and your portion will be this amount. How would you like to take care of that?" Because of HIPPA regulations, we do not discuss specifics about a patient's treatment or cost of a procedure out loud in the presence of other patients. For this reason, we point to the information on the route sheet without reading it aloud.

Some practices take a deposit in order to reserve the doctor's time when the appointment is made and some offices even have success collecting the entire payment at the time of scheduling. While this does not work for all offices, others have executed this well.

The Bloody Prophy Practice

One of the biggest challenges that new practice owner's face is educating patients about periodontal disease and introducing periodontal protocols into a practice. This is particularly challenging when the previous ownership has not been diagnosing or treating appropriately.

A metric that we always check during our due diligence period prior to purchasing a practice or when coaching a member through a transition is periodontal procedure percentage. If this number is in the single digits or low double digits, we know we are most likely dealing with a bloody prophy practice. In many cases it seems as though these practices have denied the existence of periodontal disease for years if not decades. Often, patients of these practices were treated with a routine prophylaxis without knowing that they had deep pocketing, bleeding or probing and significant bone loss. Once again, communication is very important in education and conversion of these patients to appropriate care and stabilization of their condition. A conversation may sound something like this:

"Mrs. Schmidt, when we do our exams, we start by checking the foundation first which is the gums and bone before moving to the teeth. When looking at your gum tissue, we are seeing

many areas of puffiness and bleeding. You may have noticed some of the numbers that Mary was calling out when she was checking the health of your gum tissue. Numbers 1-3 indicate a normal area, 4 indicates borderline and 5 and above indicates gum disease and infection. This basically indicates that the gum tissue is pulling away from the bone creating inflammation and infection called periodontal disease. The reason that this occurs is…"

As you explain the root causes and consequences of periodontal disease, expect Mrs. Schmidt to ask, "I just had a check-up and cleaning 6 months ago, why didn't Dr. Seller tell me about this?" A good reply would sound something like this:

"Many dentists like to be as conservative as possible by not recommending any unnecessary treatment and this is a good thing, but WHAT WE NOW KNOW, is that untreated periodontal disease will not only lead to bad breath and tooth loss, it also is very dangerous for your overall health. In fact, studies have found that it can lead to a higher risk of heart attacks and strokes, and many other chronic diseases."

A nice addition to this script is from the book Beat the Heart Attack Gene by Dr. Bradley Bale and Amy Doneen. There are a handful of pages that can be referenced, copied, and shaped with your more skeptical patients. While it may take a significant investment in time, your patience and consistent message will eventually lead to a much healthier patient base under your care.

Amalgam Crowns

A familiar scenario that we see play out over and over again in practices sold by late career dentists is the "watch and patch" practice. Much like the "Bloody Prohy Practice," these practices have evolved away from proactive restorative practices into observe and patchwork practices that provide the minimal amount of dentistry possible in order to keep the patient in function. As we have all learned in dental school, providing this type of care has its place - as a temporary fix in emergency situations or in community-based clinic settings or missionary dental settings when there is no other alternative. But what we also know is that putting off inevitable treatment can lead to much larger and even more expensive procedures or permanent tooth loss.

Utilizing an intraoral camera is probably the most helpful tool in creating urgency and showing the patient exactly why you are making the recommendations you are making. Additionally, when presenting their treatment options, try to present what could potentially occur as far as additional costs (RCI< surgical extraction, bone graft, implant placement, etc.) if they wait too long to proceed with the treatment.

If a patient still persists in asking for patchwork treatment, you can simply say something like, "I'm sorry Mrs. Schmidt, I believe that what you are asking is below the standard of care and I don't feel comfortable with that compromise." While this is a hard line, it may be necessary at times depending on the situation.

I'm Retiring, You get a Raise!

One of our DSN Members shared a situation that she had to deal with early in her ownership journey. Shortly after the purchase of a dental practice, she discovered that the departing doctor gave the entire staff significant pay increases just prior to the transition. This was obviously an unanticipated surprise and put her in quite a precarious situation. She ultimately had to have some difficult conversations and it added more stress to an already stressful time.

In order to decrease the likelihood that this happens to you, be certain that the seller has given you information about the staffs' pay rates and any benefits all the way up to the date of closing. There are documents in Chapter 2 and contracts in Chapter 4 that will help you through this process.

The Landlord from Hell

In many transitions, the selling doctor will sell their practice but retain the real estate as an investment and rent it back to the buyer. This can be an ideal arrangement but there are occasions when it doesn't go so smoothly.

We have heard stories and personally dealt with landlords that were unresponsive or unwilling to deal with issues relating to the property. From AC units, to leaky faucets, to cracking walls, to foundation issues. At the end of the lease term the landlord might not be open to extending the lease or to renegotiating the terms moving forward. (This happened to both of us.)

In order to protect yourself, your personal Board of Directors should include a real estate attorney and a lease negotiation. Being represented by a professional with this type of expertise will definitely decrease your stress and the likelihood that you'll be taken advantage of.

Welcome to Business Ownership!

One particular story that drives home the importance of being adequately prepared for as many contingencies as possible came to us from a DSN Member in the midwest. Here is his account in his own words:

I had just purchased my practice and building and was leaving my previous practice to meet my new team at my new practice. I had a feeling of joy and excitement that comes from accomplishing a goal that I had envisioned since the day I started dental school. There was a light snowfall which gave a white blanket of brightness to the winter dreariness. I knew that this was going to be the beginning of a new chapter, a journey filled with ups and downs and new opportunities for growth. I had not even stepped foot in the practice as the new owner yet when I got a call from the seller. He calmly informed me that the sewage pump in the basement of my new building was broken and it had happened in the hour since we had signed all the closing documents. Raw sewage was now backing up into the basement and as the new owner of the building, it was my responsibility to take care of it. Lucky me! The joys of business and building ownership started pretty much right away for me!

When becoming a practice and building owner, it's important to have a plan in place that is triggered in the event of an emergency. Assembling a reliable and trustworthy group of repair companies and trade-specific specialists is a great place to start. If something breaks on your dental delivery unit who will you call? If there's an electrical issue who will be your go-to contact? If a toilet is broken or overflowing, who will be your preferred plumber? If water starts spewing out of a faucet or wall, where is the shut off valve?

Once you have put together your list of contacts, it's important that each person on your team knows where to find it and understands basic building emergency procedures and who to call if the doctor/owner is not available. We have also had good success taking a simple video walk through of the building with specific information and instructions for the team.

The Staff is Untrainable!

Imagine this familiar scenario… you have done your best to onboard your new team and to provide them with all of the resources that you feel are necessary for them to be successful in their positions. While it seems like they understand your goals and expectations, they are not performing up to your standards. It's as if all of your efforts have yielded no results.

When this occurs, it's a good time to reflect upon the root cause of the disconnect. Maybe these team members would respond more favorably if the information was presented in a different manner or via a different modality? Perhaps they need more support or accountability measures in place? Maybe you need to modify your leadership style or delivery?

In a Continuing Education video we have done on DSN about Managing Change, we discuss the large 6 points about the process to change. Remember, to affect change, we need to have:
1. Awareness
2. Buy-In
3. Skills
4. Desire
5. Action Plan
6. Resources

Scan the QR code to the right to access the CE video on 'Managing Change'

So, before coming to a definitive conclusion about the value or capability of a team member, sometimes it's helpful to assess whether you have been clear about expectations, have supported him or her in every way possible and have allowed sufficient time to adjust to the change in ownership. We have found that some of our most talented, valuable, and trusted employees have had a shaky start, and giving up on them too soon would have been a hasty decision.

On the other hand, if you believe that you have done everything in your power to get them trained and they still fail to fit the culture or meet your skill-set standards, it may be time to free them to a new future.

You Get Stuck with Unforeseen Expenses

Every acquisition that we've ever been involved with has resulted in unforeseen expenses. A sterilizer breaks. A server goes down two weeks after the warranty expires. The AC unit only blows hot air. The chair in room one won't recline. These types of "emergencies" can throw a serious wrench in your day, week or month, but are just part of what we are taking on with business ownership.

We believe that even though these types of expenses can sting for a new owner, especially if they occur in clusters and in a relatively short time from closing, that it pays off to fix them the right way. Planning for contingencies is paramount to a successful transition. In order to account for these unpredictable occurrences, it's helpful to have a line of credit available to deploy as needed and avoid costly shut-downs.

Accounts Receivable are Not Being Received

Oftentimes new owners struggle to collect AR that they have purchased from the selling doctor. Our best guess as to why this scenario occurs so often is that patients may feel as though they do not need to pay a new doctor for work done by the previous dentist and the fact that payments may be delayed from insurance companies during the credentialing process. If you find yourself in this scenario we recommend reviewing Chapter 4 as a refresher as to the most effective and efficient methods of collecting AR. We often see after the fact that people have paid too much for AR. With this in mind, if you are considering buying the AR with the practice, factor in the cost of uncollectible monies from patients who refuse to pay the new owner. Also keep in mind the time value of money. Simply put, the longer it takes to get paid, the less the money is worth to you.

The Associate Doctor is your New Employee

When we inherit an associate dentist during a practice sale there are a myriad of considerations that have to be made. One of the trickiest scenarios that we've seen is when the associate doctor was not aware that a sale was taking place and was caught off guard. What can make this even more difficult is when the doctor was led to believe that they were going to be a partner or given the opportunity to buy the practice outright.

When this occurs, and you wish to retain him or her as an associate, it's best to be completely transparent and begin anew. These scenarios can place you right in the middle of an emotionally charged situation, but keep in mind that this is now your practice, you did not make the decisions that led to their current experience. You also know that you will be fair and supportive in your new role as practice owner. Open conversations about contract details and compensation need to be had uncovering as many details as possible with the help of professional advisors and counsel.

There will be a delicate balance to this process and it will test your diplomacy and leadership style right out of the gate. Now is the time to define your expectations as clearly as possible, the level of systemization you intend to deploy, your culture and clinical philosophies and how he or she will fit into your long term plan for the practice.

Notes:

_____

_____

_____

_____

_____

_____

_____

_____

_____

_____

_____

_____

_____

_____

_____

_____

_____

_____

_____

_____

_____

_____

_____

_____

Chapter 13

More Resources and Open Dental Startup Resources

Other Resources

Inside the Dental Success Network, there is a room specifically meant for doctors who are starting and taking over a practice, "Starting up Right: Acquisition and Denovo Secrets". This is where you can either search for posts about a topic, or ask your own question to the faculty and members of that group. It is always good to have people in your corner and colleagues to turn to who have been there, and want to help and support you in your journey.

Also as you traverse this journey, rely on your own physical and mental health. We recommend using the 4 Futures Journal created by co-author Mark Costes and Alastair Macdonald, and edited by co-author Addison Killeen. This is the journal we use everyday, and we think it might be of help to you as well. The framework is helpful because it has many pages set up perfectly for the endless to-do lists you will encounter! (TheFourFutures.com)

Practice Launchpad

 The final recommendation we can make is to check out the Practice Launchpad, a private coaching firm dedicated to startups and acquisitions. This group of coaches includes Dr. Taher Dhoon, Dr. Chris Green, and us, your authors. If you are interested in learning more about how we help startups and acquisitions, check out the website www.thepracticelaunchpad.com. In this coaching group you get unfiltered access to the coaches, unlimited resources, and even greater savings on some of the common pieces in the process including floor plan design, systemization, and HR consulting. If you prefer a deeper level of instruction, check out this resource.

Final Notes & OpenDental Packet

We know that the acquisition process is a marathon, and we sincerely hope that this book has helped you through that process. We have seen it all, and we hope that any mistakes we made in the past will help you to avoid making the same mistake in the future! If you ever need guidance along the way, we hope that you can refer back to this book for the solutions you seek.

The next section is the OpenDental Startup Guide, a 55 page packet that goes along with a video series in the Dental Success Network. This guide will help you as you set up the database from scratch. The online documents also have active links to all the appropriate resources available to make this setup process simple and straightforward. We know this will help!

Finally, we wish you good luck and much success. You have gotten this far, we know that you will do well as you grow this new venture!

Opendental Setup Checklist

2021 EDITION

ental Success Network

aster Checklist

- DSN Vendor Discounts & Bridges

- Providers & List

- Operatories

- Schedule Views

- Procedure List and Fee Schedules

- Definitions

- Appointment Views

- Procedure Buttons

- Program Buttons

  - Auto Notes Templates

  - Procedure Note Template in Procedure

  - Definitions - Quick Add

  - Setup RX Pad

  - Educational Video Tracts for different positions

Master Checklist

Before you Begin		OD Web Link	Download
Data Paths	Make sure the paths to Open Dental Folders work on all computers	Data Paths Setup	Video & Notes Below
Bridges: - Digital Imaging - Other	Program Bridges need to be set up on the server and workstations - **Select Digital Imaging software** - **Determine any other 3rd party softwares**	Program Bridges DSN Vendor Discounts	Visit Website for specific Vendor Discounts
Clearinghouse	Select the clearinghouse you will send e-claims to, then set up.	E-Claims	

Initial Setup		OD Web Link	Download
General Practice Information	Turn on features (Clinics, Medical, EHR)	Show Features	
	Set up Dentists and Hygienists as Users	Provider List	
	If using clinics, enter clinic names, addresses, defaults (Only for Multiple Clinic Users)	Clinic Setup	
	Enter practice name, address, default providers.	Practice Setup	
Scheduling	Enter employee names.	Employee List	
	Set up Operatories (Assign Dentists, hygienists, clinics)	Op Setup	
Fee Schedules	Set up provider schedules. This affects open/close times in the appointment module.	Schedule Setup	
	Create Fee Schedule- Download template and change by % - **Mark any hygiene procedures as 'is hyg. Procedure'** - **Enter any non-standard codes**	Procedure Code List	Fee Schedule Example Non-Standard Codes and Usage
	Customize Definitions and options	Definitions Setup	
Users and Security	Printing and Scanning - **Set default printers** - **Set default scanners**	Printer Setup Imaging Setup	
	Create Users, assign groups, assign security settings	Security	Example Security Settings
	Define pay periods and rules for Time Clock	Time Card Setup	

Appointments		OD Web Link	Download
Views	Set up appointment schedule Views, HIPAA Compliant View	Appointment View Setup	Video and Samples
Recall	Verify default recall types.	Recall Types	
	Set defaults for the recall list.	Recall List Defaults	
Charting		OD Web Link	Download
	Set up Procedure Buttons	Procedure Button Setup	Video and Document
	Auto-Notes	Auto Note Setup	Video and Template
	Procedure Notes and Notes Standard for Every Procedure	Procedure Notes	
Preferences and Customization		OD Web Link	Download
	Set default preferences for each module	Module Preferences	Change Setting
	Set the title bar, language options, and task list defaults	Misc Setup	
	For printed claims, set the default claim form. (Advanced)	Claim Form Setup	
	Define custom background, text, and notification colors.	Definition Setup	
	Schedule- set up block scheduling.		Video and Spreadsheet
	Set up Rx Pad		Video and Notes below
Install into System		OD Web Link	Download
	Allergies	Allergy List	
	Medications	Medication List	
	Problems	Problem List	
	Referrals	Referral List	
	Dental Laboratory List	Lab Setup	
FINAL MUST-DO	BACKUPS - Cloud and Local		Video

1. DSN Vendor Discounts & Bridges
[LINK to Discounts](#) for DSN Members

- Add-On Softwares to Consider
  - Flex   Mango Phones- DSN Discount
  - Modento - DSN Discount
- E-Claims
  - Dental X-Change
  - Renaissance
- ApteryX
  - X-Ray Imaging

2. Providers & List

- Fill out the list below in preparation to input all providers:

Provider List			
Doctor 1	Name:	DOB:	License State:
Abbreviation:	State Rx:	DEA:	License #:
	Medicaid ID	NPI:	Color Choice:
	Hourly Production Goal:		
Doctor 2	Name:	DOB:	License State:
Abbreviation:	State Rx:	DEA:	License #:
	Medicaid ID:	NPI:	Color Choice:
	Hourly Production Goal:		
Doctor 3	Name:	DOB:	License State:
Abbreviation:	State Rx:	DEA:	License #:
	Medicaid ID:	NPI:	Color Choice:
	Hourly Production Goal:		
Hygiene 1	Name:	DOB:	License State:

Abbreviation:	State Rx:	DEA:	License #:
	Medicaid ID:	NPI:	Color Choice:
	Hourly Production Goal:		
Hygiene 2	Name:	DOB:	License State:
Abbreviation:	State Rx:	DEA:	License #:
	Medicaid ID:	NPI:	Color Choice:
	Hourly Production Goal:		
Hygiene 3	Name:	DOB:	License State:
Abbreviation:	State Rx:	DEA:	License #:
	Medicaid ID:	NPI:	Color Choice:
	Hourly Production Goal:		
Hygiene 4	Name:	DOB:	License State:
Abbreviation:	State Rx:	DEA:	License #:
	Medicaid ID:	NPI:	Color Choice:
	Hourly Production Goal:		
Hygiene 5	Name:	DOB:	License State:
Abbreviation:	State Rx:	DEA:	License #:
	Medicaid ID:	NPI:	Color Choice:
	Hourly Production Goal:		

Employee List

Name:	Wireless Phone:	Email Work:
Email Personal:		
Name:	Wireless Phone:	Email Work:
Email Personal:		
Name:	Wireless Phone:	Email Work:

Email Personal:		
Name:	Wireless Phone:	Email Work:
Email Personal:		
Name:	Wireless Phone:	Email Work:
Email Personal:		
Name:	Wireless Phone:	Email Work:
Email Personal:		
Name:	Wireless Phone:	Email Work:
Email Personal:		
Name:	Wireless Phone:	Email Work:
Email Personal:		
Name:	Wireless Phone:	Email Work:
Email Personal:		
Name:	Wireless Phone:	Email Work:
Email Personal:		
Name:	Wireless Phone:	Email Work:
Email Personal:		

Operatories

Op 1	Op 2	Op 3	Op 4	Op 5	Op 6	Op 7
Name?	Name?	Name?	Name?	Name?	Name?	Name?
Abbrev:	Abbrev:	Abbrev:	Abbrev:	Abbrev:	Abbrev:	Abbrev:
Circle: Doc / Hyg	Circle: Doc / Hyg	Circle: Doc / Hyg	Circle: Doc / Hyg	Circle: Doc / Hyg	Circle: Doc / Hyg	Circle: Doc / Hyg
Provider:	Provider:	Provider:	Provider:	Provider:	Provider:	Provider:

Schedule Views

Schedule Setup: Download Spreadsheet (Doubles as Block Scheduling Sheet)

Procedure List and Fee Schedules

Download Procedure Codes **&** Fee Schedule

6. Security Settings Examples

⊞ Security

Global Security Settings

| Users | User Groups |

User Group:

- Admin Group
- Assistant
- Front Desk
- Hygiene
- Office Manager
- Regular Users

Permissions for group:

- ☐ Main Menu
  - ☐ File
    - ☑ Graphics Edit
    - ☑ Choose Database
  - ☑ Setup - Covers a wide variety of setup functions
    - ☐ Chart - EHR
      - ☑ EHR Emergency Access
      - ☑ EHR Measure Event Edit
    - ☐ Advanced Setup
      - ☑ Replication Setup
    - ☑ Auto/Quick Note Edit
    - ☐ Dental School
      - ☑ Instructor Edit
      - ☑ Student Edit
      - ☑ Admin Evaluation Edit
    - ☑ Schedules - Practice and Provider
    - ☐ Security
      - ☑ Security Admin
      - ☑ Add New User
  - ☐ Lists
    - ☑ Procedure Code Edit
    - ☑ Fee Schedule Edit
    - ☑ Provider Fee Edit
    - ☑ Problem Edit
    - ☑ Providers
      - ☑ Providers - Alphabetize
    - ☐ Referrals
      - ☑ Referral Add
      - ☑ Referral Edit
      - ☑ Referral, Attach to Patient
      - ☑ Referral, Delete from Patient
  - ☑ Reports
    - ☑ Production and Income - View All Providers
    - ☑ Daily payments - View All Providers
    - ☑ Reports - Graphical Setup
    - ☑ Reports - Graphical
    - ☑ User Query
    - ☑ User Query Admin
    - ☑ Command Query
    - ☑ Procedures Not Billed to Insurance, New Claims button (if days newer than 1)
  - ☐ Tools
    - ☐ Misc Tools
      - ☑ Medication Merge
      - ☑ Patient Merge
      - ☑ Provider Merge
      - ☑ Referral Merge
    - ☑ Audit Trail
    - ☑ Repeating Charge Tool
    - ☑ Wiki Admin
    - ☑ Wiki List Setup
  - ☐ Clinics
    - ☑ Unrestricted Patient Search
  - ☐ eServices
    - ☑ eServices Setup
- ☐ Main Toolbar
  - ☑ Commlog Edit
  - ☑ Email Send
  - ☑ Webmail Send
  - ☑ Sheet Edit
    - ☑ Sheet Delete
  - ☑ Task Edit

User Group:

- **Admin Group**
- Assistant
- Front Desk
- Hygiene
- Office Manager
- Regular Users

Permissions for group:

- ☑ Task Edit
- ☑ Task Note Edit
- ☑ TaskList Create
- ☑ Popup Edit (other users)
- ☑ Appointments Module
  - ☑ Appointment Create
  - ☑ Appointment Move
  - ☑ Appointment Edit
  - ☑ Completed Appointment Edit
  - ☑ eCW Appointment Revise
  - ☑ Insurance Plan Verification Assign
  - ☑ Appointment Confirmation Status Edit
  - ☑ Blockouts
- ☑ Family Module
  - ☑ Insurance Plan Edit
    - ☑ Change existing Ins Plan using Pick From List
    - ☑ Insurance Verification
  - ☑ Insurance Plan Change Assignment of Benefits
  - ☑ Insurance Plan Change Subscriber
  - ☑ Insurance Plan Ortho Edit
  - ☑ Carrier Create
  - ☑ Patient Billing Type Edit
  - ☑ Patient Primary Provider Edit
  - ☑ Patient Restriction Edit
  - ☑ Archived Patient Edit
  - ☑ Patient Social Security Number View
  - ☑ Patient Birthdate View
- ☑ Account Module
  - ▣ Claim
    - ☑ Claim Send
    - ☑ Claim Sent Edit
    - ☑ Claim Delete
    - ☑ Claim History Edit
    - ☑ Claim View
    - ☑ Claim Procedure Provider Edit When Attached to Claim
    - ☑ Claim Procedure Received Edit
    - ☑ Update Custom Tracking
    - ☑ PreAuth Sent Edit
  - ☑ Account Procs Quick Add
  - ▣ Insurance Payment
    - ☑ Insurance Payment Create
    - ☑ Insurance Payment Edit
    - ☑ Insurance Write Off Edit
  - ▣ Payment
    - ☑ Payment Create
    - ☑ Payment Edit
    - ☑ Pay Split Create after Global Lock Date
  - ▣ Payment Plan
    - ☑ Pay Plan Edit
  - ▣ Adjustment
    - ☑ Adjustment Create
    - ☑ Adjustment Edit
    - ☑ Adjustment Edit Zero Amount
- ☑ TreatmentPlan Module
  - ☑ Edit Treatment Plan
  - ☑ Edit Treatment Plan Presenter
  - ☑ Sign Treatment Plan
- ☑ Chart Module
  - ▣ Procedure
    - ☑ Edit EO or EC Procedures
    - ☑ Show Procedure Fee

User Group:

Permissions for group:

Admin Group
Assistant
Front Desk
Hygiene
Office Manager
Regular Users

- ☑ Insurance Payment Create
- ☑ Insurance Payment Edit
- ☑ Insurance Write Off Edit
- ▪ Payment
  - ☑ Payment Create
  - ☑ Payment Edit
  - ☑ Pay Split Create after Global Lock Date
- ▪ Payment Plan
  - ☑ Pay Plan Edit
- ▪ Adjustment
  - ☑ Adjustment Create
  - ☑ Adjustment Edit
  - ☑ Adjustment Edit Zero Amount
- ☑ TreatmentPlan Module
  - ☑ Edit Treatment Plan
  - ☑ Edit Treatment Plan Presenter
  - ☑ Sign Treatment Plan
- ☑ Chart Module
  - ▪ Procedure
    - ☑ Edit EO or EC Procedures
    - ☑ Show Procedure Fee
    - ☑ TP Procedure Delete
    - ☑ Procedure Note (full)
    - ☑ Procedure Note (same user)
    - ☑ Group Note Edit (other users, signed)
  - ▪ Completed Procedure
    - ☑ Create Completed Procedure (or set complete)
    - ☑ Edit Completed Procedure
    - ☑ Change Status or Delete a Completed Procedure
    - ☑ Edit Note on Completed Procedure
    - ☑ Add Adjustment to Completed Procedure
    - ☑ Miscellaneous edit on Completed Procedure
  - ▪ Rx
    - ☑ Rx Create
    - ☑ Rx Edit
  - ☑ Ortho Chart Edit (full)
  - ☑ Ortho Chart Edit (same user, signed)
  - ☑ Perio Chart Edit
  - ▪ Anesthesia
    - ☑ Intake Anesthetic Medications into Inventory
    - ☑ Edit Anesthetic Records; Edit/Adjust Inventory Counts
- ☑ Image Module
  - ☑ Image Delete
- ☑ Manage Module
  - ☑ Accounting
    - ☑ Accounting Create Entry
    - ☑ Accounting Edit Entry
  - ☑ Billing
  - ☑ Deposit Slips
  - ☑ Backup
  - ▪ Time Card
    - ☑ Edit All Time Cards
    - ☑ Time Card Delete Entry
  - ▪ Equipment
    - ☑ Equipment Setup
    - ☑ Equipment Delete
- ▪ Merge Tools
  - ☑ Insurance Carrier Combine
  - ☑ Insurance Plan Combine
- ▪ Web Applications
  - ☑ Mobile Web

User Group:

Admin Group
Assistant
Front Desk
Hygiene
Office Manager
Regular Users

Permissions for group:

- ▦ Main Menu
  - ▦ File
    - ☑ Graphics Edit
    - ☑ Choose Database
  - ☑ Setup - Covers a wide variety of setup functions
    - ▦ Chart - EHR
      - ☐ EHR Emergency Access
      - ☐ EHR Measure Event Edit
    - ▦ Advanced Setup
      - ☐ Replication Setup
    - ☑ Auto/Quick Note Edit
    - ▦ Dental School
      - ☐ Instructor Edit
      - ☐ Student Edit
      - ☐ Admin Evaluation Edit
    - ☑ Schedules - Practice and Provider
    - ▦ Security
      - ☐ Security Admin
      - ☐ Add New User
  - ▦ Lists
    - ☐ Procedure Code Edit
    - ☐ Fee Schedule Edit
    - ☑ Provider Fee Edit
    - ☐ Problem Edit
    - ☐ Providers
      - ☐ Providers - Alphabetize
    - ▦ Referrals
      - ☑ Referral Add
      - ☑ Referral Edit
      - ☑ Referral, Attach to Patient
      - ☐ Referral, Delete from Patient
  - ☐ Reports
    - ☐ Production and Income - View All Providers
    - ☐ Daily payments - View All Providers
    - ☐ Reports - Graphical Setup
    - ☐ Reports - Graphical
    - ☐ User Query
    - ☐ User Query Admin
    - ☐ Command Query
    - ☑ Procedures Not Billed to Insurance, New Claims button (if days newer than 1)
  - ▦ Tools
    - ▦ Misc Tools
      - ☐ Medication Merge
      - ☐ Patient Merge
      - ☐ Provider Merge
      - ☐ Referral Merge
    - ☐ Audit Trail
    - ☐ Repeating Charge Tool
    - ☐ Wiki Admin
    - ☐ Wiki List Setup
  - ▦ Clinics
    - ☐ Unrestricted Patient Search
  - ▦ eServices
    - ☐ eServices Setup
- ▦ Main Toolbar
  - ☑ Commlog Edit (if days newer than 2)
  - ☐ Email Send
  - ☐ Webmail Send
  - ☐ Sheet Edit
    - ☐ Sheet Delete
  - ☐ Task Edit

User Group:	Permissions for group:

User Group:
- Admin Group
- Assistant
- Front Desk
- Hygiene
- Office Manager
- Regular Users

Permissions for group:

- ☐ Task Edit
- ☐ Task Note Edit
- ☐ Task List Create
- ☐ Popup Edit (other users)
- ☑ Appointments Module
  - ☑ Appointment Create
  - ☑ Appointment Move
  - ☑ Appointment Edit
  - ☑ Completed Appointment Edit
  - ☑ eCW Appointment Revise
  - ☑ Insurance Plan Verification Assign
  - ☑ Appointment Confirmation Status Edit
  - ☑ Blockouts
- ☑ Family Module
  - ☑ Insurance Plan Edit
    - ☐ Change existing Ins Plan using Pick From List
    - ☐ Insurance Verification
  - ☐ Insurance Plan Change Assignment of Benefits
  - ☐ Insurance Plan Change Subscriber
  - ☐ Insurance Plan Ortho Edit
  - ☑ Carrier Create
  - ☐ Patient Billing Type Edit
  - ☐ Patient Primary Provider Edit
  - ☐ Patient Restriction Edit
  - ☐ Archived Patient Edit
  - ☑ Patient Social Security Number View
  - ☑ Patient Birthdate View
- ☑ Account Module
  - ◼ Claim
    - ☐ Claim Send
    - ☐ Claim Sent Edit
    - ☐ Claim Delete
    - ☐ Claim History Edit
    - ☑ Claim View
    - ☐ Claim Procedure Provider Edit When Attached to Claim
    - ☐ Claim Procedure Received Edit
    - ☐ Update Custom Tracking
    - ☐ PreAuth Sent Edit
  - ☐ Account Procs Quick Add
  - ◼ Insurance Payment
    - ☐ Insurance Payment Create
    - ☐ Insurance Payment Edit
    - ☐ Insurance Write Off Edit
  - ◼ Payment
    - ☑ Payment Create
    - ☑ Payment Edit (if days newer than 1)
    - ☑ Pay Split Create after Global Lock Date
  - ◼ Payment Plan
    - ☐ Pay Plan Edit
  - ◼ Adjustment
    - ☑ Adjustment Create
    - ☑ Adjustment Edit (if days newer than 1)
    - ☐ Adjustment Edit Zero Amount
- ☑ Treatment Plan Module
  - ☑ Edit Treatment Plan
  - ☑ Edit Treatment Plan Presenter
  - ☑ Sign Treatment Plan
- ☑ Chart Module
  - ◼ Procedure
    - ☑ Edit EO or EC Procedures
    - ☑ Show Procedure Fee

User Group:

- Admin Group
- Assistant
- Front Desk
- Hygiene
- Office Manager
- Regular Users

Permissions for group:

- ☐ Insurance Payment Create
- ☐ Insurance Payment Edit
- ☐ Insurance Write Off Edit
- ▣ Payment
  - ☑ Payment Create
  - ☑ Payment Edit (if days newer than 1)
  - ☑ Pay Split Create after Global Lock Date
- ▣ Payment Plan
  - ☐ Pay Plan Edit
- ▣ Adjustment
  - ☑ Adjustment Create
  - ☑ Adjustment Edit (if days newer than 1)
  - ☐ Adjustment Edit Zero Amount
- ☑ TreatmentPlan Module
  - ☑ Edit Treatment Plan
  - ☑ Edit Treatment Plan Presenter
  - ☑ Sign Treatment Plan
- ☑ Chart Module
  - ▣ Procedure
    - ☑ Edit EO or EC Procedures
    - ☑ Show Procedure Fee
    - ☑ TP Procedure Delete
    - ☑ Procedure Note (full)
    - ☑ Procedure Note (same user)
    - ☑ Group Note Edit (other users, signed)
  - ▣ Completed Procedure
    - ☑ Create Completed Procedure (or set complete)
    - ☑ Edit Completed Procedure
    - ☑ Change Status or Delete a Completed Procedure
    - ☑ Edit Note on Completed Procedure
    - ☑ Add Adjustment to Completed Procedure
    - ☑ Miscellaneous edit on Completed Procedure
  - ▣ Rx
    - ☑ Rx Create
    - ☑ Rx Edit
  - ☑ Ortho Chart Edit (full)
  - ☑ Ortho Chart Edit (same user, signed)
  - ☑ Perio Chart Edit
  - ▣ Anesthesia
    - ☑ Intake Anesthetic Medications into Inventory
    - ☑ Edit Anesthetic Records; Edit/Adjust Inventory Counts
- ☑ Image Module
  - ☐ Image Delete
- ☑ Manage Module
  - ☐ Accounting
    - ☐ Accounting Create Entry
    - ☐ Accounting Edit Entry
  - ☐ Billing
  - ☐ Deposit Slips
  - ☐ Backup
  - ▣ Time Card
    - ☐ Edit All Time Cards
    - ☐ Time Card Delete Entry
  - ▣ Equipment
    - ☐ Equipment Setup
    - ☐ Equipment Delete
- ▣ Merge Tools
  - ☐ Insurance Carrier Combine
  - ☐ Insurance Plan Combine
- ▣ Web Applications
  - ☐ Mobile Web

Users | User Groups

User Group:

Admin Group
Assistant
Front Desk
Hygiene
Office Manager
Regular Users

Permissions for group:

- Main Menu
  - File
    - ☐ Graphics Edit
    - ☐ Choose Database
  - ☐ Setup - Covers a wide variety of setup functions
    - Chart - EHR
      - ☐ EHR Emergency Access
      - ☐ EHR Measure Event Edit
    - Advanced Setup
      - ☐ Replication Setup
    - ☑ Auto/Quick Note Edit
    - Dental School
      - ☐ Instructor Edit
      - ☐ Student Edit
      - ☐ Admin Evaluation Edit
    - ☑ Schedules - Practice and Provider
    - Security
      - ☑ Security Admin
      - ☐ Add New User
  - Lists
    - ☐ Procedure Code Edit
    - ☐ Fee Schedule Edit
    - ☐ Provider Fee Edit
    - ☐ Problem Edit
    - ☐ Providers
      - ☐ Providers - Alphabetize
    - Referrals
      - ☑ Referral Add
      - ☑ Referral Edit
      - ☑ Referral, Attach to Patient
      - ☑ Referral, Delete from Patient
  - ☑ Reports
    - ☑ Production and Income - View All Providers
    - ☑ Daily payments - View All Providers
    - ☑ Reports - Graphical Setup
    - ☑ Reports - Graphical
    - ☑ User Query
    - ☑ User Query Admin
    - ☑ Command Query
    - ☑ Procedures Not Billed to Insurance, New Claims button (if days newer than 1)
  - Tools
    - Misc Tools
      - ☑ Medication Merge
      - ☑ Patient Merge
      - ☑ Provider Merge
      - ☑ Referral Merge
    - ☐ Audit Trail
    - ☑ Repeating Charge Tool
    - ☑ Wiki Admin
    - ☑ Wiki List Setup
  - Clinics
    - ☑ Unrestricted Patient Search
  - eServices
    - ☑ eServices Setup
- Main Toolbar
  - ☑ Commlog Edit
  - ☑ Email Send
  - ☑ Webmail Send
  - ☑ Sheet Edit
    - ☑ Sheet Delete
  - ☑ Task Edit

User Group:

Permissions for group:

Admin Group
Assistant
Front Desk
Hygiene
Office Manager
Regular Users

- ☑ Task Edit
- ☑ Task Note Edit
- ☑ Task List Create
- ☑ Popup Edit (other users)
- ☑ Appointments Module
  - ☑ Appointment Create
  - ☑ Appointment Move
  - ☑ Appointment Edit
  - ☑ Completed Appointment Edit
  - ☑ eCW Appointment Revise
  - ☑ Insurance Plan Verification Assign
  - ☑ Appointment Confirmation Status Edit
  - ☑ Blockouts
- ☑ Family Module
  - ☑ Insurance Plan Edit
    - ☑ Change existing Ins Plan using Pick From List
    - ☑ Insurance Verification
  - ☑ Insurance Plan Change Assignment of Benefits
  - ☑ Insurance Plan Change Subscriber
  - ☑ Insurance Plan Ortho Edit
  - ☑ Carrier Create
  - ☑ Patient Billing Type Edit
  - ☑ Patient Primary Provider Edit
  - ☑ Patient Restriction Edit
  - ☑ Archived Patient Edit
  - ☑ Patient Social Security Number View
  - ☑ Patient Birthdate View
- ☑ Account Module
  - ▨ Claim
    - ☑ Claim Send
    - ☑ Claim Sent Edit
    - ☑ Claim Delete
    - ☑ Claim History Edit
    - ☑ Claim View
    - ☑ Claim Procedure Provider Edit When Attached to Claim
    - ☑ Claim Procedure Received Edit
    - ☑ Update Custom Tracking
    - ☑ PreAuth Sent Edit
  - ☑ Account Procs Quick Add
  - ▨ Insurance Payment
    - ☑ Insurance Payment Create
    - ☑ Insurance Payment Edit
    - ☑ Insurance Write Off Edit
  - ▨ Payment
    - ☑ Payment Create
    - ☑ Payment Edit (if days newer than 1)
    - ☑ Pay Split Create after Global Lock Date
  - ▨ Payment Plan
    - ☑ Pay Plan Edit
  - ▨ Adjustment
    - ☑ Adjustment Create
    - ☑ Adjustment Edit
    - ☐ Adjustment Edit Zero Amount
- ☑ Treatment Plan Module
  - ☑ Edit Treatment Plan
  - ☑ Edit Treatment Plan Presenter
  - ☑ Sign Treatment Plan
- ☑ Chart Module
  - ▨ Procedure
    - ☑ Edit EO or EC Procedures
    - ☑ Show Procedure Fee

User Group:

- Admin Group
- Assistant
- **Front Desk**
- Hygiene
- Office Manager
- Regular Users

Permissions for group:

- ☑ Insurance Payment Create
- ☑ Insurance Payment Edit
- ☑ Insurance Write Off Edit
- ▣ Payment
  - ☑ Payment Create
  - ☑ Payment Edit (if days newer than 1)
  - ☑ Pay Split Create after Global Lock Date
- ▣ Payment Plan
  - ☑ Pay Plan Edit
- ▣ Adjustment
  - ☑ Adjustment Create
  - ☑ Adjustment Edit
  - ☐ Adjustment Edit Zero Amount
- ☑ Treatment Plan Module
  - ☑ Edit Treatment Plan
  - ☑ Edit Treatment Plan Presenter
  - ☑ Sign Treatment Plan
- ☑ Chart Module
  - ▣ Procedure
    - ☑ Edit EO or EC Procedures
    - ☑ Show Procedure Fee
    - ☑ TP Procedure Delete
    - ☑ Procedure Note (full)
    - ☑ Procedure Note (same user)
    - ☑ Group Note Edit (other users, signed)
  - ▣ Completed Procedure
    - ☑ Create Completed Procedure (or set complete)
    - ☑ Edit Completed Procedure
    - ☑ Change Status or Delete a Completed Procedure
    - ☑ Edit Note on Completed Procedure
    - ☑ Add Adjustment to Completed Procedure
    - ☑ Miscellaneous edit on Completed Procedure
  - ▣ Rx
    - ☑ Rx Create
    - ☑ Rx Edit
  - ☑ Ortho Chart Edit (full)
  - ☑ Ortho Chart Edit (same user, signed)
  - ☑ Perio Chart Edit
  - ▣ Anesthesia
    - ☑ Intake Anesthetic Medications into Inventory
    - ☑ Edit Anesthetic Records; Edit/Adjust Inventory Counts
- ☑ Image Module
  - ☑ Image Delete
- ☑ Manage Module
  - ☑ Accounting
    - ☑ Accounting Create Entry
    - ☑ Accounting Edit Entry
  - ☑ Billing
  - ☑ Deposit Slips
  - ☑ Backup
  - ▣ Time Card
    - ☐ Edit All Time Cards
    - ☐ Time Card Delete Entry
  - ▣ Equipment
    - ☑ Equipment Setup
    - ☑ Equipment Delete
- ▣ Merge Tools
  - ☐ Insurance Carrier Combine
  - ☐ Insurance Plan Combine
- ▣ Web Applications
  - ☐ Mobile Web

Users | User Groups

User Group:

Admin Group
Assistant
Front Desk
Hygiene
Office Manager
Regular Users

Permissions for group:

- ▪ Main Menu
  - ▪ File
    - ☑ Graphics Edit
    - ☑ Choose Database
  - ☐ Setup - Covers a wide variety of setup functions
    - ▪ Chart - EHR
      - ☑ EHR Emergency Access
      - ☐ EHR Measure Event Edit
    - ▪ Advanced Setup
      - ☐ Replication Setup
    - ☑ Auto/Quick Note Edit
    - ▪ Dental School
      - ☐ Instructor Edit
      - ☐ Student Edit
      - ☐ Admin Evaluation Edit
    - ☐ Schedules - Practice and Provider
    - ▪ Security
      - ☐ Security Admin
      - ☐ Add New User
  - ▪ Lists
    - ☐ Procedure Code Edit
    - ☐ Fee Schedule Edit
    - ☐ Provider Fee Edit
    - ☐ Problem Edit
    - ☑ Providers
      - ☑ Providers - Alphabetize
    - ▪ Referrals
      - ☑ Referral Add
      - ☑ Referral Edit
      - ☑ Referral, Attach to Patient
      - ☑ Referral, Delete from Patient
  - ▪ Reports
    - ☐ Production and Income - View All Providers
    - ☐ Daily payments - View All Providers
    - ☐ Reports - Graphical Setup
    - ☐ Reports - Graphical
    - ☐ User Query
    - ☐ User Query Admin
    - ☐ Command Query
    - ☑ Procedures Not Billed to Insurance, New Claims button (if days newer than 1)
  - ▪ Tools
    - ▪ Misc Tools
      - ☐ Medication Merge
      - ☐ Patient Merge
      - ☐ Provider Merge
      - ☐ Referral Merge
    - ☐ Audit Trail
    - ☐ Repeating Charge Tool
    - ☐ Wiki Admin
    - ☐ Wiki List Setup
  - ▪ Clinics
    - ☑ Unrestricted Patient Search
  - ▪ eServices
    - ☐ eServices Setup
- ▪ Main Toolbar
  - ☑ Commlog Edit
  - ☐ Email Send
  - ☐ Webmail Send
  - ☐ Sheet Edit
    - ☐ Sheet Delete
  - ☑ Task Edit

User Group:

Admin Group
Assistant
Front Desk
Hygiene
Office Manager
Regular Users

Permissions for group:

- ☑ Task Edit
- ☑ Task Note Edit
- ☑ Task List Create
- ☑ Popup Edit (other users)
- ☑ Appointments Module
  - ☑ Appointment Create
  - ☑ Appointment Move
  - ☑ Appointment Edit
  - ☑ Completed Appointment Edit
  - ☑ eCW Appointment Revise
  - ☑ Insurance Plan Verification Assign
  - ☑ Appointment Confirmation Status Edit
  - ☑ Blockouts
- ☑ Family Module
  - ☑ Insurance Plan Edit
    - ☑ Change existing Ins Plan using Pick From List
    - ☑ Insurance Verification
  - ☑ Insurance Plan Change Assignment of Benefits
  - ☑ Insurance Plan Change Subscriber
  - ☑ Insurance Plan Ortho Edit
  - ☑ Carrier Create
  - ☑ Patient Billing Type Edit
  - ☑ Patient Primary Provider Edit
  - ☐ Patient Restriction Edit
  - ☑ Archived Patient Edit
  - ☑ Patient Social Security Number View
  - ☑ Patient Birthdate View
- ☑ Account Module
  - ▣ Claim
    - ☑ Claim Send
    - ☐ Claim Sent Edit
    - ☐ Claim Delete
    - ☐ Claim History Edit
    - ☑ Claim View
    - ☐ Claim Procedure Provider Edit When Attached to Claim
    - ☐ Claim Procedure Received Edit
    - ☐ Update Custom Tracking
    - ☐ PreAuth Sent Edit
  - ☐ Account Procs Quick Add
  - ▣ Insurance Payment
    - ☐ Insurance Payment Create
    - ☐ Insurance Payment Edit
    - ☐ Insurance Write Off Edit
  - ▣ Payment
    - ☑ Payment Create (if days newer than 1)
    - ☑ Payment Edit (if days newer than 1)
    - ☐ Pay Split Create after Global Lock Date
  - ▣ Payment Plan
    - ☐ Pay Plan Edit
  - ▣ Adjustment
    - ☐ Adjustment Create
    - ☐ Adjustment Edit
    - ☐ Adjustment Edit Zero Amount
- ☑ TreatmentPlan Module
  - ☑ Edit Treatment Plan
  - ☑ Edit Treatment Plan Presenter
  - ☑ Sign Treatment Plan
- ☑ Chart Module
  - ▣ Procedure
    - ☑ Edit EO or EC Procedures
    - ☑ Show Procedure Fee

User Group:

- Admin Group
- Assistant
- Front Desk
- **Hygiene**
- Office Manager
- Regular Users

Permissions for group:

- ☐ Insurance Payment Create
- ☐ Insurance Payment Edit
- ☐ Insurance Write Off Edit
- ▣ Payment
  - ☑ Payment Create (if days newer than 1)
  - ☑ Payment Edit (if days newer than 1)
  - ☐ Pay Split Create after Global Lock Date
- ▣ Payment Plan
  - ☐ Pay Plan Edit
- ▣ Adjustment
  - ☐ Adjustment Create
  - ☐ Adjustment Edit
  - ☐ Adjustment Edit Zero Amount
- ☑ Treatment Plan Module
  - ☑ Edit Treatment Plan
  - ☑ Edit Treatment Plan Presenter
  - ☑ Sign Treatment Plan
- ☑ Chart Module
  - ▣ Procedure
    - ☑ Edit EO or EC Procedures
    - ☑ Show Procedure Fee
    - ☑ TP Procedure Delete
    - ☑ Procedure Note (full)
    - ☑ Procedure Note (same user)
    - ☑ Group Note Edit (other users, signed)
  - ▣ Completed Procedure
    - ☑ Create Completed Procedure (or set complete)
    - ☑ Edit Completed Procedure
    - ☑ Change Status or Delete a Completed Procedure
    - ☑ Edit Note on Completed Procedure
    - ☑ Add Adjustment to Completed Procedure
    - ☑ Miscellaneous edit on Completed Procedure
  - ▣ Rx
    - ☑ Rx Create
    - ☐ Rx Edit
  - ☑ Ortho Chart Edit (full)
  - ☑ Ortho Chart Edit (same user, signed)
  - ☑ Perio Chart Edit
  - ▣ Anesthesia
    - ☑ Intake Anesthetic Medications into Inventory
    - ☑ Edit Anesthetic Records; Edit/Adjust Inventory Counts
- ☑ Image Module
  - ☑ Image Delete
- ☑ Manage Module
  - ☐ Accounting
    - ☐ Accounting Create Entry
    - ☐ Accounting Edit Entry
  - ☐ Billing
  - ☐ Deposit Slips
  - ☐ Backup
  - ▣ Time Card
    - ☐ Edit All Time Cards
    - ☐ Time Card Delete Entry
  - ▣ Equipment
    - ☐ Equipment Setup
    - ☐ Equipment Delete
- ▣ Merge Tools
  - ☐ Insurance Carrier Combine
  - ☐ Insurance Plan Combine
- ▣ Web Applications
  - ☐ Mobile Web

| Users | User Groups |

User Group:

- Admin Group
- Assistant
- Front Desk
- Hygiene
- **Office Manager**
- Regular Users

Permissions for group:

- ◻ Main Menu
  - ◻ File
    - ☑ Graphics Edit
    - ☑ Choose Database
  - ☑ Setup - Covers a wide variety of setup functions
    - ◻ Chart - EHR
      - ☑ EHR Emergency Access
      - ☑ EHR Measure Event Edit
    - ◻ Advanced Setup
      - ☑ Replication Setup
    - ☑ Auto/Quick Note Edit
    - ◻ Dental School
      - ☑ Instructor Edit
      - ☑ Student Edit
      - ☑ Admin Evaluation Edit
    - ☑ Schedules - Practice and Provider
    - ◻ Security
      - ◻ Security Admin
      - ☑ Add New User
  - ◻ Lists
    - ☑ Procedure Code Edit
    - ☑ Fee Schedule Edit
    - ☑ Provider Fee Edit
    - ☑ Problem Edit
    - ☑ Providers
      - ☑ Providers - Alphabetize
    - ◻ Referrals
      - ☑ Referral Add
      - ☑ Referral Edit
      - ☑ Referral, Attach to Patient
      - ☑ Referral, Delete from Patient
  - ☑ Reports
    - ☑ Production and Income - View All Providers
    - ☑ Daily payments - View All Providers
    - ☑ Reports - Graphical Setup
    - ☑ Reports - Graphical
    - ☑ User Query
    - ☑ User Query Admin
    - ☑ Command Query
    - ☑ Procedures Not Billed to Insurance, New Claims button (if days newer than 1)
  - ◻ Tools
    - ◻ Misc Tools
      - ☑ Medication Merge
      - ☑ Patient Merge
      - ☑ Provider Merge
      - ☑ Referral Merge
    - ☑ Audit Trail
    - ☑ Repeating Charge Tool
    - ☑ Wiki Admin
    - ☑ Wiki List Setup
  - ◻ Clinics
    - ☑ Unrestricted Patient Search
  - ◻ eServices
    - ☑ eServices Setup
- ◻ Main Toolbar
  - ☑ Commlog Edit (if days newer than 5)
  - ☑ Email Send
  - ☑ Webmail Send
  - ☑ Sheet Edit (if days newer than 2)
    - ☑ Sheet Delete
  - ☑ Task Edit

User Group:

Permissions for group:

Admin Group
Assistant
Front Desk
Hygiene
Office Manager
Regular Users

- ☑ Sheet Delete
- ☑ Task Edit
- ☑ Task Note Edit
- ☑ Task List Create
- ☑ Popup Edit (other users)
- ☑ Appointments Module
  - ☑ Appointment Create
  - ☑ Appointment Move
  - ☑ Appointment Edit
  - ☑ Completed Appointment Edit
  - ☑ eCW Appointment Revise
  - ☑ Insurance Plan Verification Assign
  - ☑ Appointment Confirmation Status Edit
  - ☑ Blockouts
- ☑ Family Module
  - ☑ Insurance Plan Edit
    - ☑ Change existing Ins Plan using Pick From List
    - ☑ Insurance Verification
  - ☑ Insurance Plan Change Assignment of Benefits
  - ☑ Insurance Plan Change Subscriber
  - ☑ Insurance Plan Ortho Edit
  - ☑ Carrier Create
  - ☑ Patient Billing Type Edit
  - ☑ Patient Primary Provider Edit
  - ☑ Patient Restriction Edit
  - ☑ Archived Patient Edit
  - ☑ Patient Social Security Number View
  - ☑ Patient Birthdate View
- ☑ Account Module
  - ▦ Claim
    - ☑ Claim Send
    - ☑ Claim Sent Edit
    - ☑ Claim Delete (if days newer than 180)
    - ☑ Claim History Edit (if days newer than 5)
    - ☑ Claim View
    - ☑ Claim Procedure Provider Edit When Attached to Claim
    - ☑ Claim Procedure Received Edit
    - ☑ Update Custom Tracking
    - ☑ PreAuth Sent Edit (if days newer than 5)
  - ☑ Account Procs Quick Add
  - ▦ Insurance Payment
    - ☑ Insurance Payment Create
    - ☑ Insurance Payment Edit
    - ☑ Insurance Write Off Edit
  - ▦ Payment
    - ☑ Payment Create
    - ☑ Payment Edit
    - ☑ Pay Split Create after Global Lock Date
  - ▦ Payment Plan
    - ☑ Pay Plan Edit
  - ▦ Adjustment
    - ☑ Adjustment Create
    - ☑ Adjustment Edit
    - ☑ Adjustment Edit Zero Amount
- ☑ Treatment Plan Module
  - ☑ Edit Treatment Plan
  - ☑ Edit Treatment Plan Presenter
  - ☑ Sign Treatment Plan
- ☑ Chart Module
  - ▦ Procedure
    - ☑ Edit EO or EC Procedures

Users | User Groups

User Group:
- Admin Group
- Assistant
- Front Desk
- Hygiene
- Office Manager
- Regular Users

Permissions for group:

- ☑ Insurance Payment Create
- ☑ Insurance Payment Edit
- ☑ Insurance Write Off Edit
- ◻ Payment
  - ☑ Payment Create
  - ☑ Payment Edit
  - ☑ Pay Split Create after Global Lock Date
- ◻ Payment Plan
  - ☑ Pay Plan Edit
- ◻ Adjustment
  - ☑ Adjustment Create
  - ☑ Adjustment Edit
  - ☑ Adjustment Edit Zero Amount
- ☑ TreatmentPlan Module
  - ☑ Edit Treatment Plan
  - ☑ Edit Treatment Plan Presenter
  - ☑ Sign Treatment Plan
- ☑ Chart Module
  - ◻ Procedure
    - ☑ Edit EO or EC Procedures
    - ☑ Show Procedure Fee
    - ☑ TP Procedure Delete
    - ☑ Procedure Note (full)
    - ☑ Procedure Note (same user)
    - ☑ Group Note Edit (other users, signed)
  - ◻ Completed Procedure
    - ☑ Create Completed Procedure (or set complete)
    - ☑ Edit Completed Procedure
    - ☑ Change Status or Delete a Completed Procedure
    - ☑ Edit Note on Completed Procedure
    - ☑ Add Adjustment to Completed Procedure
    - ☑ Miscellaneous edit on Completed Procedure
  - ◻ Rx
    - ☑ Rx Create
    - ☑ Rx Edit
  - ☑ Ortho Chart Edit (full)
  - ☑ Ortho Chart Edit (same user, signed)
  - ☑ Perio Chart Edit
  - ◻ Anesthesia
    - ☑ Intake Anesthetic Medications into Inventory
    - ☑ Edit Anesthetic Records; Edit/Adjust Inventory Counts
- ☑ Image Module
  - ☑ Image Delete
- ☑ Manage Module
  - ☑ Accounting
    - ☑ Accounting Create Entry
    - ☑ Accounting Edit Entry
  - ☑ Billing
  - ☑ Deposit Slips
  - ☑ Backup
  - ◻ Time Card
    - ◻ Edit All Time Cards
    - ◻ Time Card Delete Entry
  - ◻ Equipment
    - ☑ Equipment Setup
    - ☑ Equipment Delete
- ◻ Merge Tools
  - ☑ Insurance Carrier Combine
  - ☑ Insurance Plan Combine
- ◻ Web Applications
  - ☑ Mobile Web

Adj Types -

- ○ Add Employee Discount (-)
- ○ Check all others to either add or remove ones you don't think you'll use

Appointment Colors

- ○ Change 'Practice Closed' to slightly darker grey

Appointment Confirmed

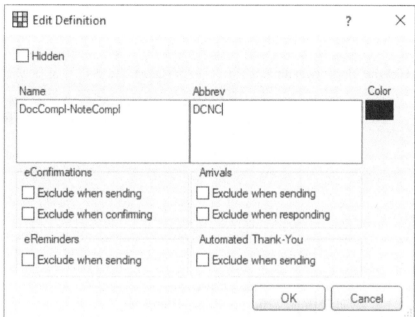

- ○ Add Type
- ○ This is used for once Doctor/Hygiene has completed their notes
- ○ Should appear like this:

Definitions			
Name	Abbrev	Color	Hide
Not Called	NotCalled		
Unconfirmed	Unconfirmed		
Appointment Confirmed	Confirmed		
Left Msg	LeftMsg		
Arrived	Arrived		
Ready to go back	Ready		
In Treatment Room	In Room		
Front Desk	FrontDesk		
DocCompl-NoteCompl	DCNC		
E-mailed	E-mailed		
Texted	Texted		
eConfirmSent	eConfirmSent		
eConfirmCallBack	eConfirmCallBack		
eConfirmFailure	eConfirmFailure		
Created from Web Sched	WebSched		

○

Appointment Procs Quick Add: see Step 9 Below

Blockout Types

- ○ Create all the following blockouts as shown below

Edit Blockout Type

☐ Hidden

Name

High Prod

Usage

☐ Block appointments scheduling
☐ Disable Cut/Copy/Paste

Color

[ ]

[OK]   [Cancel]

- ○
- ○ Only Click the 'Block appointments scheduling' for Lunch and Meeting as shown below

Definitions			
Name	**Flags**	**Color**	**Hide**
Staff Meeting	NS		
Lunch	NS		
High Prod			
Low Prod			
Surgury			
Consult			
Emergency			
Seat			
NP-SRP			

- ○
- ○ Go to Spreadsheet
  - ■ Pick the hours your practice will be open
  - ■ Pick the ideal length of the Planned appointments
  - ■ Pick the ideal XX-OOO-XX Times for 'captive doctor time'
    - ● Set the middle of the blockout to be the darker colors
  - ■ Plan out the ideal day/week/ to hit the target numbers for:
    - ● #s of New Patients per month (then divide by 4 to hit weekly target)
    - ● #s of High Prod/Surgery/Low Prod blocks to hit daily Production $ target

Appointment Views

- Keys to Appointment Views
  - Create 3 types
    - <u>All Information</u>

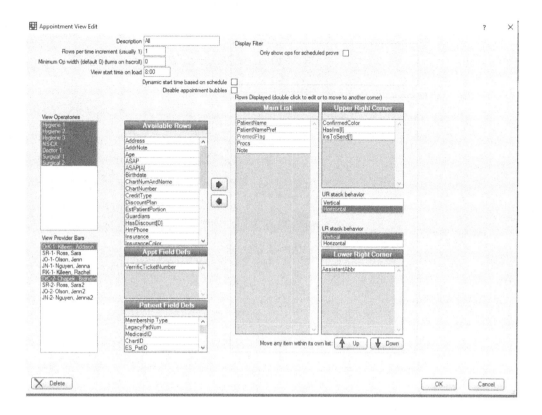

- **HIPAA Compliant View**

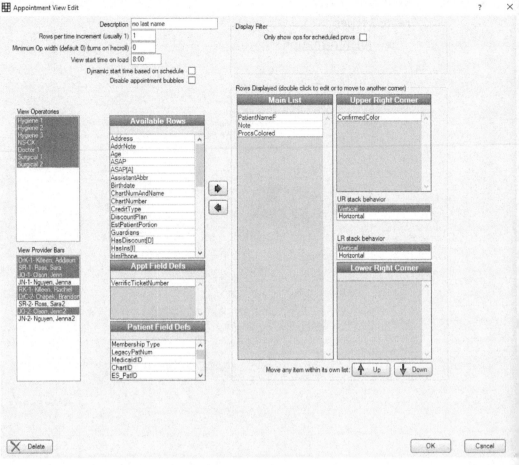

- **Single Provider** Goal and Production View
- Key to this one is that you can still 'View' the entire schedule, but only the provider selected under 'View Provider Bars' is actually used to figure out production on the 'Appointment' Screen

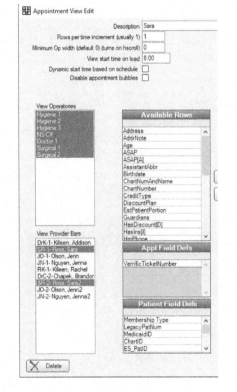

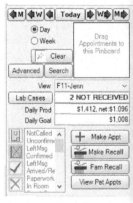

Procedure Buttons

- Setup the Categories to match these, or nearly all of these below:

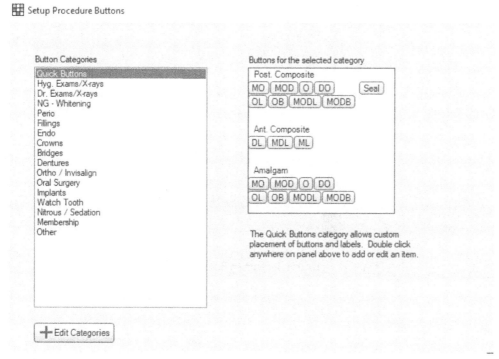

- And under each of these Categories, you will add a Procedure, which Category it falls under, the Image (a 20x20 pixel image- Paint is good to create your own), **LINK HERE for IMAGE FOLDER**, and then
    - Add Procedure Codes you want to 'Explode' when you Treatment Plan this procedure

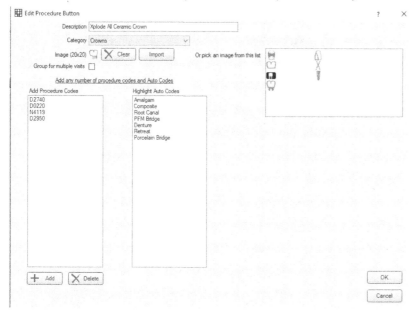

Button Categories

Quick Buttons
Hyg. Exams/X-rays
Dr. Exams/X-rays
NG - Whitening
Perio
Fillings
Endo
Crowns
Bridges
Dentures
Ortho / Invisalign
Oral Surgery
Implants
Watch Tooth
Nitrous / Sedation
Membership
Other

Buttons for the selected category

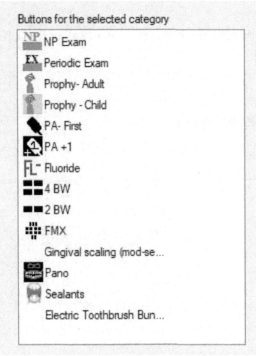

NP Exam
Periodic Exam
Prophy- Adult
Prophy - Child
PA- First
PA +1
Fluoride
4 BW
2 BW
FMX
Gingival scaling (mod-se...
Pano
Sealants
Electric Toothbrush Bun...

⊞ Setup Procedure Buttons

Button Categories

Quick Buttons
Hyg. Exams/X-rays
Dr. Exams/X-rays
NG - Whitening
Perio
Fillings
Endo
Crowns
Bridges
Dentures
Ortho / Invisalign
Oral Surgery
Implants
Watch Tooth
Nitrous / Sedation
Membership
Other

Buttons for the selected category

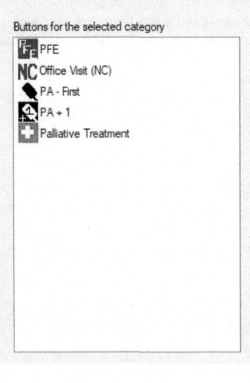

PFE
Office Visit (NC)
PA - First
PA + 1
Palliative Treatment

Setup Procedure Buttons

Button Categories

Quick Buttons
Hyg. Exams/X-rays
Dr. Exams/X-rays
NG - Whitening
Perio
Fillings
Endo
Crowns
Bridges
Dentures
Ortho / Invisalign
Oral Surgery
Implants
Watch Tooth
Nitrous / Sedation
Membership
Other

Buttons for the selected category

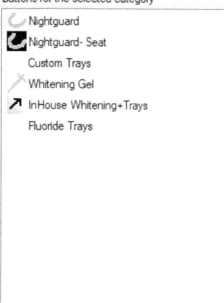

Nightguard
Nightguard- Seat
Custom Trays
Whitening Gel
InHouse Whitening+Trays
Fluoride Trays

Setup Procedure Buttons

Button Categories

Quick Buttons
Hyg. Exams/X-rays
Dr. Exams/X-rays
NG - Whitening
Perio
Fillings
Endo
Crowns
Bridges
Dentures
Ortho / Invisalign
Oral Surgery
Implants
Watch Tooth
Nitrous / Sedation
Membership
Other

Buttons for the selected category

4+ SRP 4+ Quad
1-3 SRP 1-3 Teeth
Perio Maint
Perio Charting
Comprehensive Perio Ex...
Gingival scaling (mod-se...

⊞ Setup Procedure Buttons

Button Categories

Quick Buttons
Hyg. Exams/X-rays
Dr. Exams/X-rays
NG - Whitening
Perio
Fillings
Endo
Crowns
Bridges
Dentures
Ortho / Invisalign
Oral Surgery
Implants
Watch Tooth
Nitrous / Sedation
Membership
Other

Buttons for the selected category

🗃 Amalgam
🗃 Composite
   Direct Pulp Cap

⊞ Setup Procedure Buttons

Button Categories

Quick Buttons
Hyg. Exams/X-rays
Dr. Exams/X-rays
NG - Whitening
Perio
Fillings
Endo
Crowns
Bridges
Dentures
Ortho / Invisalign
Oral Surgery
Implants
Watch Tooth
Nitrous / Sedation
Membership
Other

Buttons for the selected category

Endo Code
✚ Emergency Relief of End...

Setup Procedure Buttons

Button Categories

- Quick Buttons
- Hyg. Exams/X-rays
- Dr. Exams/X-rays
- NG - Whitening
- Perio
- Fillings
- Endo
- **Crowns**
- Bridges
- Dentures
- Ortho / Invisalign
- Oral Surgery
- Implants
- Watch Tooth
- Nitrous / Sedation
- Membership
- Other

Buttons for the selected category

- Xplode All Ceramic Crown
- Xplode PFM Crown
- Xplode Gold Crown
- Post & Core
- Recement Crown
- PFM crown
- Gold crown
- All Ceramic crown
- Build Up

Setup Procedure Buttons

Button Categories

- Quick Buttons
- Hyg. Exams/X-rays
- Dr. Exams/X-rays
- NG - Whitening
- Perio
- Fillings
- Endo
- Crowns
- **Bridges**
- Dentures
- Ortho / Invisalign
- Oral Surgery
- Implants
- Watch Tooth
- Nitrous / Sedation
- Membership
- Other

Buttons for the selected category

- Ceramic Bridge
- PFM Bridge
- Build-up
- Post & Core
- Seat Bridge
- Recement Bridge
- Section Bridge

⊞ Setup Procedure Buttons

Button Categories

Quick Buttons
Hyg. Exams/X-rays
Dr. Exams/X-rays
NG - Whitening
Perio
Fillings
Endo
Crowns
Bridges
Dentures
Ortho / Invisalign
Oral Surgery
Implants
Watch Tooth
Nitrous / Sedation
Membership
Other

Buttons for the selected category

Complete Max
Complete Mand
Max Partial- Resin
Mand Partial- Resin
Max Partial - Cast Metal
Mand Partial - Cast Metal
Max Immediate Denture
Mand Immediate Partial
Add tooth to partial
Max Hard Reline
Mand Hard Reline

Setup Procedure Buttons

Button Categories

Quick Buttons
Hyg. Exams/X-rays
Dr. Exams/X-rays
NG - Whitening
Perio
Fillings
Endo
Crowns
Bridges
Dentures
Ortho / Invisalign
Oral Surgery
Implants
Watch Tooth
Nitrous / Sedation
Membership
Other

Buttons for the selected category

Comp Adult Ortho
Comp Teenager Ortho
Limited Adult Ortho
Limited Teen Ortho
Ortho Check $0
Ortho Retainer
3D 3D SCAN
1 Invis1- Low Interest
2 Invis2- High Interest

Setup Procedure Buttons

Button Categories

Quick Buttons
Hyg. Exams/X-rays
Dr. Exams/X-rays
NG - Whitening
Perio
Fillings
Endo
Crowns
Bridges
Dentures
Ortho / Invisalign
Oral Surgery
Implants
Watch Tooth
Nitrous / Sedation
Membership
Other

Buttons for the selected category

Simple Extraction
Surgical Ext
Soft Tissue Imp
Partial Bony Ext
Complete Bony
Alveol w/ 4+Ext
Alveol w 1-3Ext
Alveolo-w/oE4+
Alveolo-w/oExt 1-3
Incise and Drain
Lateral Aug- Bone Graft
Socket Pres- Bone
Sinus Bump/Graft
Sinus Lateral

Button Categories	Buttons for the selected category
Quick Buttons	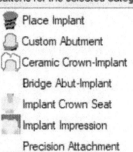 Place Implant
Hyg. Exams/X-rays	Custom Abutment
Dr. Exams/X-rays	Ceramic Crown-Implant
NG - Whitening	Bridge Abut-Implant
Perio	Implant Crown Seat
Fillings	Implant Impression
Endo	Precision Attachment
Crowns	Precision Change Part
Bridges	
Dentures	
Ortho / Invisalign	
Oral Surgery	
Implants	
Bone Graft	
Membranes	
Nitrous / Sedation	
Watch Tooth	
Membership	
Other	

Button Categories

Quick Buttons
Hyg. Exams/X-rays
Dr. Exams/X-rays
NG - Whitening
Perio
Fillings
Endo
Crowns
Bridges
Dentures
Ortho / Invisalign
Oral Surgery
Implants
Bone Graft
Membranes
Nitrous / Sedation
Watch Tooth
Membership
Other

Buttons for the selected category

PRF Membrane
Resorb Membrane
Non-Resorb Membrane

Button Categories

Quick Buttons
Hyg. Exams/X-rays
Dr. Exams/X-rays
NG - Whitening
Perio
Fillings
Endo
Crowns
Bridges
Dentures
Ortho / Invisalign
Oral Surgery
Implants
Bone Graft
Membranes
Nitrous / Sedation
Watch Tooth
Membership
Other

Buttons for the selected category

 Socket Preservation
 Socket Pres +1
 Ridge Preservation Post-...
Bone Graft w Implant Pla...
 Sinus Lateral
Sinus Direct
 Ridge Augmentation

⊞ Setup Procedure Buttons

Button Categories

Quick Buttons
Hyg. Exams/X-rays
Dr. Exams/X-rays
NG - Whitening
Perio
Fillings
Endo
Crowns
Bridges
Dentures
Ortho / Invisalign
Oral Surgery
Implants
Watch Tooth
Nitrous / Sedation
Membership
Other

Buttons for the selected category

Watch Tooth

Watch Surface

⊞ Setup Procedure Buttons

Button Categories

Quick Buttons
Hyg. Exams/X-rays
Dr. Exams/X-rays
NG - Whitening
Perio
Fillings
Endo
Crowns
Bridges
Dentures
Ortho / Invisalign
Oral Surgery
Implants
Watch Tooth
Nitrous / Sedation
Membership
Other

Buttons for the selected category

Nitrous

IV Sedation First 15

IV +15 Min

Button Categories

- Quick Buttons
- Hyg. Exams/X-rays
- Dr. Exams/X-rays
- NG - Whitening
- Perio
- Fillings
- Endo
- Crowns
- Bridges
- Dentures
- Ortho / Invisalign
- Oral Surgery
- Implants
- Watch Tooth
- Nitrous / Sedation
- **Membership**
- Other

Buttons for the selected category

- Memb- Kid
- Memb-Adult
- Memb-Perio
- Kid Yearly
- Adult Yearly
- Perio Yearly

Button Categories

- Quick Buttons
- Hyg. Exams/X-rays
- Dr. Exams/X-rays
- NG - Whitening
- Perio
- Fillings
- Endo
- Crowns
- Bridges
- Dentures
- Ortho / Invisalign
- Oral Surgery
- Implants
- Watch Tooth
- Nitrous / Sedation
- Membership
- **Other**

Buttons for the selected category

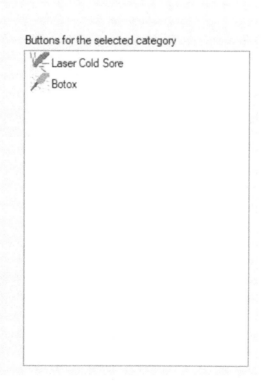

- Laser Cold Sore
- Botox

r procedures that are common:

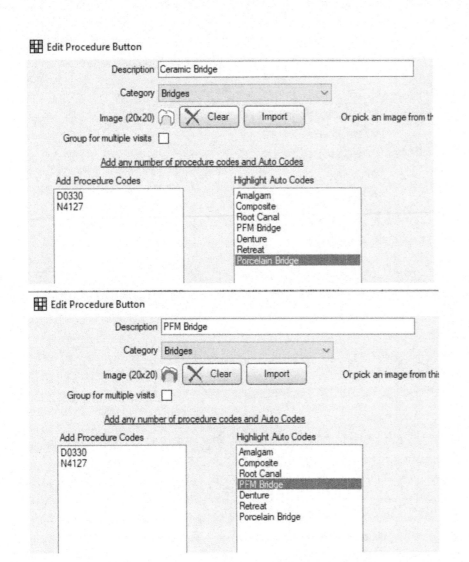

⊞ Edit Procedure Button

Description Ceramic Bridge

Category Bridges ⌄

Image (20x20) 🦷 ✕ Clear   Import   Or pick an image from th

Group for multiple visits ☐

Add any number of procedure codes and Auto Codes

Add Procedure Codes

D0330
N4127

Highlight Auto Codes

Amalgam
Composite
Root Canal
PFM Bridge
Denture
Retreat
Porcelain Bridge

⊞ Edit Procedure Button

Description PFM Bridge

Category Bridges ⌄

Image (20x20) 🦷 ✕ Clear   Import   Or pick an image from thi

Group for multiple visits ☐

Add any number of procedure codes and Auto Codes

Add Procedure Codes

D0330
N4127

Highlight Auto Codes

Amalgam
Composite
Root Canal
PFM Bridge
Denture
Retreat
Porcelain Bridge

Program Buttons

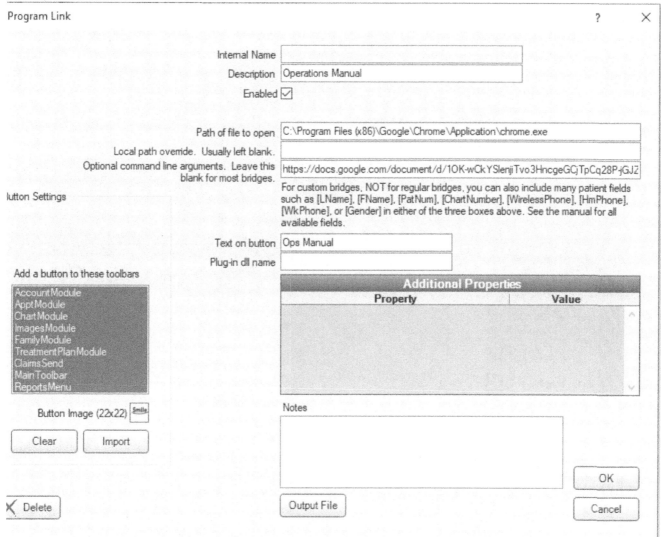

- If you have an operations manual or key documents you want to link to from OD, go to Setttings>Program Links
- Enter in any Description, then Path to open (Like Chrome), then the Optional Command line arguments - the Web URL
- Also you can input a 22x22 pixel image to show.
- Highlight all the places you want the button to show on the left hand column
- Many do this for:
  - Ops Manual
  - Flex or Modento Link
  - Insurance Verification Companies (Verrific will do this for you)
  - Insurance Portals
  - Invisalign Website
  - Itero Doctor Website

Program Link   ?   ✕

Internal Name [   ]

Description [Flex   ]

Enabled ☑

Path of file to open [C:\Program Files (x86)\Google\Chrome\Application\chrome.exe]

Local path override. Usually left blank. [   ]

Optional command line arguments. Leave this [https://capitaldental.myflex.app:45622/]
blank for most bridges.

For custom bridges, NOT for regular bridges, you can also include many patient fields
such as [LName], [FName], [PatNum], [ChartNumber], [WirelessPhone], [HmPhone],
[WkPhone], or [Gender] in either of the three boxes above. See the manual for all
available fields.

Text on button [Flex   ]

Plug-in dll name [   ]

Button Settings

Add a button to these toolbars

AccountModule
ApptModule
ChartModule
ImagesModule
FamilyModule
TreatmentPlanModule
ClaimsSend
MainToolbar
ReportsMenu

Button Image (22x22) ✕

[Clear]   [Import]

Additional Properties	
Property	**Value**

Notes

[   ]

[OK]

✕ Delete   [Output File]   [Cancel]

Auto Notes Templates

Go to Settings - Auto Notes

Delete all existing notes and prompts

Then go to Import- see image->

Download a .json file

You'll see a message confirming 41

AutoNotes imported

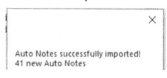

Auto Notes successfully imported!
41 new Auto Notes

Go into these 'Available Prompts' to
Change:

- Doctor
- Assistant

Review all other prompts for types of etch, anesthetic, composite, materials, etc. that are unique to your operation

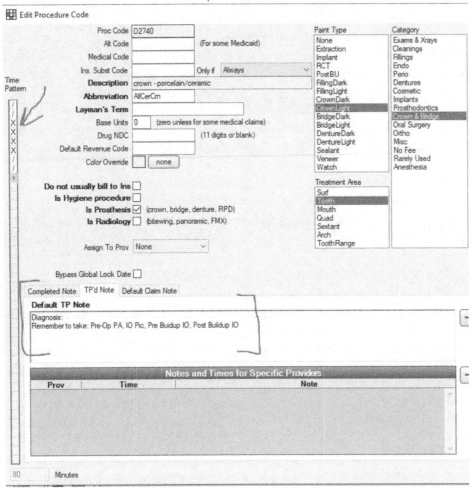

- Make sure to add these notes into any crown you do
- And for Crown Seat procedures, Add:
  - "Post op: Take IO Pic & BW"

Definitions - Quick Add

Add in these Definitions to the Procedure Quick Add Buttons

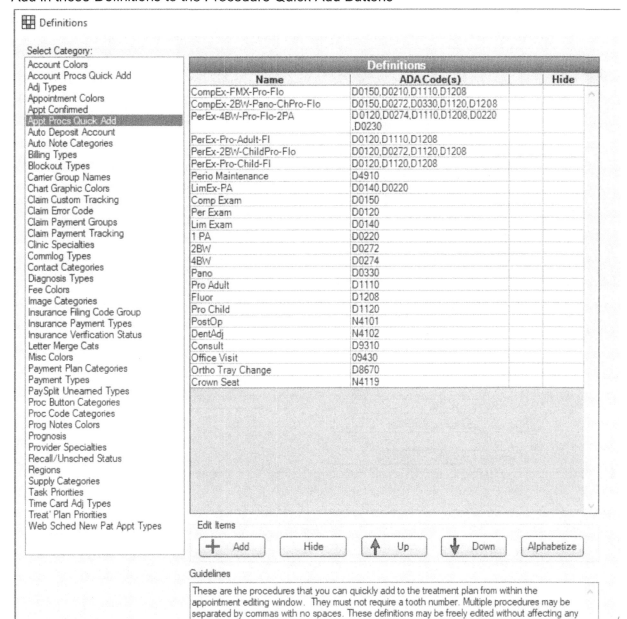

	Definitions		
Name	ADA Code(s)		Hide
CompEx-FMX-Pro-Flo	D0150,D0210,D1110,D1208		
CompEx-2BW-Pano-ChPro-Flo	D0150,D0272,D0330,D1120,D1208		
PerEx-4BW-Pro-Flo-2PA	D0120,D0274,D1110,D1208,D0220,D0230		
PerEx-Pro-Adult-Fl	D0120,D1110,D1208		
PerEx-2BW-ChildPro-Flo	D0120,D0272,D1120,D1208		
PerEx-Pro-Child-Fl	D0120,D1120,D1208		
Perio Maintenance	D4910		
LimEx-PA	D0140,D0220		
Comp Exam	D0150		
Per Exam	D0120		
Lim Exam	D0140		
1 PA	D0220		
2BW	D0272		
4BW	D0274		
Pano	D0330		
Pro Adult	D1110		
Fluor	D1208		
Pro Child	D1120		
PostOp	N4101		
DentAdj	N4102		
Consult	D9310		
Office Visit	09430		
Ortho Tray Change	D8670		
Crown Seat	N4119		

Select Category:
- Account Colors
- Account Procs Quick Add
- Adj Types
- Appointment Colors
- Appt Confirmed
- Appt Procs Quick Add
- Auto Deposit Account
- Auto Note Categories
- Billing Types
- Blockout Types
- Carrier Group Names
- Chart Graphic Colors
- Claim Custom Tracking
- Claim Error Code
- Claim Payment Groups
- Claim Payment Tracking
- Clinic Specialties
- Commlog Types
- Contact Categories
- Diagnosis Types
- Fee Colors
- Image Categories
- Insurance Filing Code Group
- Insurance Payment Types
- Insurance Verification Status
- Letter Merge Cats
- Misc Colors
- Payment Plan Categories
- Payment Types
- PaySplit Unearned Types
- Proc Button Categories
- Proc Code Categories
- Prog Notes Colors
- Prognosis
- Provider Specialties
- Recall/Unsched Status
- Regions
- Supply Categories
- Task Priorities
- Time Card Adj Types
- Treat' Plan Priorities
- Web Sched New Pat Appt Types

Edit Items

[+ Add] [Hide] [↑ Up] [↓ Down] [Alphabetize]

Guidelines

These are the procedures that you can quickly add to the treatment plan from within the appointment editing window. They must not require a tooth number. Multiple procedures may be separated by commas with no spaces. These definitions may be freely edited without affecting any patient records.

14. Setup RX Pad Sheet and Routing Pad Sheet
- Get icon of your Practice Logo, put on Desktop
- Setup-Sheets
  - Move the RX pad into the custom column, then edit to be like this shape:

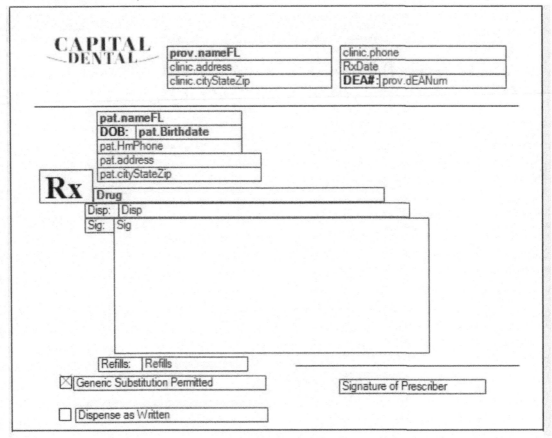

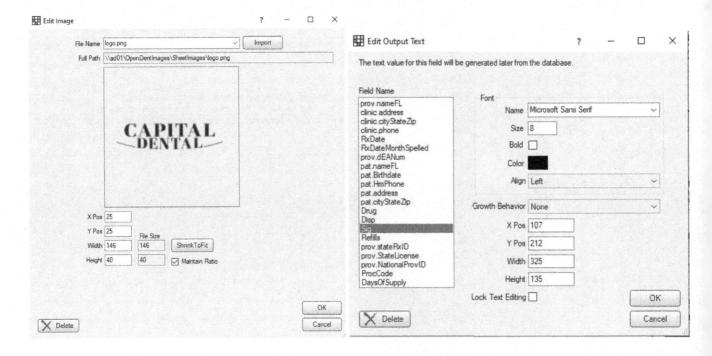

Routing Slip:

```
┌─────────────────────────────┐
│        Routing Slip         │
└─────────────────────────────┘
```

[nameFL]		Guarantor: [guarantorNameFL]
appt.timeDate		Balance: [balTotal]
appt.length		-Ins Est: [balInsEst]
appt.providers		=Total: [balTotalMinusInsEst]
Procedures:		
appt.procedures		
Note: appt.Note		

Patient Info

Age: [age]

Recall Due Date: [dateRecallDue]

Medical notes: [MedUrgNote]

Other Family Members

otherFamilyMembers

'GIENE

s Doctor Met Patient?   YES   NO   Compliment_____

ays Taken Today?   PANO   BW   FMX   PA_____   Recap:_____

Pics Taken?   YES   NO   Personal:_____

eas of treatment recommended:

                         __ Urgent   __ Preventative __ Elective / Costmetic

junct Services Recommended:

    Implants   Whitening   NG   Fluoride Trays   Sealants   Invisalign

Treatment Plan	**Visit set complete: Y N**
[treatmentPlanProcsPriority]	Next visit:_____
	Date to return: 1wk 2wk 4 wks_____
	Time needed: _____ / _____ / _____
	Appointment Scheduled: Date _____
	Recare scheduled: Y N
	Referral asked for: Y N

15. Educational Video Tracts for different positions (Coming Soon)

16. Medications List

- Follow the instructions in the video to upload

17. Backup Procedures & Best Practices (Coming Soon)

18. Splash Screen .jpeg

The splash screen appears briefly upon launching Open Dental.

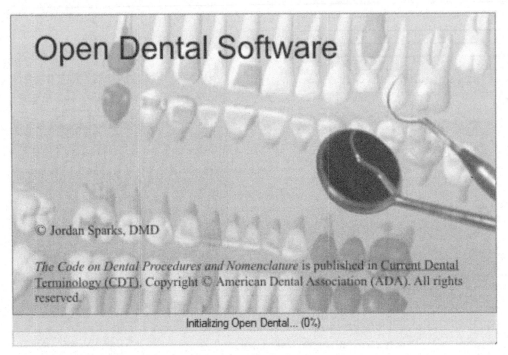

The image above is the default Open Dental splash screen.

In special cases, users may want to use their own custom the splash screen.

1. Create a .jpg file of your splash screen. The recommended image size is 500x300 px.
2. Name the file splash.jpg.
3. Place the file in the Open Dental program file on each workstation. This file will then be used in place of the original Open Dental splash screen.

Top Tricks

Control 'D' = Date

- Instantly putting in the date- any time, any place, Hit (Control D) and it will insert it

You can open multiple windows of OpenDental at once

- Usually have 2-3 open at a time for front desk users to not lose their place during some tasks, payment entering, etc.

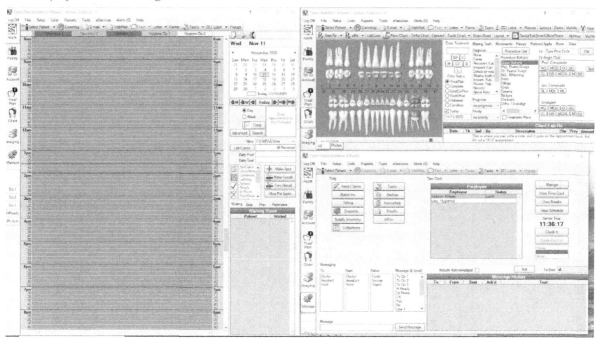

Don't accidentally Quit OpenDental

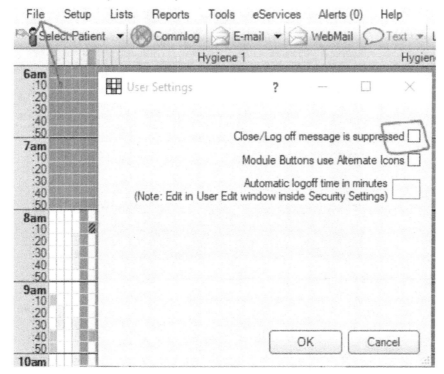

- Patient Notes
    - This process will allow you to put patient notes on the Appointment Screen without having a fake appointment. To start, click 'View Patient Appointments'
    - Then 'NOTE for Patient'
    - Then enter any note that needs to be remembered for the patient.

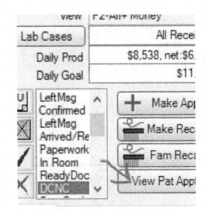

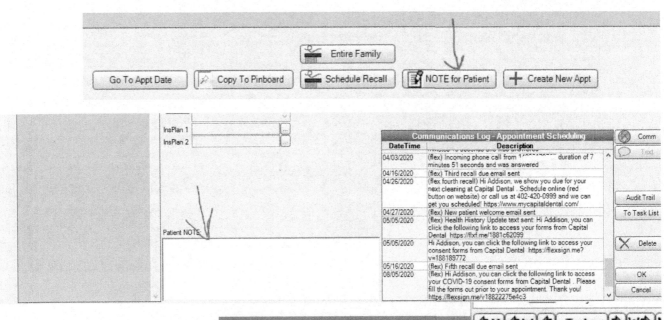

- And remember that you can always set it to 'Completed' after you've completed the task/note!
- It will then turn the note dark grey

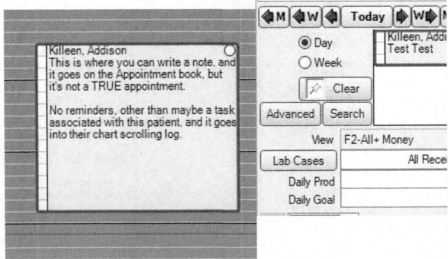

11/14/2020		*** Patient NOTE *** - 10:30 AM						
This is where you can write a note, and it goes on the Appointment book, but it's not a TRUE appointment.								
No reminders, other than maybe a task associated with this patient, and it goes into their chart scrolling log.								

Waiting Room Time Turn Red

- After X number of minutes, the time clock on the patient can turn red

Module Preferences

Appts | Family | Account | Treat' Plan | Chart | Images | Manage

Broken Appointment Automation

Broken appointment procedure type `Both`

Make broken appointment commlog ☐
Make broken appointment adjustment ☐

Broken appt default adj type `BROKEN Appt - No Show`

Time Arrived trigger `Arrived/Ready`
Time Seated (in op) trigger `In Treatment Room`
Time Dismissed trigger `Front Desk`
Search Behavior `Provider Time`

Appointment time locked by default ☐
Appointment bubble max note length (0 for no limit) `0`
Filter the waiting room based on the selected appointment view ☐
Waiting room alert time in minutes (0 to disable) `5`

Add daily adjustments to net production ☐
Force op's hygiene provider as secondary provider ☐
Appointments Module production uses operatories ☐
Appointments require procedures ☑
Appointment without procedures default length `30`
Allow setting future appointments complete ☐
Allow setting appointments without procedures complete ☑

Allow 'Block appointment scheduling' blockouts to replace conflicting blockouts ☐
Do not allow recall appointments on the Unscheduled List ☑
Number of days out to automatically refresh Appointments Module (-1 for all) `4`
Prevent changes to completed appointments with completed procedures ☐
Appointments allow overlap ☐
Force users to break scheduled appointments before rescheduling ☐

Appearance

Default appointment bubble to 'disabled' for new appointment views [
Appointment bubble popup delay [
Use solid blockouts instead of outlines on the Appointments Module [
Show ! on appts for ins not sent, if added to Appt View (might cause slowdown) [
Waiting room alert color ▮
Appointment time line color ▮
Appointments Module defaults to week view [
Appointment click delay `0.2 seconds`
Refresh every 60 seconds, keeps waiting room times refreshed [
Appointment font size. Default is 8. Decimals allowed `8`
Width of provider time bar on left of each appointment `11`

Comm Log Colors
- Change comm log colors for ease of viewing

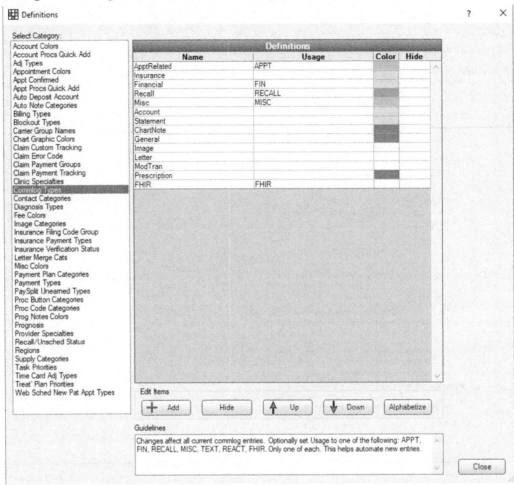

Name	Usage	Color	Hide
ApptRelated	APPT		
Insurance			
Financial	FIN		
Recall	RECALL		
Misc	MISC		
Account			
Statement			
ChartNote			
General			
Image			
Letter			
ModTran			
Prescription			
FHIR	FHIR		

Guidelines

Changes affect all current commlog entries. Optionally set Usage to one of the following: APPT, FIN, RECALL, MISC, TEXT, REACT, FHIR. Only one of each. This helps automate new entries.

04/16/2020		Comm - Recall					Admin	
	(flex) Third recall due email sent							
04/26/2020		Comm - Recall					Admin	
	(flex fourth recall) Hi Addison, we show you due for your next cleaning at Capital Dental . Schedule online (red button on website) or call us at 402-420 -0999 and we can get you scheduled! https://www.mycapitaldental.com/							
04/27/2020		Comm - ApptRelated					Admin	
	(flex) New patient welcome email sent							
05/05/2020		Comm - ApptRelated					Admin	
	(flex) Health History Update text sent: Hi Addison, you can click the following link to access your forms from Capital Dental. https://flxf.me/1881c62099							
05/05/2020		Comm - ApptRelated					Admin	
	Hi Addison, you can click the following link to access your consent forms from Capital Dental. https://flexsign.me?v=188189772							
05/05/2020		Comm - Financial					Dr. Killeen	
	Test Test Test - PAY SOME MONEY							
05/16/2020		Comm - Recall					Admin	
	(flex) Fifth recall due email sent							
08/03/2020		limited oral evaluation - problem focused	C	DrK-1	7.00	D0140		
08/05/2020		Comm - ApptRelated					Admin	
	(flex) Hi Addison, you can click the following link to access your COVID-19 consent forms from Capital Dental . Please fill the forms out prior to your appointment. Thank you! https://flexsign.me/v18822275e4c3							

- Viewing Settings on the Chart

- You can change settings on what to see on each computer
- Make Pre-set and toggle using F1, F2, F3, etc.
-

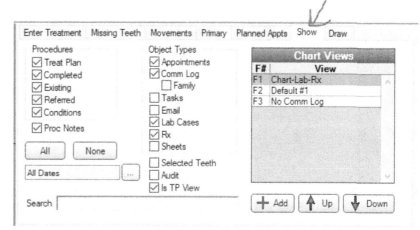

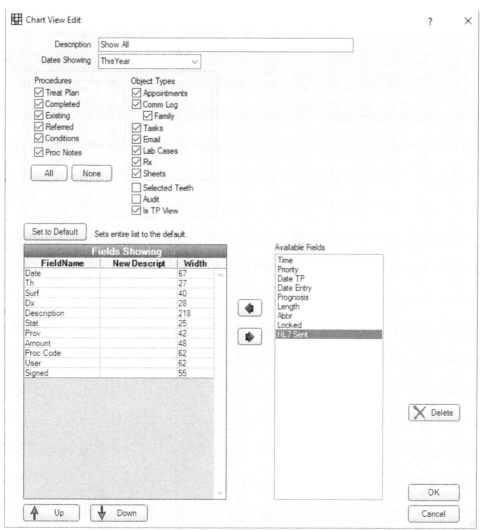

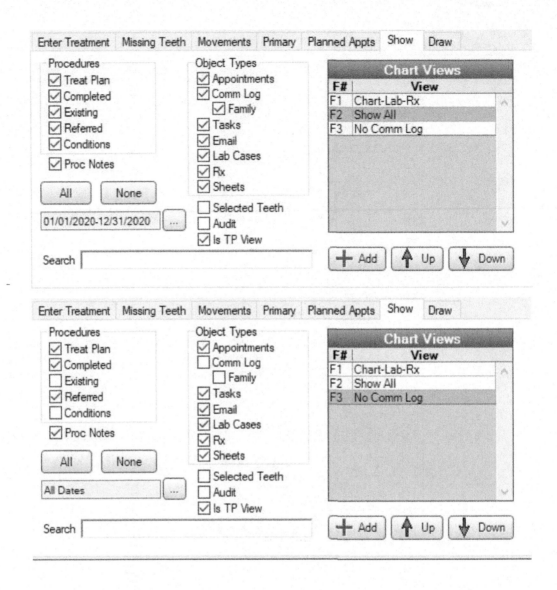

| Enter Treatment | Missing Teeth | Movements | Primary | Planned Appts | Show | Draw |

Procedures
- ☑ Treat Plan
- ☑ Completed
- ☑ Existing
- ☑ Referred
- ☑ Conditions
- ☑ Proc Notes

[All] [None]

`01/01/2020-12/31/2020` [...]

Search [ ]

Object Types
- ☑ Appointments
- ☑ Comm Log
  - ☑ Family
- ☑ Tasks
- ☑ Email
- ☑ Lab Cases
- ☑ Rx
- ☑ Sheets
- ☐ Selected Teeth
- ☐ Audit
- ☑ Is TP View

Chart Views

F#	View
F1	Chart-Lab-Rx
F2	Show All
F3	No Comm Log

[+ Add] [↑ Up] [↓ Down]

| Enter Treatment | Missing Teeth | Movements | Primary | Planned Appts | Show | Draw |

Procedures
- ☑ Treat Plan
- ☑ Completed
- ☐ Existing
- ☑ Referred
- ☐ Conditions
- ☑ Proc Notes

[All] [None]

`All Dates` [...]

Search [ ]

Object Types
- ☑ Appointments
- ☐ Comm Log
  - ☐ Family
- ☑ Tasks
- ☑ Email
- ☑ Lab Cases
- ☑ Rx
- ☑ Sheets
- ☐ Selected Teeth
- ☐ Audit
- ☑ Is TP View

Chart Views

F#	View
F1	Chart-Lab-Rx
F2	Show All
F3	No Comm Log

[+ Add] [↑ Up] [↓ Down]

- Viewing the Patient Dashboard Tools- Patient Dashboard
  - Setup a Default one...then change to the information you want to show, example:

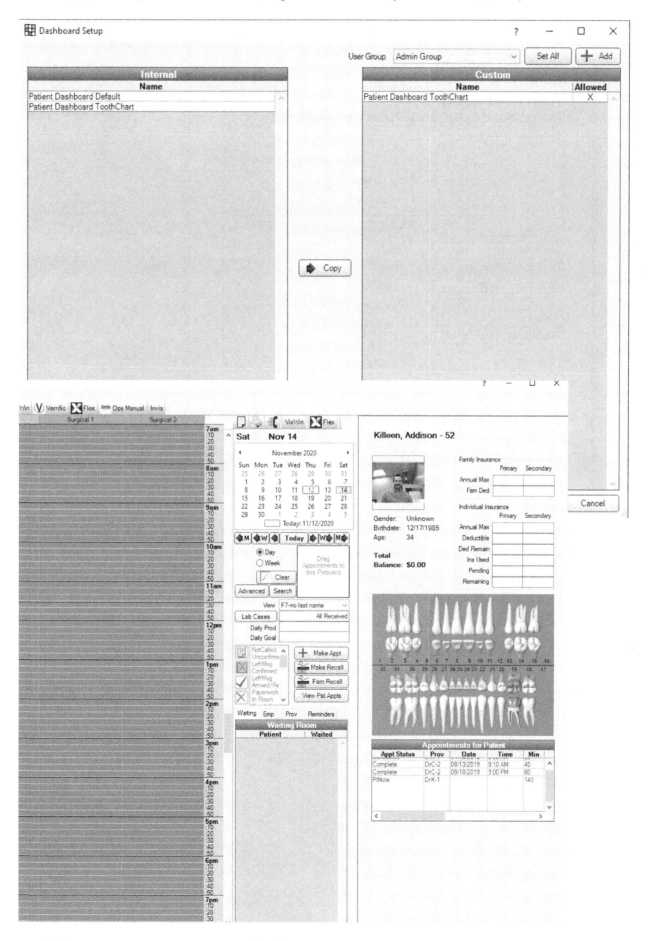

○ A Universal Example below

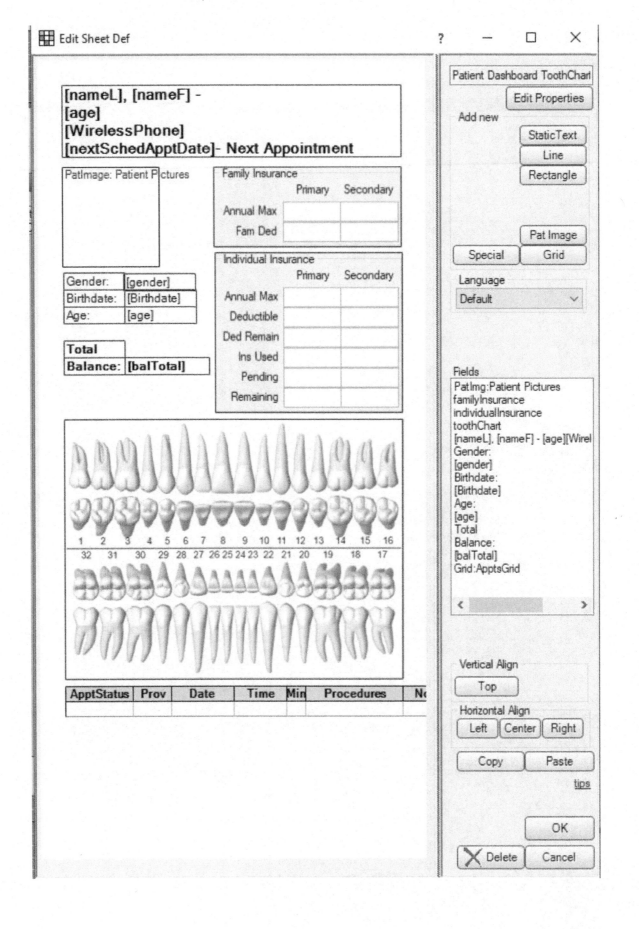

hen a HIPAA Compliant example for use in operatories:

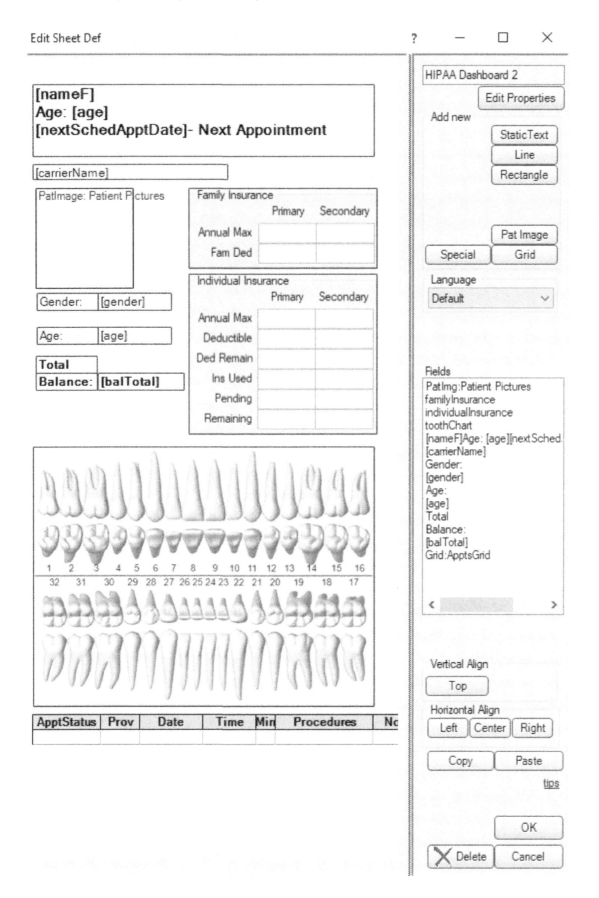

Made in United States
North Haven, CT
13 September 2022